INSTRUCTOR'S MANUAL

to accompany

FUNDAMENTALS OF CORPORATE FINANCE

Third Edition

Stephen A. Ross
Randolph W. Westerfie
Bradford D. Jordan

Prepared by
Thomas H. Eyssell
University of Missouri–St. Louis

IRWIN

Chicago · Bogota · Boston · Buenos Aires · Caracas
London · Madrid · Mexico City · Sydney · Toronto

PREFACE
FROM THE AUTHORS

This Instructor's Manual is intended for use with the 3rd edition of *Fundamentals of Corporate Finance*. This preface describes the various features of this manual and provides some tips on using it. It also discusses the transparency package and videos that accompany this edition of the text.

QUICK SUMMARY OF THE INSTRUCTOR'S MANUAL

The Instructor's Manual (IM) has three main sections. The first section runs about 300 pages and contains chapter outlines and other lecture materials designed for use with the Annotated Instructor's Edition of the text. There is an annotated outline for each chapter in this section, and, included in the outlines, there are lecture tips, ethics notes, and suggested overhead transparencies. The second section of the IM contains approximately 100 pages of detailed solutions to all of the end of chapter problems. The third section contains selected transparency masters.

THE ANNOTATED INSTRUCTOR'S EDITION

The Annotated Instructor's Edition of the text contains extensive references to the IM regarding lecture tips, ethics notes, and the availability of transparencies. The lecture tips vary in content and purpose; they may provide an alternative perspective on a subject, suggest important points to be stressed, give further examples, or recommend other readings. The ethics notes present background on topics that can be used to motivate classroom discussion of *finance-related* ethical issues. The back cover of the Instructor's Edition contains further information.

THE TRANSPARENCY SET

The 3rd edition of *Fundamentals* features an extensive transparency set. There are approximately 400 different exhibits, figures, tables, and problems for classroom use. Our goal is to provide complete coverage of the text topics, thereby allowing the instructor to pick and choose among the various overheads and custom-tailor course offerings. For instructors who so desire, there are a sufficient number of transparencies for a full course without the need for supplemental materials.

Also, for those of you who prefer to adapt and improve on our materials, we are pleased to announce that the transparency set is now available on Microsoft* PowerPoint", the popular presentation graphics program. Please contact your local Richard D. Irwin representative for further details or call Irwin customer service at (800) 634-3961.

Transparency Types

To provide for some variation in the overheads and to allow for differences in use among instructors, we created six different types:

1. **Chapter Outlines** For each chapter, the first transparency is simply a broad outline of the chapter contents. We use these to start a lecture and briefly overview the chapter subjects before plunging in. We also reuse them to summarize and reinforce the main elements of a subject before we move on.

2. **Important Figures and Tables** These transparencies are taken from the text and correspond to the most important chapter exhibits. They generally provide a convenient means of discussing and explaining the chapter materials. They are very useful for making certain that students understand what is being explained and why.

3. **Key Issues** The key issues transparencies provide a means of organizing discussion on various topics. They are intended to help frame questions and broad issues that students need to understand and be able to address.

4. **Supplemental Examples and Exhibits** For some subjects, examples and illustrations not found in the text are supplied as a way to expand on some subjects, reinforce chapter discussions, or provide additional examples of important calculations.

5. **Interactive Problems** Almost every chapter contains some interactive overheads. These usually involve important calculations or problems in which some numbers or comments are missing and replaced with blanks. Because the instructor can ask students for the needed information, these transparencies provide a good springboard for classroom participation, and they break up some of the monotony that can exist when overheads are used. They are also a good way of making sure that students are paying attention and not just taking dictation. As a convenience for users, the third section of the IM contains completed transparency masters for this group of overheads. These masters make it clear what numbers need to be filled in and where they need to go.

6. **Solution Transparencies** For each chapter, we selected some representative end of chapter problems and created transparencies for classroom use. Like the interactive problem overheads, these usually contain a few blanks that can be filled in during a discussion of the problem as a means of motivating student attention and involvement. Complete solutions to these problems are found in the second part of the IM.

About the Ready Notes

The Ready Notes are intended to improve notetaking by students. All of the overheads in the transparency set have been reduced in size (to provide room to write) and then bound in an inexpensive supplement. Having these available frees students from the need to copy background information, tabular material, or figures. Instead, they can concentrate on what is being said and what is important about the material. We have found that students who use the Ready Notes pay much better attention and are much more willing to participate in classroom discussion, particularly in very large classes. The Ready Notes are perforated and three-hole punched so that they can be detached and combined in a loose-leaf notebook with other materials if that is desirable.

In addition, the Ready Notes can be custom published for instructors who wish to combine their own materials with some or all of the available transparencies. Instructors simply supply copies of class materials, including such things as syllabi, old exams, problems, cases, and exhibits, along with a list of the *Fundamentals* transparencies to be included. See your local Richard D. Irwin representative for further details.

Tips for Transparency Use

Different instructors will prefer to present material and discuss topics in different ways. The sequencing and numbering of the overheads in the transparency set is simply a reflection of the page order in which material appears in the Annotated Instructor's Edition of the text. This sequencing is not necessarily optimal for presentation purposes, and the transparencies can be readily reordered. For example, on a few occasions, a discussion in the text will reference a table or figure that, for design reasons, appears on a previous or subsequent page. When this occurs, the transparencies may not be in the best order for classroom explanation and discussion. Similarly, the solution transparencies are placed at the end of each chapter, but instructors may wish to work problems on particular subjects immediately following a discussion to reinforce the important elements.

VIDEOS

We chose a total of eleven videos to accompany the 3rd edition of *Fundamentals*. These videos feature Paul Solman, the Emmy award-winning business and economics correspondent for the MacNeil/Lehrer NewsHour, on a variety of text-related topics. They each run about eight to ten minutes and are a useful (and fun) way of breaking up some of the material as well as illustrating real-world applicability and relevance. A brief description of the videos and some suggested uses follow.

Video #1: *Exxon: Corporate Goals and Social Welfare*

Should a corporation pursue social goals? With the Exxon Valdez supertanker oil spill as the backdrop, this video examines what many feel is a potential for conflict between the goal of the corporation and the goals of society. It goes well with Problem 3 at the end of Chapter 1, and it is a useful lead-in to a class discussion of social responsibility and ethics. It contains footage of Exxon's annual meeting following the spill, so students can get a feel for how contentious shareholder meetings can be. This material also goes well with the discussion of corporate governance in Chapter 12.

Video #2: *Valuing the Stock Market*

How does a company's book, or accounting, value relate to its value as a going concern? This video examines Gillette's market and book values and discusses how accounting information can be used to at least roughly value a firm. It goes well with Chapters 2 and 3 because it dwells on market versus book values and the uses of accounting information. It also goes well with a discussion of fundamental analysis in the context of semistrong market efficiency in Chapter 11.

Video #3: *Bond Buccaneers*

This video goes well with Chapter 6 because it discusses bond basics and bond trading. The bonds discussed are defaulted LDC obligations (the political equivalent of junk bonds), so the video adds an interesting and useful international flavor to the material.

Video #4: *Financial Reality and the Entrepreneur*

How do new products and their inventors get funded? This video spotlights high-tech inventor and entrepreneur Raymond Kurzweil's innovative electronics products and his tactics for acquiring the necessary financial backing to bring them to market. It goes with Chapters 8 and 9 on capital budgeting because it illustrates the origin of new ideas through entrepreneurship. It also shows how real-world capital budgeting decisions involve much more than simple number-crunching. The video also goes well with Chapter 13 on raising long-term financing.

Video #5: *Test Your Insider I.Q.*

When do diligent research and smart investing become illegal insider trading? This video discusses just what is and what is not insider trading, and it emphasizes that the distinction is sometimes a little murky. It goes well with a discussion of market efficiency and the value of private information (Chapter 11). It also provides a good springboard for a discussion of broader ethical issues concerning insider information.

Video #6: Junk Bonds

Are junk bonds really junk? This video discusses how junk bonds came to play such an important role in American corporate finance, and it dispels some of the misconceptions surrounding junk bond financing. It goes well with Chapter 12 on long-term debt. It also goes with Chapter 15 on capital structure and Chapter 21 on takeovers.

Video #7: Celtics IPO

Who would have bet against Larry Bird and his teammates in their heyday? And when the Boston Celtics decided to raise money with an initial public offering, or IPO, the stock looked like a sure winner, but were investors the victims of a winner's curse? This video discusses the Boston Celtic's IPO, and it goes extremely well with the IPO discussion in Chapter 13. It is very useful for illustrating the dangers of IPO investing.

Video #8: The Importance of the Bond Market

This video focuses on the underwriting process for new bond issues using the example of an Archer Daniels Midland $250 million issue. It contains very topical coverage of short- and long-term interest rates and the effect of inflation on interest rates. It also provides background and detail on the borrowing process from the company's and the underwriter's point of view. It goes well with Chapter 13 on issuing securities to the public. It also could be used with Chapter 6 on bond valuation or Chapter 14 on the cost of debt financing.

Video #9: Leveraged Legacy

Leveraged buyouts, or LBO's, have received a lot of bad press. Using Duracell as an example, this video shows how LBO's, when properly done, can revitalize a company and help it just keep going and going and going . . . . This LBO discussion goes well with Chapter 15 on capital structure and Chapter 20 on acquisitions. It provides a good balance to a lot of the negative publicity surrounding junk bond financing by describing the successful Duracell LBO.

Video #10: European Currency Crisis

This video goes well with Chapter 21 on international finance or as a general international finance supplement. It focuses on the turmoil existing in Europe following England's withdrawal of support for the European community's exchange rate mechanism and other events. It provides a good discussion of exchange rates and international interest rates.

Video #11: Debt Swap

International investing creates unique opportunities for creative financing and financial engineering. This video discusses one such financial arrangement, a three-way international (in Mexico) debt and equity swap. It goes very well with discussions of international financing (in Chapter 21), financial engineering (Chapter 22), and long-term financing with unusual debt instruments (Chapter 12).

ACKNOWLEDGEMENTS

We would first like to thank one of our colleagues, Cheri Etling of Wichita State, for proofing and checking the end-of-chapter solutions found in the IM. This type of work is not a great deal of fun, and we appreciate her careful efforts. We also thank David R. Kuipers, a University of Missouri doctoral student, for proofing the answers. Most of the ethics materials were contributed by Darryl E. J. Gurley of Northeastern University, to whom we are very grateful.

In closing, we always welcome comments, criticisms, and suggestions. Please contact us and let us know what you like and don't like.

T.H.E
S.A.R.
R.W.W.
B.D.J.

August, 1994

Alternative Course Formats

Fundamentals of Corporate Finance, 3rd ed., can be readily adapted to meet the individual preferences of course instructors and the differing backgrounds and needs of introductory finance students. Three course outlines are described below, but these are only possibilities and many other permutations exist. Chapters marked * may be assigned as outside reading if time is short. Chapters marked ** may be covered in part or omitted without loss of continuity if time is short. The chapters on options and leasing are available from Richard D. Irwin, Inc., and can be packaged with the text. Please contact your Irwin representative for further information.

Course Outline
A Broad Survey Course

Chapter	Topic
1	Introduction to Corporate Finance
2	Financial Statements, Taxes, and Cash Flow
3	Working with Financial Statements
4**	Long-Term Financial Planning and Corporate Growth
5	First Principles of Valuation: The Time Value of Money
6	Valuing Stocks and Bonds
7	Net Present Value and Other Investment Criteria
8	Making Capital Investment Decisions
9	Project Analysis and Evaluation
10	Some Lessons from Capital Market History
11	Return, Risk, and the Security Market Line
12*	Long-Term Financing: An Introduction
13*	Issuing Securities to the Public
14	Cost of Capital
15**	Financial Leverage and Capital Structure Policy
16	Dividends and Dividend Policy
17	Short-Term Finance and Planning

A Course Emphasizing Valuation and Current Issues

Chapter	Topic
1	Introduction to Corporate Finance
2	Financial Statements, Taxes, and Cash Flow
5	First Principles of Valuation: The Time Value of Money
6	Valuing Stocks and Bonds
7	Net Present Value and Other Investment Criteria
8	Making Capital Investment Decisions
10	Some Lessons from Capital Market History
11	Return, Risk, and the Security Market Line
12*	Long-Term Financing: An Introduction
13*	Issuing Securities to the Public
14	Cost of Capital
15	Financial Leverage and Capital Structure Policy
16	Dividends and Dividend Policy
O	Options and Corporate Securities
20	Mergers and Acquisitions
21	International Corporate Finance
L**	Leasing
22**	Risk Management

A Course Emphasizing Traditional Topics

Chapter	Topic
1	Introduction to Corporate Finance
2	Financial Statements, Taxes, and Cash Flow
3	Working with Financial Statements
4	Long-Term Financial Planning and Corporate Growth
5	First Principles of Valuation: The Time Value of Money
6	Valuing Stocks and Bonds
7	Net Present Value and Other Investment Criteria
8	Making Capital Investment Decisions
9**	Project Analysis and Evaluation
10	Some Lessons from Capital Market History
11	Return, Risk, and the Security Market Line
12*	Long-Term Financing: An Introduction
13*	Issuing Securities to the Public
14	Cost of Capital
17	Short-Term Finance and Planning
18	Cash and Liquidity Management
19	Credit Management
L*	Leasing

Table of Contents

Part I: Course and Lecture Materials

Chapter		Page

1.	Introduction to Corporate Finance	1
2.	Financial Statements, Taxes, and Cash Flow	11
3.	Working with Financial Statements	20
4.	Long-Term Financial Planning and Growth	38
5.	First Principles of Valuation: The Time Value of Money	50
6.	Valuing Stocks and Bonds	66
7.	Net Present Value and Other Investment Criteria	78
8.	Making Capital Investment Decisions	88
9.	Project Analysis and Evaluation	106
10.	Some Lessons from Capital Market History	120
11.	Return, Risk, and the Security Market Line	132
12.	Long-Term Financing: An Introduction	148
13.	Issuing Securities to the Public	159
14.	Cost of Capital	170
15.	Financial Leverage and Capital Structure Policy	181
16.	Dividends and Dividend Policy	193
17.	Short-Term Finance Planning and Management	205
18.	Cash and Liquidity Management	218
19.	Credit and Inventory Management	229
20.	Mergers and Acquisitions	242
21.	International Corporate Finance	254
22.	Risk Management: An Introduction to Financial Engineering	266
	Supplement: Options and Corporate Securities	276
	Supplement: Leasing	290

Part II: End-of-Chapter Solutions

Chapter		Page
1.	Introduction to Corporate Finance	301
2.	Financial Statements, Taxes, and Cash Flow	303
3.	Working with Financial Statements	310
4.	Long-Term Financial Planning and Growth	318
5.	First Principles of Valuation: The Time Value of Money	327
6.	Valuing Stocks and Bonds	334
7.	Net Present Value and Other Investment Criteria	340
8.	Making Capital Investment Decisions	346
9.	Project Analysis and Evaluation	353
10.	Some Lessons from Capital Market History	358
11.	Return, Risk, and the Security Market Line	362
12.	Long-Term Financing: An Introduction	366
13.	Issuing Securities to the Public	370
14.	Cost of Capital	373
15.	Financial Leverage and Capital Structure Policy	378
16.	Dividends and Dividend Policy	383
17.	Short-Term Finance Planning and Management	387
18.	Cash and Liquidity Management	393
19.	Credit and Inventory Management	397
20.	Mergers and Acquisitions	402
21.	International Corporate Finance	406
22.	Risk Management: An Introduction to Financial Engineering	410
	Supplement: Options and Corporate Securities	414
	Supplement: Leasing	419
Transparency Masters		422

PART I

COURSE MATERIALS

AND

LECTURE NOTES

CHAPTER 1
INTRODUCTION TO CORPORATE FINANCE

TRANSPARENCIES

> **T1.1:** Chapter Outline
> **T1.2:** A Simplified Organizational Chart
> **T1.3:** Forms of Organization and the Goal of Financial Management
> **T1.4:** The Agency Problem and Financial Markets
> **T1.5:** Cash Flows between the Firm and Financial Markets

CHAPTER ORGANIZATION

> **T1.1: Chapter Outline**

1.1 CORPORATE FINANCE AND THE FINANCIAL MANAGER
What Is Corporate Finance?
The Financial Manager
Financial Management Decisions

1.2 THE CORPORATE FORM OF BUSINESS ORGANIZATION
Sole Proprietorship
Partnership
Corporation
A Corporation by Another Name...

1.3 THE GOAL OF FINANCIAL MANAGEMENT
Possible Goals
The Goal of Financial Management
A More General Goal

1.4 THE AGENCY PROBLEM AND CONTROL OF THE CORPORATION
Agency Relationships
Management Goals
Do Managers Act in the Stockholders' Interests?

1.5 FINANCIAL MARKETS AND THE CORPORATION
Cash Flows to and from the Firm
Primary versus Secondary Markets

1.6 OUTLINE OF THE TEXT

1.7 SUMMARY AND CONCLUSIONS

ANNOTATED CHAPTER OUTLINE

1.1 CORPORATE FINANCE AND THE FINANCIAL MANAGER

A. What Is Corporate Finance?

Corporate finance is the study of the answers to the following questions:

1. *What long-term investments should we make?*

2. *Where will we get the funds to pay for our investment?*

3. *How will we collect from customers and pay our bills?*

In other words, the answers to the capital budgeting question, the capital structure question, and the net working capital question are all part of corporate finance.

B. The Financial Manager

> **T1.2: A Simplified Organizational Chart**

The *Chief Financial Officer, CFO.*

Controller—handles cost and financial accounting, tax payments and information systems.

Treasurer—handles cash management, financial planning, and capital expenditures.

Corporate finance is concerned with the issues faced by the treasurer.

C. Financial Management Decisions

The financial manager is concerned with three primary corporate financial decisions.

Capital budgeting—process of planning and managing a firm's investments in fixed assets. The key concerns are the *size*, *timing*, and *riskiness* of cash flows.

Capital structure—mix of debt and equity used by a firm. What are the least expensive sources of funds? Is there a best mix? When and where to raise funds?

Working capital management—managing short-term assets and liabilities. How much cash and inventory to keep around? What is our credit policy? Where will we obtain short-term loans?

1.2 THE CORPORATE FORM OF BUSINESS ORGANIZATION

> **T1.3: Forms of Organization and Goal of Financial Management**

A. Sole Proprietorship

A business owned by one person. Simple, but involves *unlimited liability*. Its life is limited to the owner's, and the equity that can be raised is limited to the proprietor's wealth.

B. Partnership

A business in which there are multiple owners.

General partnership—all partners share in gains or losses; all have unlimited liability for all partnership debts.

Limited partnership—one or more *general partners* will run the business and have unlimited liability. A *limited partner's* liability is limited to her contribution to the partnership.

C. Corporation

A business created as a distinct legal entity composed of one or more individuals or entities.

Corporations are the most important form of business organization in the U.S. There are several advantages to the corporate form:

1. *Limited liability for stockholders.*

2. *Unlimited life for the business.*

3. *Ownership can be easily transferred.*

These characteristics make it easier for corporations to raise capital. The primary disadvantage to the corporate form is *double taxation.*

Lecture Tip, page 7: The following example provides a brief case summary which may be used for a class discussion concerning the issues of possible corporate civil neglect and/or the extent to which corporate owners should be protected by limited liability.

Dow Corning is a joint venture of Corning Corporation and Dow Chemical Corporation, with each owning 50 percent of Dow Corning's outstanding shares. In 1975, Dow Corning introduced a new use for silicone—breast implants. In 1990, a civil jury awarded a California woman $7.3 million on the claim that her leaking implants caused autoimmune disorder. Dow Corning announced it would appeal the judgment.

In January 1991, the New York Times *reported that Dow Corning had faced 250-300 similar cases over the implants' life but, until 1990, the victims agreed to suppression orders. These orders effectively kept the public uninformed regarding safety issues associated with silicon breast implants.*

Dow Corning established the Dow Information Center Hotline to provide information concerning the safety of implants. In June 1991, Newsweek reported that, for many years, internal Dow Corning documents had noted potential health risks associated with implants. The article charged that Dow Corning used the legal process to keep the internal studies from reaching the public. In February 1992, the Food and Drug Administration concluded the implants' safety had not been established and restricted their use to clinical studies. In response, Dow Corning closed its implant manufacturing facilities.

The instructor can present this situation to the class and inquire as to the ethics of using the legal system to limit adverse information and to what extent responsibility should be assumed by both Corning and Dow Chemical, given their limited liability as the owners of Dow Corning.

Lecture Tip, page 7: Although the corporate form of organization has the advantage of limited liability, it has the disadvantage of double taxation. A small business of 35 or fewer stockholders is allowed by the Internal Revenue Service to form an S Corporation. The S Corporation organizational form provides limited liability but allows pretax corporate profits to be distributed on a pro rata basis to individual shareholders, who would be obligated to only pay personal taxes on the distributed income.

D. A Corporation by Another Name...

Laws and regulations differ from country to country but the essential features of public ownership and limited liability remain.

Lecture Tip, page 8: A recent development in organizational form is the "LLC", or limited-liability corporation. LLCs are a hybrid form of organization that fall between partnerships and corporations; i.e., investors in LLCs have the protection of limited liability but firm income escapes the double taxation associated with the corporate form of organization. Instead, it flows through to the investors, to be taxed as their personal income. LLCs first appeared in Wyoming in 1977, but have skyrocketed in popularity since 1988 due to a favorable ruling by the Internal Revenue Service, as well as to the explosion in the cellular communications field, in which many firms are organized as LLCs. As of November, 1993, the LLC has been approved in 37 states, from fewer than ten in 1991. Perhaps the biggest beneficiaries of this new organizational form will be small and medium-sized businesses such as law and medical practices. The instructor may wish to use the creation of the LLC to (a) demonstrate the evolutionary nature of the marketplace, (b) generate a discussion of the agency-cost implications, or (c) raise the question of why different types of firms take different organizational forms.

1.3 THE GOAL OF FINANCIAL MANAGEMENT

A. Possible Goals

The possible goals are legion—some involve profit, some not.

B. The Goal of Financial Management

From the stockholders' perspective, the goal in buying a firm's stock is to gain financially.

The goal of financial management is to maximize the current value per share of the existing stock.

C. A More General Goal

A more general goal of financial management is to maximize the market value of the owners' equity.

1.4 THE AGENCY PROBLEM AND CONTROL OF THE CORPORATION

> **T1.4: The Agency Problem and Financial Markets**

A. Agency Relationships

The relationship between stockholders and management is called an *agency relationship*.

This occurs when one party (*principal*) pays another (*agent*) to represent them. The possibility of conflicts of interest between the parties is termed the *agency problem*.

B. Management Goals

Agency costs—two types: *direct* and *indirect*. Direct costs come about in compensation and perquisites for management. Indirect costs are the result of monitoring managers and of suboptimal decisions (from the owners' perspective) by management.

Ethics Note, page 11: *When shareholders elect a board of directors to oversee the corporation, the election serves as a control mechanism for management. The board of directors holds all legal responsibility for corporate actions. However, this responsibility is to the corporation itself and not necessarily to the stockholders. The following is an interesting springboard for a discussion of directors' and managers' duties:*

In 1986, Ronald Perelman engaged in an unsolicited takeover offer for Gillette. Gillette's management filed litigation against Perelman and subsequently entered into a standstill agreement with Perelman. This action eliminated the premium that Perelman offered shareholders for their stock in Gillette.

A group of shareholders filed litigation against the board of directors in response to its actions. It was subsequently discovered that Gillette had entered into standstill agreements with ten additional companies. When questioned regarding the rejection of Perelman's offer, management responded that there were projects on line that could not be discussed (later revealed to be the sensor razor, which proved to be the most profitable new venture in Gillette's history). Thus, despite appearances, management's actions may have been in the best interests of the corporation, and this situation indicates that management may consider factors other than the bid alone when considering a tender offer.

Ethics Note, page 11: *The following situation can be presented to the class as an example of the magnitude of one type of agency expense, and one corporation's attempt to control perquisites and thereby reduce direct agency costs:*

On March 26, 1992, Digital Equipment Corporation moved to curb expense accounts and eliminate an estimated $30 million in annual abuses. An internal memo had stated that abuses were getting worse, noting $1,000 bar bills as an example of such abuses. The $30 million might appear trivial when compared to the estimated total expense costs of $6.5 billion. However, DEC was facing a $110 million loss for the first half of its fiscal year and desired to send a message to both employees and stockholders that it intended to control both costs and abuses. This warning came on the heels of a work force cut of 10,500 employees between September 1989 and March 1992. These cuts were a result of poor forecasting of sales growth and a misestimation of the economic recession.

Lecture Tip, page 11: *Insight into the agency relationship can be provided with an example of the classroom environment. For example, the class must work end-of-chapter problems and submit them to you, the instructor, for grading. You find it necessary to institute a costly monitoring device which consumes much of your effort and time, parallel to a corporation's internal audit, to ensure that the students, as employees, act in a particular manner. More generally, if students could be trusted to simply learn the material, then costly exams and grading would be unnecessary. Instead, costly monitoring must be performed.*

Examples of agency conflicts can also be found in various periodicals which can be considered for outside class readings. A few suggested examples are provided below:

1) *"Did the Time Decision Torpedo the Hostile Bid?" Mergers and Acquisitions, January/February 1990, by J. Lerner. This article discusses the Time/ Warner merger, which occurred despite Paramount's higher bid for Time. The article also discusses the 1989 Delaware Chancery Court ruling which allowed Time's and Warner's Boards of Directors to pursue the merger even though Time's shareholders might prefer the immediate gains offered by Paramount's cash bid.*

2) *"Who Owns This Company, Anyhow?," Fortune, July 29, 1991, by Rob Norton. This article discusses the rising ownership of stock by institutions and further discusses the closer attention institutions are directing to how companies are managed and how executives are compensated. It discusses the market for corporate control as a crude device for disciplining managers.*

3) *"The Shareholder As Second-Class Citizen," Accountancy, April, 1991, by Denis Keenan. This article discusses shareholder ownership in the UK. The article also makes reference to rising institutional ownership and suggests that some boards appear to run companies in complete disregard of smaller shareholders, paying themselves too much, not allowing a discussion of issues during the general meeting, and so on.*

C. Do Managers Act in the Stockholders' Interests?

Managerial compensation—firm performance and management compensation and prospects are linked.

Lecture Tip, page 12: A 1993 study performed at the Harvard Business School indicates that the total return to shareholders is closely related to the nature of CEO compensation; specifically, higher returns were achieved by those CEOs whose pay package included more option and stock components. (See The Wall Street Journal, November 12, 1993, p. B1)

As persuasive as the empirical evidence is, however, occasionally students will cite apparent counterexamples. In 1992, high-level managers at General Dynamics shared millions of dollars in bonuses while simultaneously engaging in massive layoffs, because the firm's stock exceeded a prespecified target price for ten consecutive days. Cases such as this can be used to illustrate the importance of appropriate contracting, as well as the existence of stakeholder/stockholder conflicts.

Control of the Firm—management can be replaced by several methods which involve stockholders.

Stakeholders—someone other than a stockholder or creditor who potentially has a claim on a firm.

Lecture Tip, page 14:   *A good practitioner-oriented discussion of the impact of stakeholders on decision-making is found in a 1987 Wall Street Journal article by Charles Exley, Jr., then-chairman and president of NCR Corp. The thrust of Mr. Exley's comments is that giving more consideration to the interests of non-stockholder stakeholders is good business, and results in the decentralization of management. Frequently, a discussion of stakeholder interests (as opposed to a discussion exclusively geared toward stockholder interests) leads to a better understanding of the nature of the corporate form of organization, the role of the corporation in society (and the question of "corporate social responsibility"), as well as to the role of contracting in the labor and financial markets.*

Lecture Tip, page 14:   *California Public Employees' Retirement System (CalPERS) is the largest institutional shareholder in the United States, controlling $68 billion of pension funds. Traditionally, CalPERS acts as an activist shareholder, sponsoring proxy initiatives on topics ranging from corporate strategy to executive compensation. In the fall of 1991, CalPERS began meeting with corporate executives regarding their initiatives. During the winter of 1992, CalPERS offered 11 different initiatives for shareholder vote, regarding the composition of directors, executive pay, and corporate strategy.*

Ownership of common stock provides a right to sponsor initiatives for shareholder vote, but is CalPERS an ordinary shareholder? The instructor might ask the class if the voting rights should pass through to the stakeholders in CalPERS or should the investment managers of the fund determine the voting practices of the shares held?

Lecture Tip, page 14:   *A periodical reference concerning the stakeholders' interest in the firm can be found in the following article:*

"Do Poison Pills Make You Strong?," The Economist, June 29, 1991. This article discusses the nature of the share contract and the stakeholder interest in the firm. The article also provides an insight into the economics of contracts between the firm and its stakeholders, and the residual risk stakeholders encounter.

Ethics Note, page 14:   *An interesting aspect of the question of stakeholder concerns is that it leads rather smoothly into a discussion of ethical decision-making. Theories of ethical behavior invariably focus on the rights of all parties to a decision, as opposed to just one or two. For example, the "utilitarian" model defines an action as acceptable if it maximizes the benefit, or minimizes the harm, to stakeholders in the aggregate. The "golden rule" model, on the other hand, deems an decision ethical if all stakeholders are treated as the decision-maker would wish to be treated. And finally, the Kantian "basic rights" model defines acceptable actions as those which minimize the violation of stakeholders' rights.*

1.5 FINANCIAL MARKETS AND THE CORPORATION

T1.5: Cash Flows between the Firm and Financial Markets

A. Cash Flows to and from the Firm

A firm issues securities to realize cash for investment in assets. The operating cash flows generated from the investment in assets allows for payment of taxes, reinvestment in new assets, and payment of interest and dividends to the investors in the firm's securities. The financial markets bring the buyers and sellers of debt and equity securities together.

B. Primary versus Secondary Markets

Primary market—refers to the original sale of securities. *Public offers, SEC registration,* and *underwriters* are part of this market.

Lecture Tip, page 15: Students are often curious about the nature of the information that is made public at the time of a primary offering. An interesting example of full disclosure appeared in The Wall Street Journal several years ago in the form of excerpts from a prospectus for a company called Indian Bingo, Inc.

> *"To hear Indian Bingo tell it, prospective investors should think carefully before deciding to shell out $1 per share for the company's proposed initial public offering of five million common shares.*
>
> *"Indian Bingo says in a preliminary registration statement filed with the Securities and Exchange Commission that it wants to get into the business of operating bingo games on indian reservations. But Indian Bingo points out that the company would be a 'high-risk' investment. Among the reasons: the company is a month old, such bingo games may be held illegal, third-party studies of such activities haven't been made, the company doesn't yet have any source of income and the underwriter hasn't any experience as a securities dealer.*
>
> *Also, "one of [the firm's] main consultants has served time in prison for obstruction of justice, and another has served time for conspiracy and mail fraud. Both have also received civil sanctions from the SEC for allegedly fraudulent activities, according to federal court records and SEC documents. Together, the two consultants and their family will control more than 50% of Indian Bingo's stock."*

Secondary market—refers to the resale of securities. *Stock exchanges (NYSE, AMEX)* and the *over-the-counter, OTC, market (NASDAQ)* are part of this market.

Listing—stocks that trade on an exchange are said to be *listed*.

1.6 OUTLINE OF THE TEXT

Part One:	Overview of Corporate Finance
Part Two:	Financial Statements and Long-Term Financial Planning
Part Three:	Valuation of Future Cash Flows
Part Four:	Capital Budgeting
Part Five:	Risk and Return
Part Six:	Long-Term Financing
Part Seven:	Cost of Capital and Long-Term Financial Policy
Part Eight:	Short-Term Financial Planning and Management
Part Nine:	Topics in Corporate Finance

1.7 SUMMARY AND CONCLUSIONS

CHAPTER 2
FINANCIAL STATEMENTS, TAXES, AND CASH FLOW

TRANSPARENCIES

T2.1: Chapter Outline
T2.2: The Balance Sheet
T2.3: GAAP versus Cash Flow Time Line
T2.4: Taxes
T2.5: Marginal versus Average Corporate Tax Rates
T2.6: Cash Flow Example (2 pages)
T2.7: Cash Flow Summary
T2.8: Hermetic, Inc., Balance Sheet
T2.9: Hermetic, Inc., Income Statement
T2.10: Hermetic, Inc., Cash Flow from Assets
T2.11: Solution to Problem 2.6
T2.12: Solution to Problem 2.11
T2.13: Solution to Problem 2.12
T2.14: Solution to Problem 2.13

CHAPTER ORGANIZATION

T2.1: Chapter Outline

2.1 THE BALANCE SHEET
Assets: The Left-Hand Side
Liabilities and Owners' Equity: The Right-Hand Side
Net Working Capital
Liquidity
Debt versus Equity
Market Value versus Book Value

2.2 THE INCOME STATEMENT
GAAP and the Income Statement
Non-cash Items
Time and Costs

2.3 TAXES
Corporate and Personal Tax Rates
Average versus Marginal Tax Rates

2.4 CASH FLOW
Cash Flow from Assets
Cash Flow to Creditors and Stockholders

2.5 SUMMARY AND CONCLUSIONS

ANNOTATED CHAPTER OUTLINE

2.1 THE BALANCE SHEET

> **T2.2: The Balance Sheet**

A. Assets: The Left-Hand Side

What the firm owns. Current versus Fixed. Tangible versus Intangible.

B. Liabilities and Owner's Equity: The Right-Hand Side

What the firm owes. Current and long-term. *Shareholders' equity* is assets less liabilities.

*Lecture Tip, page 23: Students sometimes find it difficult to see the relationship between the decisions made by financial managers and the values that subsequently appear on the firm's financial statements. A good way for them to gain a better understanding of the "big-picture" aspects of financial decision-making is for the instructor to emphasize the fact that all decisions in finance ultimately fall into one of two categories: those that involve the acquisition (or divestiture) of assets, i.e., **investment** decisions; and those that involve obtaining funds - **financing** decisions. The appearance of the balance sheet is the direct result of these decisions. Put another way, the asset side of the balance sheet reflects all of the investment decisions made from the day of the firm's inception to the creation of the latest set of financial statements, and the liabilities and equity side reflect all of the financing decisions made over the same period.*

Lecture Tip, page 24: You may find it useful at this point to. spend a few minutes reinforcing the concepts of shareholders' equity and retained earnings. Some will have forgotten the accounting components of shareholders' equity - the common stock, surplus, retained earnings, and treasury stock accounts. Others will benefit from an explanation of why the retained earnings balance doesn't represent spendable funds. A solid grasp of the accounting basics will avoid much confusion in subsequent chapters.

C. Net Working Capital

The difference between a firm's current assets and its current liabilities.

D. Liquidity

The order of assets on the balance sheet reflects their liquidity. Liability order reflects time to maturity.

Liquidity as a continuum reflects an ability to convert an asset to cash with little or no loss of value.

Liquidity has an opportunity cost—the more liquid an asset is, the less profitable it usually is.

Lecture Tip, page 24: Some students seem to get a little confused when they try to understand that excessive cash can be undesirable. For example, they sometimes leave an accounting principles class with the belief a large current ratio is always favorable.
     The instructor may wish to mention that a cash balance is a use of funds that has an opportunity cost. Students can be asked what a company could do with cash if it were not on deposit in a bank account. The best answer is that it could be paid out to stockholders. Other answers include paying off debt and investing in productive assets. In broader terms, students need to understand that the change in a firm's holding of cash is not the same as its cash flow. The (misnamed) accounting statement of cash flows tends to create this confusion. This statement is deferred to Chapter 3 to avoid any further reinforcement of this error.

E. Debt versus Equity

Precedence of debt over equity to firm's cash flows.

Gains or losses of the business may be magnified for stockholders by financial leverage.

F. Market Value versus Book Value

Irrelevance of book (historical cost) value and importance of market (exchange) value for decision making.

Some of the most important assets and liabilities do not appear on the balance sheet, e.g., talented managers and products that bring lawsuits. Especially true in service industries.

Lecture Tip, page 25: It is noted in Chapter 2 that accounting, or historical, costs are not especially important to financial managers while market values are. Some students have difficulty recognizing that the passage of time and changing circumstances will almost always mean that the price an asset would fetch if sold today is quite different from its book, or historical, value. Sometimes an example or two of familiar instances is enough to make the point. For instance, the market values versus historical costs less depreciation of used cars (both ordinary and collectable) and houses (in, say, California versus Texas) may help.

It may be that some students, while acknowledging the difference between historical cost and market value, ask why market value is considered the more important of the two. The simplest answer is market value represents the cash price people are willing and able to pay. After all, it is cash that must ultimately be paid or received for investments, interest, principal, dividends, and so forth.

Lecture Tip, page 25: *It may be beneficial for the instructor to discuss why book values are below market values in Example 2.2. The instructor can mention that favorable earnings expectations for Klingon Corp. cause a higher market valuation of the assets relative to their historical (book) costs, and the equity valuation benefits from the market's appraisal of this future earning power.*

Lecture Tip, page 25: *Example 2.2 can be easily extended to demonstrate that shareholders bear the cost of declining market values. Consider the balance sheet below.*

KLINGON CORPORATION
Balance Sheets
Market Value versus Book Value

	Book	Mkt (U)	Mkt (D)		Book	Mkt (U)	Mkt (D)
Assets				*Liabilities and Shareholders' Equity*			
Net working capital	$400	$600	$200	Long-term debt	$500	$500	$500
Net fixed assets	700	1,000	500	Shareholders' equity	600	1,100	200
	$1,100	$1,600	$700		$1,100	$1,600	$700

Clearly, higher (lower) market values of assets increase (decrease) the market value of shareholders' equity, even though book value is unaffected. This simple example provides a compelling argument for the use of market values in decision-making.

Lecture Tip, page 26: *The above example also provides a rationale for the accounting practice of "marking-to-market". However, students should be reminded that this occurs with only a portion of the firm's assets - primarily marketable securities and inventory. As such, it is unlikely that the aggregate balance sheet values provided by the firm will accurately reflect market values, even when prepared by the most scrupulous of accountants.*

2.2 THE INCOME STATEMENT

T2.3: GAAP versus Cash Flow Time Line

A. GAAP and the Income Statement

Accounting's "realization" principle for revenue, the "matching" principle for costs, and their incongruence with actual cash flow timing.

*Lecture Tip, page 27: Previously it was noted that investment decisions are reflected on the left-hand side of the balance sheet, while financing decisions are reflected on the right-hand side. In an analogous fashion, the instructor may wish to emphasize that the income statement format utilized throughout the text reflects **investment** decisions in its "top half" (i.e., from Sales down to Earnings Before Interest and Taxes), and reflects **financing** decisions in the "bottom half" (from EBIT down to Net Income and EPS.)*

Ethics Note, page 27: The instructor may wish to discuss Blockbuster Video's accounting practices and ask whether they were potentially deceptive. Some facts are presented here; for greater detail, see "Shorts, Lies, and Videotape" in CFO *Magazine December, 1991.*

Blockbuster expanded from 100 video rental "superstores" to 700 between 1987 and 1989. Profits rose to $15.5 million in 1988 with sales of $137 million and the stock rose sevenfold. However, on May 8, 1989, Bear Stearns & Co. reported that Blockbuster's 100% rise in 1988 per-share profits was achieved with excessively aggressive accounting practices. When Blockbuster bought an existing video chain, it stretched out the accounting charge for the acquisition's goodwill over 40 years. This resulted in lower expenses and higher profits in the short term. But if growth slackened, the extended goodwill schedule would hurt later earnings.

Additionally, the acquisitions were financed with stock instead of cash, and this required Blockbuster to keep its share price high by maintaining high earnings' growth. Sales of franchises and videotapes to new franchisees were included in operating income. A franchisee paid Blockbuster a $9,000 opening fee, a $35,000 initial franchisee fee, and a $35,000 software licensing fee to use Blockbuster's computer system. Initial inventory was also purchased from the head office. In 1988, Blockbuster received 28 percent of its revenue from these payments.

If Blockbuster continued opening stores, this practice would be fine, but if franchise growth stopped, it would hurt earnings. Also, if the current amortization schedule was shortened to five years, Bear Stearns figured EPS would have changed from the reported $.58 to merely $.32. Blockbuster also depreciated its videotapes over long periods of time by industry standards, again increasing earnings.

B. Non-cash Items

For many firms, the most important non-cash item is depreciation.

Lecture Tip, page 28:   Students sometimes fail to grasp the distinction between the economic life of an asset, the useful life of an asset for accounting purposes, and the useful life of an asset for tax purposes. "Economic life" refers to the period of time over which the asset is expected to generate cash flows, and is obviously important to those making capital budgeting decisions. "Useful life" for accounting purposes, on the other hand, is largely determined by the firm's accountants (guided by GAAP) and affects the level of depreciation taken for book purposes. Finally, useful life for tax purposes is determined by the Internal Revenue Service. For example, the IRS provides rules for categorizing assets into class life groups (for example, autos fall into the three-year category) and mandates the annual depreciation rates for each group.

C. Time and Costs

Long run versus short run: The key is variability of costs; all costs are virtually fixed for very small periods while nearly all costs are variable if enough time is allowed.

Variable and fixed costs, useful in analyzing cash flows and preparing budgets, are not the same as product and period costs identified by accountants.

Lecture Tip, page 29:   Distinguishing between fixed and variable costs can have important implications for estimating and budgeting cash flows. It is sometimes helpful to remind students that variable costs are those cash outflows which change with the level of output, while fixed costs are constant. Moreover, when discussing the long-run versus short-run, students don't always recall the economic concept of the short-run as the period when virtually all costs are fixed as opposed to the long-run when virtually all costs are variable. An important thing to note is that what are short-run and long-run time periods will vary for different types of businesses.

2.3 TAXES

T2.4: Taxes
T2.5: Marginal versus Average Corporate Tax Rates

Lecture Tip, page 29:   The text notes the ever-changing nature of the tax code. This is well-illustrated by the "now-you-see-it now-you-don't" aspects of the Investment Tax Credit (ITC) since 1962. The table below details the strange history of this feature of the Code.

1962	Seven percent ITC created to stimulate capital investment.
1966	ITC suspended
1967	Seven percent credit reinstated
1969	ITC eliminated
1971	Seven percent credit reinstated
1975	Credit increased to 10 percent
1986	ITC eliminated (again)

A. Corporate and Personal Tax Rates

With the enactment of Omnibus Budget Reconciliation Act of 1993, corporate tax rates are not strictly increasing; the marginal rates are 15%, 25%, 34%, 39%, 34%, 39%, 34%, 35%, 38%, and then 35% again.

B. Average versus Marginal Tax Rates

The average rate rises to the marginal rate at $50,000,000 of taxable income. The "blips" of 39% and 38% add taxes which offset the initial lower brackets.

Example: Average versus Marginal

Taxable income		$150,000
.15 × $50,000	=	7,500
.25 × $25,000	=	6,250
.34 × $25,000	=	8,500
.39 × (150,000 − 100,000)	=	19,500
Total taxes	=	$ 41,750

Average tax rate = $41,750/150,000 = 27.8%; Marginal tax rate = 39%

Lecture Tip, page 30: It is useful to stress the situations in which marginal tax rates are relevant and those in which average tax rates are relevant. For purposes of computing a company's total tax liability, the average tax rate is the correct rate to apply to before-tax profits. However, in evaluating the cash flows which would be generated from a new investment, the marginal tax rate would be correct since the new investment would generate profits that would be taxed above the company's existing profit figure. The student may wish to remember that the relevant tax rate to apply to capital investment decisions (Chapter 8) is the marginal tax rate. The student should also note that, for corporations with taxable income greater than $335,000, the marginal tax rate and the average tax rate are equal (there is effectively a flat-rate tax), but it is still important to note the distinction between marginal and average tax rates.

2.4 CASH FLOW

T2.6: Cash Flow Example (2 pages)
T2.7: Cash Flow Summary

Based upon the balance sheet identity, Assets = Liabilities + Equity, the equivalent cash flow statement is

Cash Flow from Assets = Cash Flow to Creditors + Cash Flow to Owners.

A. Cash Flow from Assets

$$CF(A) = \text{Operating Cash Flow} \pm \text{Capital Spending}$$
$$\pm \text{ Additions to Net Working Capital}$$

Operating cash flow is:
Earnings before interest and taxes (EBIT)
+ Depreciation
− Current Taxes

(Net) Capital Spending is:
Ending fixed assets
− Beginning fixed assets
+ Depreciation

Additions to Net Working Capital (NWC) is:
Ending NWC − Beginning NWC

Negative Cash Flow from Assets is not unusual for growing firms.

B. Cash Flow to Creditors and Stockholders

Cash Flow to Bondholders (Creditors) is:
Interest paid
+ Principal paid
− New borrowing

Cash Flow to Stockholders (Owners) is:
Dividends paid
+ Stock repurchased
− New stock issued

2.5 REVIEW PROBLEM

This section is a review problem. An original example based upon Hermetic, Inc. is presented in the transparencies below.

```
T2.8:     Hermetic, Inc., Balance Sheet
T2.9:     Hermetic, Inc., Income Statement
T2.10:    Hermetic, Inc., Cash Flow from Assets
```

2.6 SUMMARY AND CONCLUSIONS

T2.11: Solution to Problem 2.6
T2.12: Solution to Problem 2.11
T2.13: Solution to Problem 2.12
T2.14: Solution to Problem 2.13

CHAPTER 3
WORKING WITH FINANCIAL STATEMENTS

TRANSPARENCIES

T3.1:   Chapter Outline
T3.2:   Hermetic, Inc., Balance Sheet
T3.3:   Hermetic, Inc., Income Statement
T3.4:   Statement of Cash Flows
T3.5:   Hermetic, Inc., Statement of Cash Flows
T3.6:   Hermetic, Inc., Common-Size Balance Sheet (2 pages)
T3.7:   Hermetic, Inc., Common-Size Income Statement
T3.8:   Things to Consider: Financial Ratios
T3.9:   Categories of Financial Ratios
T3.10: Common Financial Ratios
T3.11: The Du Pont Identity
T3.12: Ratio Comparison across Business Types
T3.13: A Brief Case History of Hermetic, Inc.
T3.14: Solution to Problem 3.6
T3.15: Solution to Problem 3.13
T3.16: Solution to Problem 3.32

CHAPTER ORGANIZATION

T3.1: Chapter Outline

3.1 CASH FLOW AND FINANCIAL STATEMENTS: A CLOSER LOOK
Sources and Uses of Cash
The Statement of Cash Flows

3.2 STANDARDIZED FINANCIAL STATEMENTS
Common-Size Statements
Common-Base-Year Financial Statements: Trend Analysis

3.3 RATIO ANALYSIS
Short-Term Solvency Measures
Long-Term Solvency Measures
Asset Management or Turnover Measures
Profitability Measures
Market Value Measures

3.4 THE DU PONT IDENTITY
ROE = ROA × Equity multiplier

3.5 USING FINANCIAL STATEMENT INFORMATION
Why Evaluate Financial Statements?
Choosing a Benchmark
Problems with Financial Statement Analysis

3.6 SUMMARY AND CONCLUSIONS

ANNOTATED CHAPTER OUTLINE

3.1 CASH FLOW AND FINANCIAL STATEMENTS: A CLOSER LOOK

Lecture Tip, page 46: Students sometimes get the impression that,because one must exercise care when using accounting data, it is of little value in decision-making. Why, they ask, should we bother with financial statement analysis? A constructive answer to this question is provided by Robert Higgins, who states in his financial analysis text that

> *"objectively determinable current values of many assets do not exist. Faced with a trade-off between relevant, but subjective current values, and irrelevant, but objective historical costs, accountants have opted for irrelevant historical costs. This means that it is the user's responsibility to make adjustments"*

to financial statement data where appropriate. In other words, financial statement information (and, by implication, financial statement analysis) is important because it is often the only source of information available.

A. Sources and Uses of Cash

T3.2: Hermetic, Inc., Balance Sheet

---

1. Activities that bring in cash are sources.
   Firms raise cash by selling assets, borrowing money or selling securities.

2. Activities that involve cash outflows are uses.

Firms use cash to buy assets or make payments to providers of capital.

3. Mechanical rules for determining Sources and Uses:

Sources	Uses
Decreases in assets	Increases in assets
Increases in equity and liabilities	Decreases in equity and liabilities

Lecture Tip, page 47: Student often experience difficulty when conceptualizing an increase in the cash balance, an asset, as a use of cash (they typically think of an increase in cash as a source of cash). It may be helpful to stress that a cash increase (a use) on the balance sheet must be realized through a reduction in another asset account (a source) or through an increase in a liability or an equity account (a source). Put another way, building up bank balances is definitely a use of cash because that same cash could be used to pay dividends.

B. The Statement of Cash Flows

Idea is to group cash flows into one of three categories

operating activities
investment activities
financing activities

T3.3: Hermetic, Inc., Income Statement

T3.4: Statement of Cash Flows

A General Statement of Cash Flows

Operating Activities

+ Net Income
+ Depreciation

+ Any decrease in current assets (except cash)
+ Any increase in current liabilities

− Any increase in current assets (except cash)
− Any decrease in current liabilities

Investment Activities

    + Ending net fixed assets
    − Beginning net fixed assets
    + Depreciation

Financing Activities

    ± Change in notes payable
    ± Change in long-term debt
    ± Change in common stock
    − Dividends

Putting it all together:

    ± Net cash flow from operating activities
    ± Fixed asset acquisition
    ± Net cash flow from financing activities

    = Net increase (decrease) in cash

T3.5: Hermetic, Inc., Statement of Cash Flows

3.2 STANDARDIZED FINANCIAL STATEMENTS

A. Common-Size Statements

Useful in comparisons of unequal size firms

T3.6: Hermetic, Inc., Common-Size Balance Sheet (2 pages)
T3.7: Hermetic, Inc., Common-Size Income Statement

---

1. Common-Size Balance Sheet
    Express individual accounts as a percent of total assets

2. Common-Size Income Statement
    Express individual items as a percent of sales

B. Common-Base-Year Financial Statements: Trend Analysis

Select a base year, then express each item or account as a percentage of the base-year value of that item (useful for picking up trends).

1. Combined Common-Size and Base-Year Analysis

Express each item in base year as a percent of either assets or sales. Then, compare each subsequent year's common-size percent to the base-year percent (abstracts from the growth in assets and sales).

3.3 RATIO ANALYSIS

```
T3.8:  Things to Consider: Financial Ratios
```

Things to Consider Concerning Financial Ratios

What aspects of the firm are we attempting to analyze? Generally, the aspects of interest are "fuzzy" (e.g., liquidity or utilization) and often both abstract and relative.

What information goes into a particular ratio and how does that information relate to the aspect of the firm being analyzed?

What is the unit of measurement? (e.g., dollars? days? turns?)

What would a "good" ratio look like? A "bad" one?

```
T3.9:  Categories of Financial Ratios
```

Categories of Financial Ratios

- Short-Term Solvency - Ability to pay bills in the short-run
- Long-Term Solvency - Ability to meet long-term obligations
- Asset Management - Intensity and efficiency of asset use
- Profitability - The bottom line
- Market Value - Going beyond financial statements

Lecture Tip, page 55: Students attempting to grasp financial statement analysis for the first time are often overwhelmed by what they perceive to be an incomprehensible series of "equations" and, as a result, fail to understand the "big picture". It can be useful to provide for them a simple framework. Ratio categories can be thought of as the financial "dimensions" of the firm, and are, therefore, analogous to the physical dimensions of an object. In either case, how we describe something is as function of the measures used to describe it. (Note: this "financial dimensions" idea is also developed in the Student Problem Manual.)

T3.10: Common Financial Ratios

A. Short-Term Solvency Measures (Liquidity Ratios)

1. <u>Current Ratio</u>
   Current assets/Current liabilities
   Hermetic $745/$435 = 1.71

2. <u>Quick Ratio</u>
   (Current assets − inventory)/Current liabilities
   Hermetic $(745 − 385)/$435 = .83

3. Other Liquidity Ratios
   <u>Cash ratio</u>
   Cash/Current liabilities
   Hermetic $50/$435 = .115 or about 12%

   <u>NWC/Total assets</u>
   Hermetic $(745 − 435)/$1845 = .17 or 17%

   <u>Interval measure</u>
   Current assets/Average daily operating costs
   Hermetic $745/($480/365) = 566.5 days

Lecture Tip, page 55: When asked to define liquidity, students invariably state that it refers to the ability to convert an asset into cash quickly. The instructor can stress the inadequacy of this definition by next asking the class to imagine that they own a new Corvette and if they believe they could sell it quickly for $100. The response will be yes. Is the car, therefore, necessarily a liquid asset? Of course not. This example usually ensures that students will remember the second half of the definition of liquidity - "with little or no loss in value" the next time the question arises.

Lecture Tip, page 56: Students often think that a high current ratio is favorable. The instructor might suggest that the class reconsider the statement of cash flows. All asset balances must be supported by funds sources which have a cost to the firm. If the ratio is higher than the industry norm, the firm would be maintaining larger amounts of long-term debt or equity relative to current assets. If a company can operate with lower levels of current assets without negatively impacting operations,this situation would be preferred since it would lower costs. (The use of a benchmark is discussed in Section 3.5.)

Lecture Tip, page 57: The instructor may want students to consider the interaction of ratios at this point in the text. The instructor could suggest a company scenario in which the current ratio exhibits no change over a two or three year trend. However, the quick ratio experiences a steady decline. This would indicate that the company is operating with lower levels of the more liquid assets relative to current liabilities. The instructor could alert the student to the possible dangers:

1. The company is operating with lower levels of the more liquid assets, and this situation should be monitored. A problem could arise should a large amount of current liabilities be due for payment. However, this may not be a major concern if the company had access to available lines of credit at a bank.

2. This situation also indicates that larger levels of inventory, relative to current liabilities, have accumulated in the firm. The instructor could state that an examination of other ratios is required to further explore this situation. It would be helpful to examine the level of inventory relative to sales (a lead into the turnover section).

B. Long-Term Solvency Measures (Financial Leverage)

Lecture Tip, page 58: This group of ratios really measures two different aspects of leverage - the level of indebtedness, and the ability to service debt. The former is indicative of the firm's debt capacity, while the latter more closely relates to the likelihood of default.

Further, it is sometimes helpful to alert students to some of the nuances of the ratios within these subgroups. For example, the total debt ratio measures what proportion of the firm's assets are financed with borrowed money, while the debt/equity ratio compares the amount of funds supplied by creditors and owners.

1. Total Debt Ratio
   (Total assets − Total equity)/Total assets
   Hermetic $(1,845 − 1,185)/$1,845 = .36 or 36%

   Variations:
   Debt/Equity = (Total assets − Total equity)/Total equity
   Equity multiplier = Total assets/Total equity = 1 + Debt/Equity

2. Long-term Debt Ratio
   Long-term debt/(Long-term debt + Total equity)
   Hermetic $225/$(225 + 1,185) = .16 or 16%

3. Times Interest Earned (TIE)
   EBIT/Interest
   Hermetic $200/$20 = 10 times

4. Cash Coverage
   (EBIT + Depreciation)/Interest
   Hermetic $(200 + 30)/$20 = 11.5 times

Lecture Tip, page 59: The importance of coverage ratios is sometimes overlooked, particularly when one considers their importance to creditors of all stripes. In their revision to Graham and Dodd's famous text, Security Analysis, Cottle, Murray, and Block describe five coverage ratios and include in the denominator such items as interest expense, rent, sinking fund payments, and lease payments. Particularly important is the fact that the format of the ratio(s) used depends greatly on the purpose of the analysis. (See Chapter 20, Security Analysis, fifth, edition, New York: McGraw-Hill, 1991.)

C. Asset Management Measures (Turnover Ratios)

1. Inventory Turnover
      COGS/Inventory
      Hermetic $480/$385 = 1.25 times

      Days sales in inventory: 365/Inventory turnover
      Hermetic 365/1.25 = 292 days

2. Receivables Turnover
      Sales/Accounts receivable
      Hermetic $710/$310 = 2.29 times

      Days sales in receivables (days sales outstanding)
      365/Receivables turnover
      Hermetic 365/2.29 = 159 days

3. Asset Turnover Ratios (variations on a theme)
      NWC turnover = Sales/NWC

      Fixed asset turnover = Sales/Net fixed assets

      Total assets turnover = Sales/Total assets
      Hermetic $710/$1,845 = .385 times

Lecture Tip, page 60: The instructor may wish to mention that there may be significant inconsistencies in the methods used to compute ratios by financial advisory firms (Example: Table 3.10, a page from Robert Morris Associates) due to the nature of the industry (in reference to footnote 4). When using ratios supplied by others, it is important to be aware of the exact financial items used. A manufacturer would typically consider inventory at cost and thus relate inventory to cost of goods sold. However, a retailer might maintain its inventory level based on retail price. In the latter case, inventory should be related to sales to compute inventory turnover. The markup would cancel in the numerator and denominator and give an accurate indication of turnover based on cost.

Lecture Tip, page 61: In discussing the nature of financial statement analysis, the instructor may wish to emphasize frequently that it is a means to an end, rather than an end in itself. This suggests that financial ratios are "red flags", and that a good analyst will use them to determine what to investigate further.

Consider the following example. Calvada, Inc.'s average collection period ratio is significantly higher than the industry norm. What questions might one ask?

1. What are the firm's credit terms? The industry's terms, on average?
2. Has the ACP been trending upward? Or is this an aberration?
3. Which customers are contributing to the relatively high ACP?
4. Is this an industrywide phenomenon? Economywide?

Clearly, these are questions that cannot all be answered easily. The instructor may wish to emphasize that a good analyst will consider questions like these in making a final determination about the firm's ability to manage its assets.

Lecture Tip, page 62: Students should be warned that, just as one must take care in making generalizations across industries, intra-industry generalizations should also be made with great caution. For example, a fixed asset turnover ratio that is high relative to that of the industry can be the result of efficient asset utilization, or it can indicate that the firm is utilizing old (and perhaps inefficient) equipment, while others in the industry have invested in modern equipment. This example also provides the instructor the opportunity to illustrate the underlying linkages inherent in financial statement analysis. In this case, the firm using inefficient equipment would display a favorable fixed asset turnover ratio, but would also be likely to display a higher level of expenses, and, unless offset by other factors, lower profitability.

D. Profitability Measures (The Bottom Line)

These measures are based upon <u>book</u> values, not market values, and so may not convey much useful information.

     1. <u>Profit margin</u>
        Net income/Sales
        Hermetic $126.55/$710 = 17.8%

     2. <u>Return on Assets</u>
        Net income/Total assets
        Hermetic $126.55/$1,845 = 6.8%

     3. <u>Return on Equity</u>
        Net income/Total equity
        Hermetic $126.55/$1,185 = 10.7%

Lecture Tip, page 63: The instructor may wish to emphasize that, in most instances, return on equity is the most important accounting indication of management's success in accomplishing the shareholders' valuation objective. The significance of this ratio will be further explored in Section 3.4, "The Du Pont Identity."

E. Market Value Measures (for publicly traded firms)

     1. Price/Earnings ratio
     2. Market-to-book ratio

Lecture Tip, page 64: While some investors seem to view price-earnings ratios as universally applicable measures, differences in generally accepted accounting practices used to compute the numerator, earnings per share, make international comparisons risky. For example, for many years, conventional wisdom has held that the high P/Es of Japanese stocks have been due in part to the more conservative nature of Japanese accounting practices, which tends to depress reported earnings and, therefore, increase P/Es.

An interesting discussion of this issue appears in the November 14, 1988 issue of Pensions and Investment Age. On the one hand, Gary Schieneman, vice president of international equity research with Prudential-Bache applies U.S. accounting standards to 25 Japanese firms in 17 industries and finds little evidence of a systematic downward bias in reported earnings. On the other hand, Paul Aron, vice-chairman emeritus at Daiwa Securities, Inc. contends that, after adjusting for methodological problems, 75% of the firms in Mr. Schieneman's sample did indeed underreport earnings relative to those computed using U.S. standards. Regardless of who is correct, though, the most telling aspect of the discussion is Mr. Schieneman's comment in summing up: "I don't think earnings mean a whole lot in Japan."

Lecture Tip, page 64: The instructor could ask students to consider how the market-to-book ratio could be interpreted if the student was considering the purchase of the company's stock. Some might feel a ratio less than one would be preferred since the stock is selling below the equity value on the books. One could use this point to comment that the market is evaluating the company's future earning power while the book value figures reflect the cost at which stock had previously been issued and the amount of the past retained earnings on the company's balance sheet. The students could then be asked to consider which is more important. The instructor could also mention that valuation techniques concerning a company's future earnings will be explored in Chapter 5 and later chapters. Additionally, the efficiency of the market's pricing will be examined, beginning with Chapter 10, "Capital Market History."

3.4 THE DU PONT IDENTITY

> ### T3.11: The Du Pont Identity

How does financial leverage transform return on assets into return on equity?

$$Return\ on\ Equity = \frac{Net\ Income}{Total\ equity} = \frac{Net\ Income}{Assets} \times \frac{Assets}{Equity}$$

That is, ROE = Return on assets × Equity multiplier

Decomposing ROA into profit margin and asset turnover gives

$$ROE = \frac{Net\ Income}{Sales} \times \frac{Sales}{Assets} \times \frac{Assets}{Equity}$$

Profit margin × Asset turnover × Equity multiplier
Operating efficiency × Asset use × Financial leverage
Hermetic = .178 × .385 × 1.56 = 10.7%

3.5 USING FINANCIAL STATEMENT INFORMATION

A. Why Evaluate Financial Statements?

1. Internal Uses: Evaluating performance, spotting trouble, generating projections
2. External Uses: Making credit decisions, evaluating competitors, assessing acquisitions

Lecture Tip, page 67: Much of financial statement analysis is rooted in a manufacturing tradition with the large industrial corporation at its center. That is, many of the notions about statement analysis grew out of a view of business in which specialized plant and equipment is used to turn raw goods into finished goods which are sold on credit.

This view was modified by the advent of the large, retail corporation, but the emphasis on balance sheet assets (receivables, inventories, plant and equipment) and the measures associated with them remain.

Because of this manufacturer/retailer tradition, much of the conventional wisdom about statement analysis is inappropriate to many of today's business situations. Take, for example, professional services firms such as those formed by lawyers, accountants, doctors, management consultants, computer programmers, and engineers. Or consider television networks, radio stations, colleges and universities. The most valuable assets of such firms are not on the balance sheet, their liquidity is not in a stock of current assets, and their liabilities are not all represented. Rather, their assets are human capital, licenses, viewership, and reputation; their liquidity lies in an ability to generate revenues; and their liabilities include negligence, malpractice, and malfeasance.

Thus, financial statement analysis as we know it is a product of our economic history. We can expect it to evolve to encompass new economic realities, but as it does it is important to understand its perspective and the limitations imposed by it.

B. Choosing a Benchmark

<u>Example: Ratio Comparison Across Business Types—What's My Line?</u>[1]

Identify the electric utility (B), retail jeweler (E), auto manufacturer (A), Japanese trading company (D), and supermarket chain (C) using their common-size statements and financial ratios

<u>Key common-size accounts in the comparison:</u>
Inventories, receivables, property and equipment, debt

<u>Key ratios in the comparison:</u>
Profit margin, inventory turnover, total asset turnover

---

[1]The example is adapted from Fruhan, Kester, Mason, Piper, and Ruback, *Case Problems in Finance*, 10th ed. (Homewood, Illinois: Richard D. Irwin, Inc.), 1992, p. 20, with the permission of the publisher.

T3.12: Ratio Comparison across Business Types

The principle is essentially management by exception.

1. Time-trend Analysis
   Significant changes to be looked into.

2. Peer Group Analysis
   Significant differences are to be examined.
   Industry group comparisons are common (SIC).

C. Problems with Financial Statement Analysis

-no underlying financial theory
-finding comparable firms
-what to do with conglomerates
-differences in accounting practices
-differences in fiscal year
-differences in capital structure
-seasonal variations
-one-time events

Ethics Note, page 72:   An interesting example of an additional problem faced by professional analysts is demonstrated by the Trump-Roffman case. In 1990. Marvin Roffman, an analyst at Janney Montgomery Scott, Inc. stated in a Wall Street Journal article that, on the basis of his examination of the financial data, he had "severe reservations about the future" of the Trump Taj Mahal in Atlantic City. In response, Donald Trump threatened to sue Janney Montgomery Scott. Roffman wrote, and subsequently retracted, a public apology to Trump, and was dismissed. He successfully sued and received a large settlement. Nonetheless, his case illustrates the dangers one faces as a practicing analyst. (For further details of this case, see the New York Times, June 6, 1991.)

T3.13: A Brief Case History of Hermetic, Inc.

Lecture Tip, page 72:   The following example is useful in illustrating the kinds of problems that can come up in comparing financial statements.

A "Spot the Potential Problems" Example

Hermetic is a wholesale firm with a January 1 to December 31 fiscal year. Several competitors use a July 1 to June 30 fiscal year. Most of Hermetic's sales are to small retailers on credit. Some competitors are cash-and-carry only. About 50% of Hermetic's annual sales occur in the last quarter, October to December.

Hermetic generally uses trade credit from manufacturers to finance its inventories. At the end of the year, however, Hermetic takes advantage of after-season clearance sales by manufacturers to stock up on inventory, financing the purchases with bank loans.

While Hermetic uses First-In-First-Out inventory accounting, many of its competitors use Last-In-First-Out. Furthermore, Hermetic owns its warehouses and equipment while some competitors lease theirs.

Implications:

The January to December fiscal year and year-end inventory build-up have given rise to relatively high (compared to other times of the year) levels of receivables, inventory, payables, and notes—producing the following ratios:

Inventory turnover: $480/$385 = 1.25 turns
Days sales in inventory: 365/1.25 = 292 days

Receivables turnover: $710/$310 = 2.29 turns
Days in receivables: 365/2.29 = 159 days

Total asset turnover: .385 turns
Total debt ratio: $(1,845 − 1,185)/$1845 = 36%

By averaging quarterly or semi-annual balance sheet values the fiscal year and seasonal sales effects can be mitigated.

The inventory accounting may lead to Hermetic showing a higher level of inventory (increasing price environment) or lower level (declining price environment) compared to competitors.

If competitors have not had to capitalize their leases, Hermetic will show substantially higher plant and equipment amounts, and may have a lower ROA and ROE as a result. Of course, lease payments are cash flows while depreciation is not, but the income statement doesn't make that distinction.

3.6 SUMMARY AND CONCLUSIONS

T3.14: Solution to Problem 3.6
T3.15: Solution to Problem 3.13
T3.16: Solution to Problem 3.32

MINI-CASE: COMPAQ COMPUTER CORPORATION

"The computer industry . . . is in a time of fundamental transition, and the velocity of change is increasing."

John Akers, former Chairman
International Business Machines Corporation
(quoted in Standard and Poor's Industry Survey, 1993 edition)

Recent years have proven to be difficult financially for the personal computer industry. The requirement to innovate and stay ahead of the technological curve while at the same time cutting costs, meeting slackening demand, and facing growing competition from abroad have all contributed to ever-slimmer profit margins.

COMPAQ Computer Corporation was incorporated in 1982 and quickly grew to become a major adversary of IBM in the personal computer market. However, in the early 1990s, COMPAQ began to suffer financial difficulties (along with many other personal computer manufacturers) and, in October 1992 was forced to lay off 1,000 employees in response to pressures to cut costs. One reason the difficulties arose was that, while more and more people began to substitute microcomputers for mainframes, they also recognized that low-cost "clones" could perform just as well as brand-name equipment. This forced major firms such as IBM and COMPAQ to engage in aggressive price-cutting to a degree unthinkable just a few years earlier. COMPAQ's problems were exacerbated by the fact that its share of the personal computer market fell from 4.6 percent in 1990 to 4.1 percent in 1991, a drop of over 12 percentage points. The uncertainty surrounding COMPAQ is reflected in the variation in its stock price in 1991: the stock traded as high as $74.25 and as low as $22.125.

Assume that you are an analyst for a major financial institution and have been asked to assess COMPAQ's current financial position. Financial statement information appears below.

COMPAQ Computer Corporation
Income Statement

	1991	1990
Sales	$3,271,367	$3,598,768
Cost of Sales	2,053,576	2,057,886
Gross Profit	1,217,791	1,540,882
Research and Development	197,277	185,726
Selling, General & Administrative Expenses	852,491	1,160,970
Other Income and Expense	(144,856)	(42,195)
Earnings Before Tax	154,036	641,433
Taxes	42,932	216,205
Net Income	130,869	454,910

COMPAQ Computer Corporation
Balance Sheet

	1991	1990
Current Assets		
Cash and Marketable Securities	452,174	434,700
Accounts Receivable	624,376	626,548
Inventories	436,824	543,630
Prepaid Expenses and Other Current Assets	269,203	83,054
Total Current Assets	1,782,577	1,687,932
Net Fixed Assets	883,765	892,132
Other Assets	160,044	137,465
Total Assets	2,826,326	2,717,529

	1991	1990
Current Liabilities		
Accounts Payable	195,582	292,367
Income Taxes Payable	33,103	50,631
Other Current Liabilities	409,258	300,035
Total Current Liabilities	637,943	643,033
Long-Term Debt	73,456	73,996
Deferred Income Taxes	184,283	141,487
Common Stock (par = $.01)	842	861
Capital Surplus	536,814	595,973
Retained Earnings	1,393,048	1,262,179
Stockholders' Equity	1,930,704	1,859,013
Total Liabilities and Stockholders' Equity	2,826,386	2,717,539

Source: Moody's Industrial Manuals, 1992 and 1993 editions.

Questions

1. Industry average values for selected ratios appear below.[1]

	1991	1990
Current Ratio	2.61	2.26
Debt to Total Capitalization	8.7%	14.33%
Equity Multiplier	1.89	2.36
Total Asset Turnover	1.94	2.33
Net Profit Margin	5.49%	6.09%
Return on Assets	10.53%	12.84%
Return on Equity	20.13%	33.49%

    Compute analogous ratios for COMPAQ. How does COMPAQ compare to its industry peers in terms of liquidity? Leverage? Asset utilization? Profitability? Are any trends apparent in the data?

2. Compute the Du Pont identity for COMPAQ and for the industry for 1990 and 1991. Did COMPAQ achieve its ROE values in the same way as other firms in the industry? Do your results provide any clues to COMPAQ's management philosophy?

3. Interpret your results. Based on 1991 values, would you characterize COMPAQ as a firm that is performing better than or worse than its industry peers?

4. Would you recommend that the stock be purchased by investors? Is COMPAQ's stock more suitable as an investment for a young person with many income-producing years ahead, or to a retiree seeking current income?

---

[1]   These data are based on individual firm values appearing in Standard and Poor's Industry Survey. Industry peers include the following firms: AST Research, Apple Computer, Commodore International, COMPAQ, Dell Computer Corp., Tandy Corp., and Zeos International, Ltd.

SOLUTIONS TO THE COMPAQ COMPUTER CORPORATION MINI-CASE

This case is designed to accomplish two things. First, it provides students the opportunity to exercise their analytical skills using "real-world" data from a firm that they have heard of. Second, the questions are somewhat open-ended, and they allow the instructor to raise issues that foreshadow several topics to be covered in future chapters. You may wish to distribute the mini-case as a homework assignment, use it as a quiz following Chapter 3, or break the class into groups and have one group present the results to the rest of the class.

1. Ratio comparisons:

	Industry 1991	COMPAQ 1991	Industry 1990	COMPAQ 1990
Current Ratio	2.61	2.79	2.26	2.62
Debt to Total Capitalization[1]	8.7%	3.4%	14.33%	3.6%
Equity Multiplier	1.89	1.46	2.36	1.46
Total Asset Turnover	1.94	1.16	2.33	1.32
Net Profit Margin	5.49%	4.0%	6.09%	12.6%
Return on Assets	10.53%	4.6%	12.84%	16.7%
Return on Equity	20.13%	6.7%	33.49%	24.4%

Liquidity: COMPAQ is slightly more liquid than its peers in both years. This is a good place to emphasize, however, the importance of inventory management in an industry such as this. A good analyst would attempt to ascertain the relative inventory levels of COMPAQ and its competitors.

Further, you should point out that the increases in the current ratios above might reflect inventory accumulation due to the slackening of demand noted in the case text. The latter possibility is particularly disturbing when one considers that this was a period of aggressive price-cutting in order to move merchandise.

Leverage: COMPAQ has significantly less financial leverage than its peers. You might wish to ask the students why this is the case. Is COMPAQ's management more fiscally conservative than its competitors? Does COMPAQ have more business risk than its competitors? Several issues can be raised which lead into foreshadowing discussions of future topics.

Of course, COMPAQ's relatively low equity multiplier will affect its ROE. (See question 3 below.)

Asset Utilization: COMPAQ's total asset turnover ratio is also significantly less than the industry norm in both years. Further investigation should be undertaken to ascertain if this is due to excess inventory (noted above) or to relatively high fixed asset levels. This is a good point at which to emphasize interrelatedness of financial ratios. Students are sometimes slow to recognize that inferences drawn from the calculation of one set of ratios can be verified (or refuted) by calculating those ratios in another set.

Profitability: This may be the most dramatic comparison to be made. While the industry's net profit margin falls to 5.49% from 6.09%, COMPAQ's PM falls by over two-thirds (!) to 4.0% from 12.6%. Students should be asked how a such a result might occur. Possible answers: Drastic price-cutting (as in this case), marked reductions in volume, large increases in operating expenses, etc. Which of the possibilities is most likely here?

A similar pattern is observed in the ROA and ROE measures. In the next question we investigate the latter.

2. Du Pont identity: ROE = Net profit margin × Total asset turnover × Equity multiplier

| Industry (1991) | 5.49 x 1.94 x 1.89 = 20.13% |
| COMPAQ (1991) | 4.0 x 1.16 x 1.46 = 6.77% |

| Industry (1990) | 6.09 x 2.33 x 2.36 = 33.49% |
| COMPAQ (1990) | 12.64 x 1.32 x 1.46 = 24.36% |

Configuring the numbers in this manner confirms our suspicions that the decline in COMPAQ's ROE is largely the result of the dramatic decline in its PM. COMPAQ's asset efficiency and leverage are both less than the industry values, but they decline in a manner roughly consistent with those of the industry.

It is sometimes useful for students to speculate on the firm's management philosophy on the basis of the quantitative analysis. For example, one might ask students if there is any indication that COMPAQ's management overreacted to increased competition in 1991? Under what conditions might it be a good strategy to cut prices? Can this strategy be sustained?

3. Interpretation: Clearly, COMPAQ underperformed the industry during the period examined. One approach to take here is to facilitate 15-20 minutes of open-ended discussion in order to compare different points of view concerning COMPAQ's performance. Some students (e.g., MIS majors) will undoubtedly be familiar with COMPAQ and the personal computer industry. Others will not, but will be more familiar with the vagaries of accounting data. Marketing students will enjoy looking a the problem from their own viewpoint. The bottom line is that a wide-ranging discussion will not only cement the ratio definitions in students' minds, it will convince them of the vast amount of information contained in a relatively few numbers - information that can be "unlocked" with a few simple calculations.

4. Recommendation: This question is designed to lead to a discussion of the apparent risk and return characteristics of COMPAQ stock and, more generally, to a discussion of investor behavior and security valuation, which leads in to Chapter 6.

---

[1]   Following the definitions used in the Industry Survey, the debt-to-total capitalization ratio is equal to Long-term debt/(Stockholders' equity + long-term debt + deferred income taxes).

CHAPTER 4
LONG-TERM FINANCIAL PLANNING AND GROWTH

TRANSPARENCIES

T4.1: Chapter Outline
T4.2: Financial Planning Model Ingredients
T4.3: Example: A Simple Financial Planning Model
T4.4: The Percentage of Sales Approach
T4.5: Pro Forma Statements
T4.6: The Percentage of Sales Approach: A Financing Plan
T4.7: The Percentage of Sales Approach: An Alternative Scenario
T4.8: Growth and External Financing
T4.9: Growth and Financing Needed For the Hoffman Company
T4.10: Internal Growth Rate
T4.11: Sustainable Growth Rate
T4.12: Questions the Financial Planner Should Consider
T4.13: Solution to Problem 4.9
T4.14: Solution to Problem 4.16

CHAPTER ORGANIZATION

T4.1: Chapter Outline

4.1 WHAT IS FINANCIAL PLANNING?
Growth as a Financial Management Goal
Dimensions of Financial Planning
What Can Planning Accomplish?

4.2 FINANCIAL PLANNING MODELS: A FIRST LOOK
A Financial Planning Model: The Ingredients
A Simple Financial Planning Model

4.3 THE PERCENTAGE OF SALES APPROACH
An Illustration of the Percentage of Sales Approach

4.4 EXTERNAL FINANCING AND GROWTH
EFN and Growth

Financial Policy and Growth

4.5 SOME CAVEATS OF FINANCIAL PLANNING MODELS

4.6 SUMMARY AND CONCLUSIONS

ANNOTATED CHAPTER OUTLINE

4.1 WHAT IS FINANCIAL PLANNING?

A. Growth as a Financial Management Goal

Growth is a by-product of increasing value.

B. Dimensions of Financial Planning

Planning horizon (usually 2-5 years)

Aggregation (lumping accounts together)

Lecture Tip, page 84:   Students may grasp the notion of best- and worst-case scenarios incompletely, without realizing it. For example, if asked to describe a worst-case situation, a student might answer "If sales drop by 40%." You may wish to emphasize that, in reality, it is often the confluence of several (sometimes related) factors in combination that constitute a worst- or best case. One might better describe a worst-case scenario as one in which sales drop by 40% due to an economic downturn, which, in turn, causes a buildup in finished goods, and is reflected in a slowing of payments from customers, and perhaps, a reduction in the firm's ability to borrow on a short-term basis. Financial management involves the ability to deal with these situations simultaneously - only with a financial planning model of some type can one hope to estimate the multiple effects of these events on cash flows.

C. What Can Planning Accomplish?

Interactions (between investments and financing)

Options (investment and financing)

Avoiding Surprises (contingency plans)

Feasibility and Internal Consistency

4.2 FINANCIAL PLANNING MODELS: A FIRST LOOK

T4.2: Financial Planning Model Ingredients

A. A Financial Planning Model: The Ingredients

Sales Forecast
-most other considerations depend upon it

Pro Forma Statements
-the output summarizing different projections

Asset Requirements
-investment needed to support sales growth

Financial Requirements
-debt and dividend policies

The "Plug"
-designated source(s) of external financing

Economic Assumptions
-state of economy, interest rates, inflation

T4.3: Example: A Simple Financial Planning Model

Lecture Tip, page 87: Some students may complain that the effects of aggregation produce "unrealistic" results, as in aggregating depreciation and interest expense in costs, or pooling all sorts of assets to get the capital intensity ratio. While correct, this criticism is misdirected. The point of the method discussed is not to produce a detailed financial plan, but to highlight the relationships, especially between investments and financial policy, to be considered when planning for growth. The appendix presents a more detailed plan, while still finer and more sophisticated methods are in use.

4.3 THE PERCENTAGE OF SALES APPROACH

The idea is that sales generate retained earnings. Retained earnings, plus external funds raised, support an increase in assets. More assets lead to more sales, and the cycle starts again.

A. An Illustration of the Percentage of Sales Approach

The Income Statement

Given forecasted sales and a constant profit margin, what retained earnings can be expected?

<u>Define:</u>

S = previous period's sales
g = projected growth rate of sales
A = previous period's ending total assets
PM = profit margin
b = retention or plowback ratio

Addition to retained earnings = PM × S(1 + g) × b

The Balance Sheet

What assets are needed to support sales growth? If we assume 100% capacity utilization, a simplified approach is to use:

A × g = Increase in assets

Alternatively, we might use a *capital intensity ratio* (= Assets/Sales) to find the assets necessary to support $1 of sales. This can be different for different types of assets, e.g., a ratio of .5:1 for current assets and 1.5:1 for fixed assets.

However figured, if the increase in total assets exceeds the addition to retained earnings, the difference is *external financing needed*, EFN.

T4.4: **The Percentage of Sales Approach**
T4.5: **Pro Forma Statements**
T4.6: **The Percentage of Sales Approach: A Financing Plan**
T4.7: **The Percentage of Sales Approach: An Alternative Scenario**

<u>Aside</u>: If asset use is less than 100% of capacity, fixed assets will not necessarily need to increase by g. Sales supportable by full capacity = S ÷ % use.

Example: EFN

Sales, S,	= $9,362	Profit margin, PM,	= 14.34%
Current assets	= $2,364.60	Plowback ratio, b,	=50%
Net fixed assets	= $16,374.80	Payables	= 7% of assets

What external funds are needed for sales to increase 10%?

Addition to retained earnings:
$$= PM \times S(1+g) \times b$$
$$= (.1434)(\$9,362.1)(1.1)(.5) = \$738.39$$

Increase in assets:
$$= A \times g \text{ (assuming 100\% capacity use)}$$
$$= (\$18,739.4)(.1) = \$1,873.9$$

Optional: suppose fixed assets are currently used at 90% of capacity. They will support sales of $10,402.3 (= $9,362.1/.9), so no new fixed assets would be needed. Current assets needed = (Current assets $\times$ g) = $236.5:

$$EFN = \$1,873.9 - 738.39 = \$1,135.51$$

Symbolically,

$$EFN = (A \times g) - [S(1 + g) \times PM \times b].$$

Optional: Suppose payables increase with sales. The increase in spontaneous funds would be 7% $\times$ A $\times$ g = (.07)(18,739.4)(.1) = $131.2:

$$EFN = \$1,873.9 - 738.39 - 131.2 = \$1,004.31$$

Lecture Tip, page 90: In the first three chapters of the text, we have described "the financing decision"in one of two ways: either in relatively broad terms, referring simply to the means by which funding is acquired with which to accomplish our investment objectives, or relatively specifically - e.g., in terms of capital structure. At this point, the financing decision is characterized in another way: as one aspect of the practice of working capital management. The instructor may wish to take this opportunity to set the stage for the material in Chapters 17-19. Specifically, one may find it helpful to introduce the concept of "spontaneous" financing, i.e., that financing which arises in the normal course of business, requires little (if any) face-to-face negotiation with the lender, and which is less likely to result in bankruptcy proceedings in the event of default. Students should be reminded that while long-term financing decisions may have greater potential impacts on firm value, they are made relatively infrequently. Short-term investment and financing decisions are made virtually continuously and affect the "lifeblood" - daily cash flows" - of the business.

Lecture Tip, page 91: The instructor may wish to integrate the various issues presented in Chapters 2, 3 and 4 at this time. The company's plan for the sales increase must be supported by an investment in additional current and fixed assets (cash uses). On the liability side, current liabilities will increase (a source) due to the increase in the purchase of inventory. At this point, we have accounted for the investment in fixed assets and addition to net working capital (a net use).
    The balancing must come from some cash source: either from a retention of the current year's operating cash flow or through the issuance of new debt or new

equity. These latter two items (new debt or new equity) represent the external financing needs or alternatives the company would consider for its cash sources.

Regression analysis is a commonly used technique to forecast financial requirements. The line of best fit relating sales to various individual asset categories will provide the analyst with a more accurate prediction of how a particular balance sheet account will change for varied levels of projected sales.

4.4 EXTERNAL FINANCING AND GROWTH

Other things the same, more growth means more external financing will be needed.

Lecture Tip, page 93: You may wish to point out that the relationship between firm growth and external financing needs is of utmost importance to firms in the early stages of the product life-cycle. Typically, these are firms which have developed a new product or technology, are experiencing rapid sales growth, have continuing capital needs, and must be extremely careful in forecasting cash flows. Since many of these firms are relatively small and/or new, their financing problems are often exacerbated by a lack of access to the capital markets. As such, the "internal growth rate" and "sustainable growth rate" concepts are of particular importance to the financial decision-makers at these firms.

T4.8: Growth and External Financing
T4.9: Growth and Financing Needed for the Hoffman Company

A. EFN and Growth

Assuming no spontaneous sources of funds, EFN can be expressed as the increase in total assets less addition to retained earnings.

The increase in assets required is simply equal to the original assets multiplied by the growth rate. For low growth rates, a firm will run a surplus, resulting in a decline in the debt/equity ratio. As the growth rate increases, the surplus becomes a deficit as the requirement for new assets exceeds the addition to retained earnings.

B. Financial Policy and Growth

T4.10: Internal Growth Rate
T4.11: Sustainable Growth Rate

The internal growth rate is the growth rate that the firm can maintain with internal financing only.

Internal growth rate = (ROA × b) / (1 − ROA × b)

where b = plowback ratio.

The sustainable growth rate is the maximum growth rate a firm can achieve without external equity financing while maintaining a constant debt/equity ratio.

Sustainable growth rate = (ROE × b) / (1 − ROE × b).

Lecture Tip, page 97: Some students will wonder why managers would wish to avoid issuing equity to meet anticipated financing needs. This is a good opportunity to bring in concepts from previous chapters (e.g., stockholder/bondholder conflicts of interest and the resultant agency costs), as well as introduce topics to be covered in future chapters (information asymmetry and the signalling aspects of equity issuance - Chapter 12, issuance costs - Chapter 13, the relatively high cost of equity capital - Chapter 14, capital structure - Chapter 15, and control issues - Chapter 21).

Determinants of growth:

From the Du Pont identity, ROE can be viewed as the product of profit margin, assets turnover, and the equity multiplier. Anything that increases ROE will increase the sustainable growth rate by making the numerator larger and the denominator smaller.

So, the sustainable growth depends on:

  a. Operating efficiency, reflected in profit margin
  b. Asset use efficiency, reflected in total asset turnover or capital intensity
  c. Financial policy, reflected in debt/equity ratio
  d. Dividend policy, reflected in retention or plowback ratio

Lecture Tip, page 100: Wanting sales or revenues to grow by X% a year as a goal of the firm is properly understood as meaning: "Other things the same, we want sales to grow." The "other things the same" part is often not well understood. Here are some ideas to consider:

-cutting margins might make sales "grow," but is it desirable? (can be related to demand elasticity)
-cutting the dividend might "pay" for growth, but is that desirable?
-increasing the proportion of borrowing might "pay" for growth, but is it desirable?
-employing more assets per dollar of sales might make sales "grow," but is it desirable?

4.5 SOME CAVEATS OF FINANCIAL PLANNING MODELS

The problem is that the models are really accounting statement generators rather than determinants of value. They ignore cash flows, timing, and risk.

Lecture Tip, page 101: As presented here, growth "happens" as a consequence of financial policy and profitability. Of course, ultimately growth depends on selling more of something and some students may feel the chapter's treatment neglects relevant marketing aspects. Here, the point is to draw attention to the investment and financing implications of growth.

Some may also be concerned that there is little management involvement when most of the investment and financing relationships are treated as given. While this is necessarily true to start with, potentially all aspects of profitability, asset investment, and financial policy are candidates for "management."

Lecture Tip, page 101: The hoary adage "Garbage in, garbage out" is particularly apt when it comes to assessing the usefulness of financial planning models. Students (and practitioners) often find these models seductively complex and seemingly complete, ignoring the fact that the output is only as good as the inputs, which, in turn, may be of questionable accuracy. In order to reduce the possibility that poor decisions are made on the basis of plan output, the analyst should ask the following questions:

-Are the results (additional asset requirements, net income, etc.) reasonable?
-Have I considered all possible outcomes?
-How reasonable are the assumptions employed in generating the financial results?
-Which assumptions and variables have the greatest impact on projected cash flows?
-What have I forgotten?

T4.12 Questions the Financial Planner Should Consider

4.6 SUMMARY AND CONCLUSIONS

T4.13: Solution to Problem 4.9
T4.14: Solution to Problem 4.16

HANDOUT: A FINANCIAL PLANNING MODEL FOR THE ROBERTS COMPANY[1]

In this handout, we discuss how to get started with building a financial planing model in somewhat greater detail. Our goal is to build a simple model for the Roberts Company that incorporates some features commonly found in planning models.

Table 1
ROBERTS COMPANY
Income Statement and Balance Sheet

Income Statement

Sales	(S)	$500
Costs	(C)	235
Depreciation	(DEP)	120
Interest	(INT)	45
Taxable income	(TI)	$100
Taxes (34%)	(T)	34
Net Income	(NI)	$ 66
Addition to retained earnings (ARE)		$ 22
Dividends	(DIV)	$ 44

Balance Sheet

Assets			Liabilities and Owners' Equity		
Current assets	(CA)	$ 400	Total debt	(D)	$ 450
Net fixed assets	(FA)	600	Owners' equity	(E)	550
			Total liabilities and		
Total assets	(TA)	$1000	owners' equity	(L)	$1000

This model will include our percentage of sales approach as a special case, but it will be more flexible and a little more realistic. It is by no means complete, but should give you an idea how to proceed.

Table 1 shows the financial statements for the Roberts Company in more detail than the financial statements shown earlier. We have separated out depreciation and interest, and included abbreviations that will be used to refer to various statement items.

We use new borrowing as the plug in our model, and we assume that Roberts does not issue new equity. This means that we allow the debt/equity ratio to change if needed. Our model takes a sales forecast as its input and supplies the pro forma financial statements as its output.

---

[1] This example draws, in part, from R.A. Brealey and S. C. Myers, *Principles of Corporate Finance*, 3rd ed. (New York:McGraw-Hill, 1988), Chapter 28.

To create our model, we take the financial statements and replace the numbers with formulas describing their relationships. In addition to the symbols above, we will use E_0 to stand for beginning equity. With this in mind, Table 2 contains the resulting model.

Table 2
ROBERTS COMPANY
Long-Term Financial Planning Model
Income Statement

Sales	S = Input by user
Costs	$C = a_1 \times S$
Depreciation	$DEP = a_2 \times FA$
Interest	$\underline{INT = a_3 \times D}$
Taxable income	$TI = S - C - DEP - INT$
Taxes	$\underline{T = a_4 \times TI}$
Net income	$\underline{NI = TI - T}$

Addition to retained earnings	$ARE = NI - DIV$
Dividends	$DIV = a_5 \times NI$

Balance Sheet

Assets		*Liabilities and Owners' Equity*	
Current assets	$CA = TA - FA$	Total debt	$D = TA - E$
Net fixed assets	$\underline{FA = a_6 \times TA}$	Owners' equity	$\underline{E = E_0 + ARE}$
		Total liabilities and	
Total assets	$\underline{TA = a_7 \times S}$	owners' equity	$\underline{L = TA}$

In Table 2, the symbols a_1 through a_7 are called the *model parameters*. These describe the relationships among the variables. For example, a_7 is the relationship between sales and total assets, and it can be interpreted as the capital intensity ratio:

$$TA = a_7 \times S \quad \text{or} \quad a_7 = TA/S = \text{Capital intensity ratio.}$$

Similarly, a_3 is the relationship between total debt and interest paid, so a_3 can be interpreted as an overall interest rate. The tax rate is given by a_4, and a_5 is the dividend payout ratio.

This model uses new borrowing as the plug by first setting total liabilities and owners' equity equal to total assets. Next, ending owners' equity is calculated as the beginning amount, E_0, plus the addition to retained earnings, ARE. The difference, TA-E, is the new total debt needed to balance.

The primary difference between this model and our earlier EFN approach is that we have separated out depreciation and interest. Notice that a_2 expresses depreciation as a fraction of beginning fixed assets. This, along with the assumption that the interest paid depends on total debt, is a more realistic approach than we used earlier. However, since interest and depreciation now do not necessarily vary directly with sales, we no longer have a constant profit margin.

The model parameters a_1-a_7 can be based on a simple percentage of sales approach, or they can be determined by any other means the model builder wishes. For example, they might be based on average values for the last several years, industry standards, subjective estimates, or even company targets. Alternatively, sophisticated statistical techniques can be used to estimate them.

We will finish this discussion by estimating the model parameters for Roberts using simple percentages and then generating pro forma statements for a $600 predicted sales level. We estimate the parameters as:

$$a_1 = \$235/\$500 \quad = .47 = \text{Cost percentage}$$
$$a_2 = \$120/\$600 \quad = .20 = \text{Depreciation rate}$$
$$a_3 = \$45/\$450 \quad = .10 = \text{Interest rate}$$
$$a_4 = \$34/\$100 \quad = .34 = \text{Tax rate}$$
$$a_5 = \$44/\$66 \quad = .67 = \text{Payout ratio}$$
$$a_6 = \$600/\$1,000 \quad = .60 = \text{Fixed assets/Total assets}$$
$$a_7 = \$1,000/\$500 \quad = 2.0 = \text{Capital intensity ratio}$$

With these parameters and a sales forecast of $600, our pro forma financial statements are shown in Table 3. Our model tells us is that a sales increase of $100 will require $200 in net new assets (since the capital intensity ratio is 2). To finance this, we will use $24 in internally generated funds. The balance, $176, must be borrowed. This is the increase in total debt on the balance sheet: $626-450 = $176. If we pursue this plan, our profit margin will decline and the debt/equity ratio will rise.

Table 3
ROBERTS COMPANY
Income Statement and Balance Sheet

Income Statement

Sales	(S)	$600 = Input
Costs	(C)	282 = .46 × $600
Depreciation	(DEP)	144 = .20 × $720
Interest	(INT)	63 = .10 × $626
Taxable income	(TI)	$111 = $600 - 282 - 144 - 63
Taxes (34%)	(T)	38 = .34 × $111
Net Income	(NI)	$ 73 = $111 - 38
Addition to retained earnings (ARE)		$ 24 = $73 - 49
Dividends	(DIV)	$ 49 = .67 × $73

Balance Sheet

Assets			Liabilities and Owners' Equity			
Current assets	(CA)	$ 480 = $1,200 - 720	Total debt	(D)	$ 626	= $1,200 - 574
Net fixed assets	(FA)	720 = .6 × $1,200	Owners' equity	(E)	574	= $550 + 24
			Total liabilities &			
Total assets	(TA)	$1,200 = 2.0 × $600	owners' equity	(L)	$1,200	= $1,200

Questions and Problems

1. **Pro Forma Statements from a Model**   Consider the following simplified financial statements from the Dotsa Lot Company.

DOTSA LOT COMPANY
Income Statement and Balance Sheet
Income Statement

Sales	$500
- Costs	400
Taxable income	$100
- Taxes (34%)	34
Net income	$ 66
Retained earnings	$22
Dividends	44

Balance Sheet

Assets		Liabilities and Owners' Equity	
Current assets	$ 400	Total debt	$ 450
Net fixed assets	600	Owners' equity	550
Total assets	$1,000	Total liabilities	
		& owners' equity	$1,000

Prepare a financial planning model along the lines of our model for the Roberts Company. Estimate the values for the model parameters using percentages calculated from these statements. Verify the values in the pro forma statements by recalculating the model by hand.

2. **A Modification**   Modify the model in the previous question so that borrowing doesn't change and new equity sales is the plug.

3. **A Further Modification** (Challenge Question) How would you modify the model for the Roberts Company if you wanted to maintain a constant debt/equity ratio?

4. **Borrowing and the Financial Model** (Challenge Question) In our financial planning model for Roberts, show that it is possible to solve algebraically for the amount of new borrowing. Can you interpret the resulting expression?

CHAPTER 5
FIRST PRINCIPLES OF VALUATION: THE TIME VALUE OF MONEY

TRANSPARENCIES

T5.1: Chapter Outline
T5.2: Future Value for a Lump Sum
T5.3: Interest on Interest Illustration
T5.4: Future Value of $100 at 10 Percent (Table 5.1)
T5.5 Present Value for a Lump Sum
T5.6: Present Value of $1 for Different Periods and Rates
T5.7: The Basic Present Value Equation
T5.8: An Example: A Penny Saved
T5.9: The Basic Present Value Equation—Revisited
T5.10: Future Value Calculated (Fig. 5.6 - 5.7)
T5.11: Present Value Calculated (Fig. 5.8 - 5.9)
T5.12: Annuities and Perpetuities (4 pages)
T5.13: A 0% Financing Example
T5.14: Future Value for Annuities—A Short Cut
T5.15: Effective Annual Rates and Compounding (3 pages)
T5.16: Cheap Financing versus Rebate
T5.17: Ripov Retailing: An Example
T5.18: Solution to Problem 5.6
T5.19: Solution to Problem 5.41
T5.20: Solution to Problem 5.66

T5A.1: Amortization Schedule: Fixed Principal
T5A.2: Amortization Schedule: Fixed Payments
T5A.3: A Mortgage Application

CHAPTER ORGANIZATION

> **T5.1: Chapter Outline**

5.1 FUTURE VALUE AND COMPOUNDING
Investing for a Single Period
Investing for More than One Period
A Note on Compound Growth

5.2 PRESENT VALUE AND DISCOUNTING
The Single Period Case
Present Values for Multiple Periods

5.3 MORE ON PRESENT AND FUTURE VALUES
Present versus Future Value
Determining the Discount Rate
Finding the Number of Periods

5.4 PRESENT AND FUTURE VALUES OF MULTIPLE CASH FLOWS
Future Value with Multiple Cash Flows
Present Value with Multiple Cash Flows

5.5 VALUING LEVEL CASH FLOWS: ANNUITIES AND PERPETUITIES
Present Value for Annuity Cash Flows
Future Value for Annuities
Perpetuities

5.6 COMPARING RATES: THE EFFECT OF COMPOUNDING PERIODS
Effective Annual Rates and Compounding
Calculating and Comparing Effective Annual Rates
EARs and APRs
Taking It to the Limit: A Note on Continuous Compounding

5.7 SUMMARY AND CONCLUSIONS

APPENDIX 5A—LOAN TYPES AND LOAN AMORTIZATION

5A.1 PURE DISCOUNT LOANS

5A.2 INTEREST-ONLY LOANS

5A.3 AMORTIZED LOANS

ANNOTATED CHAPTER OUTLINE

5.1 FUTURE VALUE AND COMPOUNDING

Lecture Tip, page 112: Many students find the phrases "time value of money" and "a dollar today is worth more than a dollar later" to be somewhat cryptic. In some ways, it might be better to say "the money value of time" and to state that a dollar today doesn't trade for less than a dollar later.

Indeed, many of the phrases and much of the terminology surrounding exchanges of money now for money later are confusing to students. For example, present value as the name for money paid or received earlier in time and future value as the name for money paid or received later in time are a constant source of confusion. How, students ask, can money to be paid next year be a "present" value; how can money received today be a "future" value? They must be made aware that we mean earlier money and later money (or leftmost and rightmost amounts on the time line).

Many students never fully comprehend that present value, future value, interest rates, and interest rate factors are simply a convenient means for communicating the terms of exchange for what are essentially different kinds of money. One way to emphasize both the exchange aspect of the time value of money and that present dollars and future dollars are different kinds of money is to compare them to U.S. dollars and Canadian dollars.

Both are called dollars, but they're not the same thing. And just as U.S dollars rarely trade 1 for 1 for Canadian dollars, neither do present dollars trade 1 for 1 for future dollars. Just as there are exchange rates for U.S. dollars into Canadian and vice-versa, present value and future value factors represent exchange rates between earlier money and later money. Also, the same reciprocity that exists between the foreign exchange rates exists between future value and present value interest factors.

A. Investing for a Single Period

T5.2: Future Value for a Lump Sum
T5.3: Interest on Interest Illustration
T5.4: Future Value of $100 at 10 Percent (Table 5.1)

Given r, the interest rate, every $1 today will produce $(1 + r)$ of future value (FV). So, $FV = \$X(1 + r)$, where X is principal.

Example:
$100 at 10% interest gives $100(1.1) = \$110$.

B. Investing for More than One Period

Reinvesting the interest—*compounding*—interest on interest

$$FV = \$X(1 + r)(1 + r) = \$X(1 + r)^2$$

Example:
$100 at 10% for 2 periods: $100(1.1)(1.1) = $100(1.1)^2 = $121

In general, for t periods, $FV = \$X(1 + r)^t$ where $(1 + r)^t$ is the future value interest factor, FVIF(r,t).

Example:
$100 at 10% for 10 periods: $100(1.1)^{10} = $259.37

FVIF(r,t): Factor can be obtained in various ways
    -factor tables such as A.1 of Appendix in text
    -scientific calculator with y^x key
    -financial calculator

Lecture Tip, page 113: It may be helpful to emphasize this compounding example on the chalkboard. The instructor could demonstrate the compounding of $100 at 10 percent by showing the future value at the end of year one. The instructor could then separate the $110 into $100 principal and $10 interest. One could then demonstrate that the $100 principal will then earn another $10 over the second year and the $10 interest earned at the end of the first year will earn $1 interest over the second year, resulting in a $121 end-of-year-two value.

Example:

Present	End Yr. 1 Value	End Yr. 2 Value	
$100 ------>	$100	Principal------>	$110
	$ 10	Interest ------->	$ 11
$100	$110		$121

By stressing this paragraph's example and the initial example in the text, the students' intuition of compounding or interest-on-interest may be enhanced. This example is extended over five periods in Table 5.1 in the text. A failure to understand this compounding impact will create trouble for some students throughout the course.

Lecture Tip, page. 117: Students are often helped by concrete examples tied to real life. For example, one might illustrate the effect of compound growth by asking the following question in class: "Assume you just started a new job and your current annual salary is $25,000. Suppose that the rate of inflation stays at around 4% annually for the next 40 years, and you receive annual cost-of-living increases tied to the inflation rate. What will your ending salary be?"
    Most students are happy to hear that, given the assumed conditions, their final annual salary will be $120,025. (=$25,000 × (1.04)⁴⁰) They are often less happy,

however, when they find that today's $15,000 automobile will cost $72,015 under the same assumptions.

This example can be extended in many directions. For example, you might next ask how much their final salary will be 40 years hence, should they receive better-than-average raises of, say, 5% annually. The difference is striking: $25,000 × (1.05)^{40} = $176,000; or approximately $56,000 in additional purchasing power in that year alone! (Admittedly, the difference is smaller than it appears when one realizes that it is quoted in future dollars and, therefore, wouldn't even be enough to buy us that $15,000 car 40 years hence.)

C. A Note on Compound Growth

Compound growth is not limited to money; it shows up in many things (e.g., populations).

Lecture Tip, page 118: You may wish to take this opportunity to remind students that, since compound growth rates are found using only the beginning and ending values of a series, they convey <u>nothing</u> about the values in-between. For example, a firm may state that "EPS has grown at a 10% annually compounded rate over the last decade" in an attempt to impress investors of the quality of earnings. However, this statement is true whenever $EPS_{11}/EPS_1 = (1.10)^{10} = 2.5937$. So, the firm could have earned $1 per share ten years ago, suffered a string of losses, and then earned $2.59 per share this year. Clearly, this is not what is implied from management's statement above. (Note: the subscripts indicate a span of 11 - 1 = 10 years.)

5.2 PRESENT VALUE AND DISCOUNTING

A. The Single Period Case

Given r, what amount today (*Present Value or PV*) will produce a given future amount?

Since future amount = $X(1 + r)$, PV = future amount/(1 + r).

<u>Example:</u>
$110 in 1 period at 10% has a PV of $110/(1.1) = $100.

Discounting—the process of finding PV

Lecture Tip, page 119: It may be helpful to utilize the example of $100 compounded at 10 percent to emphasize the present value concept. One can emphasize the basic formula: $PV \times (1 + r)^t = FV$; therefore, $PV = FV \times [1 / (1 + r)^t]$. The student should recognize that the discount factor is the inverse of the compounding factor. The instructor could ask the class to determine the present value of $110 and $121 if the amounts are received in one year and two years respectively, and the interest rate is 10 percent. The instructor could then demonstrate the mechanics:
$100 = $110 \times [1 / (1 + .10)^1] = $110 \times .0909$
$100 = $121 \times [1 / (1 + .10)^2] = $121 \times .8264$

The students will recognize that it was an initial investment of $100 and an interest rate of 10 percent that created these two future values.

B. Present Values for Multiple Periods

PV of future amount in t periods at r is:

PV = future amount × [1/(1 + r)^t], where [1/(1 + r)^t] is the discount factor or Present Value Interest Factor, PVIF(r,t).

Example:
$259.37 10 periods from now has a PV at 10% of $259.37 × [1/(1.1)^{10}] = $100 (the PVIF is .3855).

DCF (Discounted Cash Flow)—the process of valuation by finding the present value.

Lecture Tip, page 120: *The following example can be used to dramatize the effect of discounting over long periods.*

Vincent Van Gogh's 'Sunflowers' was sold at auction in 1987 for approximately $36 million. It had sold in 1889 for $125. At what discount rate is $125 the present value of $36 million, given a 98-year timespan?

$125/$36 million = PVIF(r,98) = .0000034722 = (1 + r)$^{-98}$. Solving for r, we find that the implied discount rate is approximately 13.685%.

Of course, the example can be turned around. "If your great-grandfather had purchased the painting in 1889 and your family sold it for $36 million, the average annually compounded rate of return on the $125 investment was ___?" Stating the problem this way and working it as a compounding problem helps students to see the relationship between discounting and compounding.

Lecture Tip, page 122: *This paragraph, along with figure 5.3, should be stressed. Some students will have trouble understanding that a given future amount is worth less today as the interest rate increases. One may want to remain with the earlier example and provide a very simple example of a future amount of $110 to be received in one year. The student would recognize that if the interest rate is 10%, she would be willing to invest $100 today. The instructor could then ask the students what they would be willing to pay for the $110 in one year if the interest rate was 20 percent. They should realize that they would have to pay less than $100 if they are to realize a 20 percent return on an amount invested today. One could then emphasize that as rates increase, the present value of a fixed future amount decreases. Emphasize that this is the opposite of what would occur if we considered the effect of increasing rates on a given amount we would invest today.*

5.3 MORE ON PRESENT AND FUTURE VALUES

A. Present versus Future Value

T5.5: Present Value for a Lump Sum
T5.6: Present Value of $1 for Different Periods and Rates (Fig. 5.3)

Present Value factors are reciprocals of Future Value factors:

$$PVIF(r,t) = 1/(1 + r)^t \text{ and}$$
$$FVIF(r,t) = (1 + r)^t$$

So $PVIF(r,t) = 1/FVIF(r,t)$ and vice-versa.

Example:
$$FVIF(10\%,4) = (1.1)^4 = 1.464 \text{ and } PVIF(10\%,4) = 1/(1.1)^4 = .683$$

Basic present value equation: $PV = FV \times [1/(1 + r)^t]$

Lecture Tip, page 122: *Students who fail to grasp the concept of time value often do so because it is never really clear to them that, given a 10% opportunity rate, $11 to be received in one year is **equivalent** to having $10 today. Or $9.09 one year ago. Or $8.26 two years ago, etc. At its most fundamental level, compounding and discounting is nothing more than using a set of formulas to find equivalent values at any two points in time. In economic terms, one might stress that equivalence just means that a rational person will be **indifferent** between $10 today and $11 in one year, given a 10% opportunity rate, because s/he could (a) take the $10 today and invest it to have $11 in one year, or (b) sell the right to receive $11 in one year for $10 today.*

A corollary to this concept is that one can't (or shouldn't) add, subtract, multiply, or divide money values in different time periods unless those values are stated in equivalent terms, i.e., at a single point in time.

B. Determining the Discount Rate

T5.7: The Basic Present Value Equation
T5.8: An Example: A Penny Saved

Finding r in the basic present value equation

$$PV = FV \times [1/(1 + r)^t] \text{ or } FV = PV(1 + r)^t$$

-financial calculator (supply PV, FV, and t; compute r)
-[t^{th} root of FV/PV] − 1
-look up either PVIF (PV/FV) or FVIF (FV/PV) in appropriate table

Example:

What interest rate makes a PV of $100 become a FV of $150 in 6 periods?

-FV/PV = $150/100 =1.5, the 6th root of 1.5 is 1.0699, making r = 7%
-FV/PV gives an FVIF of 1.5, look across 6 periods in Table A.1 of Appendix, r = 7%
-PV/FV gives a PVIF of .6666, look across 6 periods in Table A.2, r = 7%

Lecture Tip, page 123: This paragraph should be strongly emphasized. With the examples used thus far, there have always been four parts to the equation, one of which has been unknown. In finding the future value, we must know the present value, the interest rate and the time of the investment. In finding the present value, we must know the future value, the interest rate and the time of the investment. Although it may seem obvious, the instructor could ask the class "what must be known if we are attempting to determine the discount rate of an investment?" (PV, FV and t). The instructor could then use the previous example and ask the class to determine the discount rate or return on an investment if they invested $100 today and received $121 in two years. The students should remember that 10 percent generated the identity. The instructor could then show the solution process using Table A.1 or A.2. One could then proceed to examples covering longer time spans and demonstrate the repetition of the solution.

C. Finding the Number of Periods

T5.9: The Basic Present Value Equation—Revisited

Finding t in the basic present value equation

$PV = FV \times [1/(1 + r)^t]$ (or $FV = PV(1 + r)^t$)

 -financial calculator (supply PV, FV, and r; compute t)
 -using $FV = PV(1 + r)^t$, make $(FV/PV) = (1 + r)^t$, $\ln(FV/PV) = t[\ln(1 + r)]$, then
     $t = [\ln(FV/PV)/\ln(1 + r)]$
 -using PVIF (= PV/FV) or FVIF (= FV/PV), look under r in appropriate table.

Example: How many periods before $100 today grows to be $150 at 7%?

-FV/PV = 150/100 = 1.5; 1 + r = 1.07; ln(1.5) = .405465 and ln(1.07) = .067659,
     so ln(FV/PV)/ln(1 + r) = .405465/.067659 = 6 periods.
-FV/PV gives an FVIF of 1.5, look under 7% in Appendix A, Table A.1, t = 6 periods.

Rule of 72—the time to double your money, (FV/PV) = 2, is approximately (72/r%) periods. The rate needed to double your money is approximately (72/t)%.

Example: To double your money at 10% takes approximately (72/10) = 7.2 periods.
Example: To double your money in 6 years takes approximately (72/6) = 12%.

5.4 PRESENT AND FUTURE VALUES OF MULTIPLE CASH FLOWS

A. Future Value with Multiple Cash Flows

> **T5.10: Future Value Calculated (Fig. 5.6 - 5.7)**

There are two ways to calculate future values of multiple cash flows:

Compound the accumulated balance forward one period at a time, or calculate the future value of each cash flow and add them up.

B. Present Value with Multiple Cash Flows

> **T5.11: Present Value Calculated (Fig. 5.8 - 5.9)**

There are two ways to calculate present values of multiple cash flows:

Discount the last amount back one period and add them up as you go, or discount each amount to time 0 and then add them all up.

5.5 VALUING LEVEL CASH FLOWS: ANNUITIES AND PERPETUITIES

> **T5.12: Annuities and Perpetuities (4 pages)**
> **T5.13: A 0% Financing Example**

A. Present Value for Annuity Cash Flows

Ordinary Annuity—multiple, identical cash flows occurring at the <u>end</u> of each period for a fixed number of periods.

The present value of an annuity of $C per period for t periods at r percent interest is:

Annuity present value = $C $\times$ (1 − PVIF(r,t))/r   or
APV = $C $\times$ (1 − [1/(1 + r)^t])/r

<u>Example:</u>   If you are willing to make 36 monthly payments of $100 at 1.5% per period, what size loan (APV) can you obtain? PVIFA(1.5%, 36) = 27.66, so $C $\times$ PVIFA(r,t) = $100 $\times$ 27.66 = $2,766

Finding the payment, C, given APV, r, t.

$$\text{Since APV} = C \times \text{PVIFA}(r,t), \quad C = \text{APV}/\text{PVIFA}(r,t)$$

Example: If you borrow $400, promising to repay in 4 monthly installments at 1% a month, how much are your payments?

APV $= C \times \text{PVIFA}(r,t)$ gives $400 = C \times \{1 - [1/(1.01)^4]\}/r$
$400 $= C \times 3.9$, so $C = \$400/3.9 = \$102.56$.

Finding the Number of Payments given APV, r, and C.

$\text{APV} = C \times (1 - (1/(1 + r)^t))/r$ so $1 - (\text{APV}/C \times r) = [1/(1 + r)^t]$
The latter is the PVIF(r,t), so proceed as before with logs (take inverses of both sides first) or look in the table under r%.

Example: How many $100 payments will pay off a $5,000 loan at 1% per period?

$1 - (\text{APV}/C \times r) = [1/(1 + r)^t]$ gives $1 - [(\$5,000/\$100)(.01)] = [1/(1.01)^t]$ so that $0.5 = 1/(1.01)^t$. Taking reciprocals of both gives $2 = (1.01)^t$, thus $\ln(2) = (t)\ln(1.01)$ gives $t = 69.66$ periods.

Finding the rate, r, given APV, C, and t.
    Use a financial calculator, tables, or trial and error (no analytic solution).
Table method—since APV = C × PVIFA(r,t), APV/C = PVIFA(r,t). See Table A.3.

Example: A finance company offers to loan you $1,000 today if you will make 48 monthly payments of $32.60. What rate is implicit in the loan? APV = C × PVIFA(r,t) means $1,000 = $32.60 × PVIFA(r,48) so APV/C = $1,000/$32.60 = 30.67 = PVIFA(r,48). A PV table gives 2% (per month) for r.

Lecture Tip, page 133: The instructor should emphasize that the annuity factor approach is a short-cut approach in the process of calculating the present value of multiple cash flows; however, the cash flow stream is a level stream of payments. The instructor could demonstrate using the example provided in the text:

PV $= \$500/(1.1)^1 + 500/(1.1)^2 + 500/(1.1)^3$
    $= \$454.55 + \$413.22 + \$375.66 = \$1,243.43$

PV $= \$500 \times \{1/(1.1)^1 + 1/(1.1)^2 + 1/(1.1)^3\}$
    $= \$500 \times \{[1 - (1/1.1)^3]/.1\}$
    $= \$500 \times 2.48685 = \$1,243.43$

It may also be helpful to have the class examine the PVIF tables and recognize that a factor in the PVIFA table is simply an addition of the column in the PVIF table over the time period in which a level cash flow stream is realized.

Lecture Tip, page 134: Although it is unlikely that today's students will ever have to prepare an amortization table manually, virtually all of them will need to understand the mechanics involved, either for personal reasons (buying a home or car) or professional reasons (computing interest tax shields on a term loan, performing a lease-versus-buy analysis). The example below is useful in emphasizing the utility of this concept.

Your firm wishes to purchase a 2-ton turret lathe which costs $500,000. The First National Bank will loan the entire amount for five years at 10%. The loan will be amortized over its life, with equal payments beginning one year from today and ending five years from today. How much will each payment be? How much interest will be paid over the life of the loan? How much interest will be paid in year 3? How much is owed at the end of year 3?

The loan amount is actually the present value of the payments made, so

$$\$500,000 = C \times \text{PVIFA}(10,5)$$
$$C = \$500,000/\text{PVIFA}(10,5)$$
$$= \$500,000/3.7908 = \$131,898.74.$$

With this information the table can be prepared to answer the other questions.

Period	Beginning Balance	Payment	Interest Due	Reduction in Principal	Ending Balance
1	$500,000	$131,898.74	$50,000	$81,898.74	$418,101.26
2	$418,101.26	$131,898.74	$41,810.13	$90,088.61	$328,012.65
3	$328,012.65	$131,898.74	$32,801.27	$99,097.48	$228,915.18
4	$228,915.18	$131,898.74	$22,891.52	$109,007.22	$119,907.96
5	$119,907.96	$131,898.74	$11,990.79	$119,907.95	≈ 0
		$659,493.70	$159,493.70	$500,000.00	

(Note: Columns may not sum exactly due to rounding.)

Lecture Tip, page 135: The previous lecture tip describes the preparation of an amortization table for a relatively short-lived loan. Suppose the same questions were asked in the context of a 30-year mortgage. Some shortcuts are suggested below.
  You wish to purchase a $170,000 home. Putting 10% down, you will borrow $153,000 at 7.75%, with monthly payments for 30 years. How much will each payment be? How much interest will be paid over the life of the loan? How much is owed at the end of year 20? How much interest will be paid in year 20?
  Clearly, we don't want to prepare a 360-period amortisation table to find the answers to these questions. Instead, do the following.

(1)   Find the payment: $C = \$153,000/\text{PVIFA}(.0775/12,360)$
            $= \$153,000/139.5844 = \$1096.11.$

(2)   Find the total interest cost: Interest paid = total payments - principal

$$= (\$1096.11 \times 360) - 153,000$$
$$= \$394,599.87 - 153,000 = \$241,599.87$$

(Students are usually shocked to find out how much interest is paid on a 30-year mortgage!)

(3)   *Tip: The outstanding balance of any loan equals the present value of the remaining payments. So, after 240 monthly payments, the outstanding balance equals*

$$\$1096.11 \times \text{PVIFA}(.0775/12,120)$$
$$\$1096.11 \times 83.3259 = \$91,334.41$$

(Students are also surprised to find that, after making ⅔ of the scheduled mortgage payments, approximately 60% of the loan remains unpaid.)

(4)   *Tip: The interest paid in any year is equal to the sum of the payments made over the period less the change in principal. Specifically,*

After 228 monthly payments (i.e., 19 years' worth), the outstanding loan balance is

$$\$1096.11 \times \text{PVIFA}(.0775/12,132) = \$1096.11 \times 88.6424 = \$97,161.79.$$

The change in principal is $97,161.79 - 91,334.41 = $5827.38; since 12 payments totalling $13,153.32 were made, interest of $13,153.32 - 5827.38 = $7325.94 was paid.

Lecture Tip, page 136: *The instructor may wish to summarize the discussion with a reference to the tables. The process of solving for a discount rate, or the number of periods required to meet a future value, is the same process whether dealing with one known future value or a known annuity. We must solve for a factor by relating either the annuity or future value to the present value. This ratio is the factor we find in the tables:*

1)   *If we are concerned only with one future payment, we would utilize Table A.2.*
2)   *If we are concerned with an annuity, we would utilize Table A.3.*
3)   *If we are determining the return or interest rate, we would identify the period the future cash flow would be realized (or the period in which the last annuity payment is realized) and then search across that time period's row until we find the factor or ratio. The column in which we find the factor identifies the return.*
4)   *If we are searching for the time period involved, we would identify the return we expect and search down that column until we find the factor we have calculated. We would then identify the period involved by identifying the row in which the factor is located.*

B. Future Value for Annuities

One way—first, discount payments, then find the future value. Annuity future value = Annuity present value $\times (1 + r)^t$.

T5.14: Future Value for Annuities—A Short Cut

Another way—annuity future value factor is:
(Future value factor − 1)/r, that is, FVIFA(r,t) = [(1 + r)^t − 1]/r.

$$AFV = C \times ((1 + r)^t − 1)/r$$

Example: If you make 20 payments of $1,000 at the end of each period at 10% per period, how much will your account grow to be? [(1.10)^{20} − 1]/.10 = 57.275 so AFV = $1,000 × 57.275 = $57,275.

Lecture Tip, page 137: It should be emphasized that Table A.4 assumes the first payment is made one period from the present, with the final payment made at the end of the annuity's life. Example: $1 deposited over three years at 10 percent with the first payment deposited one year from today:

FV in three years = $1 × 3.31 = $3.31.

However, if the first of three payments is deposited today, the value in three years would have the added benefit of compounding the initial payment over the three year period. We can solve for this problem with an adjustment to the table. If the annuity is over "t" years, we use a factor equal to (FVIFA,r,t + 1) − 1. In the case of the above example,

FV in three years   = $1 × [(FVIFA,.10,4) − 1]
                      = $1 × (4.6410 − 1)
                      = $1 × (3.6410) = $3.641

The difference between the two amounts is due to the three-year compounding effect of the $1 deposit made at the beginning of the annuity's life instead of at the end:

$3.641 − $3.31 = $1 × [(1.1)^3 − 1] = .331

The student could then be asked to consider the interest savings a homeowner might realize if she would make an early payment on a mortgage which has a remaining life of 20 years. One could also use this as an introduction to "the effect of compounding periods" section, since homeowners' mortgage payments are paid monthly.

Lecture Tip, page 140: You may wish to sum up this section by describing some of the "Great Underlying Rules of Finance":

GURF 1: A dollar at time t has an equivalent value in period t + n and in period t - n.
GURF 2: Unless otherwise specified, annuity cash flows occur at the end of each period.
GURF 3: Higher market (opportunity) rates imply lower present values and higher future values, cet. par. Lower rates imply the opposite.

C. Perpetuities

Perpetuity—series of level cash flows forever

Perpetuity present value = C/r, since PPV × r must give payment, C.

Preferred stock is an important example of a perpetuity.

5.6 COMPARING RATES: THE EFFECT OF COMPOUNDING PERIODS

> **T5.15: Effective Annual Rates and Compounding (3 pages)**
> **T5.16: Cheap Financing and Rebate**

A. Effective Annual Rates and Compounding

Stated or quoted interest rate—rate before considering any compounding effects, such as 10% compounded quarterly.

Effective annual interest rate—rate, on an annual basis, that reflects compounding effects, e.g., 10% compounded quarterly gives an effective rate of 10.38% (from $(1.025)^4 - 1$).

B. Calculating and Comparing Effective Annual Rates (EAR)

To get the effective rate, divide the quoted annual rate by # of periods in a year (semi-annual = 2, quarterly = 4, monthly = 12, etc.), add 1, raise to the # of periods power, then subtract 1. That is,

$$\text{EAR} = [1 + (\text{quoted rate})/m]^m - 1 \quad \text{where } m = \text{\# of periods per year}$$

Example: 18% compounded monthly is $[1 + (.18/12)]^{12} - 1 = 19.56\%$ effective rate.

Use either the effective rate with years or the periodic rate (quoted/m) and appropriate number of periods (years × m) when finding present or future values.

Example: What is the present value of $100 in two years at 10% compounded quarterly? Use either an effective rate of $[(1.025)^4 - 1]$ for 2 years or 2.5% for 8 periods to get PVIF(10.38%,2) or PVIF(2.5%,8) = .8207 for PV = $82.07.

*Lecture Tip, page 142: The instructor might stir interest in this section by asking how many students have taken out a loan to pay for (finance) the car they are driving. One might then ask one of the students to reveal the **annual** interest rate she/he is paying on the loan. Students will typically quote the loan in terms of the APR. The instructor could* *mention that the student is actually paying more than the rate she/he had just quoted and demonstrate the calculation of the EAR.*

C. EARs and APRs

T5.17: Ripov Retailing: An Example

Annual Percentage Rate (APR)—simply the rate per period × # periods per year, making it a quoted or stated rate.

Ethics Note, page 143: A class discussion concerning the ethical implications of a business practice attempting to circumvent usury laws and the calculation of the true EAR is provided below:

  You are interested in the purchase of a new car. Trust Me Used Car Sales *offers you a $25,000 new car for a $903.33 monthly payment over the next five years. Usury laws (interest rate limits established by the state for credit transactions) disallow rates greater than 21%.*

  The instructor could begin by asking the class to determine, or provide, the EAR on the transaction (IRR = 24%). The instructor might then ask if this transaction is "fair." Many students will have difficulty in establishing what is meant by fair. Responses might range from "if this is the market price, then there is no problem" to "if this is illegal, then we should not do it."

  The instructor could introduce a follow-up question by asking, "would this transaction be fair if the established usury limit is 50% as in Delaware?"

  Use of this problem can lead to a meaningful class discussion as well as provide an example for understanding the rudiments of annuities. Additionally, Circuit Courts of Appeals often ignore usury limits due to the harm that such limits might cause a business.

D. Taking It to the Limit: A Note on Continuous Compounding

Let q stand for the quoted rate (in decimal form). What happens as m in $(1 + q/m)^m$ or $1/[(1 + q/m)^m]$ gets arbitrarily large? The limit as m gets large of $(1 + q/m)^m$ is e^q and the limit as m gets large of $1/[(1 + q/m)^m]$ is e^{-q}. These are the FVIF and PVIF for continuous compounding and discounting for 1 period.

EAR = $e^q - 1$ under continuous compounding

Example: 10% compounded continuously has an EAR = $e^{.10} - 1 = 10.52\%$.

5.7 SUMMARY AND CONCLUSIONS

> **T5.18:** Solution to Problem 5.6
> **T5.19:** Solution to Problem 5.41
> **T5.20:** Solution to Problem 5.66

APPENDIX 5A—LOAN TYPES AND LOAN AMORTIZATION

5A.1 PURE DISCOUNT LOANS

Borrower pays a single lump sum (principal and interest) at maturity.

Example: A U.S. Treasury bill

5A.2 INTEREST-ONLY LOANS

Borrower pays interest only each period and entire principal at maturity.

Example: A typical corporate bond

5A.3 AMORTIZED LOANS

> **T5A.1:** Amortization Schedule: Fixed Principal
> **T5A.2:** Amortization Schedule: Fixed Payments
> **T5A.3:** A Mortgage Application

Borrower repays part or all of the principal over the life of the loan. Two methods are 1) fixed amount of principal to be repaid each period, which results in uneven payments, and 2) fixed payment, which results in uneven principal reduction.

CHAPTER 6
VALUING STOCKS AND BONDS

TRANSPARENCIES

T6.1: Chapter Outline
T6.2: Bond Features
T6.3: Bond Rates and Yields
T6.4: Valuing a Bond
T6.5: A Discount Bond
T6.6: A Premium Bond
T6.7: Bond Price Sensitivity to YTM
T6.8: General Expression for the Value of a Bond
T6.9: Interest Rate Risk and Time to Maturity (Fig. 6.2)
T6.10: Bond Pricing Theorems
T6.11: Sample *Wall Street Journal* Bond Quotation (Fig. 6.3)
T6.12: Common Stock Cash Flows
T6.13: Dividend Growth Model
T6.14: Stock Price Sensitivity to Dividend Growth, g
T6.15: Stock Price Sensitivity to Required Return, r
T6.16: More on Dividend Growth (2 pages)
T6.17: Sample Stock Market Quotation from *Wall Street Journal* (Fig 6.5)
T6.18: Solution to Problem 6.9
T6.19: Solution to Problem 6.22
T6.20: Solution to Problem 6.30

CHAPTER ORGANIZATION

T6.1: Chapter Outline

6.1 BONDS AND BOND VALUATION
Bond Features and Prices
Bond Values and Yields
Interest Rate Risk
Finding the Yield to Maturity: More Trial and Error
Bond Price Reporting

6.2 COMMON STOCK VALUATION
Common Stock Cash Flows
Common Stock Valuation: Some Special Cases
Components of the Required Return
Stock Market Reporting

6.3 SUMMARY AND CONCLUSIONS

ANNOTATED CHAPTER OUTLINE

6.1 BONDS AND BOND VALUATION

A. Bond Features and Prices

Bonds—long term IOU's, usually interest-only loans (interest is paid by the borrower every period, and the principal is repaid at the end of the loan).

Coupons—the regular interest payments (if fixed amount—*level coupon*)

Face or par value—amount repaid at the end of the loan

Coupon rate—annual coupon/face value

Maturity—number of years until face value is paid

> **T6.2: Bond Features**
> **T6.3: Bond Rates and Yields**
> **T6.4: Valuing a Bond**

B. Bond Values and Yields

The cash flows from a bond are typically the coupons and face value. Finding the market price of a bond requires discounting the coupons and face value at the market rate.

Yield to maturity (YTM)—the required market rate or rate that makes the discounted cash flows from a bond equal to the bond's price.

Example:
Suppose Wilhite Co. were to issue $1,000 bonds with 20 years to maturity. The annual coupon is $110. Similar bonds have a yield to maturity of 11%.

Present value of face value = $1,000/(1.11)^{20}$ = $124.03

Annuity present value of coupons $= \$110 \times (1 - 1/(1.11)^{20})/.11$
                                        $= \$110 \times 7.9633 = \$875.96$

Adding the discounted face value and coupons together
$\$124.03 + \$875.96 = \$1,000$

Since the YTM and coupon rate are the same, price = face value.

Discount bond—a bond that sells for less than its par or face value. This is the case when the YTM is greater than the coupon rate.

T6.5: A Discount Bond

Example: Discount bond
        If the YTM on bonds similar to that of the Wilhite Co. ($1,000 bond, $110 coupon, 20 years to maturity) were 13%, instead of 11%, the bonds would sell for:

Present value of face value $= \$1,000/(1.13)^{20} = \$86.78$

Annuity present value of coupons $= \$110 \times (1 - 1/(1.13)^{20})/.13$
                                        $= \$110 \times 7.0248 = \$772.72$

Adding the discounted face value and coupons together: $\$86.78 + \$772.72 = \$859.50$

The difference between this price, $859.50, and the par price of $1,000 is $140.50. This is equal to the present value of the difference between YTM coupons and Wilhite's coupons: $130 − $110 = $20 per year for 20 years at 13% $= \$20 \times PVIFA(13\%,20) = \$20 \times 7.0248 = \$140.50$.

Premium bond—a bond that sells for more than its par or face value. This is the case when the YTM is less than the coupon rate.

Lecture Tip, page 167: The instructor should stress the issue that the coupon interest rate and par value are fixed by contract when the bond is issued. Therefore, the components in the numerator will never change over the life of the bond. However, after issuance, as the bond approaches maturity, the time remaining and the yield to maturity will change, causing the bond's value to either increase or decrease.

Lecture Tip, page 168: The instructor may wish to further explore the loss in value of $115 ($1,000 − $885) which the bond experienced due to the rise in interest rates. The instructor should remind the class that when the 8% coupon bond was issued, bonds of similar risk and maturity were yielding $80 per year.
        One year later, the ten-year bond has nine years remaining to maturity. However, bonds of similar risk are now issued to yield 10% ($100 per year) over a nine-year period. The bond which we are examining yields only $80 per year or $20 less than a

new bond which sells for $1,000. The instructor should emphasize this point and the issue of the preceding paragraphs—the old bond must sell for less than $1,000 based on present value mathematics:

Discount
= ($80 − $100) × (PVIFA,10%,9)
= −$20 × 5.7590
= −$115.18
= Value of old 8% bond − Value of new 10% bond
= $884.82 − $1,000
= −$115.18.

T6.6: A Premium Bond

Example: Premium bond

If the YTM on bonds similar to that of the Wilhite Co. ($1,000 bond, $110 coupon, 20 years to maturity) were 9% instead of 11% the bonds would sell for:

Present value of face value = $1,000/(1.09)^{20} = $178.43

Annuity present value of coupons
= $110 × (1 − 1/(1.09)^{20})/.09
= $110 × 9.1285 = $1,004.14

Adding the discounted face and coupons together: $178.43 + $1,004.14 = $1,182.57

The difference between this price, $1,182.57 and the par price of $1,000, $182.57, is equal to the present value of the difference between Wilhite's coupons and YTM coupons, i.e., $110 − $90, or $20 per year for 20 years at 9% = $20 × PVIFA(9%,20) = $20 × 9.1285 = $182.57.

General expression for the value of a bond:

Bond value = Present value of the coupons + Present value of the face amount

Bond value = [C × (1 − 1/(1 + YTM)^t)/YTM] + [F × 1/(1 + YTM)^t]

T6.7: Bond Price Sensitivity to YTM
T6.8: General Expression for the Value of a Bond

semiannual coupons—halve the annual coupon amount, halve the *quoted* annual YTM, and double the number of years.

Example:
A $1,000 bond with an 8% coupon rate maturing in 10 years will have what price if the market quoted YTM is 10%?

Present value of face value = $1,000/(1.05)^{20}$ = $376.89

Annuity present value of coupons   = $40 × (1 − 1/(1.05)^{20})/.05$
                                     = $40 × 12.4622 = $498.49

Adding the discounted face value and coupons together: $376.89 + $498.49 = $875.38

C. Interest Rate Risk

T6.9: Interest Rate Risk and Time to Maturity

Interest rate risk—refers to changes in bond prices arising from fluctuating interest rates (varying YTMs).

Ceteris paribus, the longer the time to maturity, the greater the interest rate risk.
Ceteris paribus, the lower the coupon rate, the greater the interest rate risk.

Lecture Tip, page 171: Upon learning about the concept of interest rate risk, students sometimes conclude that bonds with low interest-rate risk (i.e., high-coupon bonds) are necessarily "safer" than otherwise identical bonds with lower coupons. In reality, quite the contrary is true: the increasing volatility of market interest rates over the last two decades has greatly increased the importance of interest rate risk in bond valuation. The days when bonds represented a perfect "widows and orphans" investment are long gone.
You may wish to point out that one potentially undesirable feature of high-coupon bonds is the required reinvestment of coupons at the computed yield-to-maturity if one is to actually earn that yield. Those who purchased bonds issued in the early 1980s (when even high-grade corporates had coupons over 11%) found, to their dismay that interest payments could not be reinvested at similar rates a few years later without taking greater risk. A good example of the tradeoff between interest rate risk and reinvestment risk is the purchase of a zero-coupon bond - one eliminates reinvestment risk but maximizes interest-rate risk!

D. Finding the Yield to Maturity: More Trial and Error

It is usually a trial and error process to find the YTM via the general formula above. Knowing if the bond sells for a premium (YTM must be below coupon rate) or discount (YTM must be above coupon rate) is a help, but using a financial calculator is (by far) the quickest, easiest, and most accurate method.

Lecture Tip, page 171: The class should be informed that finding the yield to maturity can be a tedious process of trial and error. It may help to pose a hypothetical situation *in which a 10-year, 10% bond sells for $1,050. The instructor could ask the students whether paying a higher price than $1,000 would yield an investor more or less than 10%. Hopefully, the students will recognize that if they pay $1,000 for $100 per year, the bond would yield 10% but if they paid more than $1,000, the bond would be yielding less than 10%. Thus, a starting point to determine the yield would be the 9% factors (not 11%). However, if that same bond happened to be selling for $1,200, one might want to try 8% as a starting point, since we would be paying a higher price than par and realizing a lower yield.*

Lecture Tip, page 171: *Although the advent of inexpensive financial calculators has lessened the relevance of yield-to-maturity approximation formulas, some students will be interested in using such formulas to avoid much of the trial-an-error involved in solving the bond valuation formula for the YTM. Rodriguez suggests the following:*

$$Estimated\ YTM = [C + (F - V)/t]/[(F + 2V)/3]$$

where: $C =$ *the dollar coupon,*
$F =$ *the face value of the bond,*
$V =$ *the current market value of the bond, and*
$t =$ *the number of periods to maturity.*

For the example, assume we wish to estimate the YTM of a bond with five year to maturity, which pays annual coupons of $100, has a $1,000 face value, and currently sells for $900. Using the bond pricing equation and a financial calculator, we obtain a YTM of 12.83%. According to the formula above, the estimated YTM is

$$[\$100 + (\$1,000 - 900)/5]/[(\$1,000 + 2(\$900))/3]$$
$$= \$120/\$933.33$$
$$= 12.86\%.$$

Lecture Tip, page 172: *Some instructors will wish to discuss the components of bond required returns in a fashion analogous to the stock return discussion on pages 182-183 of the text. As with common stocks, the required return on a bond can be decomposed into current income and capital gains components. The yield-to-maturity (YTM) equals the current yield plus the capital gains yield.*

Consider the premium bond described at the top of page 168 of the text. The bond has a $1000 face value, $120 annual coupons, and 12 years to maturity. As shown, when the required return on bonds of similar risk is 11%, the market value of the bond is $1,064.92. But what if one purchases this bond and sells it one year later at the going price? Assume no change in market rates. The current income portion of the bondholder's return equals the interest received divided by the initial outlay; i.e.,

$$Current\ yield = \$120/1,064.92 = .1127 = 11.27\%.$$

The capital gains yield equals the change in bond price divided by the initial outlay. Given no change in market rates, the "one-year-later" price must be

$$\$120 \times (1 - 1/1.11^{11})/.11 + \$1,000/1.11^{11}$$
$$= \$120 \times 6.2065 + \$1,000/3.1518$$
$$= \$744.78 + \$317.28$$
$$= \$1,062.06$$

Therefore, the capital gains yield is ($1,062.06 - 1,064.92)/$1,064.92 = - .27%. Summing, the YTM = 11.27% + (-.27%) = 11.00. In other words, buying a premium bond and holding it to maturity ensures capital losses over the life of the bond; however, they will be exactly offset by the higher-than-market coupon. Of course, the opposite holds true for discount bonds.

Because bond valuation is just an application of the time value model discussed in Chapter 5, we can add to our list of "Great Underlying Rules of Finance":

GURF 4: Bond prices and market interest rates always move inversely.
GURF 5: Given two bonds identical but for time to maturity, the price of the longer bond will always change more than that of the shorter bond for a given change in market interest rates.
GURF 6: Given two bonds identical but for coupon, the price of the lower coupon bond will always change more than that of the higher coupon bond for a given change in market interest rates.

T6.10: Bond Pricing Theorems

E. Bond Price Reporting

T6.11: Sample *Wall Street Journal* Bond Quotation

6.2 COMMON STOCK VALUATION

Stock valuation is more difficult than bond valuation because the cash flows are not explicit, the life is forever, and the market rate is not easily observed.

A. Common Stock Cash Flows

T6.12: Common Stock Cash Flows

The cash flow to holders of common stock consists of dividends plus a future sale price. By recursively substituting the next dividend plus end-of-period price for the future cash flows, the current price of a stock can be written

$$P_0 = \frac{D_1}{(1+r)^1} + \frac{D_2}{(1+r)^2} + \frac{D_3}{(1+r)^3} + \frac{D_4}{(1+r)^4} + \dots$$

Ethics Note, page 176: The importance of the components of the valuation model are brought into sharp focus in a discussion of pension funding decisions. Pension and Investments reports that in November, 1993 the Securities and Exchange Commission issued a "new, unprecedented warning . . . to use only 'high-grade' market rates for discounting" for valuing pension assets. The article reports that many overfunded plans could "slip into underfunded status." A practical result of the use of inappropriate return estimates is found in the case of Witco Chemical, which took large charges against earnings in 1993 related to its use of an inappropriate rate for computing its unfunded pension liability. Students might first be asked to guess how one determines an "appropriate" return estimate for pension funding purposes. Then, they might be asked to whom the actuary owes greater responsibility - future pension recipients, management, shareholders, or the Pension Benefit Guaranty Corporation? It is easy to see that the ethical issues underlying the actuarial calculations can become quite complex.

B. Common Stock Valuation: Some Special Cases

T6.13: Dividend Growth Model

Zero growth—implies $D_1 = D_2 = D_3 = D$, a constant

Since the cash flow is always the same, the PV is that for a perpetuity, C/r, or: $P_0 = D/r$

Example:
        At a 10% market rate, a stock expected to pay a $2 dividend forever would be worth $2/.10 = $20.

Constant growth—$D_1 = D_0 \times (1 + g)$; $D_2 = D_1 \times (1 + g)$;
        in general $D_t = D_0 \times (1 + g)^t$

<u>Example:</u>

If the current dividend is $2 and the expected growth rate is 5%, what is D_5?

$$D_0 \times (1.05)^5 = \$2 \times 1.276 = \$2.55$$

An amount that grows at a constant rate forever is called a *growing perpetuity*. In this case the expression for the value of a stock now becomes:

$$P_0 = \frac{D_0(1+g)^1}{(1+r)^1} + \frac{D_0(1+g)^2}{(1+r)^2} + \frac{D_0(1+g)^3}{(1+r)^3} + \ldots$$

As long as $g < r$, the present value at the rate r of dividends growing at the rate g is:

$$P_0 = \frac{D_0(1+g)}{r-g} = \frac{D_1}{r-g}$$

In general, the price at any time t is written:

$$P_t = \frac{D_t(1+g)}{r-g} = \frac{D_{t+1}}{r-g}$$

<u>Example:</u>

It is 4 years since the dividend was $2 as in the example above. What price do we expect to see?

$$P_4 = D_5/(r - g) = \$2.55/.05 = \$51$$

T6.14: **Stock Price Sensitivity to Dividend Growth, g**
T6.15: **Stock Price Sensitivity to Required Return, r**
T6.16: **More on Dividend Growth (2 pages)**

<u>General Formula for a *Growing Perpetuity*</u>

Present value of a growing perpetuity $= C_0(1 + g)/(r - g)$

Non-constant growth—usually a mix of "supernormal" growth early on and then a constant, "normal" growth rate later. Here we discount the individual "high" growth dividends and discount the dividend growth model stock value at the future, constant growth date.

Example:
        The next three dividends for Fudgit Co. are expected to be $0.50, $1.00, and $1.50. Then the dividends are expected to grow at a constant 5% forever. If the required return on Fudgit is 10%, what is P_0?

$$P_0 = \frac{D_1}{(1+r)^1} + \frac{D_2}{(1+r)^2} + \frac{D_3}{(1+r)^3} + \frac{P_3}{(1+r)^3}$$

where $P_3 = [D_3 \times (1 + g)]/(r - g) = \$1.5(1.05)/(.10 - .05) = \$1.575/.05 = \$31.50$

$$P_0 = \frac{.50}{(1.1)^1} + \frac{1.00}{(1.1)^2} + \frac{1.50}{(1.1)^3} + \frac{31.50}{(1.1)^3}$$

$$= \$0.454 + \$0.826 + \$1.127 + \$23.67 = \$26.07$$

Lecture Tip, page 177: *In his book,* A Random Walk Down Wall Street, *pp. 82-89, (1985, W.W. Norton & Company, New York), Burton Malkiel does not discuss the constant growth formula, but rather gives four "fundamental" rules of stock prices. Loosely paraphrased the rules are as follows. Other things the same:*

1.   *Investors pay a higher price the larger the dividend growth rate*
2.   *Investors pay a higher price per share the larger the proportion of earnings paid out in cash dividends*
3.   *Investors pay a higher price per share the less risky the company's stock*
4.   *Investors pay a higher price per share the lower interest rates are*

        If the required return, r, is looked at as a riskless rate of interest, r_f, plus a risk premium, r_p, (so that $r = r_f + r_p$), it is easily shown that Malkiel's rules have counterparts in the dividend growth model that exert just these effects on stock price.
        Of course, the tricky part is estimating the growth rate and required return. So, while the model is precise, its predictions may be substantially different from observed stock prices depending upon the values used .

Lecture Tip, page 178: *You might find it useful to derive the constant-growth model.*

$$P_0 = \frac{D_1}{(1 + r)} + \frac{D_2}{(1 + r)^2} + \frac{D_3}{(1 + r)^3} + ... + \frac{D_t}{(1 + r)^t}$$

Equivalently,

$$P_0 = \frac{D_0(1 + g)}{(1 + r)} + \frac{D_0(1 + g)^2}{(1 + r)^2} + \frac{D_0(1 + g)^3}{(1 + r)^3} + ... + \frac{D_0(1 + g)^t}{(1 + r)^t}$$

Now multiply both sides by (1 + r)/(1 + g):

$$\frac{(1 + r)}{(1 + g)} \, P_0 = D_0 \, [1 + \frac{(1 + g)}{(1 + r)} + \frac{(1 + g)^2}{(1 + r)^2} + \frac{(1 + g)^3}{(1 + r)^3} + \ldots + \frac{(1 + g)^{t-1}}{(1 + r)^{t-1}}]$$

Subtract the second equation from the third:

$$[\frac{(1 + r) - (1 + g)}{(1 + g)}]P_0 = D_0[1 - \frac{(1 + g)^t}{(1 + r)^t}]$$

Of course, the bracketed term on the right-hand side goes to one as t approaches ∞ (assuming, as we have, that r > g). Solving for P_0 and rearranging leaves the constant-growth model.

Lecture Tip, page 180: Inquisitive students often raise questions at this point. E.g.,

1. "What is the value of a stock that pays no dividends (and never will)?" Clearly, the valuation models presented indicate the stock will have no value, but students often counter with the fact that, regardless of the lack of a dividend, a shareholder still owns a piece of the firm, which (assumedly) has some value. I respond by asking how, in cash flow terms, a share of stock differs from a perpetual zero-coupon bond (if there were such a thing). The answer is that it does not differ in the least. Most students will readily agree that a perpetual zero-coupon bond (which pays no interest and never matures) can have no market value. The same must hold for the zero-dividend common stock. (Again, we assume no dividends, liquidating or otherwise, will be paid <u>ever</u>.)

2. "How can g ever be assumed to be constant?" The answer, of course, lies in the competitive equilibrium model of classical microeconomics. Since g represents not only the growth rate in dividends but also in earnings and sales (given no change in the firm's cost structure), we are simply assuming that the product market the firm operates in "settles down" to a steady state in which competing firms earn sufficient returns to remain in business, but not large enough to attract outside capital.

3. "Why do we assume that r > g?" At least two answers are possible. First, r may be less than g <u>in the short run</u>. (Hence the supernormal growth model in the next section.) Second, in equilibrium, high returns on investment will attract capital, which, in the absence of technological change, will ensure that in succeeding periods, higher returns cannot be earned without taking greater risk. But taking greater risk will increase r, so g cannot be increased without raising r.

Lecture Tip, page 181: In this example $P_3 = D_4 / (.10 - .05)$. Some students have a tendency to incorrectly discount P_3 by $(1 + r)^4$, not $(1 + r)^3$. This is probably because D_4 is used to determine P_3. It should be stressed that we are always bringing the next dividend back one period. The timing of P_3 determines the time period for the factor used.

C. Components of the Required Return

Rearrange $P_0 = D_1/(r - g)$ to give $r = D_1/P_0 + g$
Dividend yield—D_1/P_0
Capital gains yield—g (price appreciation), *and*
r = dividend yield + capital gains yield

International Note, page 183: An interesting question arises as to the relative importance of the components of required (or total) return in the stocks of different countries when one considers the differences in dividend yields and P/E ratios in U.S. and Japanese stocks, respectively. The Financial Times reports that, near the end of 1993, the average dividend yield on Japanese stocks was approximately .8 percent, or about one-third that of U.S. stocks. On the other hand, the P/E ratios of U.S. stocks ranged in the mid-20s, the same story reports that Japanese P/E ratios nearing 90 were not uncommon. You may wish to ask students to speculate on why such differences could arise. This facilitates discussion of differential tax laws, accounting rules, market interest rates, etc. In this context, you might wish to ask students to evaluate a statement from a contemporaneous article in the South China Morning Post: "Japanese companies pay comparatively smaller dividends, so net earnings per share takes on less importance" to investors.

D. Stock Market Reporting

Lecture Tip, page 184: It may stimulate the class interest to require the students to purchase a recent Wall Street Journal and have them examine the financial section. Pick out a familiar stock and have the class perform some of the calculations presented in the text. Then have the students examine the dividend column for various stocks and point out the number of *non*dividend paying stocks there are. This could reinforce the text discussion of how the market values the future dividend stream.

T6.17:   Sample Stock Quotation from the *Wall Street Journal* (Fig. 6.4)

6.3 SUMMARY AND CONCLUSIONS

T6.18:   Solution to Problem 6.9
T6.19:   Solution to Problem 6.22
T6.20:   Solution to Problem 6.30

CHAPTER 7
NET PRESENT VALUE AND OTHER INVESTMENT CRITERIA

TRANSPARENCIES

T7.1:   Chapter Outline
T7.2:   NPV Illustrated
T7.3:   Payback Rule Illustrated
T7.4:   Ordinary and Discounted Payback (Table 7.3)
T7.5:   Discounted Payback Illustrated
T7.6:   Average Accounting Return Illustrated
T7.7:   Internal Rate of Return Illustrated
T7.8:   Net Present Value Profile
T7.9:   Multiple Rate of Return
T7.10: NPV Profile: Multiple IRR Problem
T7.11: IRR, NPV, and Mutually Exclusive Projects
T7.12: Percentage of Responding Firms Using Capital Budgeting Methods
T7.13: Solution to Problem 7.3
T7.14: Solution to Problem 7.8
T7.15: Solution to Problem 7.17

CHAPTER ORGANIZATION

> **T7.1: Chapter Outline**

7.1 NET PRESENT VALUE
   The Basic Idea
   Estimating Net Present Value

7.2 THE PAYBACK RULE
   Defining the Rule
   Analyzing the Payback Period Rule
   Redeeming Qualities
   Summary of the Payback Rule

7.3 THE DISCOUNTED PAYBACK RULE

7.4 THE AVERAGE ACCOUNTING RETURN
Analyzing the Average Accounting Return Method

7.5 THE INTERNAL RATE OF RETURN
Problems with the IRR
Redeeming Qualities of the IRR

7.6 THE PROFITABILITY INDEX

7.7 THE PRACTICE OF CAPITAL BUDGETING

7.8 SUMMARY AND CONCLUSIONS

ANNOTATED CHAPTER OUTLINE

"What Assets Should We Buy?" - The Capital Budgeting Decision

7.1 NET PRESENT VALUE

A. The Basic Idea

Net present value—a measure of the difference between the market value of an investment and its cost. While cost is often relatively straight forward, finding the market value of assets or their benefits can be tricky. The principle is to find the market price of comparables or substitutes.

Lecture Tip, page 197: *Some instructors will wish to take the opportunity to use this example to illustrate the interpretation of NPV and its relationship to organizational form.*

Specifically, assume that, in order to raise the $50,000 needed to buy and rehab the house, you had sold 50,000 shares of stock in the venture for $1 apiece. Your father purchased 15,000 shares, your brother purchased 15,000 shares, and you purchased the remaining 20,000. How much are the shares worth upon the sale of the house for $60,000? Your father's share of the selling price is $18,000 (= 15,000/50,000 × $60,000), as is your brother's. Your share is $24,000 (= 20,000/50,000 × $60,000). In other words, the value created accrued to the owners of the investment. This is the essence of the NPV approach: <u>*The NPV measures the increase in firm value, which is also the increase in the value of what the shareholders own.*</u> *Thus, making decisions with the NPV approach facilitates the achievement of our goal in Chapter 1 - making decisions which will maximize shareholder wealth.*

Lecture Tip, page 197: *Although this point may seem rather obvious, it could be helpful to stress the issue of "net" in NPV. Some students may later carelessly calculate the PV*

of the inflows and fail to subtract out the cost of a capital asset. The PV of inflows is not NPV; rather NPV is the amount remaining after offsetting the PV of the inflows with the PV of the outflows. The NPV amount determines the additional value created by the firm undertaking the investment.

B. Estimating Net Present Value

Discounted cash flow (DCF) valuation—finding the market value of assets or their benefits by taking the present value of future cash flows, i.e., by estimating what the future cash flows would trade for in today's dollars.

T7.2: NPV Illustrated

Net present value rule—an investment should be accepted if the net present value is positive and rejected if it is negative.

In other words, if the market value of the benefits is larger than the cost, an investment will increase value.

Lecture Tip, page 199: The instructor may wish to give the student a perspective on the meaning of NPV. In terms of the present, if we accept a negative NPV project of -$2,422, the student might view this as an equivalent to the company investing $2,422 today with nothing received in return. Therefore, the total value of the firm would decrease by $2,422. This, of course, assumes that the various components (cash flows estimated, discount factor, etc.) used in the computation are correct.

Lecture Tip, page 199: First, it should be noted that, in practice, financial managers are rarely presented with zero-NPV projects for at least two reasons. First, in an abstract sense, zero is just another of the infinite number of values the NPV can take; as such, the likelihood of obtaining any single number is small. Second, (and more pragmatically), in most large firms, capital investment proposals are submitted to the finance group from other areas (e.g., the industrial engineering group) for analysis. Those submitting proposals recognize the ambivalence associated with zero NPVs and are often less likely to send them to the finance group in the first place.

Conceptually, a zero-NPV project earns exactly its required return. Assuming that risk has been adequately accounted for, investing in a zero-NPV project is equivalent to purchasing a financial asset in an efficient market. (Capital market efficiency is discussed in Chapter 10.) In this sense, one would be indifferent between the capital expenditure project and the financial asset investment. Further, since firm value is completely unaffected by the investment, there is no reason for shareholders to prefer either one.

Before leaving this topic, it should be noted that several real-world considerations make comparisons such as the one above difficult. For example, adjusting for risk in capital budgeting projects can be problematic. And, some investment projects may be associated with benefits that are difficult to quantify, but exist, nonetheless. (Consider, for example, an investment with a zero NPV but which enhances a firm's image as a good corporate citizen.) Additionally, the secondary market for most physical assets is substantially less efficient than the secondary market for financial assets. While, in theory, one could adjust the required return for differences in liquidity, the adjustment is, again, problematic. Finally, some would argue that, all else equal, some investors prefer larger firms to smaller; if true, investing in any project with a nonnegative NPV is desirable. Of course, others might argue just the opposite. Of course, the above discussion is equally applicable to the case where the IRR exactly equals the cost of capital.

7.2 THE PAYBACK RULE

Ethics Note, page 200: *The American Association of Colleges and Universities estimates that 10 percent of all college students cheat at some time during their postsecondary education careers. The instructor might pose the ethical question of whether it would be proper for a publishing company to offer a new book* How to Cheat: A User's Guide. *The company has a cost of capital of 8% and estimates it could sell 10,000 volumes by the end of year one and 5,000 volumes in each of the following two years. The immediate printing costs for the 20,000 volumes would be $20,000. The book would sell for $7.50 per copy and net the company a profit of $6.00 per copy after royalties (which would, of course, be quite small!), marketing costs, and taxes. Year one net would be $60,000.*

The instructor could ask if the investment is worth buying the publication rights and what is the payback of the investment? (Payback = $20,000/$60,000 = .33 years). Students should recognize that the quick payback results in a pure profit of $6.00 per book following the investment's recovery. However, the instructor might ask the class if the publishing of this book would encourage cheating and if the publishing company would want to be associated with this text and its message. Some students may feel that one should accept these profitable investment opportunities while others might prefer that the publication of this profitable text be rejected due to the behavior it could encourage.

A. Defining the Rule

Payback period—length of time until the accumulated cash flows equal or exceed the original investment.

Payback period rule—investment is acceptable if its calculated payback is less than some prespecified number of years.

Lecture Tip, page 201: *The payback period is computed by summing the cash inflows, beginning with period one, and stopping at the time period in which the accumulation of the cash inflows equals the initial cash outflow (as discussed in section 7.2). The instructor could mention that, in the case of an annuity, the payback can be quickly solved by forming the ratio of initial outflow to annuity payment. However, one should mention that this only applies in the case of an annuity. Problem 7.2 represents an annuity in which the short cut approach could be used while problem 7.1 presents a nonconstant payment stream.*

T7.3: Payback Rule Illustrated

B. Analyzing the Payback Period Rule

- No discounting involved
- Doesn't consider risk differences
- How to determine the cutoff point
- Bias for short-term investments

C. Redeeming Qualities

- Simple to use (mostly by ignoring long-term)
- Bias for short-term promotes liquidity
- Can be adjusted for risk in some sense (altering the cutoff)

D. Summary of the Payback Rule

Advantages
>   Easy to understand
>   Adjusts for uncertainty of later cash flow
>   Biased toward liquidity

Disadvantages
>   Ignores time value of money
>   Ignores cash flow beyond payback period
>   Biased against long-term projects

Lecture Tip, page 203: *The payback period can be interpreted as a naive form of discounting if we consider the class of investments with level cash flows over arbitrarily long lives. Since the present value of a perpetuity is the payment divided by the discount rate, a payback period cut-off can be seen to imply a certain discount rate. That is,*

> *Cost/annual cash flow = payback period cut-off*
> *Cost = annual cash flow × payback period cut-off.*

Since the PV of a perpetuity is: PV = annual cash flow × (1/r), the correspondence between the discount rate, r, and the payback period cut-off is obvious. The longer the payback period, the lower the implied value of r, and vice versa.

International Note, page 204: In the late 1970s, the author worked as a capital project analyst for a large manufacturer of oilfield equipment. The firm had plants in several politically unstable countries (e.g., Libya). Because of the possibility that these assets would be confiscated by the foreign governments via "nationalization" at any given time, the firm was quite concerned with how long the foreign plants would have to operate before they "paid themselves back". Thus, the payback period approach was heavily relied upon as a decision tool because of international uncertainties.

7.3 THE DISCOUNTED PAYBACK RULE

> **T7.4: Ordinary and Discounted Payback (Table 7.3)**
> **T7.5: Discounted Payback Illustrated**

Discounted payback period—length of time until accumulated discounted cash flows equal or exceed the initial investment.

This technique entails all the work of NPV and yet it is arbitrary. A redeeming feature is that if the project ever pays back on a discounted basis, then it must have a positive NPV.

Why bother? You need cash flow estimates and a discount rate to compute the discounted payback. You might as well go ahead and figure out the NPV and know what you're getting.

Lecture Tip, page 204: The instructor could mention that "the discounted payback is the time it takes to break even in an economic or financial sense." This indicates that if a project has a negative NPV, we would never break even in an economic sense and, therefore, the discounted payback period would not exist for the project. However, a negative NPV project could easily have a short ordinary payback period.

7.4 THE AVERAGE ACCOUNTING RETURN

> **T7.6: Average Accounting Return Illustrated**

Average accounting return (AAR):

   Some measure of accounting profit/Some measure of average accounting value

In other words, it is a benefit/cost analysis that produces a pseudo rate of return. Because of the accounting conventions involved and the lack of cashflows, it isn't clear what is calculated.

The text gives the following specific definition: Average net income/Average book value

Average accounting return rule—project is acceptable if its AAR return exceeds a target return.

A. Analyzing the Average Accounting Return Method

- Since it involves accounting figures rather than cashflows, it is not comparable to returns in capital markets;
- It treats money in all periods as having the same value;
- There is no objective way to find the cut-off rate.

Lecture Tip, page 209: Surveys indicate that few large firms employ the payback period and/or the AAR methods exclusively; rather, these techniques are used in conjunction with one or more of the DCF techniques. On the other hand, anecdotal evidence suggests that a large number of smaller firms rely more heavily on non-DCF approaches. Reasons for this include: (1) small firms don't have access to the organized capital markets; (2) the AAR is the project-level equivalent to the ROA measure used for analyzing firm profitability (ROA is discussed in Chapter 3); and, (3) some small-firm decision-makers may be less aware of DCF approaches than their large-firm counterparts.

7.5 THE INTERNAL RATE OF RETURN

Ethics Notes, page 209: To comply with the Air Quality Control Act of 1989, a company must install three smoke stack scrubber units to its ventilation stacks at an installed cost of $355,000 per unit. An estimated $100,000 per unit could be saved each year over the five-year life of the ventilation stacks. The cost of capital is 14% for the firm. The analysis of the investment results in a NPV of −$11,692.

Despite the financial assessment dictating rejection of the investment, public policy might suggest acceptance of the project. By fiat, certain types of pollution controls are required, but should the firm exceed the minimum legal limits and be responsible for the environment, even if this responsibility leads to a wealth reduction for the firm? The instructor could also pose the question, "Is environmental damage merely a cost of doing business?" Also, "could investment in a healthier working environment result in lower long-term costs in the form of lower future health costs? If so, might this decision result in an increase in shareholder wealth?" Notice that if the answer to this second question is yes, then all this means is that our original analysis omitted some side benefits to the project. This point is discussed in Chapter 8 in greater detail.

Internal rate of return (IRR)—rate that makes the present value of the future cash flows equal to the initial cost or investment. In other words, the discount rate that gives a project a $0 NPV.

IRR rule—investment is acceptable if the required return is less than the IRR. Otherwise, it should be rejected.

T7.7: Internal Rate of Return Illustrated

Net present value profile—plot of an investment's NPV at various discount rates.

T7.8: Net Present Value Profile

NPV and IRR comparison: If a project's cash flows are conventional (costs are paid early and benefits are received over the life), and if the project is independent (meaning the decision to take it does not affect any other project), then NPV and IRR will give the same accept or reject signal.

> *Lecture Tip, page 212: It may be helpful to provide an example of a decision involving dependent cash flows. The instructor could mention a capital budgeting decision in which a plot of land is purchased for the intent of building a factory which could produce a product that the marketing department estimates would have an expected future life of three years. However, the project can only be justified if, in three years at the end of the product's life cycle, the factory would undergo an expensive modification (cash outflow) and produce a second product, which would generate a cash inflow beginning one year after the factory modification. Such a project would have to be justified based on the cash flows of both projects and would generate more than one IRR. One could also use this example to consider the issue of "multiple discount rates," if desired.*

A. Problems with the IRR

> *Unconventional cash flows*—if the cash flows are of loan type, meaning money in at first and cash out later, the IRR is really a borrowing rate and <u>lower</u> is better. The IRR is sometimes called the IBR (internal borrowing rate) in this case.

> *Multiple rates of return*—if cash flows alternate back and forth between positive and negative (in and out), more than one IRR is possible. NPV rule still works just fine.

T7.9:   Multiple Rate of Return
T7.10: NPV Profile: Multiple IRR Problem

> *Mutually exclusive investment decisions*—if taking one project means another is not taken, the projects are mutually exclusive. The one with the highest IRR may not be the one with the highest NPV.

T7.11: IRR, NPV, and Mutually Exclusive Projects

> *Crossover rate*—the discount rate that makes the NPV of two projects the same (assuming, of course, their NPV profiles cross). Find the crossover rate using the NPV profile or by taking the difference in the projects' cash flows and calculate the IRR.

<u>Example:</u>
   If project A has a cost of $500 and cash flows of $325 for two periods, while project B has a cost of $400 and cash flows of $325 and $200 respectively, the incremental flows are:

Period	A	B	Incremental
0	-$500	-$400	-$100
1	325	325	0
2	325	200	125
IRR (%)	19.43	22.17	11.80

So the crossover is 11.8%. At this rate, NPV_A = $50.71 and NPV_B also = $50.71.

B. Redeeming Qualities of the IRR

People seem to prefer talking about rates of return to dollars of value.

Unlike NPV, which requires a market discount rate, IRR relies only on the project cash flows, which, if the IRR is high enough, may be all that is needed to accept or reject as a practical matter.

7.6 THE PROFITABILITY INDEX

Profitability index (PI) (or benefit/cost ratio)—present value of the future cash flows divided by the initial investment.

If a project has a positive NPV, then the PI will be greater than 1.

This method has ranking problems similar to the IRR when dealing with mutually exclusive projects, i.e., we're not necessarily looking for the biggest return per dollar, but the project that adds the greatest value.

7.7 THE PRACTICE OF CAPITAL BUDGETING

It is common practice among large firms to employ some discounted cash flow technique such as IRR or NPV along with payback period or average accounting return. It is suggested that this is one way to resolve the considerable uncertainty over future events that surrounds estimating the NPV.

T7.12: Percentage of Responding Firms using Capital Budgeting Methods

---

Lecture Tip, page 219: While the resolution of uncertainty is one reason multiple criteria may be used to judge projects, another is the judging of managers. When managers are judged and rewarded on the basis of periodic accounting figures (quarterly profits, annual earnings, etc.), there is an incentive to evaluate projects with methods such as payback or average accounting return that make these numbers look good.

7.8 SUMMARY AND CONCLUSIONS

T7.13: Solution to Problem 7.3
T7.14: Solution to Problem 7.8
T7.15: Solution to Problem 7.17

CHAPTER 8
MAKING CAPITAL INVESTMENT DECISIONS

TRANSPARENCIES

T8.1:   Chapter Outline
T8.2:   Relevant Cash Flows
T8.3:   Capital Budgeting: *Pro Formas*
T8.4:   Capital Budgeting: The DCF valuation
T8.5:   A Closer Look: NWC Spending
T8.6:   Modified ACRS Property Classes and MACRS Depreciation Allowances
T8.7:   MACRS Depreciation: An Example
T8.8:   Fairways Equipment and Operating Costs
T8.9:   Fairways Revenues, Depreciation, and Other Costs
T8.10: Fairways Pro Forma Income Statement
T8.11: Fairways Cash Flows
T8.12: Alternative Definitions of OCF
T8.13: Sample Problems (2 pages)
T8.14: A Cost-Cutting Proposal
T8.15: Sample Problem
T8.16: Setting the Bid Price (4 pages)
T8.17: Equivalent Annual Cost (3 pages)
T8.18: Solution to Problem 8.6
T8.19: Solution to Problem 8.7
T8.20: Solution to Problem 8.15
T8.21: Solution to Problem 8.18
T8.22: Solution to Problem 8.30

CHAPTER ORGANIZATION

T8.1: Chapter Outline

8.1 PROJECT CASH FLOWS: A FIRST LOOK
Relevant Cash Flows
The Stand-Alone Principle

8.2 INCREMENTAL CASH FLOWS

Sunk Costs
Opportunity Costs
Side Effects
Net Working Capital
Financing Costs
Other Issues

8.3 PRO FORMA FINANCIAL STATEMENTS AND PROJECT CASH FLOWS

Getting Started: Pro Forma Financial Statements
Project Cash Flows
Project Total Cash Flow and Value

8.4 MORE ON PROJECT CASH FLOWS

A Closer Look at Net Working Capital
Depreciation
An Example: The Majestic Mulch and Compost Company (MMCC)

8.5 ALTERNATIVE DEFINITIONS OF OPERATING CASH FLOWS

The Bottom-Up Approach
The Top-Down Approach
The Tax Shield Approach

8.6 SOME SPECIAL CASES OF DISCOUNTED CASH FLOW ANALYSIS

Evaluating Cost-Cutting Proposals
Setting the Bid Price
Evaluating Equipment with Different Lives

8.7 SUMMARY AND CONCLUSIONS

ANNOTATED CHAPTER OUTLINE

8.1 PROJECT CASH FLOWS: A FIRST LOOK

> **T8.2: Relevant Cash Flows**

A. Relevant Cash Flows

Relevant cash flows—cash flows that come into or out of being because a project is undertaken, thus we are interested in incremental cash flows.

Incremental cash flows—any and all changes in the firm's future cash flows that are a direct consequence of taking the project.

Lecture Tip, page 230: It should be strongly emphasized that the identification of a project's cash flows represents changes occurring in the financial statements as a result of accepting a project. The instructor may wish to provide a few examples of possible projects which would cause the student to consider the nature of an incremental item.

Examples:
a) The development of a plant on land currently owned by the company versus the same development, but the land must be purchased. This example would also allow the instructor to discuss the concept of opportunity cost as in the text.

b) Tax shelter provided by depreciation: The relevant depreciation effect if we replace an old machine with a three-year remaining life and $5,000 per year depreciation. The instructor could state that a new machine would cost $45,000 and be depreciated over a five-year life ($9,000 per year depreciation assuming straight-line). The students should be aware that the incremental tax shelter is t × ($9,000 − $5,000) for years one through three. The instructor might also ask the students to consider the incremental tax shelter in years four through five [t × ($9,000 − 0)].

B. The Stand-Alone Principle

Viewing projects as "mini-firms" with their own assets, revenues, and costs allows us to evaluate the investments separately from the other activities of the firm.

8.2 INCREMENTAL CASH FLOWS

A. Sunk Costs

Sunk cost—a cash flow already paid or already promised to be paid. Obviously, these costs should not be included in the incremental flows of a project.

Example:
    A firm has a policy of paying the tuition bills for any of its newly hired managers who attend an accredited MBA program on their own time. Two managers already taking MBA classes are assigned to develop a new product. Should their tuition costs be included in the project's cash flows?

Lecture Tip, page 231: Personal examples of sunk costs may be helpful for the student's understanding of this issue. The instructor might ask the student to consider a hypothetical situation in which a college student had purchased a typewriter for $300 while in high school. A computer is now available with an elaborate word processing package for $400. Although the student may be reluctant to purchase the new computer because of the previous decision to purchase the typewriter, the student should question the factors that would be relevant in the decision. The current cost (computer cost less any cash from the possible sale of typewriter) relative to the future benefits (time saved on retyping errors, completing many homework assignments sooner, etc.).

B. Opportunity Costs

Opportunity costs—any cash flows lost or foregone by taking one course of action rather than another. These apply to any asset or resource that has value if sold rather than used.

Example:
> Would land, already owned by a firm but not being used, be "free" when considering the investment outlay for a plant to be built on it?

C. Side Effects

With multi-line firms, projects often affect one another—sometimes helping, sometimes hurting. The point is to be aware of such effects in calculating incremental cash flows.

Erosion—new project revenues gained at the expense of existing products/services.

Examples:

a) Every time Kellogg's brings out a new oat cereal, it probably causes some erosion of existing product sales.

b) When a university adds to its list of program offerings, some of the "new" students are really transfers from other degree programs.

Ethics Note, page 231: An episode of the "L.A. Law" television series presented an interesting example of the ethical aspects of capital budgeting. According to the script, an automobile manufacturer knowingly built cars that had a tendency to explode when involved in accidents of a certain type. Rather than redesign the cars (at substantial additional cost), the manufacturer calculated the expected costs of future lawsuits and determined that it would be cheaper to sell an unsafe car and defend itself against lawsuits than to redesign the car.

> *Many would say that the above example is an inappropriate (to say the least!) and unrealistic application of cost-benefit analysis. And yet, manufacturers make similar decisions daily. Is a Yugo as safe as a Volvo in the event of a head-on collision? Empirical data suggest that it is not. So did Yugo management make unethical decisions? Or did the costs of enhanced safety features simply outweigh the incremental sales? Why did it take so long for air bags to become standard equipment on domestic cars? Why is a driver's side air bag standard equipment on a 1994 Grand Cherokee but not a 1994 Ford Explorer? Arriving at acceptable answers to questions such as these gets to the very heart of ethics in financial decision-making. The point is, in some cases the "side effects" of a capital budgeting decision may be quite complex, and, in the eyes of some, at least as important as other aspects.*

D. Net Working Capital

New projects often require incremental investments in cash, inventories, and receivables that need to be included in cash flows if they are not offset by changes in payables. Later, as projects end, this investment is often recovered.

E. Financing Costs

Do not include any interest or principal on debt, dividends, or other financing costs in computing cash flows. Financing costs represent part of the division of cash flows from a project to providers of capital.

F. Other Issues

Use cash flow, not accounting numbers.
Use <u>aftertax</u> cash flows, not pretax (the tax bill is a cash outlay even though it is based on accounting numbers).

Lecture Tip, page 232: Students sometimes become disheartened at what they perceive as complexities in the various capital budgeting calculations. You may find it useful to remind them that, in reality, setting up timelines and performing calculations are typically the least burdensome portion of the task. Rather, the difficulties arise principally in two areas: (1) generating good investment projects, and (2) developing reliable cash flow estimates for these projects.

It should be pointed out that investing in fixed assets differs from investing in financial assets in at least one important sense: that is, that one need only open The Wall Street Journal or call a broker to obtain a list of investment opportunities (good, bad, or otherwise), and then perform the appropriate analysis. Preparation of a capital budget, on the other hand, requires that people investigate and develop new project proposals, estimate the cash flows associated with these projects, and only then perform the analyses. (One might argue that the presence of large industrial engineering departments are de facto proof of the difference in these two types of investments.)

Developing reliable cash flow estimates ranges, of course, from being a relatively minor task (say, a simple replacement project), to one which is subject to a great deal of uncertainty, and which requires, in addition to all the analytical tools that one can bring to bear, years of experience. In any event, it is the author's experience that students more readily grasp the basic concepts if they are made aware of some of the more difficult real-world problems.

8.3 PRO FORMA FINANCIAL STATEMENTS AND PROJECT CASH FLOWS

A. Getting Started: Pro Forma Financial Statements

T8.3: Capital Budgeting: *Pro Formas*

Treat the project as a mini-firm:

1. Start with pro forma income statement (don't include interest) and balance sheet.
2. Determine the sales projection, variable costs, fixed costs, and capital requirements.

Lecture Tip, page 233: Some students may question why we are ignoring interest since it is clearly a cash outflow. It should be emphasized that we do not ignore interest expense; rather, we are only evaluating the asset-related cash flow. It should be stressed that interest expense is a financing cost, not an operating cost. It is chiefly a reflection of how we choose to finance a project, and, ignoring some of the finer points of capital structure, it is usually not an important factor in determining the value of the project. Another way to see this is to think of the project as a mini-firm with its own balance sheet. In capital budgeting, we are trying to determine the value of the lefthand (asset) side of the balance sheet. How a project is financed only affects the composition of the righthand side of the mini-firm's balance sheet. The impact of debt is considered in deriving the required return (cost of capital, which will be discussed in a later chapter).

B. Project Cash Flows

T8.4: Capital Budgeting: The DCF Valuation

From the pro forma statements, compute:

Cash flow from assets =	+ operating cash flow
	− capital spending
	− additions to net working capital
Operating cash flow =	+ earnings before interest and taxes (EBIT)
	+ depreciation
	− taxes

Lecture Tip, page 235: Capital spending at the time of project inception (i.e., the "initial outlay") includes the following items:

+ purchase price of the new asset
− selling price of the asset replaced (if applicable)
+ costs of site preparation, setup, and startup
+/− increase (decrease) in tax liability due to sale of old asset at other than book value
= net capital spending

We would also point out that, should it be reinstated, the applicable investment tax credit (ITC) would appear as a reduction in the initial outlay.

C. Projected Total Cash Flow and Value

Tabulate total cash flows and determine NPV, IRR, and any other measure desired.

8.4 MORE ON PROJECT CASH FLOWS

A. A Closer Look at Net Working Capital

T8.5: A Closer Look: NWC Spending

How would one reconcile accounting conventions for sales and costs with the need for cash flow information? Include additions to net working capital.

Example:
Sales for the period are $100 and costs $75. With the following balance sheet information what is net cash flow?

	19X1	19X2
Receivables	$20	$25
Inventory	30	25
Payables	15	20
Net working capital	$35	$30

The decline in inventory indicates a $5 cash inflow, the increase in payables indicates another $5 cash inflow, while the $5 increase in receivables means $5 of sales were not collected. Adjusting for these,

$$\$100 - 75 + 5 + 5 - 5 = \$30 \text{ cash flow}$$

The same result is seen by noting that net working capital declined by $5. Thus, (sales − costs − change in net working capital) = $100 − 75 − (−5) = $30.

Lecture Tip, page 238: The NWC discussion is very important and should not be overlooked by the students. It may be helpful to reemphasize the point of NWC and operating cash flow through accounting entries.

Example:
Consider the accounting entries for two separate sales at the end of the year-one for cash and the other on credit.

Cash	$10,000	Revenue	$10,000
Acc. Rec.	$ 5,000	Revenue	$ 5,000

The instructor should ask the students to consider the income statement and balance sheet impact from these two transactions at the end of the year. Assuming finished goods inventory = 80% of sales, the instructor should emphasize that cost of goods sold represents a cost that has already been paid out by the firm for these sales:

$$CofGS = \$12,000 = (\$10,000 + \$5,000) \times .8$$

Ignoring taxes, the students can see that, under accrual accounting, Revenue − Cost = $15,000 − $12,000 = +$3,000, but the company actually only received $10,000 cash and had cash expenses of $12,000. The students should easily recognize that operating cash flow = $10,000 − $12,000 = −$2,000. The instructor could then demonstrate the cash flow relationship:

Total cash flow	= Oper. Cash Flow −		Additions to NWC − . .
−$2,000	= $3,000	−	$5,000

B. Depreciation

When computing depreciation, economic life and future market value are ignored.

Modified Accelerated Cost Recovery System (MACRS)—current depreciation rules governing asset lives and allowable depreciation deductions.

T8.6: Modified ACRS Property Classes and MACRS Depreciation Allowances
T8.7: MACRS Depreciation: An Example

Book value versus market value—if an asset's value when sold (i.e., salvage value) is larger than its book value, the excess depreciation is to be recaptured. That is, taxes are due on the amount received over book value. Be careful to include such taxes in calculating aftertax cash flows.

Lecture Tip, page 240: The instructor may wish to question the students as to why a company might prefer accelerated depreciation, such as the ACRS tables, over straight-line depreciation. The students could consider the purchase of a five-year, $50,000 machine by a company with a 34% marginal tax rate.
  The instructor could mention that under both ACRS and straight-line depreciation, year-one depreciation is .2 × $50,000 = $10,000. However, under the ACRS rules, year-two depreciation is .32 × $50,000 = $16,000 versus the $10,000 under straight line.
  Cash flow effect: .34 × $16,000 = $5,440 versus .34 × $10,000 = $3,400. The realization of the higher cash flow in the early years of a project's life, relative to later years, will result in a higher NPV for the project.

C. An Example: The Majestic Mulch and Compost Company (MMCC)

<u>Another Example: Fairways Driving Range</u>

Two friends are considering opening a driving range for golfers. Because of the growing popularity of golf, they estimate such a range could generate rentals of 20,000 buckets at $3 a bucket the first year, and that rentals will grow at 750 buckets a year thereafter. The price will remain a $3 per bucket.

Equipment requirements include:

ball dispensing machine	$2,000
ball pick-up vehicle	$8,000
tractor and accessories	$8,000

All the equipment is 5-year ACRS property, and is expected to have a salvage value of 10% of cost after 6 years.

Stocking a small shop selling tees, visors, gloves, towels, sun-block, etc., plus a checking account for the business make net working capital needs $3,000 to start. This amount is expected to grow at 5% per year.

Annual fixed operating costs are expected as follows:

Land lease	$12,000
Water	1,500
Electricity	3,000
Labor	30,000
Seed & Fertilizer	2,000
Gasoline	1,500
Equipment maintenance	1,000
Insurance	1,000
Other	1,000
Total	$53,000

T8.8: Fairways Equipment and Operating Costs

Expenditures for balls and baskets, initially $3,000, are expected to grow at 5% per year. The relevant tax rate is 15% and the required return is also 15%. The project is to be evaluated over a six year life. Should the friends proceed?

Projected revenues, Fairways Driving Range:

Year	Buckets	Revenues
1	20,000	$60,000
2	20,750	62,250
3	21,500	64,500
4	22,250	66,750
5	23,000	69,000
6	23,750	71,250

Projected cost of balls and buckets:

Year	Balls & Buckets
1	$3,000
2	3,150
3	3,308
4	3,473
5	3,647
6	3,829

Depreciation on $18,000 of 5-year equipment:

Year	ACRS %	Depreciation	Book value
1	20.00%	$3,600	$14,400
2	32.00	5,760	8,640
3	19.20	3,456	5,184
4	11.52	2,074	3,110
5	11.52	2,074	1,036
6	05.76	1,036	0
		$18,000	

T8.9: Fairways Revenues, Depreciation, and Other Costs

Pro forma income statement, Fairways Driving Range:

Year	1	2	3	4	5	6
Revenues	$60,000	62,250	64,500	66,750	69,000	71,250
Variable costs	3,000	3,150	3,308	3,473	3,647	3,829
Fixed costs	53,000	53,000	53,000	53,000	53,000	53,000
Depreciation	3,600	5,760	3,456	2,074	2,074	1,036
EBIT	$400	$340	$4,736	$8,203	$10,279	$13,385
Taxes	60	51	710	1,230	1,542	2,008
Net income	$340	$289	$4,026	$6,973	$8,737	$11,377

Projected increases in net working capital

Year	Net working capital	Increase in NWC
0	$3,000	$3,000
1	3,150	150
2	3,308	158
3	3,473	165
4	3,647	174
5	3,829	182
6	4,020	−4,020

T8.10: Fairways *Pro Forma* Income Statement

Projected cash flows:

Year	EBIT	+ Depreciation	− Taxes	= Operating cash flow
0	$0	$0	$0	$0
1	400	3,600	60	3,940
2	340	5,760	51	6,049
3	4,736	3,456	710	7,482
4	8,203	2,074	1,230	9,047
5	10,279	2,074	1,542	10,811
6	13,385	1,036	2,008	12,413

Year	+ Operating cash flow	− Increase in NWC	− Capital spending	= Total cash flow
0	$ 0	$3,000	$18,000	−$ 21,000
1	3,940	150	0	3,790
2	6,049	158	0	5,891
3	7,482	165	0	7,317
4	9,047	174	0	8,873
5	10,812	182	0	10,630
6	12,413	−4,020	−1,530	17,963

Fairways Driving Range: NPV = $9,685; IRR = 27%

T8.11: Fairways Cash Flows

Lecture Tip, page 246: The impact of alternative depreciation methods is sometimes not clearly understood by students. Two approaches can be used to make the point: logic and brute force. Logic tells us that since

$$Project\ operating\ cash\ flow = EBIT + depreciation - taxes,$$

then booking depreciation sooner will increase the present value of OCFs. However, some may wish to demonstrate (or, as a homework assignment, ask the students to demonstrate) this phenomenon. You may, for example, require the class to rework the Majestic Mulch example assuming that the firm will compute depreciation using the straight-line approach. Given the assumed $160,000 salvage value at the end of 8 years, annual depreciation will be $640,000/8 = $80,000, rather than the values shown in text Tables 8.11 and 8.13. Other results will be as follows.

Year	Net Income	OCF	Project Cash Flows
0			$-820,000
1	$49,500	$129,500	95,500
2	128,700	208,700	172,700
3	168,300	248,300	230,300
4	145,200	225,200	225,950
5	128,700	208,700	216,950
6	95,700	175,700	192,200
7	62,700	142,700	159,200
8	29,700	109,700	281,300

At the assumed 15% cost of capital,. the NPV is $17,006. The IRR is 15.57%, and the payback period is approximately 4.44 years. In other words, the effect is slightly deleterious, as logic indicated.

8.5 ALTERNATIVE DEFINITIONS OF OPERATING CASH FLOWS

Or, exercises in manipulating operating cash flows. Let

OCF = operating cash flow
S = sales
C = operating costs
D = depreciation
T_c = corporate tax rate

Suppose $S = \$1,000$, $C = \$600$, $D = \$200$, and $T_c = 34\%$. Then EBIT = $S - C - D = \$1,000 - 600 - 200 = \$200$; Taxes = EBIT $\times T_c = (S - C - D) \times T_c =$

$200 \times .34 = \$68$, and Operating cash flow (OCF) = EBIT + D − Taxes = $200 + 200 − 68 = \$332$.

T8.12:   Alternative Definitions of OCF

A. The Bottom-Up Approach

$$
\begin{aligned}
OCF &= EBIT + D - (EBIT \times T_c) \\
&= (S - C - D) + D - (S - C - D) \times T_c \\
&= [(S - C - D) \times (1 - T_c)] + D \\
&= \text{Net income} + \text{depreciation} \\
&= [(\$1,000 - 600 - 200) \times .66] + \$200 = \$332
\end{aligned}
$$

This approach takes after tax income (bottom line with no interest expense) and adds back non-cash items.

B. The Top-Down Approach

$$
\begin{aligned}
OCF &= (S - C - D) + D - (S - C - D) \times T_c \\
&= (S - C) - (S - C - D) \times T_c \\
&= \text{Sales} - \text{Costs} - \text{Taxes} \\
&= \$1,000 - 600 - 68 = \$332
\end{aligned}
$$

This approach simply leaves out non-cash items.

C. The Tax-Shield Approach

$$
\begin{aligned}
OCF &= (S - C - D) + D - (S - C - D) \times T_c \\
&= [(S - C) \times (1 - T_c)] + (D \times T_c) \\
&= [(\$1,000 - 600) \times .66] + (\$200 \times .34) \\
&= \$264 + 68 = \$332
\end{aligned}
$$

Depreciation tax shield—the second part of the expression, $(D \times T_c)$.

T8.13:   Sample Problems (2 pages)

8.6 SOME SPECIAL CASES OF DISCOUNTED CASH FLOW ANALYSIS

The following are illustrated by example.

A. Evaluating Cost-Cutting Proposals

T8.14: A Cost-Cutting Proposal Illustrated
T8.15: Sample Problem

Consider a $10,000 machine that will reduce operating costs (pre-tax) by $3,000 per year over a 5-year period. Assume no changes in net working capital and a scrap value of $1,000 at the end of the period. For simplicity, assume straight-line depreciation. The tax rate is 34% and the discount rate is 10%.

Using the tax-shield approach to find OCF,

$$
\begin{aligned}
OCF &= [(S - C) \times (1 - T_c)] + (D \times T_c) \\
&= [\$(0 - (-3,000)) \times .66] + (\$2,000 \times .34) \\
&= \$1,980 + 680 = \$2,660
\end{aligned}
$$

The first part reflects the after-tax cost savings, while the second part gives the depreciation tax-shield.

The after-tax salvage value is:

Market value $-$ (Market value $-$ Book value) $\times$ T_c = $1,000 - $1000 \times .34 = $660

The relevant cash flows are:

Year	OCF	Capital spending	Total
0	$0	−$10,000	−$10,000
1	2,660	0	2,660
2	2,660	0	2,660
3	2,660	0	2,660
4	2,660	0	2,660
5	2,660	+660	3,320

At 10% the NPV is $493.30 and the IRR is 11.86%.

B. Setting the Bid Price

The lowest price to bid is one that makes NPV = 0.

T8.16: Setting the Bid Price (4 pages)

The Army is asking for bids on multiple-use digitizing devices (MUDDs). The contract calls for 4 units to be delivered each year for the next 3 years. Labor and material costs are estimated to be $10,000 per MUDD. Production space can be leased for $12,000 per year. The project will require $50,000 in new equipment which is expected to have a salvage value of $10,000 at the end of the project. Making MUDDs will mean a $10,000 increase in net working capital. The tax rate is 34% and the required return is 15%. Assume straight-line depreciation.

Year	OCF	Additions to NWC	Capital spending	Total cash flow
0	0	−10,000	−50,000	−60,000
1	OCF	0	0	OCF
2	OCF	0	0	OCF
3	OCF	+10,000	+6,600	16,600 + OCF

Taking the present value of $16,600 in period 3 and subtracting this figure from the initial outlay of $60,000 gives:

Year	0	1	2	3
Cash flow	−49,085	OCF	OCF	OCF

Operating cash flow (OCF) is now an unknown ordinary annuity payment. The 3-year present value factor for an ordinary annuity at 15% is 2.283, so:

NPV = 0   = −$49,085 + (OCF × 2.283) implies
OCF = $49,085/2.283   = $21,500

Using the bottom-up approach to get OCF, and depreciation of $50,000/3 = $16,667,

Operating cash flows = Net income + depreciation
$21,500   = Net income + $16,667
Net income   = $4,833

Next, noting annual costs are $40,000 + $12,000,

Net income = $(S − C − D) × (1 − T_c)$
$4,833   = (S × .66) − [$(52,000 + 16,667) × .66]
$50,153   = (S × .66)
Sales   = $50,153/.66 = $75,989.73

Hence sales need be $76,000 per year or $19,000 per MUDD to get the required 15% return on investment.

C. Evaluating Equipment with Different Lives

> ### T8.17: Equivalent Annual Cost (3 pages)

The following example presumes replacement chains are appropriate, assumes straight-line depreciation, a 34% tax rate, and a 15% required return.

Two types of batteries are being considered for use in electric golf carts by the City Country Club. Burnout batteries cost $36 each, have a life of 3 years, cost $100 per year to keep charged, and have a salvage value of $5. Longlasting batteries cost $60 each, have a life of 5 years, cost $88 per year to keep charged, and have a salvage value of $5.

Using the tax-shield approach, cash flows for Burnout are:

$$OCF = [(S - C) \times (1 - T_c)] + (D \times T_c)$$
$$= [\$(0 - 100) \times .66] + (\$12 \times .34) = -\$66 + 4 = -\$62$$

	Year					
	0	1	2	3	4	5
OCF	$0	−$62	−$62	−$62		
Capital spending	−36	0	0	3.3		
Total	−$36	−$62	−$62	−$58.7		

For Longlasting, the relevant cash flows are:

$$OCF = [(S - C) \times (1 - T_c)] + (D \times T_c)$$
$$= [\$(0 - 88) \times .66] + (\$12 \times .34) = -\$58 + 4 = -\$54$$

	Year					
	0	1	2	3	4	5
OCF	$0	−$54	−$54	−$54	−$54	−$54
Capital spending	−60	0	0	0	0	3.3
Total	−$60	−$54	−$54	−$54	−$54	−$50.7

We now calculate costs per year for the two alternatives to make them comparable.

Equivalent annual cost (EAC)—annuity with the same PV as the actual costs. To find the EAC, find the PV of costs and use this as the PV for an annuity with a like life. The PV of costs for Burnout and Longlasting at the 15% required return are:

Burnout PV(cash flows) = $175.4   Longlasting PV(cash flows) = $239.4

The annuity factors for 3 and 5 periods at 15% are 2.283 and 3.352 respectively, so finding the annuity with the same present value gives:

Burnout: $175.4 = EAC × 2.283 gives EAC = $76.83
Longlasting: $239.4 = EAC × 3.352 gives EAC = $71.42

Longlasting is cheaper, so we choose it.

Lecture Tip, page 255: The instructor could also ask the students to consider two alternative machines: machine A with a three-year life and machine B with a six-year life. If A is accepted, it must be replaced in three years with a new machine A. An alternative to EAC would be to calculate the PV of the costs of machine A over the six-year period and compare it to the PV of the cost of machine B over the same six-year period. This process would result in the same decision as under the EAC method.

Lecture Tip, page 256: A complete discussion of capital budgeting under inflation is beyond the scope of this book; nonetheless, we provide a few guidelines for those who are interested.

First, market rates (which underlie the discount rate - see Chapter 14 on cost-of-capital estimation) impound an inflation premium; using a market-based (i.e., nominal) discount rate, therefore, implies that one should be discounting nominal cash flows. (Alternatively, one could discount real cash flows using a real discount rate.) Second, one must account for differential effects of inflation in estimating project cash flows. Suppose the firm's labor and materials costs are expected to rise significantly in the coming years, but the firm is unable to raise prices accordingly. Each cash flow component must be projected individually (perhaps using the top-down approach) to obtain the clearest picture of project cash flows. Finally, note that while annual depreciation expense will not vary from the ACRS values, the size of the depreciation tax shield might, since inflation could push the firm into a higher tax bracket in the future.

8.7 SUMMARY AND CONCLUSIONS

T8.18: Solution to Problem 8.6
T8.19: Solution to Problem 8.7
T8.20: Solution to Problem 8.15
T8.21: Solution to Problem 8.18
T8.22: Solution to Problem 8.30

CHAPTER 9
PROJECT ANALYSIS AND EVALUATION

TRANSPARENCIES

T9.1:   Chapter Outline
T9.2:   Evaluating NPV Estimates
T9.3:   Fairways Driving Range
T9.4:   Fairways Scenario Analysis
T9.5:   Fairways Sensitivity Analysis
T9.6:   Fairways: Rentals versus NPV
T9.7:   Fairways Total Cost
T9.8:   Fairways Break-Even Analysis
T9.9:   Fairways Accounting Break-Even
T9.10: More on Break-Even Analysis
T9.11: Fairways DOL
T9.12: Managerial Options and Capital Budgeting
T9.13: Solution to Problem 9.1
T9.14: Solution to Problem 9.7
T9.15: Solution to Problem 9.13
T9.16: Solution to Problem 9.24

CHAPTER ORGANIZATION

T9.1:   Chapter Outline

9.1 EVALUATING NPV ESTIMATES
The Basic Problem
Projected versus Actual Cash Flows
Forecasting Risk
Sources of Value

9.2 SCENARIO AND OTHER "WHAT IF" ANALYSES
Getting Started
Scenario Analysis
Sensitivity Analysis
Simulation Analysis

9.3 BREAK-EVEN ANALYSIS
Fixed and Variable Costs
Accounting Break-Even
Accounting Break-Even: A Closer Look
Uses for the Accounting Break-Even

9.4 OPERATING CASH FLOW, SALES, VOLUME, AND BREAK-EVEN
Accounting Break-Even and Cash Flow
Sales Volume and Operating Cash Flow
Cash Flow, Accounting, and Financial Break-Even Points

9.5 OPERATING LEVERAGE
The Basic Idea
Implications of Operating Leverage
Measuring Operating Leverage
Operating Leverage and Break-Even

9.6 ADDITIONAL CONSIDERATIONS IN CAPITAL BUDGETING
Managerial Options and Capital Budgeting
Capital Rationing

9.7 SUMMARY AND CONCLUSIONS

ANNOTATED CHAPTER OUTLINE

9.1 EVALUATING NPV ESTIMATES

> **T9.2: Evaluating NPV Estimates**

To find an NPV is to put a market value on uncertain future cash flows. Projecting the future always involves error and potential error. Among the sources of error are biases and omissions.

A. The Basic Problem

Two reasons for positive NPV: 1) a good project, or 2) a bad job of estimating NPV.

Similarly, a negative NPV may be a bad project or a bad job of estimating NPV.

B. Projected versus Actual Cash Flows

Estimated cash flows are expectations or averages of possible cash flows, not exact figures (although, of course, if an exact figure were available you'd use it).

C. Forecasting Risk

Forecasting risk—the danger of making a bad (money losing) decision because of errors in projected cash flows. This risk is reduced if we systematically investigate common problem areas.

D. Sources of Value

The first and best guard against forecasting risk is to keep in mind that positive NPVs are considered economic rarities. For a project to have a positive NPV, it must have some competitive edge—be first, be best, be the only. Keep in mind the economic axiom that in a competitive market excess profits (the source of positive NPV) are zero.

Lecture Tip, page 268: Perhaps the single largest source of positive NPVs are monopoly rents—profits above those necessary to keep resources employed in an endeavor that accrue as the result of being the only one able or allowed to do something. Often associated with patent rights and technological edges, such rents quickly dissipate in a competitive market.

Lecture Tip, page 268: In "Corporate Strategy and the Capital Budgeting Decision" (Midland Corporate Finance Journal, Spring, 1985, pp. 22-36), Alan Shapiro states that a firm's capital budgeting program should "establish strategic options in order to gain competitive advantage." Further, successful investments, according to Shapiro, are those investments "that involve creating, preserving, and even enhancing competitive advantages that serve as barriers to entry."

The following are project characteristics associated with positive NPVs. That is, projects with one or more of these attributes are more likely to be successful than those without.

(1) Economies of scale
(2) Product differentiation
(3) Cost advantages
(4) Access to distribution channels
(5) Favorable government policy

Shapiro's article serves both to take the students past the standard number-crunching and to induce them to think of capital budgeting from the strategic, or "big-picture" standpoint: how will this project (or group of projects) benefit the firm as a whole?

9.2 SCENARIO AND OTHER "WHAT IF" ANALYSES

"And time yet for a hundred indecisions,
And for a hundred visions and revisions,
Before the taking of a toast and tea."

- T.S. Eliot

What things are likely to be wrong and what will be their effect if they are?

A. Getting Started

Start with a base case—the expected cash flows—then ask "what if . . .?"

Lecture Tip, page 268: Transparencies T9.3 through T9.11 are based on the financial information for Fairways Driving Range.

T9.3: Fairways Driving Range

Example: Simplified Fairways Driving Range

Consider the following revised example of Fairways Driving Range. Rentals are expected to be 20,000 buckets a year at $3 per bucket. Equipment costs are $20,000, depreciated straight-line over 5 years with no salvage value. Variable costs are 10% of rentals and fixed costs are $45,000 per year. Assume no increase in working capital nor any additional capital outlays. The required return is 15% and the tax rate is 15%.

Revenues	$60,000
Variable costs	6,000
Fixed costs	45,000
Depreciation	4,000
EBIT	$5,000
Taxes (15%)	750
Net income	$4,250

Thus, cash flow is $5,000 + 4,000 − 750 = $8,250. At 15%, the five-year annuity factor is 3.352, so NPV based upon expected cash flows is:

Base-case NPV = −$20,000 + ($8,250 x 3.352) = $7,654

The following are different versions of "what if . . .."

B. Scenario Analysis

1. Worst-case/Best-case scenarios: putting lower and upper bounds on cash flows. Common exercises include poor revenues with high costs, and high revenues with low costs.

If, under most circumstances, the discounted projected cash flows are sufficient to cover the outlay, we can have a high level of confidence that the NPV is positive. Beyond that, it is difficult to interpret the meaning of the scenarios.

Lecture Tip, page 269: A major misconception about a project's NPV at this point is that it depends upon how the cash flows actually turn out. This thinking misses the point that NPV is an ex ante valuation of the uncertain future. The distinction between the valuation of what is expected versus the ex post value of what transpired is often difficult for students to appreciate.

An analogy useful in getting this point across is the market value of a new car. The potential to be a "lemon" is in every car, as is the possibility of it being a "cream puff." The greater or lesser the potential for a car to turn out to be troublesome or trouble free (expectations about the future) obviously influences its market value. The point, however, is that a new car doesn't have many different market values right now—one for each conceivable repair record. Rather, there is one market value embodying the different potential outcomes and their expected value. So it is with NPV—the potential for good and bad cash flows is reflected in a single market value.

T9.4: Fairways Scenario Analysis

Lecture Tip, page 270: The instructor may wish to integrate this discussion of risk into the topics which will be discussed in Chapters 10 and 11. The variability between best and worst case in this chapter has to do with forecasting risk. Our chief concern is that our estimate of NPV (as opposed to the true, but unobservable, NPV) is wrong because we incorrectly identify the expected cash flows. In later discussion, we examine the economic risks that cause the actual cash flows to differ from the expected cash flows. It helps to point out that these risks are embodied in our required return.

Also, the cases examined here aren't literally the best and worst cases. The true worst case is something absurdly unlikely, such as an earthquake that swallows our production facilities. Instead, the worst case represents the use of pessimistic forecasts in developing the expected cash flows.

Example: Fairways Scenario Analysis

Base-case scenario: rentals are 20,000 buckets, variable costs are 10% of revenue, fixed costs are $45,000 and depreciation is $4,000 per year.

Worst-case scenario: rentals are only 15,000 buckets, while variable costs are 12% of revenue, fixed costs remain the same.

Best-case scenario: rentals are 25,000 buckets, variable costs are 8% of revenue.

Scenario	Net income	Cash flow	%Return
Base case	$ 4,250	$ 8,250	30.2
Worst case	−9,400	−5,400	na
Best case	17,000	21,000	101.9

C. Sensitivity Analysis

To conduct a sensitivity analysis, hold all projections constant except one, alter that one, and see how sensitive cash flow is to that one when it changes—the point is to get a fix on where forecasting risk may be especially severe. You may want to use the worst case-best case idea for the item being varied. Common exercises include varying sales, variable costs, and fixed costs.

T9.5: Fairways Sensitivity Analysis
T9.6: Fairways: Rentals versus NPV

Example: Fairways Sensitivity Analysis

Base case: rentals are 20,000 buckets, variable costs are 10% of revenue, fixed costs are $45,000 and depreciation is $4,000 per year.

Worst-case sales: rentals are only 15,000 buckets.

Best-case sales: rentals are 25,000 buckets.

Scenario	Revenue	Cash flow	%Return
Base case	$60,000	$ 8,250	30.2
Worst case	45,000	−4,500	na
Best case	75,000	19,725	95.1

D. Simulation Analysis

Using computers, the interactions of different inputs and likely scenarios may be realized through simulating the different possible cash flows that result. Going back to the new car analogy, simulation is a way to see the different potential outcomes to be valued.

9.3 BREAK-EVEN ANALYSIS

Break-even analysis is a widely used technique for analyzing sales volume and profitability. More to the point, it determines the sales volume necessary to cover costs and implicitly asks "Are things likely to go that well?"

> *Ethics Note, page 272: The following case might be used to discuss the nature of break-even analysis and a possible ethical quandary involved with this analysis.*
> *Researchers associated with South Miami Hospital (SMH) developed a new experimental laser treatment for heart patients. It is considered by its development team and the physicians who use the laser to be a lifesaving advance. It should be noted that*

the physicians who are touting the laser hold a significant stake in the company that produces the laser.

To offer a substitute for a balloon angioplasty to treat heart blockages, the experimental laser was developed at a cost of $250,000. SMH estimates that it will cost $20,000 to install the laser. The procedure requires a nurse at $50 per hour, a technician at $30 per hour and a physician who is paid $750 per hour. Patients are billed $3,000 for the procedure compared to $1,500 for the traditional balloon treatment.

The instructor could ask the students to determine the break-even for the new procedure. Answer:

Fixed cost   = $250,000 + $20,000   = $270,000

Variable cost = $50 + $30 + $750   = $830

Cash B.E.   = $250,000 / ($3,000 − $830)   = 115.2 hours,

or approximately 116 patients (assuming a one hour procedure per patient)

The instructor could next mention that this procedure is considered experimental and, as such, would not be covered by most insurers. The experimental nature of this procedure means that part of the development costs are being paid by the patient.

The instructor could ask the class the following two questions:

1. Is it ethical for the patient to pay for R&D costs prior to the introduction of the final product?

2. Is it proper for physicians to recommend this procedure when they have a vested interest in its usage?

A. Fixed and Variable Costs

Variable costs (VC)—costs that change as the volume of sales changes (direct labor and materials, for example).

A simplifying assumption is to make variable costs constant per unit of output, i.e.,

variable costs = quantity × cost per unit
VC   = Q × v

When this is assumed, v is also the marginal cost.

Lecture Tip, page 274: You may wish to emphasize that, in computing total variable costs, the only relevant costs are those that are directly related to the manufacture and sale of the product. Allocated (or indirect) costs (such as lease payments) should not enter into th analysis.. The example on page 303 assumes therefore that the variable costs of 55 cents per unit are the only incremental costs associated with the order.

Fixed costs (FC)—costs that are constant over a period regardless of the level of sales.

1. *Total costs, (TC)*—sum of fixed costs (FC) and variable costs (VC)

$$TC = FC + VC$$
$$TC = FC + (Q \times v)$$

T9.7: Fairways Total Cost

Example: Fairways Total Cost

Buckets	Variable cost	Fixed cost	Total cost
0	$ 0	$45,000	$45,000
15,000	4,500	45,000	49,500
20,000	6,000	45,000	51,000
25,000	7,500	45,000	52,500

2. *Average cost versus marginal cost*—total cost divided by output gives average cost. Average cost will exceed marginal cost in all cases except where fixed costs are $0. But since fixed costs are a type of sunk cost (in the current period at least) the relevant cost in considering additional production is variable or marginal cost.

Lecture Tip, page 274: The student should recognize that as quantity increases, total fixed costs remain constant, but, on a per unit basis, they decrease with increasing volume. And, as quantity increases, total cost per unit approaches variable cost per unit. If a company expects a high sales volume, the company may desire to exploit the possible economies of scale by investing more in fixed costs in an effort to lower variable cost per unit. However, this could create future financial problems if sales expectations fail to materialize. The instructor might mention that this sensitivity to earnings declines will be examined later in this chapter through the discussion of the degree of operating leverage.
    If the instructor desires to expand on this issue, he or she could introduce two alternative cost structures and have the students consider what minimum quantity of sales would be required to favor one project over another. Example:

$$FC_{(Proj. A)} + VC_{(Proj. A)} \times Q \quad = FC_{(Proj. B)} + VC_{(Proj. B)} \times Q$$
$$\$10,000 + \$6 \times Q \quad = \$25,000 + \$3 \times Q$$
$$Q^* \quad = 5,000 \text{ units}$$

The instructor could then mention that a company would have to expect beyond 5,000 units of sales to justify accepting the increased fixed costs or operating risk of project B. Additionally, the forecasting risk is much greater with project B. The instructor may wish to integrate this example with the discussion on operating leverage. Note the comment on page 315 in the "implications of operating leverage" section: "The higher

> *the degree of operating leverage, the greater is the potential danger from forecasting risk."*

B. Accounting Break-Even

The sales volume at which net income = $0

C. Accounting Break-Even: A Closer Look

What sales level gives $0 net income (assuming things are the same year to year)? This happens when sales equals total costs.

P	= price per unit
v	= (variable) cost per unit
Q	= units or quantity
FC	= fixed costs
D	= depreciation
t	= tax rate

Net income is sales less total costs less taxes $= [(Q \times P) - (FC + (Q \times v) + D)] \times (1 - t)$.

At break-even, net income = 0, so,

$$\$0 = [(Q \times P) - (FC + (Q \times v) + D)] \times (1 - t)$$

Dividing both sides by $(1 - t)$ and rearranging gives sales equals total costs,

$$Q \times P = FC + (Q \times v) + D$$

Further rearranging gives: $Q = (FC + D) / (P - v)$

That is, net income is zero at the quantity Q = fixed costs plus depreciation divided by the contribution margin (price less variable cost).

T9.8: Fairways Break-Even Analysis
T9.9: Fairways Accounting Break-Even

9.4 OPERATING CASH FLOW, SALES, VOLUME, AND BREAK-EVEN

A. Accounting Break-Even and Cash Flow

Ignoring taxes for simplification:

1. Calculate Q necessary for accounting break-even. Using the Fairways example:

$$Q = (FC + D) / (P - v)$$
$$Q = \$(45,000 + 4,000) / \$(3 - .30) = 18,148 \text{ buckets}$$

Since operating cash flow = net income + depreciation,

at Q = 18,148: operating cash flow = $0 + $4,000 = $4,000.

2. At (accounting) break-even Q, the sum of the (undiscounted) cash flows is just equal to the depreciable investment and the project's payback period is exactly equal to its life.

3. A project that just breaks even on an accounting basis will have a negative NPV at any positive discount rate.

B. Sales Volume and Operating Cash Flow

Again, ignoring taxes for simplification:

$$OCF = \text{net income} + \text{depreciation}$$
$$OCF = [((P - v) \times Q) - FC - D] + D = (P - v) \times Q - FC$$

This is a linear relation with slope $(P - v)$ and intercept FC.

C. Cash Flow, Accounting, and Financial Break-Even Points

T9.10: More on Break-Even Analysis

(Illustrated with simplified Fairways and no taxes)

Rearranging $OCF = (P - v) \times Q - FC$ and solving for Q:

$$Q = (FC + OCF) / (P - v)$$

1. Accounting Break-Even Revisited—Q at which net income is $0. To get the accounting break-even let $OCF = D$ and solve for $Q = (FC + D) / (P - v)$.

2. Cash Break-Even—Q at which cash flow is $0. Let $OCF = \$0$, then the cash break-even point (ignoring taxes) is $Q = FC / (P - v)$:

$$Q = \$45,000 / (3 - .30) = 16,667$$

3. Financial Break-Even—Q at which NPV = $0.

What OCF has a present value equal to the initial investment?

$$\$20,000 = OCF \times 3.352 \ (15\%, \text{5-year annuity factor})$$

$$OCF = \$20,000 / 3.352 = \$5,967$$

What Q gives an OCF of $5,967?

$$Q = \$(45,000 + 5,967) / \$(3 - .30) = 18,877 \text{ buckets}$$

Lecture Tip, page 283: Inquisitive students will ask how the Wettways example changes with the inclusion of taxes. Assume t ≠ 0 and dollars are in thousands. Then equation 9.2 becomes:

$$OCF = EBIT + D - Taxes = (S - VC - FC - D) + D - (S - VC - FC - D)t$$

$$= (S - VC - FC - D)(1 - t) + D$$

$$= [(P - v) \times Q - FC - D](1 - t) + D$$

Let t = .40, then the analogous "base case" (page 309) is:

$$OCF = [(\$40 - 20) \times 85 - \$500 - 700](1 - .4) + \$700 = \$1,000.$$

The effect on computed NPV is dramatic. The new base case NPV is:

$$-\$3,500 + \$1,000 \times 2.9906 = -\$509.4.$$

Carrying through to the end of the example, the effect of a positive tax is, as one would expect, to increase the financial break-even point. Specifically, we know that the minimum acceptable OCF remains unchanged. From page 313:

$$\$3,500 = OCF \times 2.9906$$

$$OCF = \$3,500/2.9906 = \$1,170.$$

Since OCF = EBIT(1 - t) + D,

$$\$1,170 = .6EBIT + \$700,00$$

$$EBIT = \$470/.6 = \$783.33.$$

Substituting into the equation for EBIT and solving for Q:

$$\$783.33 = (\$40 - 20) \times Q - \$500 - 700$$

$$Q = \$1983.33/\$20 = 99.165 \text{ units.}$$

So the firm must sell an additional 16 units to offset the effects of taxes in this example.

9.5 OPERATING LEVERAGE

There is almost always some flexibility in production in deciding between fixed and variable costs. Fixed costs, however, generally magnify forecasting errors.

A. The Basic Idea

Operating leverage − Degree to which a project or firm uses fixed costs in production. Plant and equipment (capital) and noncancellable rentals are typical fixed cost items.

B. Implications of Operating Leverage

Since fixed costs do not change with sales, they make good situations better and bad situations worse, i.e., they "lever" results.

C. Measuring Operating Leverage

Degree of operating leverage (DOL)—degree to which % change in Q affects OCF.

Percentage change in OCF = DOL × percentage change in Q

$$DOL = 1 + FC / OCF$$

DOL depends upon the Q you start with in determining OCF above.

T9.11: Fairways DOL

Example: Fairways DOL

At Q = 20,000 buckets (and ignoring taxes), OCF for Fairways is $9,000 and fixed costs are $45,000.

$$DOL = 1 + (\$45,000 / \$9,000) = 6$$

If the number of buckets increases by 5%, OCF should change by (6 × 5%) = 30%. At 21,000 buckets OCF = −$45,000 + ($2.70 × 21,000) = $11,700, a 30% increase.

Lecture Tip, page 285: An alternative calculation could also be presented to the class. With Q = 50 boats, (P − v) = $20, FC = $500, we have:

(P − v) × Q	$1,000
− FC	− 500
OCF	$ 500

DOL	= (P − v) × Q / OCF = 1 + FC / OCF
$1,000 / $500	= 1 + $500 / $500.

D. Operating Leverage and Break-Even

In general, the lower the fixed costs and the degree of operating leverage, the lower is the break-even point (however you measure it). If a project can be started with low fixed costs and later switched to high fixed costs if it turns out well, this is a valuable option.

Lecture Tip, page 286: As noted above, operating leverage results from the existence of fixed _operating_ charges in the firm's income stream. In an analogous fashion, the existence of fixed _financial_ charges (e.g., interest expense) in the firm's income stream is called "financial" leverage. The effect of financial leverage is similar: small changes in EBIT are "magnified", resulting in proportionally larger changes in net income. We defer further discussion of financial leverage since, at this time, we are concerned primarily with operating decisions.

9.6 ADDITIONAL CONSIDERATIONS IN CAPITAL BUDGETING

A. Managerial Options and Capital Budgeting

Managerial options—the opportunity to change something, which is valuable.

T9.12 Managerial Options and Capital Budgeting

---

1. *Contingency planning* involves determining what will be done if this or that actually happens. This can be explored with "what if" analysis.

○   *Option to expand*—ignoring this option can result in underestimating NPV.
○   *Option to abandon*—ignoring this option can result in underestimating NPV because the right to quit a loser is valuable.
○   *Option to wait*—waiting for favorable conditions or simply for some uncertainty to be resolved, is a valuable option.

2. *Strategic options* are possible future investments that may result from an investment under consideration.

Lecture Tip, page 290: It is interesting to note that the superiority of the NPV rule over the IRR rule is apparent in a discussion of strategic options. E.g., assume a $20 million plant can be built which will allow the firm to gain a foothold in a new product market. Due to start-up costs, the NPV is -$50,000 and the IRR is 8% (with a cost of capital of 10%). Clearly, the project should be rejected under the traditional rules; however, the "foothold" aspect of the project suggests that future sales (perhaps of related product) could make this a good strategic move. The NPV estimate tells us how much firm value will be destroyed if things don't pan out (as well as the fact that it is a small percentage of the initial project outlay); the IRR figure means very little.

B. Capital Rationing

Most notions of what is being pursued by capital budgeting rules are void when *soft* or *hard* rationing goes on. *Soft rationing* is self-imposed, often for administrative reasons that have little or nothing to do with value maximization. *Hard rationing*, the lack of funds at any rate, is often associated with financial distress.

9.7 SUMMARY AND CONCLUSIONS

T9.13: Solution to Problem 9.1
T9.14: Solution to Problem 9.7
T9.15: Solution to Problem 9.13
T9.16: Solution to Problem 9.24

CHAPTER 10
SOME LESSONS FROM CAPITAL MARKET HISTORY

TRANSPARENCIES

T10.1: Chapter Outline
T10.2: Percentage Returns (Fig. 10.2)
T10.3: Inflation and Returns (2 pages)
T10.4: Value of a $1 Investment (2 pages)
T10.5: S&P 500 Risk Premiums
T10.6: Small Stock Risk Premiums
T10.7: S&P 500 versus Small Stocks
T10.8: A $1 Investment in Different Types of Portfolios (Fig. 10.4)
T10.9: Year-to-Year Total Returns on Common Stocks
T10.10: Year-to-Year Total Returns on Small-Company Stocks
T10.11: Average Returns and Volatility
T10.12: Year-to-Year Total Returns on Bonds and Bills (Fig. 10.7)
T10.13: Year-to-Year Inflation (Fig. 10.8)
T10.14: Using Capital Market History
T10.15: Average Annual Returns: 1926-1990 (Table 10.2)
T10.16: Frequency Distribution of Returns on Stocks: 1926-1990 (Fig 10.9)
T10.17: Historical Returns, Standard Deviations, and Distributions (Fig. 10.10)
T10.18: The Normal Distribution (Fig. 10.11)
T10.19: Reaction of Stock Prices to New Information
T10.20: Solution to Problem 10.3
T10.21: Solution to Problem 10.12

CHAPTER ORGANIZATION

T10.1: Chapter Outline

10.1 RETURNS
Dollar Returns
Percentage Returns

10.2 INFLATION AND RETURNS
Real versus Nominal Returns
The Fisher Effect

10.3 THE HISTORICAL RECORD
A First Look
A Closer Look

10.4 AVERAGE RETURNS: THE FIRST LESSON
Calculating Average Returns
Average Returns: The Historical Record
Risk Premiums
The First Lesson

10.5 THE VARIABILITY OF RETURNS: THE SECOND LESSON
Frequency Distributions and Variability
The Historical Variance and Standard Deviation
The Historical Record
Normal Distribution
The Second Lesson
Using Capital Market History

10.6 CAPITAL MARKET EFFICIENCY
Price Behavior in an Efficient Market
The Efficient Market Hypothesis
Some Common Misconceptions about the EMH
The Forms of Market Efficiency

10.7 SUMMARY AND CONCLUSIONS

ANNOTATED CHAPTER OUTLINE

Historically, there has been a reward for bearing risk, and, the more risk taken, the larger have been the rewards.

10.1 RETURNS

A. Dollar Returns

Income component—direct cash payments such as dividends or interest

Price change—loosely, capital gain or loss

Total dollar return = dividend income + capital gain (or loss)

The return calculation is unaffected by the decision to cash out or hold securities.

Lecture Tip, page 303: The issues discussed on pages 303 and 304 need to be stressed. Many students will feel that if you don't sell the security, you won't have to consider the capital gain or loss involved. The instructor may wish to mention that this is true for tax purposes—only realized income must be reported. However, in measuring a security's pretax performance, whether some investor chooses to liquidate his or her position is immaterial. Also, if we did not annualize total returns, we would have a very difficult task comparing and evaluating the various securities available in the market.

T10.2: Percentage Returns

B. Percentage Returns

Refers to the rate of return per dollar invested.

Percentage Return = Dividend Yield + Capital Gains Yield

Dividend Yield $= D_{t+1}/P_t$ *Capital Gains Yield* $= (P_{t+1} - P_t)/P_t$

10.2 INFLATION AND RETURNS

T10.3: Inflation and Returns (2 pages)

A. Real versus Nominal Returns

Nominal returns—returns <u>not</u> adjusted for inflation; percentage change in nominal dollars.

Real returns—returns that have been adjusted for inflation; percentage change in purchasing power.

Lecture Tip, page 306: The instructor may wish to introduce the impact of taxes on real purchasing power. The instructor could mention that the real return on risk-free Treasury bills was slightly below 1% over the period 1929 to 1990. If the inflation rate averaged 5%, our nominal return would have been be about 6%. If we are in a 28% marginal federal tax bracket (and we ignore state taxes) and these rates continue, a $100 investment would realize $6 before tax, but, on an aftertax basis, we would realize $4.32—below the inflation rate of 5%. This return would not afford us the ability to purchase an item in the future that we could purchase today for $100 (assuming the product experienced the same inflation rate as the average product in the inflation index).

B. The Fisher Effect

1. The Fisher effect is a theoretical relationship between nominal returns, real returns, and the expected inflation rate. Let R be the nominal rate, r be the real rate, and h be the expected inflation rate; then,

$$(1 + R) = (1 + r) \times (1 + h)$$

hence $R = r + h + (r \times h)$. Since $(r \times h)$ is usually small, the nominal rate is often simply thought of as the real rate plus the expected inflation rate.

2. A <u>definition</u> whereby the real rate can be found by deflating the nominal rate by the inflation rate: $r = (1 + R)/(1 + h) - 1$.

International Note, page 307: Rational investors understand the effects of inflation on their returns and, as a result, we see new instruments developed during inflationary periods to help them maintain real returns. For example, in 1980, the United Kingdom issued bonds with coupon rates linked to that country's retail price index. These bonds have proven to be very popular with investors. Similar instruments have been utilized in Latin American countries, where rapid inflation is a recurring problem. Domestically, we have witnessed the growth in popularity of adjustable-rate mortgages (which shift the risk of interest rate increases from the lender to the borrower) during the 1980s, followed by a decline in their use in the early 1990s as the rate of inflation fell. All of these illustrations are examples of <u>financial contracting</u> by market participants in order to adjust to changing economic conditions.

10.3 THE HISTORICAL RECORD

The following are the basis for the nominal pretax rates of return reported by Ibbotson and Sinquefield:

-**Common stocks**: 500 largest U.S. companies (the S&P 500 index)
-**Small stocks**: smallest 20% of U.S. firms listed on the NYSE
-**Long-term corporate bonds**: high-quality, 20 years to maturity
-**Long-term government bonds**: U.S. government bonds, 20 years to maturity
-**T-bills**, 3 months to maturity
-also annual rates of inflation measured by the CPI

Lecture Tip, page 307: Many students may not recall their statistics, and a brief review may be in order.

Security returns are examples of random variables—categories of numbers for which in any particular instance more things can happen than will happen—and the things that can happen have an associated probability of occurrence.

Random variables are typically characterized by their probability distributions (i.e., a graph, table, or function that relates the potential values of the random variable to its associated probabilities) along with measures of its central tendency and dispersion (the deviation from that central tendency). The normal distribution is a common probability distribution; mean, median, and mode measure central tendency, while variance and standard deviation are common measures of dispersion.

A. A First Look

T10.4:   Value of a $1 Investment (2 pages)

Lecture Tip, page 308: The set of transparencies, T 10.4, T 10.5, T 10.6 and T 10.7, are provided if the instructor wishes to further explore the historical return behavior relative to the January effect extensively discussed in the literature. The transparencies show both the historical returns with the month of January excluded and monthly risk premiums of the S&P 500 and small stocks. The instructor may wish to present this information following the examination of Figure 10.4 (Transparency 10.8).

The instructor might present some plausible reasons for the existence of the January effect. Some plausible reasons cited by financial theorists are: 1) Tax loss selling—small firms are more subject to year-end tax loss selling because of their higher volatilities; 2) Information releases—January is a month containing many important corporate news releases, or 3) Problems in measurement for small firms attributed to the bid/ask spread. For a more detailed discussion of the January effect, one could refer to the article, "Size-Related Anomalies and Stock Return Seasonality" by Donald B. Keim, published in the June, 1983 edition of the Journal of Financial Economics. *A discussion of the January effect should include some mention of the "self-fulfilling prophecy nature of the phenomenon - articles have appeared in The Wall Street Journal at the end of each of the last several years describing the effect and speculating on whether it will happen again in the current year. Not surprisingly, it has!*

T10.5:   S&P 500 Risk Premiums
T10.6:   Small Stock Risk Premiums
T10.7:   S&P 500 versus Small Stocks
T10.8:   A $1 Investment in Different Types of Portfolios (Fig. 10.4)

B. A Closer Look

T10.9:   Year-to-Year Total Returns on Common Stocks (Fig. 10.4)
T10.10: Year-to-Year Total Returns on Small-Company Stocks (Fig. 10.5)

10.4 AVERAGE RETURNS: THE FIRST LESSON

T10.11:   Average Returns and Volatility
T10.12:   Year-to-Year Total Returns on Bonds and Bills (Fig. 10.7)
T10.13:   Year-to-Year Inflation (Fig. 10.8)

A. Calculating Average Returns

$$\sum_{i=1}^{T} \frac{R_i}{T}$$ add them up, divide by T

B. Average Returns: The Historical Record

Average historical returns, 1926-1990

Investment	Average return %
Common stocks	12.1
Small stocks	17.8
Long-term corporate bonds	5.5
Long-term government bonds	4.9
U.S. Treasury bills	3.7
Inflation	3.2

C. Risk Premiums

T10.14:   Using Capital Market History

Using the T-bill rate as the <u>risk-free return</u> and common stocks as an average risk, define the *excess return* as the difference between an average risk return and returns on T-bills.

Risk premium—reward for bearing risk, the difference between a risky investment return and the risk-free rate.

Lecture Tip, page 314: The instructor should mention that this analysis of risk and return is based on annual data. If our investment horizon is extended over a longer period, common stocks, as evidenced by history, may be less of a risk than would be suggested by annual data. Although there is a fair probability that we could experience a negative return during a particular year, it is highly unlikely that we would experience a return from common stocks below that realized by T-bills if we would consider a five-year holding period. Based on historical returns, if we extended a holding period to ten years, the probability would be extremely small that common stocks would underperform T-bills. The instructor could suggest to the student that if one is saving for retirement in an I.R.A., defined contribution pension plan, or some similar vehicle, it would only be logical for the student, who will soon be an employee confronted with this decision, to place 100% of the invested funds into common stock and not worry about short-term value fluctuations. History indicates the student will be significantly ahead when ready to retire in the Bahamas.

T10.15: Average Annual Returns: 1926-1990 (Table 10.2)

D. The First Lesson

Risky investments earn a risk premium. For common stocks the average annual risk premium has been approximately 8.4% since 1926.

10.5 THE VARIABILITY OF RETURNS: THE SECOND LESSON

A. Frequency Distributions and Variability

T10.16: Distribution of Returns on Common Stocks, 1926-1990 (Fig. 10.9)

B. The Historical Variance and Standard Deviation

Historical returns constitute a sample, so sample statistics are in order.

Variance—the average squared deviation between actual returns and their mean

$$VAR\ (R) = \sigma^2 = \frac{\sum\limits_{i=1}^{T} \left(R_i - E(R)\ \right)^2}{T - 1}$$

Example: Variance of common stock returns, 1985-1988

Year	Actual return	Average return	Deviation	Squared deviation
1985	.3216	.1817	.1399	.019572
1986	.1847	.1817	.0030	.000009
1987	.0523	.1817	−.1294	.016744
1988	.1681	.1817	−.0136	.000185
Totals	.7267		0.00	.036510

So, VAR(R) = .03651/(4 − 1) = .01217 and standard deviation = .1103.

Lecture Tip, page 319: Occasionally, students ask why we include the above-mean returns in measuring dispersion, since these are desirable from the investor's viewpoint. This question provides a natural springboard for a discussion of alternative variability measures. In this lecture tip, we discuss semivariance as an alternative to variance.

In Portfolio Selection (1959), Harry Markowitz states:

"Analyses based on [semivariance] tend to produce better portfolios than those based on [variance]. Variance considers extremely high and extremely low returns equally undesirable. <u>An analysis based on [variance] seeks to seeks to eliminate extremes. An analysis based on [semivariance] on the other hand, concentrates on reducing losses.</u>" (emphasis added)

Semivariance is computed in a manner similar to the traditional variance, except that if the deviation is positive, its value is replaced by zero. For the example above,

Example: Semivariance of common stock returns, 1985-1988

Year	Actual return	Average return	Deviation	Squared deviation
1985	.3216	.1817	.0000	.000000
1986	.1847	.1817	.0000	.000000
1987	.0523	.1817	−.1294	.016744
1988	.1681	.1817	−.0136	.000185
Totals	.7267		0.00	.016929

So, SEMIVAR(R) = .016929/(4 − 1) = .005643. (Note: Although Markowitz divides by N when using historical returns, we divide by N - 1 for the sake of consistency.)

The instructor may wish to point out that the use of semivariance vastly complicates the risk-return issue, and, as a result, has never caught on among investors.

C. The Historical Record

> **T10.17: Historical Returns, Standard Deviations, and Distributions (Fig. 10.10)**

D. Normal Distribution

> **T10.18: The Normal Distribution and Common Stock Returns**

Historical returns on securities have probability distributions that are approximately normal. The normal distribution is completely described by its mean and variance. Common stock returns have a mean of 12.1% and standard deviation of about 21%. An observation on a normally distributed random variable has a 66% chance of being within plus or minus one standard deviation of the mean, and a 95% chance of being within plus or minus two standard deviations.

E. The Second Lesson

Based on the means and variances of securities' historical returns, the second lesson is:

The greater the potential reward, the greater is the risk.

F. Using Capital Market History

Based upon the historical risk premium to common stocks, an investment of "average risk" should return about 8.4% above the T-bill rate.

Lecture Tip, page 321: It is often difficult to get students to appreciate the risk involved in investing in common stocks. They see the average return and largely ignore the variance. A simple exercise illustrating the risk of the different securities can be performed using Table 10.1. Each student (or the entire class) is given some endowment "points" to invest. They are then allowed to pick a security class. Using a random number table and the last two digits of the year, the security's distribution is randomly sampled. The endowment points are then adjusted by the draw outcome. The exercise is most telling when the number of draws is limited to between 1 and 5.

10.6 CAPITAL MARKET EFFICIENCY

Efficient capital market—market in which current market prices fully reflect available information. In such a market, it is not possible to devise trading rules that consistently "beat the market" after taking risk into account.

A. Price Behavior in an Efficient Market

T10.19:   Reaction of Stock Prices to New Information

B. The Efficient Market Hypothesis

Efficient market hypothesis (EMH)—asserts that modern U.S. stock markets are, as a practical matter, efficient.

The important implication of the EMH is securities represent *zero NPV* investments—meaning that they are expected to return just exactly their risk-adjusted rate.

Competition among investors and traders makes a market efficient.

Lecture Tip, page 324: Although a full discussion of efficient markets goes beyond the scope of introductory corporate finance courses, the instructor may wish to ask the students if they have ever heard of a "hot investment buy." Most students probably have heard a friend claim to have such a tip, or the students have heard someone mention that a broker recommended the purchase of a particular company. The instructor could then question the students concerning the value of this information. "If this company was undervalued, why wouldn't the investing community, with all its high-paid security analysts, be purchasing stock since they would have access to this information prior to when we receive it from a stockbroker?"

Some students may also have the feeling that since some companies, such as Phillip Morris or Wal Mart, have realized extremely large returns over their recent history, there may be some easy money to be made. One could simply mention that the past earnings history is what has driven its price to the current lofty levels but the current price has already factored in (discounted) the market's belief of these companies' future earnings potential.

C. Some Common Misconceptions about the EMH

1. Market efficiency does <u>not</u> mean that it doesn't make a difference how you invest, since the risk/return trade-off still applies, but rather that you can't expect to consistently "beat the market" on a risk-adjusted basis using costless trading strategies.

2. Stock price fluctuations are evidence that the market is efficient since new information is constantly arriving—prices that <u>don't</u> change are evidence of inefficiency.

3. The EMH doesn't say prices are random. Rather, the influence of previously unknown information causes randomness in price *changes*. As a result, price changes can't be predicted before they happen.

Ethics Note, page 324: Program trading is simply automated trading generated by computer algorithms designed to react to changes in the market. Program trading enables traders to quickly respond to up or down market movements. Thus, program trading occurs more quickly than traditional floor trading. It has been argued that it is unethical for investment banking houses to operate automated trading programs for their own accounts. One reason is that the bank, with its high speed, automated response, may be trading ahead of its customers. If this trading affects prices, then the bank is not acting in the best interests of its customers.

There has been a great deal of discussion about the impact of program trading on market volatility, and there doesn't seem to be a real consensus. In any case, it is clear that program trading can impact the market. For example, a large, erroneously executed sell order (which was literally a clerical mistake) on March 25, 1992 resulted in a 12 point loss in the DJIA (a .31% drop in the DJIA's value). This trade occurred during the final minute of trading, 3:58 - 3:59 p.m. Had the error occurred earlier in the trading day, this action could have caused a greater drop in market value.

D. The Forms of Market Efficiency

1. *Weak form efficiency*—A form of the theory that suggests you can't beat the market by knowing past prices.

2. *Semi-strong form efficiency*—Perhaps the most controversial form of the theory, it suggests you can't consistently beat the market using publicly available information. That is, you can't win knowing what everyone else knows.

3. *Strong form efficiency*—The form of the theory that states no information of any kind can be used to beat the market. Evidence shows this form does not hold.

Capital market history and the EMH:

1. Prices respond very rapidly to new information.
2. Future prices are difficult to predict.
3. Mispriced stocks (those whose future price level can be predicted accurately) are difficult to identify and exploit.

Ethics Note, page 325: Insider trading is illegal, but determination of what constitutes insider trading is difficult. Rule 10B-5 of the Security Exchange Act of 1934 states: "It shall be unlawful for any person, directly or indirectly, by use of any means or instrumentality of interstate commerce, or of the mails, or of any facility on a national securities exchange, (1) to employ any device, scheme, or artifice to defraud, (2) to make any untrue statement of a material fact or omit to state a material fact necessary in order to make the statements made, in light of the circumstances under which they were made, not misleading, (3) to engage in any act, practice, or course of business which operates or would operate as a fraud or deceit upon any person, in connection with the purchase or sale of any security."

While from this rule any act that would materially manipulate the market would be illegal, several court cases have more clearly defined insider trading. For insider trading to exist, there must be a fiduciary relationship between the parties. Actions of the inside trader do not have to meet the legal requirements of fraud; they merely have to have the appearance of acting as a fraud or deceit. Accidental discovery does not constitute a fiduciary relationship.

The court decided in Chiarella v. United States *that an employee of a printing firm, who was requested to proofread proxies which contained unannounced tender offers (and unnamed targets) was not guilty of insider trading because the employee determined the identity of the target through his own expertise.*

However, a member of a company's board of directors, who has knowledge of the company's future prospects, may not individually trade on this information prior to public disclosure. See SEC v. Texas Gulf Sulfur, 401 F.2d 833 (2d Cir. 1968).

10.7 SUMMARY AND CONCLUSIONS

T10.20: Solution to Problem 10.3
T10.21: Solution to Problem 10.12

CHAPTER 11
RETURN, RISK, AND THE SECURITY MARKET LINE

TRANSPARENCIES

T11.1:   Chapter Outline
T11.2:   Calculating the Expected Return
T11.3:   Calculating the Variance
T11.4:   Calculation of the Expected Return (Table 11.3)
T11.5:   Expected Returns and Variances
T11.6:   Portfolio Expected Returns
T11.7:   Portfolio Variance
T11.8:   Portfolio Expected Returns and Variances
T11.9:   Announcements, Surprises, and Expected Returns
T11.10: Standard Deviations of Annual Portfolio Returns
T11.11: Portfolio Diversification (Fig. 11.1)
T11.12: Beta Coefficients for Selected Stocks (Table 11.8)
T11.13: Portfolio Betas
T11.14: Portfolio Expected Return and Beta
T11.15: Return, Risk, and Equilibrium
T11.16: The Capital Asset Pricing Model
T11.17: The Security Market Line (SML) (Fig. 11.4)
T11.18: Solution to Problem 11.9
T11.19: Solution to Problem 11.28

CHAPTER ORGANIZATION

T11.1:   Chapter Outline

11.1 EXPECTED RETURNS AND VARIANCES
Expected Return
Calculating the Variance

11.2 PORTFOLIOS
Portfolio Weights
Portfolio Expected Returns
Portfolio Variance

11.3 ANNOUNCEMENTS, SURPRISES, AND EXPECTED RETURNS
Expected and Unexpected Returns
Announcements and News

11.4 RISK: SYSTEMATIC AND UNSYSTEMATIC
Systematic and Unsystematic Risk
Systematic and Unsystematic Components of Return

11.5 DIVERSIFICATION AND PORTFOLIO RISK
The Effect of Diversification: Another Lesson from Market History
The Principle of Diversification
Diversification and Unsystematic Risk
Diversification and Systematic Risk

11.6 SYSTEMATIC RISK AND BETA
The Systematic Risk Principle
Measuring Systematic Risk
Portfolio Betas

11.7 THE SECURITY MARKET LINE
Beta and the Risk Premium
The Security Market Line

11.8 THE SML AND THE COST OF CAPITAL: A PREVIEW
The Basic Idea
The Cost of Capital

11.9 SUMMARY AND CONCLUSIONS

ANNOTATED CHAPTER OUTLINE

11.1 EXPECTED RETURNS AND VARIANCES

In this section, we are concerned with finding central tendency and dispersion measures when given probabilities of *future* events.

A. Expected Return

> **T11.2: Calculating the Expected Return**

Let S denote the total number of states of the world, R_i the return in state i, and p_i the probability of state i. Then the *expected return* (E(R)) is given by:

$$E(R) = \sum_{i=1}^{s}(p_i \times R_i)$$

Example:

(1) State of economy	(2) Probability of state	(3) Return if state occurs	Product (2)×(3)
+1% change in GDP	.25	−.05	−.0125
+2% change in GDP	.50	.15	.0750
+3% change in GDP	.25	.35	.0875
	1.00		$E(R) = .15$

Projected or expected risk premium—the expected return − risk-free rate = $E(R) - R_f$

B. Calculating the Variance

> T11.3: Calculating the Variance
> T11.4: Calculation of Expected Return
> T11.5: Expected Returns and Variances

$$Var(R) = \sigma^2 = \sum_{i=1}^{s}\left[p_i \times (R_i - E(R))^2 \right]$$

Example:

(1) State of Economy	(2) Probability of state	(3) Return if state occurs	(4) Squared deviation	Product (2)×(4)
+1% change in GDP	.25	−.05	.04	.01
+2% change in GDP	.50	.15	0	.00
+3% change in GDP	.25	.35	.04	.01
	1.00	$E(R) = .15$		$\sigma^2 = .02$

Lecture Tip, page 335: Some students experience confusion in understanding the mathematics of the variance calculation in Equation 10.6 and the variance calculation on page 335. Some may have the feeling they should divide the variance of an expected return by (n − 1). The instructor should state that the probabilities account for this division. Also, the instructor may wish to have the students think of "n" as the number of possible states we are considering and this could correspond to a given year.

<u>*Example:*</u>

Year	State	Stock's Return
1992	Boom Year	+30%
1993	Poor Year	−10%
1994	Average Year	+15%

$$\text{Average Return} = (.30 + -.10 + .15) / 3$$
$$= (1/3) \times .3 + (1/3) \times -.10 + (1/3) \times .15$$
$$= .1167$$

If we feel these events are equally likely in 1995, the variance calculation for the 1995 expected return is identical to dividing by "n."

$$\text{Variance} = [(.3 − .1167)^2 + (−.10 − .1667)^2 + (.15 − .1667)^2] / 3$$
$$= 1/3 \times (.3 − .1167)^2 + 1/3 \times (−.10 − .1667)^2 + 1/3 \times (.15 − .1667)^2$$

Notice that (1/n) is the probability of the particular state's occurrence in 1995.

Lecture Tip, page 336: It is sometimes useful to take a moment to explain to students that our calculations in the previous chapter also used "probabilities" to compute average values. Since we were using historical data, each occurrence was equally "likely", thus the probability of each occurrence was 1/n. Explaining the calculations in these terms often helps students link the concepts in Chapter 10 with those in Chapter 11.

11.2 PORTFOLIOS

A portfolio is a collection of securities, such as stocks and bonds, held by an investor.

A. Portfolio Weights

Portfolios can be described by the percentages of the portfolio's total value invested in each security, i.e., by the *portfolio weights*.

<u>Example:</u>
If two securities in a portfolio have a combined value of $10,000 and $6,000 is invested in IBM and $4,000 in GM then

weight IBM	= $6,000/$10,000	= .60 or 60%
weight GM	= $4,000/$10,000	= .40 or 40%

B. Portfolio Expected Returns

T11.6: Portfolio Expected Returns

The expected return on a portfolio is the sum of the product of the expected returns on the individual securities and their portfolio weights. Let x_i denote a security's portfolio weight; then

$$E(R_p) = \sum_{i=1}^{N} \left(x_i \times E(R_i) \right)$$

Example:

If the expected return on IBM stock is 15% and that of GM is 10%, and $6,000 is invested in IBM while $4,000 is invested in GM, the portfolio expected return is:

$$E(R_p) = \left[x_{IBM} \times E(R_{IBM}) \right] + \left[x_{GM} \times E(R_{GM}) \right] = [.60 \times .15] + [.40 \times .10] = .13$$

C. Portfolio Variance

T11.7: Portfolio Variance
T11.8: Portfolio Expected Returns and Variances

Unlike expected return, the variance of a portfolio is *not* the weighted sum of the individual security variances. Combining securities into portfolios can reduce the total variability of returns.

Example:
Consider a portfolio with equal amounts invested in three stocks:

State of economy	Probability of state	Return to stock A	Return to stock B	Return to stock C	Return on portfolio
+1% change in GDP	.25	−.05	.00	.20	.050
+2% change in GDP	.50	.15	.10	.10	.117
+3% change in GDP	.25	.35	.20	.00	.183
Expected return		.15	.10	.10	.117

The variances of the stock returns and the portfolio return are:

$$\sigma_A^2 = .25 \times (-.05 - .15)^2 + .50 \times (.15 - .15)^2 + .25 \times (.35 - .15)^2 = .02$$

$$\sigma_B^2 = .25 \times (.00 - .10)^2 + .50 \times (.10 - .10)^2 + .25 \times (.20 - .10)^2 = .005$$

$$\sigma_C^2 = .25 \times (.20 - .10)^2 + .50 \times (.10 - .10)^2 + .25 \times (.00 - .10)^2 = .005$$

$$\sigma_P^2 = .25 \times (.05-.117)^2 + .50 \times (.117-.117)^2 + .25 \times (.183-.117)^2 = .002$$

The calculations show that the portfolio variance is less than that for the individual securities in the portfolio.

Lecture Tip, page 338: In most business programs, a course in elementary statistics is a prerequisite for the introductory corporate finance course. And while students are sometimes fuzzy on the details, they usually remember the general concept of the correlation coefficient and the fact that it ranges from -1 to +1. You may find it useful to re-introduce them to the correlation concept here in order to deepen their understanding of portfolio variance.

Specifically, for a two-asset portfolio, the portfolio variance, σ_P^2, is equal to

$$x_1^2 \times \sigma_1^2 + x_2^2 \times \sigma_2^2 + (2 \times x_1 \times x_2 \times \sigma_1 \times \sigma_2 \times \rho_{12})$$

where ρ_{12} is the correlation coefficient between the returns on securities 1 and 2. Ignoring short sales, notice that the all of the terms in the equation except ρ_{12} will be positive; the sign of the correlation coefficient determines whether or not the term in parentheses increases or decreases portfolio variance. More simply, the equation clearly demonstrates that, at the extremes, holding stocks with positively (negatively) correlated returns increases (decreases) portfolio variance.

Lecture Tip, page 339: At this point, the student has experienced a large number of mathematical formulas—probability weights, portfolio weights, and so on. It may be helpful to review all of the calculations, beginning with the process of using the probability weights to calculate an individual stock's variance and ending with the process of using the portfolio weights to calculate a portfolio's variance.

11.3 ANNOUNCEMENTS, SURPRISES, AND EXPECTED RETURNS

> **T11.9: Announcements, Surprises, and Expected Returns**

A. Expected and Unexpected Returns

Total return = Expected return + Unexpected return

$$R = E(R) + U$$

Total return differs from expected return because of surprises causing unexpected returns.

B. Announcements and News

Announcement—the release of information not previously available. Announcements have two parts: *the expected part and the surprise part.*

The *expected part* is "discounted" information used by the market to formulate $E(R)$ early on, while the surprise is <u>news</u> that influences U.

"Discounted" information—information already impounded in expected return (and price). The tie-in to efficient markets is obvious. The assumption here is that markets are semi-strong efficient; that is, public information is incorporated into prices.

Lecture Tip, page 341: It may be helpful to select a recent news item from the Wall Street Journal *to illustrate these ideas. As an example, a January 30, 1992, article on page C1 was headlined "Greenspan Sends Prices Into Tailspin—Dow Plunges 47.18, Bonds Fall on Hint of Inaction at Fed." A sentence from the article reads "If investors become convinced that the Fed isn't going to help the economy, a full-blown correction could materialize, some analysts suggested." Such news items allow the instructor to question the students as to whether stock price corrections indicate market inefficiency or market adjustments to new information.*

11.4 RISK: SYSTEMATIC AND UNSYSTEMATIC

A. Systematic and Unsystematic Risk

Risk consists of surprises—unanticipated events. Surprises are of two kinds:

Systematic risk—a surprise that affects a large number of assets, each to a greater or lesser extent—sometimes called *market risk*.

Unsystematic risk—a risk or surprise that affects at most a small number of assets—sometimes called *unique risk*.

Example:

Changes in GDP, interest rates, and inflation are examples of *market risks*, affecting all firms to a greater or lesser degree.

Strikes, plant accidents, takeovers, and a CEO's resignation are examples of *unique risks*.

Lecture Tip, page 342: The difference between systematic and unsystematic risk could be expanded using the example of a strike by employees. Students will generally agree that this would be a unique or unsystematic effect for one company. However, one might ask the students to consider a strike by the UAW against the auto industry and whether this action could have a carry-over impact on other industries and possibly the entire economy. The students should recognize that it is not the event but rather the <u>impact</u> of the event which determines whether it is a systematic or unsystematic effect.

B. Systematic and Unsystematic Components of Return

Total return = Expected return + Unexpected return

$$R = E(R) + U$$

$$R = E(R) + Systematic\ portion + Unsystematic\ portion$$

Let *m* denote the *market* or *systematic portion* and ϵ represent the *unique* or *unsystematic portion* of risk. Then,

$$R = E(R) + m + \epsilon$$

11.5 DIVERSIFICATION AND PORTFOLIO RISK

A. The Effect of Diversification: Another Lesson from Market History

Portfolio variability can be quite different from the variability of individual securities (see prior example on portfolio variance).

T11.10:   Standard Deviations of Annual Portfolio Returns

A typical single stock on the NYSE has a standard deviation of annual returns of 49.24%, while the typical large (100 or more stock) portfolio of NYSE stocks has a standard deviation of annual returns just under 20%.

B. The Principle of Diversification

T11.11:   Portfolio Diversification

Principle of diversification—principle stating that combining imperfectly related assets can produce a portfolio with less variability than the typical individual asset.

The portion of variability present in a typical single security that is not present in a portfolio of securities is termed *diversifiable risk*. The level of variance that is present in collections of assets is termed *undiversifiable risk*.

C. Diversification and Unsystematic Risk

When securities are combined into portfolios, their *unique or unsystematic* risks tend to cancel each other out, leaving only the variability that affects all securities to a greater or lesser degree. Thus, *diversifiable risk* is synonymous with *unsystematic risk*. Large portfolios have little or no unsystematic risk.

International Note, page 345: Common sense tells us that, to the extent that national economies are less than perfectly positively correlated, there may be diversification benefits to be had by investing in foreign securities. Empirical research bears this notion out. For example, Solnik (Financial Analysts Journal, 1974) and Harvey (Journal of Finance, 1991) find that the returns on U.S. stocks are significantly less than perfectly positively correlated with the returns on stocks in other industrialized countries. As a result, the potential for risk reduction is greater when one includes international stocks in his/her portfolio.

D. Diversification and Systematic Risk

Systematic risk cannot be eliminated by diversification since it represents the variability due to influences that affect all securities to a greater or lesser extent. Thus, *systematic risk* and *undiversifiable risk* are analogous.

$$\text{Total risk} = \text{systematic risk} + \text{unsystematic risk}$$
$$= \text{undiversifiable risk} + \text{diversifiable risk}$$

11.6 SYSTEMATIC RISK AND BETA

A. The Systematic Risk Principle

<u>The principle:</u>
The reward for bearing risk depends only upon the systematic or undiversifiable risk of an investment (since unsystematic risk can be diversified away).

<u>The implication:</u>
The expected return on an asset depends only upon that asset's systematic risk.

<u>A corollary:</u>
No matter how much total risk an asset has, its expected return depends only upon its systematic or undiversifiable risk.

Lecture Tip, page 347: It is stated in the text that the "underlying rationale for [the systematic risk] principle is straightforward: Since unsystematic risk can be eliminated at virtually no cost (by diversifying), there is no reward for bearing it." You may find it useful to emphasize that this is both a crucial point and one that is consistent with observed investor behavior. First, anything that impedes portfolio construction can impede diversification. For example, some executives find themselves with "all their eggs in one basket" because their retirement funds consist largely of their own firms' shares. On the other hand, the rapid growth in both the number and size of mutual funds suggests that investors in toto aggressively seek to diversify their holdings. Further, it should be noted that barriers to diversification are minimal: many funds will open accounts with initial deposits as small as $1,000 (and many company-sponsored retirement plans will open accounts with much less.)

B. Measuring Systematic Risk

Beta coefficient (β)—measure of how much systematic risk an asset has relative to an average risk asset.

> **T11.12:   Beta Coefficients for Selected Companies**

Lecture Tip, page 348: This point, "the market does not reward risks that are born unnecessarily," should be strongly emphasized, possibly with a reference back to Figure 11.1. Many investment companies offer investors a choice between income-oriented mutual funds, consisting of bonds and stocks in more established companies with higher dividend payouts, and growth-oriented funds which are typically composed of stocks of smaller companies which retain a higher percentage of earnings to reinvest back into the company. Investors desiring growth-oriented funds typically assume a much greater degree of systematic risk and would expect a higher return. However, both funds eliminate the unsystematic element of risk through the diversification these funds provide.

C. Portfolio Betas

T11.13: Portfolio Betas

While portfolio variance is <u>not</u> equal to a simple weighted sum of individual security variances, portfolio betas <u>are</u> equal to the weighted sum of individual security betas.

<u>Example:</u>
     Using betas from Table 11.8 of the text:

(1) Stock	(2) Amount invested	(3) Portfolio weight	(4) Beta coefficient	Product $(3) \times (4)$
IBM	$6,000	50%	.90	.450
General Motors	$4,000	33%	1.10	.367
Wal-Mart	$2,000	17%	1.30	.217
Portfolio	$12,000	100%		1.033

11.7 THE SECURITY MARKET LINE

A. Beta and the Risk Premium

A riskless asset has a beta of 0. When a risky asset ($\beta \neq 0$) is combined with a riskless one, the resulting expected return is the weighted sum of the expected returns and the portfolio beta is the weighted sum of the betas. By varying the amount invested in each asset, we can get an idea of the relation between portfolio expected returns and betas.

<u>Example:</u>
     Let a portfolio be comprised of an investment in Stock A with a beta of 1.2 and expected return of 18%, and a T-bill with a 7% return. Using what has already been said about portfolio returns and betas, some possible portfolio results are:

Proportion invested in Stock A	Proportion invested in R_f	Portfolio expected return	Portfolio beta
0%	100%	7%	0
25%	75%	9.75%	.30
50%	50%	12.50%	.60
75%	25%	15.25%	.90
100%	0%	18%	1.20
125%	−25%	20.75%	1.56

A greater than 100% investment in the risky asset and negative weight on T-bills represent money borrowed at the riskless rate.

The portfolio expected return and beta combinations lie on a straight line with slope a equal to

$$\frac{Rise}{Run} = \frac{E(R_A) - R_f}{\beta_A} = \frac{.18 - .07}{1.2} = .092 = 9.2\%$$

1. *The Reward-to-Risk Ratio*: What is the expected return per "unit" of systematic risk? That is, what is the ratio of risk premium to amount of systematic risk? For Stock A in the above example, the ratio is $(.18 - .07)/1.2 = .092$ or 9.2%, the same as the slope of the Stock A/risk-free asset portfolio line.

2. *The Basic Argument*: Since systematic risk is all that matters in determining expected return, the reward-to-risk ratio, i.e., the risk premium per unit of systematic risk, must be the same for all assets. If it were not, people would buy up the asset offering the higher reward-to-risk ratio and ignore the asset with the lower ratio.

3. *The Fundamental Result*: In a competitive market where only systematic risk affects E(R), *the reward-to-risk ratio must be the same for all assets in the market*. In other words,

$$\frac{E(R_A) - R_f}{\beta_A} = \frac{E(R_B) - R_f}{\beta_B}$$

So the expected returns and betas of all assets must plot on the same straight line.

Lecture Tip, page 350: The instructor may wish to mention that a great number of investors, both individual and institutional, commonly borrow money from their broker to purchase stocks. The interest rate paid on margin accounts is known as the call loan rate, and is slightly above the Treasury bill rate. The intent of such loans is obvious—a higher return for the investor. However, higher potential returns imply higher risks and portfolio betas.

> **T11.14: Portfolio Expected Return and Beta**
> **T11.15: Return, Risk, and Equilibrium**

Lecture Tip, page 353: The issue of asset market equilibrium should be strongly emphasized in the class lecture. Rational investors will quickly exploit any disequilibrium in which one asset is expected to offer a higher risk-adjusted return than another.

B. The Security Market Line

The line which gives the expected return/systematic risk combinations of assets in a well functioning, active financial market is called the **security market line**.

> **T11.16: The Capital Asset Pricing Model**
> **T11.17: The Security Market Line (SML) (Fig. 11.4)**

Lecture Tip, page 355: Although the realized market risk premium has on average been about 8.4%, the historical average should not be confused with a current expectation. There is abundant evidence that the realized market return has varied greatly over time. The historical average value should be treated accordingly. On the other hand, there is currently no universally accepted means of coming up with a good ex ante *estimate of the market risk premium, so the historical average might be as good a guess as any.*

1. *Market Portfolios*: Consider a portfolio of all the assets in the market, and call it the *market portfolio*. This portfolio, by definition, has "average" systematic risk, i.e., it has a beta of 1. Since all assets must lie on the SML when appropriately priced, so must the market portfolio. Denote the expected return on the market portfolio $E(R_M)$. Then,

$$\frac{E(R_M) - R_f}{\beta_M} = \frac{E(R_M) - R_f}{1} = E(R_M) - R_f = SML \ slope$$

The slope of the **SML**, $E(R_M) - R_f$, is called the *market risk premium*.

2. *The Capital Asset Pricing Model*: Since the expected return to any asset i, $E(R_i)$, must satisfy the same reward-to-risk ratio as the market portfolio,

$$\frac{E(R_i) - R_f}{\beta_i} = E(R_M) - R_f$$

Rearranging, we have the capital asset pricing model (CAPM):

$$E(R_i) = R_f + [E(R_M) - R_f] \times \beta_i.$$

The CAPM states that the expected return on asset depends upon:

1. *The time value of money*, as measured by R_f.
2. *The reward per unit of systematic risk*, $E(R_M) - R_f$.
3. *The asset's systematic risk*, as measured by β.

11.8 THE SML AND THE COST OF CAPITAL: A PREVIEW

A. The Basic Idea

To determine the appropriate discount rate for use in evaluating an investment's worth we need to ascertain the investment's riskiness and determine the expected return on alternative investments of similar risk. That is:

1. Determine an investment's amount of systematic risk, β.
2. Find the expected return in the financial market for that β.

Lecture Tip, page 358: Students will remember that, in efficient markets, an investment in a publicly-traded company will result in a NPV of 0. The instructor may wish to mention that the EMH does not imply that a company's investments in new projects must have an NPV of 0. Companies always attempt to invest in projects with a positive NPV, and those that are consistently successful will trade at higher prices, reflecting the market's belief that they will probably continue to do so in the future (a high P/E ratio). The ability to generate positive-NPV projects reflects the fundamental differences in physical asset versus financial asset markets. That is, physical asset markets are, in general, less efficient then financial markets, and cash flows to physical assets are often owner-dependent, where cash flows to financial assets are not.

B. The Cost of Capital

Cost of capital—the minimum expected return an investment must offer to be attractive. Sometimes referred to as the *required return*. The cost of capital, when taken as the market rate on a financial asset of equal systematic risk, is an *opportunity cost*.

11.9 SUMMARY AND CONCLUSIONS

> **T11.18:** Solution to Problem 11.9
> **T11.19:** Solution to Problem 11.28

Some instructors will wish to delve into the calculation of beta coefficients. The following handout may be useful to those so inclined.

APPENDIX A: CALCULATING BETA COEFFICIENTS

In Chapter 11, it was noted that beta measures the amount of systematic risk present in a particular risky asset relative to an average risky asset. (Later, it was suggested that the market portfolio would serve as an appropriate proxy for the average risky asset.) Since risk is a function of the changes in, or "movement of" an asset's price, systematic risk must be attributable to the movement in a risky asset's price relative to the movement in the price of the average risky asset (or the market portfolio).

Given the above, we should not be surprised to find that the beta coefficient is nothing more than a statistical measure of the relationship between the returns on asset i and the market portfolio. This relationship is most often quantified via the use of simple linear regression. Specifically, we estimate the following model:

$$R_{it} = \alpha_i + \beta_i R_{Mt} + \epsilon_i$$

where: R_{it} = the return on stock i in period t,
R_{Mt} = the return on the market portfolio i in period t,
α_i, β_i = the intercept and the slope coefficients, respectively, and
ϵ_i = the random error term.

The model above is called the "market model" and is usually estimated using daily or monthly historical returns. (Although there are no universally accepted guidelines, most people use approximately 250 daily returns, or 60 monthly returns to estimate the model.) The estimated β coefficient in the model above is the beta referred to in the chapter.

Although it is beyond the scope of this book, it is possible to show that, given certain assumptions about the distribution of returns, the beta coefficient is equal to the correlation between returns on stock i and the market portfolio, times the product of the standard deviations of the returns on stock i and the market portfolio, all divided by the variance of the market returns. In equation form,

$$\beta_i = \rho_{iM}\sigma_i\sigma_M/\sigma_M^2.$$

Consider the following monthly stock return data.

Month	R_i	R_M
1	.003	.013
2	.024	.017
3	.021	.012
4	-.015	.004
5	.005	.011
6	.022	.015
7	-.021	.011
8	.017	-.010
9	.018	.011
10	.028	.013
11	.032	.021
12	-.017	-.013

$$E(R_i) = .00975 \qquad E(R_M) = .00875$$
$$\sigma_i = .0185 \qquad \sigma_M = .0103$$
$$\rho_{iM} = .50276$$

According to the above equation, $\beta_{iM} = .50276(.0185)(.0103)/(.0103^2) = .903$. Since, in a strict mathematical sense, the beta coefficient is simply an index measuring the statistical relationship between the returns on stock i and the market portfolio, we interpret our results to mean that the systematic risk of stock i is about 90 percent of that of the average stock. (Digression: This is the source of the terms "aggressive" and "defensive" as applied to stocks. Aggressive stocks are stocks with betas greater than 1.0; they are more volatile than the average stock, and are, therefore, more suited to investors willing to take risks, i.e., to be aggressive. Of course, the opposite holds true for defensive stocks.)

Notice that the beta equation also suggests that beta has the following properties.

1. The beta of the market portfolio, β_M, must equal 1.0, since

$$\beta_M = \rho_{MM}\sigma_M\sigma_M/\sigma_M^2 = [(1.0)(\sigma_M^2)]/\sigma_M^2 = 1.0.$$

2. The beta of the risk-free asset must equal zero.

$$\beta_f = \rho_{fM}\sigma_f\sigma_M/\sigma_M^2 = [(0)(0)(\sigma_M)]/\sigma_M^2 = 0.$$

Finally, it should be noted that most people need not bother to calculate betas for stocks they are interested in. Beta coefficients are computed by several firms (for example, Merrill Lynch, Standard and Poor's Corporation, Value Line, and Moody's) and appear in various publications.

CHAPTER 12
LONG-TERM FINANCING: AN INTRODUCTION

TRANSPARENCIES

T12.1: Chapter Outline
T12.2: Features of a Hypothetical bond
T12.3: The Bond Indenture
T12.4: Bond Ratings
T12.5: Preferred Stock
T12.6: Common Stock
T12.7: Effects of a Stock Sale
T12.8: Patterns of Corporate Financing (Table 12.2, 2 pages)
T12.9: The Long-Term Financial Deficit (Fig. 12.2)
T12.10: Bankruptcy Liquidation
T12.11: Absolute Priority Rule
T12.12: Bankruptcy Reorganization
T12.13: Solution to Problem 12.2
T12.14: Solution to Problem 12.8
T12.15: Solution to Problem 12.13

CHAPTER ORGANIZATION

T12.1: Chapter Outline

12.1 CORPORATE LONG-TERM DEBT
Is It Debt or Equity?
Long-Term Debt: The Basics
The Indenture

12.2 BOND RATINGS

12.3 SOME DIFFERENT TYPES OF BONDS
Zero Coupon Bonds
Floating-Rate Bonds
Other Types of Bonds

12.4 PREFERRED STOCK
Stated Value
Cumulative and Noncumulative Dividends
Is Preferred Stock Really Debt?
The Preferred Stock Puzzle

12.5 COMMON STOCK
Par and No Par Stock
Authorized versus Issued Common Stock
Capital in Excess of Par Value
Retained Earnings
Market Values versus Book Values
Shareholders' Rights
Dividends
Classes of Stock

12.6 PATTERNS OF LONG-TERM FINANCING

12.7 LONG-TERM FINANCING UNDER FINANCIAL DISTRESS AND BANKRUPTCY
Liquidation and Reorganization
Agreements to Avoid Bankruptcy

12.8 SUMMARY AND CONCLUSIONS

ANNOTATED CHAPTER OUTLINE

12.1 CORPORATE LONG-TERM DEBT

-Creditors generally have no voting rights.
-Payment of interest on debt is a tax deductible business expense.
-Unpaid debt is a liability, which if not paid may cause bankruptcy.

A. Is it Debt or Equity?

B. Long-Term Debt: The Basics

Major forms are *public issue* and *private placement*.

T12.2: Features of a Hypothetical Bond

Long-term debt—loosely, bonds with a maturity of one year or more
Short-term debt—less than a year to maturity, also called *unfunded debt*
Bond—strictly speaking, secured debt; but used to describe all long-term debt

C. The Indenture

T12.3: The Bond Indenture and Bond Types

Indenture—written agreement between the firm and the creditors detailing the terms of borrowing. Also known as *deed of trust*. Generally, the indenture includes the following provisions:

1. Bond terms
2. The total face amount of bonds issued
3. A description of any property used as security
4. The repayment arrangements
5. Any call provisions
6. Any protective covenants

1. Terms of a bond—face value, par value, and form

Registered form—ownership is recorded, payment made directly to owner
Bearer form—payment is made to holder (bearer) of bond

Lecture Tip, page 371: Although the majority of corporate bonds carry a $1,000 face value, there are an increasing number of "baby bonds", i.e., bonds with face values less than $1,000, outstanding. The use of the term "baby bond" goes back at least as far as 1970, when it was used in connection with AT&T's announcement of the intent to sell bonds with low face values. It was also used in describing Merrill Lynch's 1983 program to sell bonds with $25 face values. More recently, the term has come to mean bonds issued in lieu of interest payments by firms unable to make the payments in cash. Baby bonds issued under these circumstances are also called "PIK" (payment-in-kind) bonds, or "bunny" bonds, because they tend to proliferate in LBO circumstances.

2. Security—debt classified by collateral and mortgage

Collateral—strictly, pledged securities
Mortgage securities—secured by a mortgage on real property
Debenture—an unsecured debt with 10 or more years to maturity
Note—a debenture with 10 years or less to maturity

3. Seniority—order of precedence of claims

> *Subordinated debenture*—of lower priority than senior debt

4. Repayment—early repayment in some form is typical

> *Sinking fund*—an account managed by the bond trustee for early redemption

5. Call provision—allows company to "call" or repurchase part or all of issue

> *Call premium*—amount by which the call price exceeds the par value
> *Deferred call*—firm can't call bonds for some designated time
> *Call protected*—what a bond is during the period it can't be called

6. Protective covenants—indenture conditions that limit the actions of firms

> *Negative covenant*—"thou shalt not" sell major assets, merge, pay dividends in excess of $X, and so on
> *Positive covenant*—"thou shall" keep working capital at or above $X, provide audited financial statements, keep property insured and in good condition, etc.

Lecture Tip, page 371: The instructor might note that domestically issued bearer bonds will become obsolete in the near future. Since bearer bonds are not registered with the corporation, the bondholders could simply not report the interest income received on their tax return. In an attempt to eliminate this potential for tax evasion, all bonds issued in the United States after July 1983 must be in registered form. It is still legal to offer bearer bonds in some other nations, however.

Lecture Tip, page 372: The instructor may wish to have the class consider the difference in a secured bond's yield versus a debenture's yield. Since a secured bond offers additional protection in the event of bankruptcy, investors would have a preference for this type of security and, accordingly, be willing to accept a lower yield-to-maturity or return. The added security for the bondholder comes at a cost—a lower yield. This same principle holds in the case of senior debt versus subordinated debt. However, in the case of a bond issued by a financially strong company, such as Phillip Morris, this added protection may be irrelevant and result in an insignificant impact on yield.

12.2 BOND RATINGS

T12.4: Bond Ratings

Lecture Tip, page 374: The question sometimes arises as to why a potential issuer would be willing pay rating agencies tens of thousands of dollars in order to receive a rating, especially given the possibility that the resulting rating could be less favorable than expected. This is a good point with which to re-emphasize the pervasive nature of agency costs and point out a real-world example of their effects on firm value. Some may also wish to use this issue to discuss some of the consequences of information asymmetries in financial markets. (Note: Violations of the strong-form EMH provide another springboard for information asymmetry discussions.)

Lecture Tip, page 374: We tend to think of bond ratings primarily in terms of the impact on required returns. It should be pointed out that, historically, the "investment grade" distinction between bonds rated BBB and above by S&P and those below has placed some bonds off-limits to some portfolio managers (e.g., those running pension or insurance company portfolios). As a result, one would expect differences in liquidity between the higher- and the lower-rated bonds, cet. par.

12.3 SOME DIFFERENT TYPES OF BONDS

A. Zero Coupon Bonds

Zero coupon bonds are bonds offered at deep discounts because there are no coupons. Although no cash interest is paid, firms deduct the implicit interest while holders report it as income. Interest equals the periodic change in the amortized value of the bond.

Lecture Tip, page 375: Most students are familiar with Series EE savings bonds. The instructor could mention that these are actually zero coupon bonds. The investor pays one-half of the face value and must hold the bond for a given number of years before the face value is realized. An attractive feature of the bond is that, unlike corporate zeroes, the investor need not pay taxes on the accrued interest until the bond is redeemed. Further, it should be noted that interest on these bonds is exempt from state income taxes. And, savings bonds yields are indexed to Treasury rates.

Lecture Tip, page 375: A popular financial market innovation of the last decade are Treasury strips. The instructor could describe these instruments and use them as a springboard for a discussion of value additivity and/or an example of cash flow valuation (from Chapter 6) in practice.
   Treasury strips are created when a coupon-bearing Treasury issue is purchased, placed in escrow, and the coupon payments are "stripped away" from the principal portion. Each component is then sold separately to investors with different objectives: the coupon portion is purchased by those desirous of safe current income, while the principal portion is purchased by those with cash needs in the future. (The latter portion is, in essence, a synthetically created zero-coupon bond.) Merrill Lynch was the first to offer these instruments, calling them "TIGRs" (Treasury Investment Growth Receipts), soon to be followed by Salomon Brothers' "CATs" (Certificates of Accrual of Treasury securities).

B. Floating-Rate Bonds

Floating-rate bonds—coupon payments adjust periodically according to an index. Also:

    1. *put* provision—holder can sell back to issuer at par
    2. coupon rate has a floor and a ceiling

Lecture Tip, page 377: The instructor may wish to mention that the floating-rate bond concept is also involved with the variable rate mortgage many students may select when purchasing their future homes. Such rates are often tied to rates on marketable securities and the mortgage interest cost will be adjusted, typically on an annual basis, to reflect changes in the interest rate environment. From the bank's perspective the homeowner has signed (issued) a "floating-rate bond" which the bank holds as its investment. Additionally, many variable rate mortgages involve caps.

A detailed summary of the factors that affect interest rate changes is provided on a daily basis in the "Credit Markets" section of The Wall Street Journal.

C. Other Types of Bonds

Income bonds—coupon is paid if income is sufficient
Convertible bond—can be traded for a fixed number of shares of stock
Put bond—allows holder to redeem for par (opposite of call)

12.4 PREFERRED STOCK

Preferred stock has precedence over common stock in the payment of dividends and in case of liquidation. Its dividend is usually fixed, and the stock is often without voting rights.

T12.5: Preferred Stock

A. Stated Value

The value to be paid to preferred holders in the event of liquidation.

B. Cumulative and Noncumulative Dividends

A firm's directors can vote to omit the preferred dividend.

Cumulative dividends—current preferred dividend plus all arrearages (unpaid back dividends) to be paid before common stock dividends can be paid.

C. Is Preferred Stock Really Debt?

Why issue or hold preferred? As "stock," 70% of the dividends from preferred are tax exempt for corporate holders (most preferred is held by corporations). So the issuer doesn't get any tax break, but the yields (and dividends) on preferred are relatively low.

D. The Preferred Stock Puzzle

A substantial amount of preferred stock is issued by regulated utilities who can pass the cost along to customers.

While having some features of debt, preferred can't put the firm in bankruptcy. Also, the tax disadvantage only applies if the firm is expected to pay taxes. Finally, preferred sometimes doesn't come with voting rights.

12.5 COMMON STOCK

Common stock—a claim against the earnings and assets of the firm with lowest precedence, but often with voting rights.

T12.6: Common Stock

A. Par and No Par Stock

Par—some value assigned to stock for no particular reason
Dedicated capital—total par value of shares outstanding
No par—no par value assigned

B. Authorized versus Issued Common Stock

All shares to be sold must be *authorized* by the articles of incorporation.

Limits to authorized shares
-Some states impose taxes based on authorized shares.
-Current shareholders may not want a large number authorized.

C. Capital in Excess of Par Value

This is also known as *capital surplus* or *additional paid-in capital*.

D. Retained Earnings

T12.7: Effects of a Stock Sale

Retained earnings are earnings not paid out as dividends.

Book value—sum of par value, capital surplus and accumulated retained earnings.

E. Market Values versus Book Values

Market value—what the stock actually trades for.
Treasury stock—stock issued and then later repurchased by the firm.

F. Shareholder Rights

Shareholders have the right to elect corporate directors who set corporate policy and select operating management.

1. *Cumulative voting*—when the directors are all elected at once. Total votes that each shareholder may cast equals the number of shares × the number of directors to be elected. In general, if N directors are to be elected, it takes $1/(N + 1)$ percent of the stock + 1 share to assure a deciding vote for one directorship. Good for getting minority shareholder representation on the board.

2. *Straight (majority) voting*—the directors are elected one at a time, and every share gets one vote. Good for freezing out minority shareholders.

> *Staggered elections*—directors' terms are rotated so that they aren't elected at the same time. This makes it more difficult for a minority to elect a director, and makes takeovers harder.

3. *Proxy voting*—grant of authority by a shareholder to someone else to vote his or her shares. *Proxy fight*—struggle between management and outsiders for control of the board, waged by getting shareholders' proxies.

Lecture Tip, page 384: Students often find a digression on proxy fights interesting. It serves both to underline the importance of equity voting rights and to introduce the concept of the market for corporate control.

Consideration of Carl Icahn's attempt to gain control of Texaco via a 1988 proxy fight indicates that proxy fights need not be "successful" in order to benefit shareholders. Icahn amassed a 14% stake in the firm and offered to buy the remainder for $12.4 billion. Rebuffed by management, he launched a proxy fight which he ultimately lost, in large part because management was able to mount a successful public-relations campaign which convinced shareholders that Icahn's offer was not in their best interests. Nonetheless, as a result of Icahn's actions, management undertook a massive restructuring program which included a drastic reduction in the firm's debt load, significantly reduced exploration costs, and the divestiture of assets worth $5 billion. Management's efforts were so well-received in the financial markets that Icahn stated in 1991: "Since the proxy fight, [management] woke up. I wish to hell I'd kept the stock."

Other rights usually include:

1. sharing proportionately in dividends paid
2. sharing proportionately in any liquidation value
3. voting on matters of importance (e.g., mergers)

Sometimes shareholder rights include:

1. the right to purchase any new stock sold—the *preemptive right*

Lecture Tip, page 385: The instructor may wish to add that, even though corporate democracy rules, political democracy does have its place at the annual stockholders' meeting. All shareholders are invited and welcome, even if an individual shareholder owns only one share of a company's stock. Although the meeting's agenda might dictate otherwise, any individual shareholder would normally have the right to question management regarding the company's operations.

G. Dividends

Dividends—return on shareholder capital.

1. Payment of dividends is at the discretion of the board. A firm cannot default on an undeclared dividend, nor be made bankrupt because of nonpayment of dividends.

2. Dividends are not tax deductible for the paying firm.

3. Dividends received by individuals are usually considered ordinary income, while dividends paid by one corporation to the other are 70% tax-exempt to the recipient.

H. Classes of Stock

Many firms have more than one class of stock, one purpose of which may be to create unequal voting power.

12.6 PATTERNS OF LONG-TERM FINANCING

Lecture Tip, page 387: The instructor may wish to add that changes in the tax code may influence corporate willingness to issue debt. Tax reforms enacted during the 1980's lowered the top marginal tax rate of individuals below the top corporate tax rate. This change may have encouraged corporations to issue more debt and to retire equity, since firms could better use the interest deduction to shelter operating income from taxation.

T12.8: Patterns of Corporate Financing (Table 12.2, 2 pages)

<u>Several features of long-term financing:</u>

1. Internally generated funds have been the dominant source.
2. The primary use of such funds has been capital spending.
3. Corporations have been net issuers of securities.

T12.9: The Long-Term Financial Deficit (Fig. 12.2)

12.7 LONG-TERM FINANCING UNDER FINANCIAL DISTRESS AND BANKRUPTCY

<u>Financial distress:</u>
1. *Business failure*—business terminates with a loss to creditors
2. *Legal bankruptcy*—bankruptcy is a legal proceeding for liquidating or reorganizing
3. *Technical insolvency*—when a firm defaults on a legal obligation
4. *Accounting insolvency*—happens when total book liabilities exceed total book assets

Bankruptcy—here, the transfer of some or all the firm's assets to creditors.

A. Liquidation and Reorganization

Liquidation—termination of the business, selling off all assets.
Reorganization—keeping the business going, often issuing new securities to replace old.

T12.10: Bankruptcy Liquidation

---

1. *Bankruptcy liquidation (Chapter 7* or *straight liquidation)*—involves the following typical sequence of events:

1. A petition is filed in federal court (voluntary or involuntary).
2. A trustee-in-bankruptcy is elected by creditors to liquidate assets.
3. Bankruptcy costs paid, liquidation proceeds distributed to creditors.
4. If anything remains, shareholders get it.

T12.11: Absolute Priority Rule

Absolute Priority Rule (APR)—rule for distribution of proceeds in liquidation. In order:

1. Expenses associated with the bankruptcy
2. Other expenses arising after filing but before appointment of a trustee
3. Wages, salaries, commissions
4. Contributions to employee benefit plans
5. Consumer claims
6. Government tax claims
7. Unsecured creditors
8. Preferred stockholders
9. Common stockholders

T12.12: Bankruptcy Reorganization

---

2. *Bankruptcy Reorganization (Chapter 11)*—involves the following sequence of events:

1. Voluntary or involuntary petition is filed.
2. A judge approves/disapproves the petition and a time for filing claims is set.
3. The firm continues to run the business.
4. The firm submits a reorganization plan.
5. Creditors and shareholders divided into classes. A class accepts the plan if a dollar-amount majority agrees.
6. If accepted by creditors, the plan is confirmed by court.
7. Payments in cash, property, and securities; new securities may be issued.

B. Agreements to Avoid Bankruptcy

Voluntary arrangements to restructure debt are often made. *Extension* postpones the date of payment, while *composition* involves a reduced payment.

12.8 SUMMARY AND CONCLUSIONS

T12.13: Solution to Problem 12.2
T12.14: Solution to Problem 12.8
T12.15: Solution to Problem 12.13

CHAPTER 13
ISSUING SECURITIES TO THE PUBLIC

TRANSPARENCIES

T13.1: Chapter Outline
T13.2: The Basic Procedure for a New Issue
T13.3: A Red Herring
T13.4: A Tombstone Ad
T13.5: Alternative Issue Methods
T13.6: Initial Public Offerings Categorized by Gross Proceeds (Table 13.2)
T13.7: Top 10 U.S. Underwriters for 1993 (Table 13.3, 2 pages)
T13.8: Average Initial Returns by Month for SEC-Registered IPOs (Fig. 13.2)
T13.9: Number of Offerings by Month for SEC-Registered IPOs (Fig. 13.3)
T13.10: Costs of Going Public (Table 13.7)
T13.11: Five Conclusions on Flotation Costs
T13.12: Rights Offerings: Basics
T13.13: Rights Offerings: Value of a Right
T13.14: Rights Offerings: Issues
T13.15: New Issues and Dilution
T13.16: Solution to Problem 13.2
T13.17: Solution to Problem 13.10
T13.18: Solution to Problem 13.12

CHAPTER ORGANIZATION

T13.1 Chapter Outline

13.1 THE PUBLIC ISSUE
The Basic Procedure for a New Issue

13.2 ALTERNATIVE ISSUE METHODS

13.3 THE CASH OFFER
Choosing an Underwriter
Types of Underwriting
The Aftermarket
The Underwriters
The Offering Price and Underpricing

13.4 NEW EQUITY SALES AND THE VALUE OF THE FIRM

13.5 THE COSTS OF ISSUING SECURITIES

13.6 RIGHTS
The Mechanics of a Rights Offering
Number of Rights Needed to Purchase a Share
The Value of a Right
Underwriting Arrangements
Rights Offers: The Case of Time Warner
Effects on Shareholders
The New Issues Puzzle

13.7 DILUTION
Dilution of Proportionate Ownership
Dilution of Value: Book versus Market Values

13.8 ISSUING LONG-TERM DEBT

13.9 SHELF REGISTRATION

13.10 SUMMARY AND CONCLUSIONS

ANNOTATED CHAPTER OUTLINE

13.1 THE PUBLIC ISSUE

> *Lecture Tip, page 404: The volume of security issuance is important because it represents new funds for business investment. Further, it is apparent that the volume of new equity issues is cyclical. The instructor may wish to use as an example the volume of new offerings in 1993, which topped $1 trillion for the first time in history, after remaining at just over one-quarter billion dollars annually from 1986 to 1990. Offering levels rose to over one-half billion in 1991 and over three-quarter billion in 1992. The boom in equity offerings is reflected in a* Wall Street Journal *headline from December 1993: "Can't Get a Loan? Well, There's Always the Stock Market: These Days, Investors Will Put Money into any Company That Waves a Prospectus".*

T13.2: The Basic Procedure for a New Issue

A. The Basic Procedure for a New Issue

1. Obtain approval from Board of Directors.
2. File *registration statement* with SEC.
3. SEC requires a minimum 20-day waiting period; firm distributes *preliminary prospectus (red herring)*.
4. On the effective date the offering price is set and selling begins.

Lecture Tip, page 405: The instructor may wish to add that the registration statement requirements imposed on corporations by the SEC results in corporations rarely issuing commercial paper in maturities longer than nine months.

T13.3: A Red Herring

Lecture Tip, page 405: The instructor could ask the class why the SEC would not require a corporation to list an offering price. The class should remember the volatility that can occur in the market and the impact of systematic risk on security prices. Should market conditions improve between the date of the preliminary prospectus issuance and the date of actual sale, one might expect the securities would be valued at a higher price. The opposite could occur should market conditions deteriorate.

Ethics Note, page 405: A hallmark of the regulatory process is the attempt to ensure that investors receive enough information to make informed decisions before parting with any cash. Ideally, the prospectus serves to accomplish this. A recent Wall Street Journal *story suggests, however, that this is not always the case. According to the story, brokers at Prudential Securities, Inc. have ". . . been accused of widespread fraud . . . brokers routinely sold risky partnerships based solely on rosy sales scripts, and didn't rely on the prospectus." Further, although individuals were to receive a copy of the prospectus before investing, ". . . a state regulatory survey showed that just 15% [of those investing in the partnerships] said they received a prospectus before making a decision to buy the partnerships." This has led some to quip that the document should actually be called a "retrospectus".*

T13.4: A Tombstone Ad

13.2 ALTERNATIVE ISSUE METHODS

> **T13.5: Alternative Issue Methods**

Public Offer
>   *General cash offer*—offered to public
>   *Rights offer*—new stock offered to current shareholders
>   *IPO (Initial public offering)*—*unseasoned new issue*
>   *Seasoned new issue*—offered by firm with shares in circulation

13.3 THE CASH OFFER

Underwriters—investment firms that act as intermediaries between the issuer and the public. Services provided include:

>   1. advice on type of security and offer method
>   2. advice on price
>   3. selling

Syndicate—a group of underwriters, formed to share the underwriting risk.
Spread—the difference between the underwriter's buying price and the offering price; it is the underwriter's main source of compensation.

A. Choosing an Underwriter

Competitive offer basis—taking the underwriter that bids the most for the securities.
Negotiated offer basis—the more common (and expensive) method.

Lecture Tip, page 407: The underwriter's spread is defined as the difference between offering price and the price at which the underwriter purchases the securities from the issuing corporation. In a study of utility stock issues by Bhagat and Frost, published in the Journal of Financial Economics *in 1986, average spreads were found to be lower for competitive issues (3.1%) than for negotiated issues (3.9%). However, as the textbook states, "there is evidence that competitive underwriting is cheaper" but "the dominance of negotiated underwriting...[is] the subject of ongoing debate."*

Additionally, if a company's stock is particularly risky, the spread demanded by the underwriter would tend to be larger. This would be caused by the underwriter bidding less for the shares, relative to a given offering price.

B. Types of Underwriting

1. *Firm commitment underwriting*—the most prevalent form for seasoned new issues. The underwriter buys the entire issue of securities at an agreed upon price from the issuer, and assumes responsibility for reselling them.

2. *Best efforts underwriting*—common with IPOs, the underwriter promises to sell as much as possible at the offer price, but unsold securities are returned to the issuer.

T13.6: Initial Public Offerings Categorized by Gross Proceeds (Table 13.2)

C. The Aftermarket

The period during which the syndicate agrees to sell only for the offer price. The principal underwriter may *buy* shares below the market price to "stabilize" (a euphemism for "take the brunt of the punishment for mispricing") the market.

D. The Green Shoe Provision

Sometimes called an *overallotment option, the Green Shoe provision* gives members of the syndicate the right to buy additional shares (beyond those originally set to be sold) from the issuer at the original offer price. Since it is only invoked if the issue is selling above the offer price, it is a cost to issuers and a benefit to the underwriters.

E. The Underwriters

T13.7: Top 10 U.S. Underwriters for 1993 (Table 13.3, 2 pages)

F. The Offering Price and Underpricing

The underpricing of new issues, especially IPOs, appears to be common.

1. Evidence on underpricing
2. Why does underpricing exist?

Smaller, more speculative issues account for much of the observed underpricing.

It is argued that because "underpriced" IPOs are oversubscribed while "overpriced" issues are avoided, underpricing is necessary to allow the average (read, uninformed) investor to make a normal return across all issues. There is a sizable amount of evidence to suggest, however, that uninformed investors suffer from a "winner's curse"; i.e., they receive a greater proportion of overpriced issues.

Underpricing is a kind of insurance for underwriters against legal suits by angry stock buyers if issues were overpriced. Underwriters must balance this against the potential loss of firms' business for underpricing.

Lecture Tip, page 412: The Wall Street Journal *reports numerous examples of IPOs. As an example, a February 27, 1992 article, page C6, was titled "Index Rises 1.77% as Volume Climbs; Synopsys Leaps 75% in Initial Trading." The instructor could use this as another example of the underpricing of IPOs. The stock rose 13 1/2 points to 31 1/2 from its offering price of 18. However, the instructor may wish to add that demand was so strong that the stock opened at 28 1/2, 10 1/2 above the offering price.*

*A study by Ibbotson, Sindelar, and Ritter (*Journal of Applied Corporate Finance, *1988) found that the difference between offering price and market price at the end of the first day was 16.37% for a sample of over 8,000 IPOs issued over 1960 through 1987. More detailed results from this study are provided in the text. However, a later study by Ritter in* The Journal of Finance, *1991, titled "The Long-Run Performance of Initial Public Offerings," found IPOs tend to* underperform *the market over the three-year period following issuance. Ritter's sample of over 1,500 IPOs for the period 1975 through 1984 realized a holding period return of 34.47% over the three-year period. The return was measured from the opening day's closing price. However, a control sample, matched by industry and market value, realized a holding period return of 61.86% over the same period. Finally, a study by Eyssell and Kummer in* The Journal of Applied Business Research *indicates that post-offering performance is inversely related to the proportion of shares sold by insiders immediately following the offering.*

T13.8: Average Initial Returns by Month for SEC-Registered IPOs (Fig. 13.2)
T13.9: Number of Offerings by Month for SEC-Registered IPOs (Fig. 13.3)

Lecture Tip, page 417: The lecture tip on page 412, describing the Synopsys IPO, could also be used at this point as an example of the excessively high demand for certain IPOs. The instructor could then discuss the underwriter's allocation responsibility and the "winner's curse" phenomenon.

13.4 NEW EQUITY SALES AND THE VALUE OF THE FIRM

Stock prices tend to decline following the announcement of a new equity issue, and rise on news of a debt offering. Some suggested reasons for this include:

1. Managerial information. Some believe that stock is issued when managers know that it is overpriced. Market participants recognize this and react accordingly.

2. Debt usage. Issuing new equity may signal that the firm has too much debt.

3. Issue costs. There are substantial costs involved in issuing securities and these are typically higher for equity.

13.5 THE COSTS OF ISSUING SECURITIES

Issuing securities involves *flotation costs*. These may be classified as

1. the spread
2. other direct expenses (legal and accounting fees, registration and printing costs)
3. indirect expenses
4. abnormal returns
5. underpricing
6. the Green Shoe provision

T13.10: Costs of Going Public (Table 13.7)

The total cost of going public, 1977-1982, averaged 21.22% for firm commitment underwritings, and 31.87% for best efforts underwritings.

T13.11: Five Conclusions on Flotation Costs

Five conclusions on underwriting costs:

1. There are substantial economies of scale in issuing securities.
2. Best efforts offers cost more.
3. For smaller issues, the cost of underpricing may exceed direct issue costs.
4. Underpricing is more severe for best efforts offers than for firm commitments.
5. It costs more to float an IPO than a seasoned offering.

13.6 RIGHTS

Privileged subscription—issue of common stock offered to existing stockholders. Offer terms are evidenced by warrants or *rights*. Rights are often traded on exchanges or over the counter.

A. The Mechanics of a Rights Offering

T13.12: Rights Offerings: Basics

Early stages are the same as for general cash offer, i.e., obtain approval from directors, file a registration statement, etc. Difference is in the sale of the securities. Current shareholders get rights to buy new shares. They can (1) subscribe (buy) the entitled shares, (2) sell their rights, or (3) do nothing.

B. Number of Rights Needed to Purchase a Share

Number of new shares = Funds to be raised/Subscription price

Shareholders get one right for each share already owned. The number of rights needed to buy a new share is:

Number of rights needed to buy a share = # Old shares/# New shares

Example:
       Suppose a firm with 200,000 shares outstanding wants to raise $1,000,000 through a rights offering. Each current shareholder gets one right per share held. The following table illustrates how the subscription price, number of new shares to be issued, and the number of rights needed to buy a share are related, ignoring flotation costs.

Subscription price	Number of new shares	Number of rights needed to buy a share
$25	40,000	5
$20	50,000	4
$10	100,000	2
$ 5	200,000	1

Lecture Tip, page 425: The student should be aware that with each subscription price, the firm would raise the needed $5,000,000. The instructor could ask the class why a subscription price of $25 per share (200,000 new shares) was not presented in the table. Many students should recognize that if the subscription price is $25 when the market price is $20, no present stockholder would exercise the rights since they could purchase the stock at a lower price on the market. The instructor could mention that if the rights offer is to succeed and the company obtain its needed $5,000,000, the subscription price must be below the market price. The final paragraph in the "Effects on Shareholders" subsection (Section 13.6) discusses the arbitrary nature of the subscription price, provided it is below the market price of the company's stock. A further problem could arise if the market price falls below the subscription price. Damage from this problem may be avoided through a standby agreement with an underwriter. Such an arrangement requires the underwriter to purchase the unsubscribed shares (A further comment on this standby agreement is offered in "The New Issues Puzzle" subsection of Section 13.6).

C. The Value of a Right

T13.13: **Rights Offerings: Value of a Right**

A right has value if the subscription price is below the share price. How much a right is worth depends on how many rights it takes to buy a share, and the difference between the stock price and the subscription price. If it takes N rights to buy 1 share, the value of one right is equal to

$$(initial\ stock\ price - subscription\ price)/(N + 1).$$

D. Ex Rights

When a *privileged subscription* is used, the firm sets a *holder-of-record* date. The stock sells *rights-on*, or *cum rights*, until four business days before the holder-of-record date. After that the stock sells without the rights or *ex rights*.

The ex rights price $= 1/(N + 1) \times (N \times$ initial stock price $+$ subscription price)

Example:

Suppose the above firm decides on a subscription price of $20, with 50,000 shares to be issued. Assume the shares outstanding currently trade for $35. Using the valuation formula and letting $N = 4$, a right is worth ($35 − $20)/(4 + 1) = $15/5 = $3. The ex rights price is expected to be 1/5 × (4 × $35 + $20) = $160/5 = $32.

Lecture Tip, page 427: The instructor may wish to link the stock behavior of ex rights with ex dividends. The instructor could mention that the time line presented in Figure 13.4 applies to stocks trading ex rights as well as stocks trading ex dividend. Both dividend and rights declarations involve setting an ex date, which is four business days before to the record date. In both situations, the share price reacts on the ex date to reflect the value of the right or dividend which would not be received if the shares were purchased after the ex date.

E. The Underwriting Arrangements

Standby underwriting—firm makes a rights offering and the underwriter makes a commitment to "take up" (purchase) any unsubscribed shares. In return, the underwriter receives a *standby fee*. In addition, shareholders are usually given *oversubscription privileges*, the right to purchase unsubscribed shares at the subscription price.

F. Rights Offers: The Case of Time Warner

T13.14: Rights Offerings: Issues

Time Warner's rights offering was somewhat unusual. As originally proposed, the subscription price would vary, dependent upon the percentage of the issue actually sold. This feature was later dropped. As is typical of most rights offerings, only 2 percent of the rights were neither exercised nor sold. However, oversubscription rights were used to absorb the unsold stock. The underwriters' total compensation was approximately 4 percent of the issue for management services, standby commitments, and other services.

G. Effects on Shareholders

In the absence of taxes and transactions costs, shareholder wealth is not differentially affected whether they exercise or sell their rights. Nor does it matter what subscription price the firm sets as long as it is below the market price.

H. The New Issues Puzzle

Although there is evidence that rights offers are cheaper than general cash offers, they are relatively infrequent in the U.S. Arguments for underwritten cash offerings include:

1. Underwriters get higher prices (this is dubious, given observed underpricing).
2. Underwriters insure against a failed offering (also dubious)
3. Offering proceeds are available sooner (questionable)
4. Advice from underwriters is valuable

13.7 DILUTION

1. Dilution of percentage ownership
2. Dilution of market value
3. Dilution of book value and EPS

A. Dilution of Proportionate Ownership

This occurs when the firm sells stock through a general cash offer and new stock is sold to persons who previously weren't shareholders. For many large, publicly held firms this simply isn't an issue, the shareholders being many and varied to begin with. For some firms with a few large shareholders it may be of concern.

B. Dilution of Value: Book versus Market Values

A stock's market value will fall if the NPV of the financed project is negative and rise if the NPV is positive. Whenever a stock's book value is greater than its market value, selling new stock will result in *accounting dilution*.

T13.15: New Issues and Dilution

13.8 ISSUING LONG-TERM DEBT

A public issue of debt involves pretty much the same process as a stock issue, except that the registration statement must indicate an indenture.

More than 50% of all long-term debt is privately placed. *Term loans* are direct business loans with maturities of one to five years, usually amortized over the life of the loan. *Private placements* are long-term loans with bond-like features made by a single lender or a small group of investors.

Differences between direct private placement and public issue of debt:

1. No SEC registration for private placement.
2. Direct placements often have more restrictive covenants.
3. It is easier to renegotiate a private placement in the event of default.
4. A private placement costs less than a public issue (although the interest rates on private placements are generally higher)

Overall, the costs of issuing debt are substantially less than those for issuing equity.

International Note, page 435: The globalization of financial markets is nowhere more evident than in the recent rise in the popularity of large issues by foreign corporations and governments. In December, 1993, Argentina issued $1 billion of "global bonds". (Global bonds are offered simultaneously in all of the world's major financial markets. First issued by the World Bank in 1989, they are often, but not always, denominated in dollars.) Investor demand was so strong that the size of the issue was raised from $750 billion to $1 billion. (Perhaps even more interesting, these bonds were considered junk bonds at the time of the offering.) Furthermore, a Wall Street Journal story on the Argentina issue states that it is "only the latest in a stream of global-bond offerings that have flooded the world's markets this year".

13.9 SHELF REGISTRATION

Shelf registration—SEC Rule 415 allows companies to register all the securities they expect to issue within the next two years at the same time and sell the issues whenever they want during those two years. Both debt and equity issues can be registered.

Qualifications for shelf registration:

1. Securities must be investment grade.
2. No debt defaults in past three years.
3. Aggregate value of outstanding stock > $150 million.
4. No violations of Securities Act of 1934 in past three years.

13.10 SUMMARY AND CONCLUSIONS

T13.16: Solution to Problem 13.2
T13.17: Solution to Problem 13.10
T13.18: Solution to Problem 13.12

CHAPTER 14
COST OF CAPITAL

TRANSPARENCIES

T14.1: Chapter Outline
T14.2: Cost of Capital
T14.3: Dividend Growth Approach
T14.4: Estimating the Dividend Growth Rate
T14.5: SML Approach
T14.6: Costs of Debt and Preferred
T14.7: The Weighted Average Cost of Capital (WACC)
T14.8: Example: Water's Beginning WACC
T14.9: Divisional and Project Costs of Capital
T14.10: The Security Market Line and the Weighted Average Cost of Capital
T14.11: The Security Market Line and the Subjective Approach (Fig. 14.2)
T14.12: Example: Penultimate Paralegal
T14.13: Solution to Problem 14.16
T14.14: Solution to Problem 14.17
T14.15: Solution to Problem 14.26

CHAPTER ORGANIZATION

T14.1: Chapter Outline

14.1 THE COST OF CAPITAL: SOME PRELIMINARIES
Required Return versus Cost of Capital
Financial Policy and Cost of Capital

14.2 THE COST OF EQUITY
The Dividend Growth Model Approach
The SML Approach

14.3 THE COSTS OF DEBT AND PREFERRED STOCK
The Cost of Debt
The Cost of Preferred Stock

14.4 THE WEIGHTED AVERAGE COST OF CAPITAL

The Capital Structure Weights
Taxes and the WACC
Solving the Warehouse Problem and Similar Capital Budgeting Problems

14.5 DIVISIONAL AND PROJECT COSTS OF CAPITAL

The SML and the WACC
Divisional Cost of Capital
The Pure Play Approach
The Subjective Approach

14.6 FLOTATION COSTS AND THE WEIGHTED AVERAGE COST OF CAPITAL

The Basic Approach
Flotation Costs and NPV

14.7 SUMMARY AND CONCLUSIONS

ANNOTATED CHAPTER OUTLINE

14.1 THE COST OF CAPITAL: SOME PRELIMINARIES

T14.2:   Cost of Capital

Lecture Tip, page 445: Students often find it easier to grasp the intricacies of cost of capital estimation when they understand why it is important. The instructor may find it useful here to point out that an accurate estimate of the cost of capital is required for:

-good capital budgeting decisions - neither the NPV rule nor the IRR rule can be implemented without knowledge of the appropriate discount rate.
-financing decisions - the optimal/target capital structure is that which minimizes the cost of capital.
-operating decisions - the cost of capital is used by regulatory agencies in order to determine the "fair return" in some regulated industries (e.g., electric utilities)

A. Required Return versus Cost of Capital

Cost of capital, required return, appropriate discount rate—denote the same opportunity cost of using capital in one way as opposed to an alternative investment in the financial market having the same systematic risk.

- *required return* is from an investor's point of view
- *cost of capital* is the same return from the firm's point of view
- *appropriate discount rate* is the same return as used in a PV calculation

B. Financial Policy and Cost of Capital

Capital structure—the firm's combination of debt and equity. Taken as given for now, the capital structure decision is discussed in Chapter 15. A firm's cost of capital will reflect the average riskiness of all its securities, which individually may be less risky (bonds) or more risky (common stock).

14.2 THE COST OF EQUITY

A. The Dividend Growth Model Approach

T14.3: Dividend Growth Approach

According to the constant growth model from Chapter 6

$$P_0 = D_1/(R_E - g).$$

Rearranging terms and solving for the cost of equity gives:

$$R_E = D_1/P_0 + g$$

which is, of course, the dividend yield plus growth rate (capital gains).

1. Implementing the Approach

Price and latest dividend are directly observed—g must be estimated.
Estimating g—Typically use historical growth rates or analysts' forecasts.

T14.4: Estimating the Dividend Growth Rate

Example:

Year	Dividend	Dollar change	Percentage change
1986	$4.00	-	-
1987	4.40	$.40	10.00
1988	4.75	.35	7.95
1989	5.25	.50	10.53
1990	5.65	.40	7.62

Average growth rate = (10 + 7.95 + 10.53 + 7.62)/4 = 9.025%

2. Advantages and Disadvantages of the Approach

-Approach only works for dividend paying firms.
-R_E is very sensitive to the estimate of g.
-Historical dividend growth rates may not reliably predict future growth rates.
-Risk is only indirectly accounted for by the use of price.

Lecture Tip, page 447: The text mentions that there are other ways to compute g. Rather than use the arithmetic mean as in the example, the geometric mean (giving the average compound growth rate) could be used. OLS regression with the log of dividends as the dependent variable and time (1,2,3 etc.) as the independent variable has also been suggested.

Lecture Tip, page 448: Some students may question how one would value a non-dividend paying firm since, as the text states in the following paragraph, "the dividend growth model is obviously only applicable to companies that pay dividends." In anticipation of this question, the instructor might mention that, in the case of growth-oriented, non-dividend-paying firms, analysts might look at the trend in earnings or use similar firms to project the future date of the first expected dividend and its future growth rate. However, such processes are subject to greater estimation error and when companies fail to meet (or even exceed) estimates, the stock price can experience a high degree of variability. It should also be pointed out that no firm pays zero dividends forever - at some point, every going concern will begin to pay dividends.

Lecture Tip, page 448:   There are numerous examples of earnings disappointments provided in The Wall Street Journal. *The class might find it interesting to hear of a recent earnings disappointment and consider the percentage stock price change which a failure to meet growth expectations would cause. Examples are routinely found in the* Journal. *One such is provided in the April 1, 1992 "Abreast of the Market" section on page C2: "Bristol-Myers Squibb tumbled 2 to 76 1/4. Several analysts downgraded their ratings on the stock after the company said first-quarter sales growth was below expectations."*

B. The SML Approach

T14.5: SML Approach

R_E depends upon:

1. The risk-free rate, R_f
2. The expected market risk premium, $E(R_M) - R_f$
3. The amount of systematic risk as measured by β

By the CAPM: $R_E = R_f + \beta_E \times [E(R_M) - R_f]$

1. Implementing the Approach

Betas are widely available from various sources. T-bill rates are often used for R_f. The sticky point is the market risk premium, i.e., the market price of a unit of systematic risk. Many use the historical average value or an average of analysts' forecasts.

2. Advantages and Disadvantages of the Approach

-Consistent with capital market history, the approach adjusts for risk.
-Applicable to virtually all publicly traded stocks
-The past may not predict the future for market risk premium and beta.

Lecture Tip, page 450: Students are frequently surprised when they find that the two approaches typically result in different estimates. The instructor might wish to point out that it would be more surprising if the results were identical. Why? The underlying assumptions of the two models are very different. The constant growth model (which came to prominence in the mid-1950s) is a variant of the growing perpetuity model and requires little more in terms of assumptions than that (a) dividends are expected to grow at a constant rate forever, (b) the required return exceeds the discount rate.

The CAPM (and, therefore, the SML) approach, on the other hand, is built on the work of Markowitz and Sharpe, and therefore requires assumptions of normality of returns and/or quadratic utility functions, as well as the absence of taxes, transactions costs, and other market imperfections.

14.3 THE COSTS OF DEBT AND PREFERRED STOCK

A. The Cost of Debt

T14.6:   Costs of Debt and Preferred

Cost of debt (R_D)—the interest rate on new debt can easily be estimated using the yield-to-maturity on outstanding debt or by knowing the debt's bond rating and looking up the rate on new issues of that rating.

Example:

If Pohl Corp. issued a 10-year bond 5 years ago with a coupon rate of 13% that currently sells for $1,075, what is Pohl's cost of debt?

Assuming annual interest, the yield-to-maturity that makes an annuity of $130 per period for 5 periods plus $1,000 face value in 5 periods have a PV of $1,075 is 10.97%.

Lecture Tip, page 451: It may be beneficial to re-emphasize the distinction between coupon rate, the current yield, and the yield-to-maturity (cost of debt) to the class. The first represents the firm's promise to pay, the second represents the income portion of total return, and the third is the relevant figure for the current discussion. (The instructor may remind the class of the material in Chapter 6, "Valuing Stocks and Bonds." Otherwise, some will have a tendency to simply select the coupon rate as the cost of debt.

B. The Cost of Preferred Stock

To determine the cost of preferred stock, use the formula

$$R_P = D_P/P_0$$

14.4 THE WEIGHTED AVERAGE COST OF CAPITAL

A. The Capital Structure Weights

T14.7: The Weighted Average Cost of Capital (WACC)

E—the *market* value of the firm's equity (#shares common $\times$ price per share)
D—the *market* value of the firm's debt (#bonds $\times$ price per bond)
V—the combined *market* <u>value</u> of the firm's equity and debt, $V = E + D$
Capital structure weights—E/V and D/V

Lecture Tip, page 452: It may be helpful to mention and differentiate between the three types of weightings in the capital structure equation: book, market, and target. End-of-chapter problem 12 provides the opportunity to practice the calculation of book and market value weights. It may also be helpful to mention that the total market value of equity (the number of common shares outstanding times the current market price of a company's common share) measures the value of the three equity accounts (common stock, capital in excess of par value, and retained earnings) from the balance sheet.

B. Taxes and the WACC

Aftertax cash flows require an aftertax discount rate. Letting T_C stand for the firm's marginal tax rate:

$$WACC = (E/V) \times R_E + (D/V) \times R_D \times (1 - T_C)$$

WACC—overall return the firm must earn on its assets to maintain the value of its stock.

T14.8: Example: Water's Beginning WACC

Example:

 Water's Beginning has 1 million shares of common stock outstanding with a market price of $12 per share. The firm's outstanding bonds have ten years to maturity, a face value of $5 million, a coupon rate of 10%, and are priced at $985. The risk-free rate is 7%, and analysts' expected return for the market is 14%. Water's Beginning stock has a beta of 1.2 and the firm is in the 34% marginal tax bracket.

Capital structure weights:

$$\text{market value of equity} = 1{,}000{,}000 \times \$12 = \$12{,}000{,}000$$
$$\text{market value of debt} = \$5{,}000{,}000 \times .985 = \$4{,}925{,}000$$

$$V = \$12{,}000{,}000 + \$4{,}925{,}000 = \$16{,}925{,}000$$
$$D/V = \$4{,}925{,}000/\$16{,}925{,}000 = .29 \text{ or } 29\%$$
$$E/V = 1 - D/V = .71 \text{ or } 71\%$$

Cost of equity:

Using the SML approach:

$$R_E = 7\% + 1.2 \times (14\% - 7\%) = 7\% + 8.4\% = 15.4\%$$

Cost of debt:

The yield-to-maturity on the debt is 10.25% before taxes.

Weighted average cost of capital:

$$\text{WACC} = (E/V) \times R_E + (D/V) \times R_D \times (1 - T_C)$$

$$\text{WACC} = .71 \times 15.4\% + .29 \times 10.25\% \times (1 - .34) = 12.9\%.$$

Lecture Tip, page 453: If the firm utilizes preferred stock in addition to common equity, equation 14.6 from the text should be modified as follows:

$$\text{WACC} = (E/V) \times R_E + (D/V) \times R_D \times (1 - T_C) + (P/V) \times R_P$$

where P/V represents the market value weight of preferred stock in the firm's capital structure (and, therefore, V = E + D + P), and R_P is the cost of preferred stock as defined above.

C. Solving the Warehouse Problem and Similar Capital Budgeting Problems

Lecture Tip, page 455: The warehouse problem employs the WACC as the discount rate in a NPV calculation. At least two assumptions are required for this to be precisely correct. First, it must be assumed that the warehouse has approximately the same risk characteristics of the firm as a whole. More importantly, it is assumed that the project will be financed (i.e., new funds will be raised) in the target proportions. In reality, firms rarely engage in simultaneous *debt and equity financing. On the other hand, financial data suggest that, while financing is "lumpy", observed capital structures tend to fluctuate around a norm value, which is often assumed to be the target capital structure.*

14.5 DIVISIONAL AND PROJECT COSTS OF CAPITAL

T14.9:   Divisional and Project Costs of Capital

A. The SML and the WACC

The WACC is the appropriate discount rate only if the proposed investment is similar to the overall business and only if financed with the same capital structure weights.

Lecture Tip, page 457: The instructor might have the class consider a situation in which a company maintains a large portfolio of marketable securities on its balance sheet. The instructor could ask the class to further consider the impact this large security balance would have on a company's current and acid-test ratios and how this might impact the company's ability to meet short-term obligations. The students should easily remember that a larger liquidity ratio implies less risk (and less potential profit). Although the revenue realized from the marketable securities would be less than the interest expense on the company's comparable debt issues, these holdings would result in a lowering of the firm's beta and WACC. This example allows the student to recognize that the expected return and beta of an investment in marketable securities would be below the company's WACC, and justification for such investments must be considered relative to a benchmark other than the company's overall WACC.

T14.10:   The Security Market Line and the Weighted Average Cost of Capital

---

B. Divisional Cost of Capital

When a firm has different operating divisions with different risks, its WACC is an average of the divisional required returns. In such cases the cost of capital for different risks within the same firm needs to be established.

Lecture Tip, page 458: It may help students to distinguish between the average cost of capital to the firm and the required return on a given investment if the idea is turned around from the firm's point of view to one of an investor's. That is, consider an investor holding a portfolio of T-bills, corporate bonds and common stocks. Suppose there is an equal amount invested in each and further suppose that the securities have on average returned 5%, 10%, and 15% respectively. The average portfolio return will have been 10%. Now ask students if the investor should use the portfolio's average return of 10% to evaluate new security acquisitions, say T-bills offering 7% and common stocks expected to return 13%.

C. The Pure Play Approach

Pure play—a company that has a single line of business. The idea is to find the required return on a near substitute investment.

Lecture Tip, page 458: The instructor could add that although company betas can be easily found from such publications as Value Line *or Merrill Lynch's "beta book," such publications do not provide betas of individual company divisions. A quick method to identify divisional betas might be to identify publicly-traded companies which are in similar lines of business or* pure plays *as the text discusses. The analyst could then average these betas and apply the average value to the division or new project to determine a risk-adjusted cost of capital. However, as the text discusses, firms often rely on "The Subjective Approach" because of the difficulty in objectively establishing discount rates for individual projects.*

D. The Subjective Approach

T14.11: The SML and the Subjective Approach (Fig. 14.2)

Assigns investments to "risk" categories that have higher and higher risk premiums.

International Note, page 459: The difficulty in arriving at an appropriate estimate of the cost of capital for project analysis is magnified for firms engaged in multinational investing. In Financial Management for the Multinational Firm, *Abdullah suggests that adjustments to foreign project hurdle rates should reflect the effects of the following:*

1. foreign exchange risk
2. political risk
3. capital market segmentation
4. international diversification effects

Making these adjustments requires a great deal of judgment and expertise, as well as an understanding of underlying financial theory. Most multinational firms find it expeditious to adjust hurdle rates subjectively, rather than attempting to quantify precisely the effects of these factors for each foreign project.

Lecture Tip, page 459: What an individual firm considers a risky investment and what the financial market considers a risky investment may not be the same. Recall that the market is concerned with systematic or undiversifiable risk. If a firm is considering an investment's total risk in assigning it to a risk category, the risk categories may not line up with the SML.

14.6 FLOTATION COSTS AND THE WEIGHTED AVERAGE COST OF CAPITAL

A. The Basic Approach

Weighted average flotation cost (f_A)—the sum of all flotation costs as a percent of the amount of security issued, multiplied by the target capital structure weights.

The multiplier $1/(1 - f_A)$ is used to determine the gross amount of capital to be raised so that the after-flotation cost amount is sufficient to fund the investment.

B. Flotation Costs and NPV

If a project nominally requires an investment of amount I before flotation costs, the suggested procedure is to compute the gross capital requirement as $I \times 1/(1 - f_A)$, and to use this figure as the investment cost in calculating the NPV.

T14.12: Example: Penultimate Paralegal

Example:
      Suppose Penultimate Paraprofessionals, Inc. is considering opening another office. The expansion will cost $50,000 and is expected to generate aftertax cash flows of $10,000 per year in perpetuity. The firm has a target debt/equity ratio of .50. New equity has a flotation cost of 10% and a required return of 15%, while new debt costs 5% to issue and has a required return of 10%.

Cost of capital: $\text{WACC} = (E/V) \times R_E + (D/V) \times R_D \times (1 - T_C)$
                           $\text{WACC} = 2/3 \times 15\% + 1/3 \times 10\% \times (1 - .34) = 12.2\%.$

Flotation costs: $f_A = E/V \times f_E + D/V \times f_D$
                       $f_A = 2/3 \times 10\% + 1/3 \times 5\%$
                       $f_A = 8.33\%$

NPV: Investment = $50,000/(1 - .083)   = $54,526
       PV of cash flow = $10,000/.122   = $81,967
       NPV = −$54,526 + $81,967   = $27,441

Lecture Tip, page 463: Some students will recognize that while new debt and equity issues would be subject to flotation costs, the retained earnings component of equity would not. The retention of these earnings does have a cost, but it would be lower than the cost of issuing new equity. The key point to make is that whenever external financing is used, there is an additional cost associated with that financing, and that cost is a relevant cash flow for capital budgeting purposes.

14.7 SUMMARY AND CONCLUSIONS

T14.13: Solution to Problem 14.16
T14.14: Solution to Problem 14.17
T14.15: Solution to Problem 14.26

CHAPTER 15
FINANCIAL LEVERAGE AND CAPITAL STRUCTURE POLICY

TRANSPARENCIES

T15.1: Chapter Outline
T15.2: Financial Leverage and Capital Structure Policy
T15.3: Financial Leverage, EPS, and ROE: An Example
T15.4: Break-Even EBIT: A Quick Note
T15.5: Financial Leverage, EPS and EBIT
T15.6: Homemade Leverage: An Example
T15.7: M&M Propositions
T15.8: M&M Proposition II
T15.9: More on Business and Financial Risk
T15.10: Debt, Taxes, and Bankruptcy
T15.11: Debt, Taxes, and WACC
T15.12: Taxes, the WACC, and Proposition II
T15.13: The Optimal Capital Structure and the Value of the Firm
T15.14: The Optimal Capital Structure and the Cost of Capital
T15.15: The Extended Pie Model
T15.16: Solution to Problem 15.2
T15.17: Solution to Problem 15.11
T15.18: Solution to Problem 15.12

CHAPTER ORGANIZATION

T15.1: Chapter Outline

15.1 THE CAPITAL STRUCTURE QUESTION
Firm Value and Stock Value: An Example
Capital Structure and the Cost of Capital

15.2 THE EFFECT OF FINANCIAL LEVERAGE
The Impact of Financial Leverage
Corporate Borrowing and Homemade Leverage

15.3 CAPITAL STRUCTURE AND THE COST OF EQUITY CAPITAL
M&M Proposition I: The Pie Model
The Cost of Equity and Financial Leverage: M&M Proposition II
Business and Financial Risk

15.4 M&M PROPOSITIONS I AND II WITH CORPORATE TAXES
The Interest Tax Shield
Taxes and M&M Proposition I
Taxes, the WACC, and Proposition II

15.5 BANKRUPTCY COSTS
Direct Bankruptcy Costs
Indirect Bankruptcy Costs

15.6 OPTIMAL CAPITAL STRUCTURE
The Static Theory of Capital Structure
Optimal Capital Structure and the Cost of Capital
Optimal Capital Structure: A Recap
Capital Structure: Some Managerial Recommendations

15.7 THE PIE AGAIN
The Extended Pie Model
Marketed Claims versus Nonmarketed Claims

15.8 OBSERVED CAPITAL STRUCTURES

15.9 SUMMARY AND CONCLUSIONS

ANNOTATED CHAPTER OUTLINE

15.1 THE CAPITAL STRUCTURE QUESTION

> **T15.2:   Financial Leverage and Capital Structure Policy**

A. Firm Value and Stock Value: An Example

Using the firm value identity, the value of the firm equals the market value of debt plus the market value of equity ($V = D + E$). When the market value of debt is given and constant, any change in the value of the firm results in an identical change in the value of equity (stock). The key to this reasoning lies in the fixed payment nature of debt and the derivative value nature of stock.

Maximizing the value of the firm is the goal of managing capital structure.

Lecture Tip, page 472:   The instructor might want to stress our lack of overall understanding when it comes to the optimal capital structure for a particular business. In his essay, "The Capital Structure Puzzle," in the July 1984 Journal of Finance, *Stewart Myers summarizes the issues concerning capital structure, specifically the pecking order theory and what we know about corporate financing behavior. The instructor can refer to this article for further information regarding corporate financing behavior. It's a good article for students to read as well.*

It may be interesting to read Myers' own words from the opening paragraph of this article: "'How do firms choose their capital structure?' Again, the answer is, 'We don't know.'" Myers goes on to state that ". . . we know very little about capital structure. We do not know how firms choose the debt, equity or hybrid securities they issue . . . [T]here has been little if any research testing whether the relationship between financial leverage and investors' required return is as the pure MM theory predicts."

The instructor should stress that the work of Miller and Modigliani was the first attempt to rigorously model corporate behavior in this area. The instructor could add that Miller received the Nobel Prize in Economics in recognition of his contribution to this area. (Modigliani won earlier; his work on capital structure was cited at that time.)

B. Capital Structure and the Cost of Capital

Optimal capital structure—the debt/equity ratio that minimizes the WACC.

Lecture Tip, page 474:   The existence of an optimal/target capital structure makes intuitive sense to most students because it results in the lowest WACC and highest firm value. However, empirical evidence suggests that actual debt ratios vary widely across similar firms. As suggested above, it is quite plausible that target capital structures depend on factors which have yet to be understood.

Lecture Tip, page 474: Students sometimes fail to understand the mechanics of why "minimizing WACC maximizes firm value." The instructor might remind students that a firm is just a portfolio of projects, some with positive NPVs and some with negative NPVs. (Capital budgeting (discussed in chapters 7-9) is the process of adding to the portfolio.) Thus, firm value equals the sum of the component NPVs. It has already been shown that, cet. par., lower discount rates increase NPVs; since WACC is the average discount rate for the firm's projects, minimizing the WACC must *increase firm value.*

15.2 THE EFFECT OF FINANCIAL LEVERAGE

A. The Impact of Financial Leverage

T15.3: Financial Leverage, EPS, and ROE: An Example

<u>Financial Leverage, EPS, and ROE: An Example</u>

A proposed change in financial leverage:

	Current	Proposed
Assets	$5,000,000	$5,000,000
Debt	$0	$2,500,000
Equity	$5,000,000	$2,500,000
Debt/equity ratio	0	1
Share price*	$10	$10
Shares outstanding	500,000	250,000
Interest rate	na	10%

Assumes restructuring has no influence on share price. Alert students will recognize that whether any influence exists is what we're investigating. Also, we ignore taxes for now.

Scenario analysis of current and proposed capital structures:

Current capital structure: No debt

	Recession	Expected	Expansion
EBIT	$300,000	$650,000	$800,000
Interest	0	0	0
Net income	$300,000	$650,000	$800,000
ROE	6%	13%	16%
EPS	$0.60	$1.30	$1.60

Proposed capital structure: D/E = 1; interest rate = 10%

	Recession	Expected	Expansion
EBIT	$300,000	$650,000	$800,000
Interest	250,000	250,000	250,000
Net income	$ 50,000	$400,000	$550,000
ROE	2%	16%	22%
EPS	$0.20	$1.60	$2.20

Lecture Tip, page 476: The instructor may wish to provide the following example to better solidify the students' understanding of the variability in ROE due to leverage. At various sales levels, the instructor could ask the class to consider the difference between ROA and ROE for a firm with no debt in its capital structure. One could easily demonstrate that the two would be identical at all sales levels since assets = equity. The substitution of debt for equity results in ROE equalling ROA at only one level of sales (or, one level of EBIT in Figure 15.1). The fixed interest expense and lower number of common shares outstanding resulting from this substitution would cause ROE to change to a larger degree than the change in ROA, given any change in sales volume. The greater slope of the "with-debt" line in Figure 15.1 reflects this sensitivity.

T15.4: Break-Even EBIT: A Quick Note
T15.5: Financial Leverage, EPS, and EBIT

We may conclude from T15.3 - T15.5 that:

1. The effect of financial leverage depends upon EBIT.
2. When EBIT is high, financial leverage raises EPS and ROE.
3. The variability of EPS and ROE is increased with financial leverage.

Lecture Tip, page 477: Many students will feel that if a company expects to achieve the break-even EBIT, it should issue the debt. The instructor should emphasize that this is a break-even point relative to EBIT and EPS. Beyond this point, EPS will be larger under the debt alternative, but with additional debt, the firm will have additional financial risk which would increase the required return of its common stock. A higher required return might offset the increase in the EPS under leverage, resulting in a lower firm value, despite the higher EPS. The instructor could note that the MM models (soon to follow) will offer some insights on this relationship.

B. Corporate Borrowing and Homemade Leverage

Homemade leverage—there's nothing special about corporate borrowing.

T15.6: Homemade Leverage: An Example

Example: Homemade leverage

Suppose the firm in the previous example does not change its capital structure. An investor can replicate the returns of the proposed borrowing by making her own D/E ratio equal 1 for the investment. Suppose an investor buys 50 shares with her own money and 50 shares by borrowing $500 at 10% interest. The payoffs are:

	Recession	Expected	Expansion
EPS of unlevered firm	$0.60	$1.30	$1.60
Earnings for 100 shares	$60.00	$130.00	$160.00
Less interest on $500 at 10%	50.00	50.00	50.00
Net earnings	$10.00	$80.00	$110.00
Return on investment (net earnings /$500)	2%	16%	22%

Individual investors can also "unlever" the firm's borrowing by lending to the firm. Consider the investor who invests $250 in the stock of the levered firm and who also invests $250 in bonds paying 10%:

	Recession	Expected	Expansion
EPS for levered firm	$0.20	$1.60	$2.20
Earnings for 25 shares	$5.00	$40.00	$55.00
Plus interest on $250 at 10%	$25.00	$25.00	$25.00
Net earnings	$30.00	$65.00	$80.00
Return on investment (net earnings/$500)	6%	13%	16%

Thus, investors can do or undo any pattern of financing for themselves. And what they can do for themselves, they don't need, nor will they pay, the firm to do.

Example:
    Consider two firms, U and L, with identical assets and identical EBIT under all circumstances. Firm U is all equity financed while Firm L uses debt and equity. We ignore taxes.for simplicity:

$$V_U = E_U \qquad \text{and} \qquad V_L = E_L + D_L$$

If an investor buys 2% of E_U, she gets (2% × EBIT) in payoffs. Now, if this investor were to buy 2% of E_L and 2% of D_L (i.e., 2% of V_L) she gets (2% × (EBIT − interest)) in stock payoffs plus (2% × interest) in debt payoffs. Of course, (2% × (EBIT − interest)) + (2% × interest) = 2% × (EBIT − interest + interest) = (2% × EBIT).

Since both investments have the same payoff, they must have the same market price, i.e., 2% of E_U must be worth the same as 2% of E_L + D_L. Finally, this implies 2% of V_U must be worth the same as 2% of V_L, and ultimately that V_U must be equal to V_L.

15.3 CAPITAL STRUCTURE AND THE COST OF EQUITY CAPITAL

A. M&M Proposition I: The Pie Model

T15.7: M&M Propositions

M&M Proposition I—with no taxes and assuming individuals are able to borrow at the same rate as firms, the firm cannot affect its value by altering its capital structure.

B. The Cost of Equity and Financial Leverage: M&M Proposition II

T15.8: M&M Proposition II

M&M Proposition II—a firm's cost of equity capital is a positive linear function of its capital structure:

$$\text{WACC} = R_A = E/V \times R_E + D/V \times R_D$$

Rearranging:

$$R_E = R_A + (R_A - R_D) \times (D/E)$$

As more debt is used, the return on equity rises and the WACC remains the same.

Lecture Tip, page 481: Many students will wonder why we are even considering a situation in which taxes do not exist. Endeavors to understand the capital structure "puzzle" focus on which risk-return trade-off is most favorable for the company's stockholders. A proper understanding of capital structure policy requires the student to view the issues in stages. The first stage examines the risk-return trade-off in a world without taxes. Once we understand this trade-off, we proceed to an examination of the trade-off involving taxes and the impact of this environment on firm value.

Lecture Tip, page 482: According to Proposition II,

$$R_E = R_A + (R_A - R_D) \times (D/E).$$

One way to interpret this relationship is as follows. In the absence of debt, the required return on equity equals the return on the firm's assets; this is consistent with our contention in chapter 14 that the required return on the firm is determined in the financial markets and is directly related to the investment decisions made by management.

The second term is an incremental effect of borrowing. Without bankruptcy costs and debt-related agency costs, firms that use debt will be better off the greater the spread between the return earned on the firm's investments and the cost of borrowing.

C. Business and Financial Risk

> **T15.9: More on Business and Financial Risk**

The instructor may wish to skip over the asset beta/equity beta distinction. The key point is that Proposition II shows that return on equity depends on business and financial risk:

Business risk   -the risk inherent in a firm's operations
-depends on systematic risk of firm's assets
-determines the first component of the required return on equity, R_A.

Financial risk   -extra risk from using debt financing.
-determines the second component, $(R_A - R_D) \times D/E$

Lecture Tip, page 483: Some students may confuse the concepts of financial risk and default risk. Proposition II suggests that even if a firm could issue risk-free debt, its financial risk would exceed zero. The instructor should point out that the focus here is on the risk (and required return) <u>to the shareholder</u>. Regardless of the degree of certainty associated with the debt's promised returns to bondholders (i.e., the level of default risk), higher levels of debt imply greater volatility of earnings available to shareholders.

15.4 M&M PROPOSITIONS I AND II WITH CORPORATE TAXES

A. The Interest Tax Shield

The tax saving arising from the deductibility of interest.

B. Taxes and M&M Proposition I

Value of the interest tax shield $= T_C \times D$. M&M Proposition I with taxes is thus:

$$V_L = V_U + T_C \times D$$

T15.10: Debt, Taxes, and Bankruptcy

Lecture Tip, page 485: *The instructor may wish to have the class consider the impact a change in the corporate tax rate would have on a corporation's desire to issue debt, assuming the non-corporate tax environment experiences no changes in tax rates. It is important to state this assumption and recognize the trade-off between personal and corporate tax rates under the Miller '77 paper. However, a discussion of this issue is somewhat advanced knowledge for an introductory finance course. The final conclusion will be that higher tax rates create an environment in which corporations will have a greater incentive to shelter income, cet. par.*

T15.11: Debt, Taxes, and WACC

Lecture Tip, page 486: *The instructor may wish to take this opportunity to digress a bit on the idea that financing decisions can generate positive NPVs. Put very simply, a positive NPV decision is one for which the firm obtains something for less than its market value. Just as the relative inefficiency of the physical asset markets makes the search for positive NPV projects worthwhile there, the efficiency of the financial markets makes positive NPV financial projects unlikely. The latter circumstance changes, however, in the presence of financial market imperfections. And of course, the existence of corporate taxes constitutes a major imperfection. Further discussion of the successes and failures of financial engineering in the last two decades may serve to illustrate the core concepts: (1) firm value comes largely from the asset side of the balance sheet; and, (2) positive NPV financing projects can also be created, but in general, financing is a zero-NPV proposition.*

C. Taxes, the WACC, and Proposition II

T15.12: Taxes, the WACC, and Proposition II

Let R_U represent the *unlevered cost of capital*.

M&M Proposition II with corporate taxes states:

$$R_E = R_U + (R_U - R_D) \times (D/E) \times (1 - T_C)$$

and

$$WACC = E/V \times R_E + D/V \times R_D \times (1 - T_C)$$

15.5 BANKRUPTCY COSTS

One limit to the use of debt is *bankruptcy costs*.

A. Direct Bankruptcy Costs

Legal and administrative expenses directly associated with bankruptcy.

B. Indirect Bankruptcy Costs

Financial distress costs—the direct and indirect costs of avoiding bankruptcy.

Lecture Tip, page 490: Measurement of actual bankruptcy costs has proven to be exceedingly difficult. Nonetheless, some idea of the magnitudes of these costs is apparent from the examples below.

In January, 1991 Interco, Inc., a St. Louis-based conglomerate filed for bankruptcy in order to reorganize. By the time the firm emerged from bankruptcy protection in August, 1992, the bills for legal and accounting services exceeded $36 million. According to an article in the St. Louis Post-Dispatch, one of the legal firms involved had, at various times, "more than 100 lawyers and others billing Interco for work" related to the bankruptcy filing.

When one adds in indirect costs such as lost sales, reduced employee morale, loss of employees, lost opportunities, and so on, the <u>total</u> costs associated with bankruptcy become potentially enormous.

15.6 OPTIMAL CAPITAL STRUCTURE

-Firms borrow because tax shields are valuable.
-Borrowing is constrained by the costs of financial distress.

A. The Static Theory of Capital Structure

```
T15.13:  The Optimal Capital Structure and the Value of the Firm
```

B. Optimal Capital Structure and the Cost of Capital

```
T15.14:  The Optimal Capital Structure and the Cost of Capital
```

C. Optimal Capital Structure: A Recap

D. Capital Structure: Some Managerial Recommendations

1. *Taxes*—the higher the firm's tax rate, the more important are tax shields.
2. *Financial distress*—the lower is risk of financial distress, the more likely is borrowing.

International Note, page 495: *In theory, the static model of capital structure described in this section applies to multinational firms as well as to domestic firms. That is, the multinational firm should seek to minimize its* <u>global</u> *cost of capital by balancing the debt-related tax shields across all of the countries in which the firm does business against global agency and bankruptcy costs. Among other things, however, this assumes that worldwide capital markets are well-integrated and that foreign exchange markets are highly efficient. In such an environment, financial managers would seek the optimal global capital structure. In practice, of course, the existence of capital market segmentation, differential taxes, and regulatory frictions make the determination of the global optimum much more difficult than the theory would suggest.*

15.7 THE PIE AGAIN

A. The Extended Pie Model

T15.15: The Extended Pie Model

Cash Flow (CF) =   + Payments to stockholders (E)

+ Payments to bondholders (D)

+ Payments to governments (G)

+ Bankruptcy costs (B)

+ Other claims

B. Marketed Claims versus Nonmarketed Claims

The claims against cash flow that can be bought and sold are *marketed claims*, while those that cannot be are *nonmarketed claims*.

V_M—the value of marketed claims; V_N—the value of nonmarketed claims

V_T—the value of all claims against cash flow = $V_M + V_N$

$$V_T = E + D + G + B + \ldots$$

<u>Given the firm's cash flows</u>, the optimal capital structure is one that maximizes V_M, or equivalently, minimizes the value of V_N.

15.8 OBSERVED CAPITAL STRUCTURES

On average, U.S. nonfinancial companies borrow $1 for every $3 of equity.

Different industries typically have different debt/equity ratios, depending on income variability and the nature of their assets.

15.9 SUMMARY AND CONCLUSIONS

T15.16: Solution to Problem 15.2
T15.17: Solution to Problem 15.11
T15.18: Solution to Problem 15.12

CHAPTER 16
DIVIDENDS AND DIVIDEND POLICY

TRANSPARENCIES

T16.1: Chapter Outline
T16.2: Dividend Types (2 pages)
T16.3: Example of Procedure for Dividend Payment
T16.4: Does Dividend Policy Matter?
T16.5: Homemade Dividends
T16.6: Dividends and the Real World
T16.7: Establishing a Dividend Policy
T16.8: A Compromise Dividend Policy
T16.9: Cash Dividend versus Repurchase (2 pages)
T16.10: Accounting Treatment of Splits and Dividends
T16.11: Solution to Problem 16.10
T16.12: Solution to Problem 16.14
T16.13: Solution to Problem 16.18

CHAPTER ORGANIZATION

T16.1: Chapter Outline

16.1 CASH DIVIDENDS AND DIVIDEND PAYMENT
Cash Dividends
Standard Method of Cash Dividend Payment
Dividend Payment: A Chronology
More on the Ex-Dividend Date

16.2 DOES DIVIDEND POLICY MATTER?
An Illustration of the Irrelevance of Dividend Policy

16.3 REAL-WORLD FACTORS FAVORING A LOW PAYOUT
Taxes
Flotation Costs
Dividend Restrictions

16.4 REAL-WORLD FACTORS FAVORING A HIGH PAYOUT
Desire for Current Income
Uncertainty Resolution
Tax and Legal Benefits from High Dividends

16.5 A RESOLUTION OF REAL-WORLD FACTORS?
Information Content of Dividends
The Clientele Effect

16.6 ESTABLISHING A DIVIDEND POLICY
Residual Dividend Approach
Dividend Stability
A Compromise Dividend Policy

16.7 STOCK REPURCHASE: AN ALTERNATIVE TO CASH DIVIDENDS
Cash Dividends versus Repurchase
Real-World Considerations in a Repurchase
Share Repurchase and EPS

16.8 STOCK DIVIDENDS AND STOCK SPLITS
Some Details on Stock Splits and Stock Dividends
Value of Stock Splits and Stock Dividends
Reverse Splits

16.9 SUMMARY AND CONCLUSIONS

ANNOTATED CHAPTER OUTLINE

16.1 CASH DIVIDENDS AND DIVIDEND PAYMENT

> **T16.2: Dividend Types (2 pages)**

A. Cash Dividends

Regular cash dividend—dividends paid in the usual course of business.
Extra cash dividend—may or may not be repeated.
Special and *liquidating dividends*—one time dividend that won't be repeated.

Lecture Tip, page 506: Students may find it interesting to examine the various dividend policies companies have utilized by examining stock quotations in The Wall Street Journal. *The instructor could ask the students to bring a copy of the* Journal *and examine the* Explanatory Notes *box provided with the stock quotations. The instructor could then explain the presentation with a few examples such as the following from the April 9, 1992* Journal, *NYSE Composite Transactions:*

Stock Sym	Div	
AIR	.48	Normal dividend—previous quarter's dividend multiplied by 4: .12 × 4.
AEGON	3.72r	Cash dividend declared or paid in previous twelve months, plus a stock dividend.
AOF	.80e	Extra dividend—sum of the last four quarter's dividends.
x AHR	.75c	Stock went ex-dividend plus paid a liquidating dividend.

B. Standard Method of Cash Dividend Payment

C. Dividend Payment: A Chronology

T16.3: Example of Procedure for Dividend Payment

---

1. *Declaration date*—date the board resolves to pay a dividend.
2. *Ex-dividend date*—four business days before the record date; people who buy the stock on or after this date won't get the dividend.
3. *Record date*—firm prepares the list of shareholders to receive dividends.
4. *Payment date*—the check is in the mail.

D. More on the Ex-Dividend Date

Share price declines by approximately the dividend amount on the ex-dividend date.

Lecture Tip, page 508: The instructor may wish to have the class consider whether it would be advantageous to buy a stock on the day before the ex-dividend date. One could use the example in figure 16.2. If bought prior to the ex-dividend date, one would pay $10 per share. This would entitle the owner to receive the $1 dividend, which will be mailed to the holder of the stock on the payment date. The instructor could then ask the student to consider the value of the dividend plus the stock following the ex-dividend date. The students could then recognize that the owner would have a $1 dividend plus stock value of $9, or a combined value of $10. This would result in no arbitrage opportunity. However, the instructor could mention that those individuals who purchase prior to the ex-dividend date would have to pay taxes on the dividend received. In a sense, if the stock falls by the amount of the dividend, purchasing a stock prior to the ex-dividend date results in an after-tax value of:

(Ex-Dividend Stock Price + Dividend − Tax on Dividend) < $10.

Thus, if the marginal investor is in a positive tax bracket, there exists an incentive to avoid purchasing stock prior to the ex-dividend date, should the stock fall by the value of the dividend. If the instructor wishes to elaborate on this issue, one might mention that

A study by Avner Kalay (Journal of Finance, 1982) found that the actual average stock price decline on the ex-dividend date was less than the amount of the dividend; he found that (cum-dividend price − ex-dividend price) / dividend = .734. As the text states, one argument for this behavior is tax liability for which investors wish to be compensated. This issue is further explored in a later section of this chapter.

International Note, page 508: It was widely reported that, in 1988, nearly 13% of the daily average trading volume on the NYSE was attributable to the actions of investors utilizing dividend capture strategies. This involves purchasing a high-dividend stock just before it goes ex-dividend and selling it soon after. If the price of the stock falls by less than the amount of the dividend, and if the purchaser's marginal tax rate is low enough, the strategy represents a real-world arbitrage opportunity.

Japanese insurance firms, which were restricted to paying dividends from current income at this time, engaged in heavy trading in high-dividend stocks for the purpose of profiting from the cum-dividend - ex-dividend spread. The practice continues to this day, albeit to a lesser degree than in the past.

16.2 DOES DIVIDEND POLICY MATTER?

A. An Illustration of the Irrelevance of Dividend Policy

Lecture Tip, page 509: The proposition that dividend policy (as opposed to dividends) is irrelevant is a difficult one for many students. Intuitively, they know that other things the same higher dividends will make a firm more valuable. The difficult part is in understanding the qualification "other things the same." Of course, if the number of shares, cash flow, future investment, and borrowing could all be the same and current dividends increased, investors would pay more for the stock. But where would the money for such an increase come from? The point here is that something has to give (future dividends) if current dividends are to be increased.

T16.4: Does Dividend Policy Matter?

As long as a firm's investments and cash flows are held constant any increase in earlier dividends can only come at the cost of a decrease in later dividends.

Lecture Tip, page 510: Recall from Chapter 6 that, under certain conditions, the equilibrium price of a share of stock can be calculated as follows:

$$P_0 = D_1/(r - g).$$

In the absence of taxes, transactions costs, and information asymmetry, it can be shown that any increase in the future dividend, D_1, will reduce the level of earnings retention and reinvestment, thereby reducing the growth rate in future levels of earnings and dividends. In other words, both the numerator and the denominator rise, and the net effect on P_0 is zero. This is the same conclusion drawn in the illustration on page 510.

T16.5: Homemade Dividends

Homemade dividends—If investors want to change the cash payout pattern from their investment, they can do so by buying and selling shares. That is, they can create *homemade dividends*. And what they can do for themselves they don't pay extra for.

16.3 REAL-WORLD FACTORS FAVORING A LOW PAYOUT

A. Taxes

T16.6: Dividends and the Real World

When the marginal tax rate for individuals exceeds that for businesses, investors may prefer that earnings be retained rather than paid out as dividends, so as to reduce taxes.

Expected return, dividends, and personal taxes—some argue that when dividends are taxed at higher rates than capital gains, the higher a firm's dividends, the higher its cost of capital (and lower its stock value) to make the after-tax returns equal across firms of the same risk. But if investors self-select into *clienteles* on the basis of their tax rates, and the clienteles are satisfied, dividend policy may not affect expected returns.

Lecture Tip, page 512: Because many politicians favor a capital gains tax cut, the instructor may wish to have the class consider the impact this tax law change would have on a stockholder's preference for higher or lower dividend payments. The instructor could mention that, prior to 1986, any gain on stock held for over one year was given preferential tax treatment—only 40 percent of that gain was subject to individual income taxes. (The instructor might also mention that the time period and amount exempted from federal taxes has varied over time, depending upon tax laws enacted by the United States Congress.) The instructor could ask the class if they would have had a greater or lesser preference for dividends after the removal or reduction of the capital gains tax.

Ethics Note, page 513: Students may find stimulating a digression on the ethical aspects of the preferential tax treatment of capital gains. On the one hand, standard economic analysis suggests that reducing taxes on capital gains income will stimulate investment in assets expected to provide capital gains. According to this argument, preferential treatment will, therefore, benefit the nation's economy and its citizens.

Others feel, however, that the effect of preferential tax treatment is to unfairly benefit one group at the expense of another. Those who argue against capital gains tax cuts tend to view them as unethical because (it is contended) they benefit primarily the rich. The essence of this point of view is distilled in the following statement attributed to Congressman Richard Gephardt, in response to President Bush's endorsement of an attempt to have the top capital gains rate lowered from 33% to 19.6% in 1989:

> *"The president has a named a lot of his friends to be ambassadors; I guess this . . . proposal is to take care of those who didn't get named. The limousines are circling the White House."*

The veracity of the economic argument is an empirical question. The above quote suggests, however, that regardless of what the data ultimately show, it is unlikely that the parties to the capital gains debate will ever be completely reconciled.

B. Flotation Costs

Firms that pay high dividends and simultaneously sell stock to fund growth will incur higher total flotation costs than comparable firms with low payouts.

C. Dividend Restrictions

Most bond indentures and some state laws limit the dividends a firm can pay.

Lecture Tip, page 514: The instructor may wish to have the students reflect on the agency relationship discussed in Chapter 1. Although the discussion there mainly focused on the conflicts of interest between stockholders and management, a conflict also exists between stockholders and bondholders. As a result, bond indenture agreements contain restrictive covenants (discussed in Chapter 12). Dividend restrictions are one of the most common type of restrictive covenants. Such covenants often state that dividends cannot be paid if net working capital falls below a stated amount, or future common stock dividends can only be paid from profits generated after the signing of the loan agreement.

16.4 REAL-WORLD FACTORS FAVORING A HIGH PAYOUT

A. Desire for Current Income

Transaction costs may hamper homemade dividends. But the desire for high current income is not universal. If investors self-select into *clienteles* according to income desires (and clienteles are satisfied) it isn't clear that a firm can gain by paying higher dividends.

B. Uncertainty Resolution

Selling stock now also creates a *"bird-in-the-hand"* just as a dividend payment does. Again, we are back to "other things the same": can a higher dividend make a stock more valuable? If a firm must sell more stock or borrow more money to pay a higher dividend now, it must return less to stockholders in the future. Finally, the uncertainty over future income—i.e., the firm's business risk—isn't changed by its dividend policy.

C. Tax and Legal Benefits from High Dividends

1. Corporate investors—there is a 70% - 80% *exclusion* from taxable income of dividends received by one corporation from another.
2. Tax-exempt Investors—pension funds, trust funds, and endowment funds are tax-exempt. Some of these investors are prohibited from spending any "principal."

16.5 A RESOLUTION OF REAL-WORLD FACTORS?

A. Information Content of Dividends

Changes in the future amount of dividends (as opposed to simply a rearrangement over time) may be signalled by a change in dividends. The reaction to information conveyed by an increase or decrease in dividends is called the *information content effect*.

Lecture Tip, page 517: Some students may question why a company's stock price would react favorably to announcements of a dividend increase since capital gains might be preferred over the tax consequences of the higher dividend. Should a student ask this question, the instructor could emphasize that the signalling value of the dividend increase is positive. This positive value would be traded off against the tax loss associated with the dividend increase, resulting in a stock price increase. The instructor might also mention that false dividend signals could prove costly to a company should dividend increases not be supported by future higher earnings. Weak future earnings may result in the company being forced to later secure expensive external funds sources.

B. The Clientele Effect

As noted above, the clientele effect holds that investors self-select the dividend policy best for themselves. If clienteles are satisfied, dividend policy changes are pointless.

Lecture Tip, page 518: To put the clientele argument in a different light, consider the case of opening a new restaurant. Even though a lot of people like to eat hamburgers and french fries, if that clientele is already satisfied by a McDonalds you won't make a fortune opening a Burger King.

Lecture Tip, page 518: The dividend clientele argument suggests that high- (low-) tax investors will seek out low- (high-) dividend stocks. In analogous fashion, several theorists have argued that investors facing different marginal tax rates will sort themselves into "financial leverage clienteles"; i.e., low-tax investors will gravitate toward more highly levered firms because the firms are better able to utilize the tax shields associated with borrowing. Conversely, high-tax investors will borrow on their own accounts and hold the shares of firms with less debt. Although the empirical evidence on these clienteles is somewhat mixed, raising the issue may serve to stimulate thought about the many impacts of taxes on financial decision-making at the levels of both the firm and the individual.

16.6 ESTABLISHING A DIVIDEND POLICY

A. Residual Dividend Approach

T16.7: Establishing a Dividend Policy

Dividends are paid out of whatever earnings are left after all positive net present value investments have been funded and the desired debt/equity ratio is obtained. One result of such an approach is that quickly-expanding firms will pay little or no dividends while slower-growing firms will pay out relatively high proportions of earnings.

B. Dividend Stability

Dividends are generally more stable than earnings, and most managers feel that a stable dividend is good for the firm and stockholders.

C. A Compromise Dividend Policy

T16.8: A Compromise Dividend Policy

Ranked in order of importance, the objectives of dividend policy are:

1. Avoid rejecting positive NPV projects to pay a dividend.
2. Avoid cutting dividends.
3. Avoid issuing new equity.
4. Maintain a target debt/equity ratio.
5. Maintain a target dividend payout ratio.

Most firms appear to have a *target payout ratio*, a long-run proportion of earnings that is to be paid out in dividends.

Lecture Tip, page 525: To illustrate the importance of not cutting dividends, consider the case of Unisys (the computer firm created by the 1986 merger of Burroughs and Sperry corporations). In the last week of September, 1990, Unisys announced it was suspending payment of its regular quarterly dividend (which had been 25¢ a share). The pre-merger companies had a record of over 100 years of regular dividend payments. On the day of the announcement the stock fell by 23% to a 52 week low, the largest decline of any Big-Board traded issue that day.

16.7 STOCK REPURCHASE: AN ALTERNATIVE TO CASH DIVIDENDS

> **T16.9: Cash Dividend versus Repurchase (2 pages)**

A. Cash Dividends versus Repurchase

Instead of paying out a cash dividend, a firm may buy back its shares. Ignoring taxes and other imperfections, the cash distributed and value of outstanding shares afterward remains the same.

Example:
   Consider a firm with 50,000 shares outstanding and the following balance sheet:

<table>
<tr><th colspan="5">Market Value Balance Sheet</th></tr>
<tr><td>Cash</td><td>$ 100,000</td><td>$ 0</td><td>Debt</td></tr>
<tr><td>Other Assets</td><td>900,000</td><td>1,000,000</td><td>Equity</td></tr>
<tr><td>Total</td><td>$1,000,000</td><td>$1,000,000</td><td>Total</td></tr>
</table>

Price per share is $20, Net income is $100,000, EPS is $2.00, and the P/E ratio is 10.

Assuming no taxes, commissions, or other imperfections, the firm is considering:

   a) Paying a $1 cash dividend, or
   b) Repurchasing 2,500 shares @ $20

1. Choose the cash dividend

<table>
<tr><th colspan="5">Market Value Balance Sheet</th></tr>
<tr><td>Cash</td><td>$ 50,000</td><td>$ 0</td><td>Debt</td></tr>
<tr><td>Other Assets</td><td>900,000</td><td>950,000</td><td>Equity</td></tr>
<tr><td>Total</td><td>$ 950,000</td><td>$ 950,000</td><td>Total</td></tr>
</table>

Price per share is now $19 ($950,000/50,000). Net Income is still $100,000, so EPS still = $2.00, but the P/E ratio is now 9.5.

The total value to a stockholder of a share is still $20, $19 of stock + $1 in cash.

2. Choose the repurchase

Market Value Balance Sheet

Cash	$ 50,000	$ 0	Debt
Other Assets	900,000	950,000	Equity
Total	$ 950,000	$ 950,000	Total

Price per share remains $20 ($950,000/47,500). Net income is still $100,000, so EPS is now $2.10, but the P/E ratio is 9.5, the same as under the cash dividend.

The total value to a stockholder of a share is still $20.

B. Real-World Considerations in a Repurchase

The most important difference between a cash dividend and a repurchases is the tax treatment. The entire cash dividend is taxable, while only the *gain* (price − basis) on the repurchase is taxable.

Lecture Tip, page 527: It should be pointed out that distributing cash via share repurchases is desirable from the viewpoint of the investor even in the absence of a capital gains tax differential. Essentially, a repurchase allows the investor to choose whether to take cash now (and incur taxes) or hold on to the stock and benefit from the (unrealized) capital gain. Additionally, empirical evidence indicates that repurchase announcements are often viewed by market participants as favorable signals of future firm prospects and/or as evidence that management believes shares are currently undervalued. In either case, share prices rise on repurchase announcements, on average.

C. Share Repurchase and EPS

While EPS rises with a repurchase (there are, after all, fewer shares), the market value of those earnings, as reflected by the P/E ratio, is the same as that under a cash dividend.

16.8 STOCK DIVIDENDS AND STOCK SPLITS

Stock dividend—dividend paid in shares of stock rather than cash. Commonly expressed as a percentage, e.g., a 25% stock dividend (1 new share for every four old shares). As with a cash dividend, the stock price declines proportionally.

Stock split—again, new stock to stockholders, only this time a ratio (e.g., 2-for-1 split). Again the price drops proportionally.

Lecture Tip, page 528: *The instructor may wish to introduce this topic by asking the students if they had ever heard someone state that Company X's stock would be a good stock to purchase because it is rumored the company will soon have a stock split. One could solicit a few feelings concerning this issue prior to demonstrating the accounting treatment of dividends and splits on the following page. One could conclude by mentioning that even though the ex-dividend is known, since it follows the declaration date, unusual stock price behavior has been documented surrounding the ex-dividend date of non-taxable stock dividends and splits. Grinblatt, Masulis and Titman (Journal of Financial Economics, 1984) documented a five-day average abnormal return of two percent surrounding the ex-date. Although the rationale is not fully understood for this anomaly, the instructor might mention that, unlike the ex-dividend impact for cash dividends, this behavior cannot be argued away due to a tax impact. Results of this study might be a lead-in to the "Value of Stock Splits and Stock Dividends" subsection.*

A. Some Details on Stock Splits and Stock Dividends

T16.10: Accounting Treatment of Stock Splits and Dividends

Stock dividend—retained earnings are transferred to the par value and capital accounts. *Stock split*—par value is adjusted to reflect the split (no effect on retained earnings).

B. Value of Stock Splits and Stock Dividends

Benchmark case—no change in shareholder wealth.
Popular trading range—an argument in favor of splits that says investors don't like "high" prices because they make *round lots* (100 shares) harder to buy.

C. Reverse Splits

Three popular reasons given:

       1. reduced trading transactions costs
       2. "popular trading range" again (this time arguing prices can be too low)
       3. respectability (don't want the "penny" stock label).

Two technical reasons:

       1. stock exchanges have minimum price requirements
       2. it's a way to force out small shareholders.

Lecture Tip, page 530: *The instructor may wish to read the sentence in the text ending with "so the stock dividend doesn't really have any economic effect." The instructor could then mention that empirical research has documented large stock price gains at the announcement of a company's decision to have a stock dividend. A plausible argument for this has to do with the signaling issue. The student should recognize that the value of the stock dividend is transferred from retained earnings into the common stock and capital in excess of par accounts. The instructor could remind the student that many bond covenants restrict cash dividend payments when retained earnings fall below a minimum level. Only those companies confident of future earnings would be willing to reduce retained earnings through a stock dividend.*

16.9 SUMMARY AND CONCLUSIONS

T16.11: Solution to Problem 16.10
T16.12: Solution to Problem 16.14
T16.13: Solution to Problem 16.18

CHAPTER 17
SHORT-TERM FINANCE AND PLANNING

TRANSPARENCIES

T17.1: Chapter Outline
T17.2: Operating and Cash Cycles Illustrated
T17.3: Managers Who Deal With Short-term Financial Problems
T17.4: Hermetic, Inc., Operating Cycles
T17.5: Hermetic, Inc., Cash Cycles
T17.6: The Size of the Firm's Investment in Current Assets
T17.7: Carrying Costs and Shortage Costs
T17.8: Financing Policy for an "Ideal" Economy
T17.9: Alternative Asset Financing Policies
T17.10: A Compromise Financing Policy
T17.11: A Cash Budget for Ajax Co. (2 pages)
T17.12: Short-Term Borrowing
T17.13: Solution to Problem 17.9
T17.14: Solution to Problem 17.12
T17.15: Solution to Problem 17.16

CHAPTER ORGANIZATION

T17.1: Chapter Outline

17.1 TRACING CASH AND NET WORKING CAPITAL

17.2 THE OPERATING CYCLE AND THE CASH CYCLE
Defining the Operating and Cash Cycles
The Operating Cycle and the Firm's Organizational Chart
Calculating the Operating and Cash Cycles
Interpreting the Cash Cycle

17.3 SOME ASPECTS OF SHORT-TERM FINANCIAL POLICY
The Size of the Firm's Investment in Current Assets
Alternative Financing Policies for Current Assets
Which is Best?
Current Assets and Liabilities in Practice

17.4 THE CASH BUDGET
Sales and Cash Collections
Cash Outflows
The Cash Balance

17.5 SHORT-TERM BORROWING
Unsecured Loans
Secured Loans
Other Sources

17.6 A SHORT-TERM FINANCIAL PLAN

17.7 SUMMARY AND CONCLUSIONS

ANNOTATED CHAPTER OUTLINE

17.1 TRACING CASH AND NET WORKING CAPITAL

Lecture Tip, page 543: For some reason, many students (and some faculty!) tend to view the topics of short-term finance generally, and working capital management specifically, as less intrinsically "sexy" or important than, say, capital budgeting or the risk-return relationship. (If you doubt this, compare the number of articles dealing with working capital management to the number dealing with the CAPM in the academic finance journals in the last two decades!) Regardless of the reason, some instructors will find it useful to emphasize the importance of short-term finance in introducing Chapters 17 - 19.

First of all, discussions with CFOs quickly lead to the conclusion that, as important as capital budgeting and capital structure decisions are, they are made less frequently, while the day-to-day complexities involving the management of working capital (especially cash and inventory) consume tremendous amounts of management time. Second, it is clear that while poor long-term investment and financing decisions will adversely impact firm value, poor short-term financial decisions will impair the firm's ability to <u>remain operating</u>. Finally, one might take a more abstract view and point out that virtually everything in Finance ultimately comes down to the measurement of cash flows and the timing thereof; short-term finance simply details the nuts-and-bolts of the "nonsynchronicity" problem.

A. Defining Cash in Terms of Other Elements

Net working capital + Fixed assets = Long-term debt + Equity
Net working capital = (Cash + Other current assets) − Current liabilities

Substituting for NWC in the balance sheet identity and rearranging gives

Cash = Long-term debt + Equity + Current liabilities − Current assets (other than cash) − Fixed assets

Using this equation,

> Activities that Increase Cash:
> > Increasing long-term debt
> > Increasing equity
> > Increasing current liabilities
> > Decreasing current assets (other than cash)
> > Decreasing fixed assets
>
> Activities that Decrease Cash:
> > Decreasing long-term debt
> > Decreasing equity
> > Decreasing current liabilities
> > Increasing current assets (other than cash)
> > Increasing fixed assets

Lecture Tip, page 543: Concept question 17.1b asks the students to consider whether net working capital always increases when cash increases. It may be helpful to have the students consider the net working capital identity in a situation where a firm acquires cash via a long-term versus short-term source. As an example, the students should recognize that cash will increase when a firm borrows either long-term or short-term debt. If long-term debt is issued, the cash account (debit entry) would increase without any corresponding increase (credit entry) in the current liabilities. Thus, net working capital increases. However, if short-term debt is issued, the increase in cash would be offset by an increase in a current liability, resulting in no change in net working capital.

17.2 THE OPERATING CYCLE AND THE CASH CYCLE

A. Defining the Operating and Cash Cycles

1. *Operating cycle*—average time required to acquire inventory, sell it, and collect for it. Its two components are:

   a) *Inventory period*—time to acquire and sell inventory
   b) *Accounts receivable period*—time to collect on sale

2. *Cash cycle*—average time between "cash out" for inventory and "cash in" from collections:

   Cash cycle = Operating cycle − Accounts payable period

where *accounts payable period* is time between receipt of inventory and payment for it

Lecture Tip, page 545: Students should easily recognize that a company would prefer to take as long as possible before paying bills. The instructor could mention that some people view an account payable as free credit since no cash is initially paid. However, a supplying firm may add in the cost of this so-called free credit into the selling price of its product. Note that the operating cycle begins when inventory is purchased (a debit entry to inventory is matched with a credit entry to accounts payable). The cash cycle begins with the payment of the accounts payable created when inventory was initially purchased (a debit entry to accounts payable matched with a credit to cash).

T17.2: Operating and Cash Cycles Illustrated

B. The Operating Cycle and the Firm's Organization Chart

Short-term financial management in a large firm involves coordination between the credit manager, marketing manager, and controller. Potential for conflict may exist if particular managers concentrate on individual objectives as opposed to overall firm objectives.

T17.3: Operating and Cash Cycles Illustrated

C. Calculating the Operating and Cash Cycles

T17.4: Hermetic, Inc., Operating Cycles
T17.5: Hermetic, Inc., Cash Cycles

Example:
    Use Hermetic, Inc., financial statements (Chapter 2) to calculate operating and cash cycles.

The Operating Cycle

Lecture Tip, page 548: In this chapter (and in the following calculations), we use average values of inventory, accounts receivable, and accounts payable to compute values of inventory, accounts receivable, and accounts payable turnover, respectively. The instructor may wish to remind students that the balance sheet represents a financial "snapshot" of the firm and as such, balance sheet values are literally correct at only a single point in time. (In economic terms, balance sheet values are "stock" rather than "flow" values. The latter are represented by income statement values.) One way to mitigate (but not eliminate) the distortions caused by dividing a stock value by a flow value is to use the average ((beginning value + ending value)/2) stock value computed over the same period.

Example:

1. Finding the Inventory period:

Inventory turnover = COGS/Avg inventory = $480/$352.5 = 1.362 turns
Inventory period = 365/Inventory turnover = 365/1.362 = 268 days

2. Finding the accounts receivable period:

Receivables Turnover = Credit sales/Avg receivables = $710/$285 = 2.491 turns
Receivables period = 365/Receivables turnover = 365/2.491 = 146.527 or 147 days

3. Finding the operating cycle:
Operating cycle = Inventory period + Receivables period = 268 + 147 = 415 days

The Cash Cycle

1. Finding the payables turnover:

Payables turnover = COGS/Avg payables = $480/$235 = 2.043
Payables period = 365/payables turnover = 365/2.043 = 178.659 or 179 days

2. Finding the cash cycle:

Cash cycle = Operating cycle − Payables period = 415 − 179 = 236 days

Lecture Tip, page 550: The following section, "Interpreting the Cash Cycle," presents some general conclusions on the cash cycle. It may be beneficial to have the students consider the cash cycle of Slowpay. The students could reconsider the issues of a high versus a low turnover, discussed in Chapter 3. Many may feel the main demand on funds for Slowpay is attributed to the high inventory period of 73 days. However, the students should consider the implications of attempts to speed up the inventory turnover through reduced inventory purchases or attempts to accelerate sales. Such efforts may result in expanded credit terms and a slower receivables turnover. The instructor could also mention that optimal levels of working capital will be discussed in the following section.

D. Interpreting the Cash Cycle

The cash cycle increases as the inventory and receivables periods lengthen and decreases as the payables period lengthens. The longer the cash cycle, the more financing needed.

Lecture Tip, page 550: The discussion above suggests that, depending on inventory needs and financing costs, some firms will find it useful to hire others to "store inventory" for them. In fact, McDonnell-Douglas Aircraft in St. Louis does exactly that - small firms are paid to guarantee the delivery of raw materials (copper, sheet steel, etc.) to the firm at moment's notice. And while these firms also do some preliminary cutting and machining, their primary role is to hold inventory that McDonnell-Douglas would otherwise have to hold. As a result, McDonnell-Douglas' financing needs are lessened.

The relationship between inventory turnover and financing needs is also apparent in industries with extremely long or short cash cycles. For example, cash cycles are relatively long in the jewelry retailing industry, and particularly short in the grocery industry. The financing implications are obvious.

17.3 SOME ASPECTS OF SHORT-TERM FINANCIAL POLICY

If receipts could be perfectly timed to match outlays there wouldn't be any need for cash balances and net working capital could be zero. It is the mismatch between cash in and cash out (plus uncertainty about future events) which motivates businesses to hold net working capital balances.

Flexible (conservative) policy—high levels of current assets relative to sales, and relatively more long-term debt.

Restrictive (aggressive) policy—low levels of current assets relative to sales, and relatively more short-term debt.

T17.6: The Size of the Firm's Investment in Current Assets

A. The Size of the Firm's Investment in Current Assets

Flexible policy actions include:
1. Keeping large cash and securities balances.
2. Keeping large amounts of inventory.
3. Granting liberal credit terms, resulting in large receivables.

Restrictive policy actions include:
1. Keeping low cash and securities balances.
2. Keeping small amounts of inventory.
3. Allowing few or no credit sales and minimizing receivables.

T17.7: Carrying Costs and Shortage Costs

There are costs and benefits to flexible and restrictive policies. The policies represent trade-offs between costs that rise with investment and costs that fall with investment.

Carrying costs—costs that rise with increases in the level of investment in current assets.

In general, liquid assets have low yields. Thus, there ere are substantial *opportunity costs* involved with holding relatively high levels of current assets.

Shortage costs—costs that fall with increases in the level of investment in current assets.

There are two kinds of shortage costs:

1. *Trading or order costs*—commissions, set-up, paperwork, etc...
2. *Costs related to safety reserves*—lost sales, business disruptions, lost goodwill.

Lecture Tip, page 552: The students have probably heard the policy of just-in-time inventory discussed in another business class. The instructor might ask the students to consider the risks of such a policy and what cost the company is attempting to minimize (carrying cost) and what cost may be increased (shortage cost).

B. Alternative Financing Policies for Current Assets

1. An Ideal Case: always finance short-term assets with short-term liabilities, long-term assets with long-term liabilities.

T17.8: Financing Policy for an "Ideal" Economy

---

2. Different Policies in Financing Current Assets

T17.9: Alternative Asset Financing Policies

Lecture Tip, page 554: Some students may tend to think of permanent asset levels as fixed assets. The instructor may wish to emphasize that permanent assets entail both long-term assets and a component of current assets. Some students may not readily see a component of short-term assets as permanent assets and may be confused with figure 17.3, representing an "ideal economy" in which current assets = short-term debt. The instructor may wish to provide a very simplified example as presented below:

	January	*February*	*March*	*April*
Current Assets	*$20,000*	*$30,000*	*$20,000*	*$20,000*
Fixed Assets	*$50,000*	*$50,000*	*$50,000*	*$50,000*
Short-term Debt	*?*	*?*	*?*	*?*
Long-term Debt	*?*	*?*	*?*	*?*

The instructor could then ask the student to consider the alternative financing policies presented in Figure 17.5. Policy F (flexible) would entail long-term debt of $80,000. In March, the company would have excess cash of $10,000 which could be invested in marketable securities. This policy would result in a lower interest revenue relative to the interest expense it would be paying on the $10,000 of long-term debt. Under Policy R *(restrictive), the company would borrow $70,000 of long-term debt since total assets never fall below $70,000 (permanent level). In February, total assets are $80,000, and the additional $10,000 would be supported by $10,000 of short-term debt, which would be paid off in March, when assets fall back to $70,000.*

C. Which is Best?

T17.10: A Compromise Financing Policy

Things to be considered:

1. *Cash reserves*—safety versus profitability.
2. *Maturity hedging*—short-to-short, long-to-long, and ne'er the twain shall meet.
3. *Relative interest rates*—short-term rates are generally lower, but also more volatile.

Lecture Tip, page 556: A good example of the inclination to maturity-hedge is provided by pointing out that, when one borrows to buy a long-term asset for personal use, the length of the loan approximates the life of the asset. Homes are traditionally financed with 30-year mortgages, and new cars are commonly financed for 48-60 months. Why not borrow $200,000 to buy a home on a one-year note, with the intent to refinance at the end of 12 months? Two reasons: first, transactions costs (i.e., the cost of closing, etc.) would be prohibitive, and second, the borrower would incur a significant risk that an increase in market rates could impair his/her ability to obtain new financing. (Quick-witted students will ask how this example differs from the use of a one-year adjustable mortgage. The main differences are: Adjustable mortgages are "renewable" annually at the option of the borrower; and rate changes are typically limited by contract.)

D. Current Assets and Liabilities in Practice

17.4 THE CASH BUDGET

Cash budget—a schedule of projected cash receipts and disbursements.

A. Sales and Cash Collections

A cash budget begins with a *sales forecast* (daily, weekly, monthly, or quarterly). This forecast is then used to generate estimates of cash inflows and cash outflows.

Are any sales on credit and, if so, what is the *average accounts receivable period*? That is, how long after a sale will the firm collect?

B. Cash Outflows

Accounts payable—how long after a purchase before the firm pays?

Wages, taxes, and other expenses—usually given as a percent of sales.

Capital expenditures—from the capital budget.

Long-term financing expenses—interest, sinking funds, dividends.

Short-term borrowing—used as a "plug" later.

C. The Cash Balance

T17.11: A Cash Budget for Ajax Co. (2 pages)

Example: A Cash Budget
    Monthly cash budget: First quarter for the Ajax Company.

-All sales on credit. The sales forecast is:

JAN	$55,000	MAR	$65,000
FEB	$65,000	APR	$60,000

-November sales were $80,000; December sales were $95,000; the average accounts
    receivable period is 45 days; December 31st receivables were $135,000.
-Wages, taxes, and other expenses are 30% of sales.
-Raw materials are purchased on credit with an average payable period of 30 days. Raw
    materials are ordered two months in advance of forecasted sales, and are 50%
    of sales.
-An annual cash dividend of $100,000 is expected to be paid in March.
-No capital expenditures are planned for the first three months.
-The beginning cash balance is $41,000. The minimum cash balance is $25,000.

Cash collections for Ajax (all figures rounded to the nearest dollar)

	JAN	FEB	MAR
Beginning receivables	$135,000	$102,500	$ 92,500
Sales	55,000	65,000	65,000
Cash collections*	87,500	75,000	60,000
Ending receivables	102,500	92,500	97,500

*Cash collections—assuming level sales throughout the month, a 45-day collection period
implies 1/2 of a month's sales are collected in the subsequent month and 1/2 in the
second month after a sale.

Cash disbursements for Ajax

	JAN	FEB	MAR
Payment of accounts	$ 32,500	$ 32,500	$ 30,000
Wages, taxes, and other expenses	16,500	19,500	19,500
Capital expenditures	0	0	0
Long-term financing expenses	0	0	100,000
Total	$49,000	$52,000	$149,500

Net cash inflow for Ajax

	JAN	FEB	MAR
Total cash collections	$ 87,500	$ 75,000	$ 60,000
Total cash disbursements	49,000	52,000	149,500
Net cash inflow	$ 38,500	$ 23,000	−$ 89,500

Cash balance for Ajax

	JAN	FEB	MAR
Beginning cash balance	$ 41,000	$ 79,500	$102,500
Net cash inflow	38,500	23,000	−$ 89,500
Ending cash balance	$ 79,500	$102,500	$ 13,000
Minimum cash balance	− 25,000	− 25,000	− 25,000
Cumulative surplus (deficit)	$ 54,500	$ 77,500	−$ 12,000

17.5 SHORT-TERM BORROWING

A. Unsecured Loans

T17.12: Short-Term Borrowing

Line of credit—formal or informal prearranged short-term loan.

Commitment fee—a charge to secure a committed line of credit.

Compensating balances—deposits in a low-interest account as part of a loan agreement.

Cost of a compensating balance—if the compensating balance requirement is on the *used* portion, less money is actually available than is borrowed. If it is on the *unused* portion, the requirement becomes a commitment fee.

Example:

Consider a $50,000 line of credit with a 5% compensating balance requirement. The quoted rate on the line is prime + 6%, and the prime stands at 11%. Suppose the firm wants to borrow $28,500. How much do they have to borrow? What is the EAR?

Loan amount: $28,500 = (1 − .05) × Amount; Amount = $28,500/.95 = $30,000

What is the effective rate? At 17% per annum, the interest on $30,000 is $5,100. Interest rate = interest paid/amount available = $5,100/$28,500 = .17895 or 17.895%

Lecture Tip, page 561: The instructor may wish to use the credit card to illustrate a line of credit. With credit cards, the consumer can utilize the line of credit to purchase goods. The line of credit remains active until we abuse the privilege (e.g., late payments). However, there is a cost for this line, much as the compensating balance issue next discussed. Many students may have access to more than one credit card. (Articles in The Wall Street Journal suggest that card issuers have targeted college students recently.) The instructor could mention that holding more cards increases the total line of credit available but increases costs from annual fees. It would not pay to secure the maximum number of credit cards since they would not need the combined lines of credit and would incur the annual fees associated with each card. Similarly, companies do not want to secure excessive lines of credit since they would be burdened with fees for credit limits they would not use.

Lecture Tip, page 563: Trade credit represents another source of unsecured financing. However, the cost of this form of borrowing is largely implicit, since it is represented by the opportunity cost of not taking the discount offered, if any. To compute the effective annual cost of trade credit, we first use the credit terms offered to determine a periodic opportunity cost. For example, if the terms are 2/10, net 30, rational managers will either pay $.98 per dollar of goods ordered on the 10th day, or the full invoice cost on day 30. In the latter case, the firm is actually paying $.02 to borrow $.98 for 20 days. In one year's worth of borrowing there are 365/20 = 18.25 such periods. Thus, the annualized cost of this financing is $(1 + \$.02/\$.98)^{18.25} - 1 = 44.56\%$.

B. Secured Loans

1. *Accounts receivable financing*

Assigning receivables—receivables are security for a loan, but the borrower remains responsible if a receivable can't be collected.

Factoring receivables—the receivable is sold at a discount to the factor.

Example:
Consider a firm with an average receivables period of 33 days. The firm can factor the receivables at a 2% discount. That is, the firm gets $0.98 for every $1.00 of receivables, i.e., in effect pays 2¢ to get 98¢ 33 days early. The interest rate for the 33 day collection period is $.02/.98 = .0204 = 2.04\%$ per period. Since there are approximately 11 33-day periods in a year, the APR $= 11 \times 2.04\% = 22.44\%$. The effective annual rate is higher still, $(1.0204)^{11} - 1 = .24875$ or 24.875%.

2. Inventory Loans

Lecture Tip, page 563: Firms most suited to employ inventory as a financing tool have inventory which is nonperishable, marketable, and not subject to obsolescence. Some view inventory financing as a means of raising additional short-term funds after receivables financing has been exhausted. Of course, in some industries (e.g., auto sales), inventory financing is standard practice.

Types of inventory loans:
Blanket inventory liens—lender gets a lien against all the borrower's inventories.

Trust receipt—lender buys the inventory which is held in "trust" by the borrower who gives a trust receipt acknowledging the arrangement.

Field warehouse financing—independent company establishes warehouse area on the borrower's premises and only releases goods upon instructions of the lender.

Ethics Note, page 564: An interesting digression on the (mis)use of inventory financing is the story of Tino De Angelis, who has come to be known as the "salad oil king".
Mr. De Angelis, a former butcher, constructed an empire with a reported value of $100 million (in 1963!) based largely on his supposed acumen in buying and selling vegetable oil. The magnitude of his operation is apparent when one considers that at one point, he had contracted to purchase 600 million pounds of the product, or one-third of the amount produced in America annually.
Unfortunately, Mr. De Angelis' business acumen was not what it seemed, and he resorted to borrowing against his inventory, which supposedly consisted of millions of gallons of vegetable oil held in huge steel vats spread across New Jersey. Even more unfortunate was the fact that his creditors eventually discovered that the vats were largely empty. The resulting default caused millions of dollars in losses to banks, insurance companies, brokerage firms, and the New York Stock Exchange. Mr. De Angelis was paroled in 1972, having served seven years of a 20-year prison sentence for his escapades.

C. Other Sources

Commercial paper—short-term IOUs issued by large, especially creditworthy firms.

Lecture Tip, page 564: In Corporate Liquidity, Kenneth Parkinson and Jarl Kallberg call commercial paper "the most important source of short-term borrowing for large U.S. companies." The commercial paper market has grown dramatically over the last decade, and will undoubtedly continue to do so. Parkinson and Kallberg describe a typical commercial paper transaction.

1.   *The issuer sells a note to an investor for an agreed-upon rate, principal, (usually in $1 million increments), and maturity date.*

2.   *The issuer contracts with its issuing bank to prepare the note and deliver it to the investor's custodial bank.*

3.   *The investor instructs its bank to wire funds to the commercial paper issuer upon delivery and verification of the note. (Since commercial paper is sold on a discounted basis, the amount of funds wired is less than the face amount of the note.) The funds are transferred to the issuer's bank and the note is held at the investor's custodial bank.*

4.   *On the maturity date, the note is returned to the issuer's paying agent and the funds (i.e., the face value of the note) are transferred to the investor. The note is marked paid and returned to the issuer.*

(The above is adapted from Kenneth Parkinson and Jarl Kallberg, Corporate Liquidity, published by Business One, Richard D. Irwin, Inc., page 256.)

Trade credit—borrowing from suppliers by purchasing goods on account.

17.6 A SHORT-TERM FINANCIAL PLAN

Using the cash budget, the firm decides how it will raise (employ) funds for cash deficit (surplus) periods. For temporary imbalances, short-term borrowing and marketable securities are in order. For permanent shortfalls or surpluses, long-term solutions include: bond or equity issues for deficits, and dividends or a repurchase for surpluses.

17.7 SUMMARY AND CONCLUSIONS

T17.13:   Solution to Problem 17.9
T17.14:   Solution to Problem 17.12
T17.15:   Solution to Problem 17.16

CHAPTER 18
CASH AND LIQUIDITY MANAGEMENT

TRANSPARENCIES

T18.1: Chapter Outline
T18.2: Cash and Liquidity Management
T18.3: Check Clearing Illustrated
T18.4: Overview of Lockbox Processing (Fig. 18.3)
T18.5: Lockboxes and Concentration Banks (Fig. 18.4)
T18.6: Zero-Balance Accounts (Fig. 18.5)
T18.7: Some Money Market Securities
T18.8: Costs of Holding Cash
T18.9: The Miller-Orr model
T18.10: Solution to Problem 18.4
T18.11: Solution to Problem 18.13

CHAPTER ORGANIZATION

T18.1: Chapter Outline

18.1 REASONS FOR HOLDING CASH
Speculative and Precautionary Motives
The Transaction Motive
Compensating Balances
Costs of Holding Cash

18.2 UNDERSTANDING FLOAT
Disbursement Float
Collection Float and Net Float
Float Management

18.3 CASH COLLECTION AND CONCENTRATION
Components of Collection Time
Cash Collection
Lockboxes
Cash Concentration
Accelerating Collections: An Example

18.4 MANAGING CASH DISBURSEMENTS
Increasing Disbursement Float
Controlling Disbursements

18.5 INVESTING IDLE CASH
Temporary Cash Surpluses
Characteristics of Short-Term Securities
Some Different Types of Money Market Securities

18.6 SUMMARY AND CONCLUSIONS

APPENDIX 18A—DETERMINING THE TARGET CASH BALANCE
The Basic Idea
The BAT Model
The Miller-Orr Model: A More General Approach
Implications of the BAT and Miller-Orr Models
Other Factors Influencing the Target Cash Balance

ANNOTATED CHAPTER OUTLINE

18.1 REASONS FOR HOLDING CASH

A. Speculative and Precautionary Motives

Speculative motive—to take advantage of unexpected opportunities (marketable securities and credit lines also satisfy this motive).

Precautionary motive—in contrast to the unexpected opportunity, the occasional unexpected outlay. (Again, credit and securities can also satisfy this motive.)

Lecture Tip, page 577: What is needed to satisfy the speculative and precautionary motives is an ability to pay quickly—a need that is met with liquidity. Although cash is the most liquid asset, assets such as marketable securities are near substitutes for cash. Furthermore, an ability to borrow quickly is also a close substitute for cash.

Lecture Tip: Although holding cash and near-cash assets imposes opportunity costs on the firm, it can be shown that the existence of this "financial slack" is consistent with shareholder wealth maximization. Specifically, it is clear that the ability to take advantage of unexpected financial opportunities - an unexpected (and probably temporary) fall in the price of raw materials, or the ability to take a discount offered on purchases - is valuable to the firm. Additionally, in a paper which appeared in the Journal of Financial Economics in 1984, Myers and Majluf demonstrated that the lack of financial slack could cause financial decision-makers to forego positive-NPV projects because of the signalling costs incurred in a common stock issue.

B. The Transaction Motive

Since cash inflows and outflows are not perfectly synchronized, the cash balance serves as a buffer between collections and disbursements.

C. Compensating Balances

Sometimes required as a condition for granting a loan, these constitute a *de facto* lower limit on cash balances.

Lecture Tip: A compensating balance requirement serves as both a term of a loan imposed by the lender and as compensation for services rendered by the bank. As such, it is sometimes negotiable. For example, the borrower can attempt to have the size of the required balance reduced, or she can negotiate the nature of the terms. Rather than requiring that, say, $100,000 be kept on deposit at all times, the lender may instead agree to allow the firm to maintain an average balance of $100,000 over a specified period. The latter case gives the borrower more flexibility. It should also be pointed out that, for firms that hold significant liquid asset balances as a matter of policy, a compensating balance requirement may not be a binding constraint. Finally, it should be noted that, for many firms, it is cheaper to borrow funds and pay explicit fees for bank services rendered, rather than maintain large balances in non-interest bearing accounts.

D. Costs of Holding Cash

The opportunity cost to holding cash balances is the return that could be earned if the funds were invested in other asset(s). However, converting other assets into cash (or borrowing) has costs. The target cash balance must take both of these into account.

Lecture Tip, page 577: It may be helpful to have students consider their personal cash balances. Some may deposit their paychecks or student loan proceeds in a non-interest-paying checking account to use throughout the quarter. The instructor could demonstrate that these students are foregoing interest they might receive on a savings account, even though the balance might approach a low level by the end of the term. But if a student wants to maximize the interest he could receive on the savings account, he would have to carefully monitor the checking account balance to ensure that it maintains a minimum amount to cover checks written. The instructor could mention that a happy balance (no pun intended) exists between having too much idle cash in the account and too little.

The instructor could demonstrate this situation in terms of an equilibrium for a company—the marginal benefit of the liquidity that a large cash balance provides versus the marginal value of the interest received on Treasury bills; i.e., the investment of cash balances into Treasury bills is a zero net present value investment.

18.2 UNDERSTANDING FLOAT

A. Disbursement Float

T18.2: Cash and Liquidity Management

Book or *ledger balance*—what the firm's records show its cash balance to be.

Available or *collected balance*—what the bank says the cash balance is.
Float = available balance − book balance
Disbursement float—happens when the firm <u>writes</u> checks that don't clear immediately.

B. Collection Float and Net Float

Collection float—happens when the firm <u>deposits</u> checks that aren't cleared immediately.
Net float = disbursement float + collection float

Lecture Tip, page 579: It may help to personalize the issue of float. The instructor could ask the students if any of the students have written a check a day or two prior to receiving their weekly payroll check, even though, on the day on which the check was mailed, their checking balance was not sufficient to cover it. The students could view the payroll check received as a collection which they deposit prior to the mailed checks being returned for payment to the students' bank. When a student deposits the check, the bank's record of the checking account balance would be larger than the amount in the student's personal checking account records (book balance). On the day of the deposit, as the text states, "the bank thinks the firm [or the student] has more cash than [he] really does."

C. Float Management

The three components of float are:

      1. *Mail float*—the time the check is in the mail
      2. *Processing float*—handling time between receipt and deposit
      3. *Availability float*—time to clear the banking system

Float management means speeding collections (reducing collection float) and slowing disbursements (increasing disbursement float).

1. Measuring Float

    There are two distinct cases:

      a) periodic collections
      b) continuous or *steady-state* collections.

For periodic collections, average daily float equals

(check amount × days delay)/(# days in period).

<u>Example: Periodic collections</u>
Suppose a $10,000 check is mailed to Priam, Inc. every two weeks. It spends 2 days in the mail, 1½ days at Priam offices, and is credited to Priam's bank account 2 days after deposit, so the total delay is 5½ days. Over the 14 day period, the float is $10,000 for 5.5 days, and $0 for 8.5 days; then the cycle starts over. The *average daily float* is (5.5 × $10,000 + 8.5 × 0)/14 or simply (5.5 × $10,000)/14 = $3,928.57.

<u>Example: Continuous collections</u>
Suppose average daily checks arriving at Hector Company amount to $2,000, and suppose further that they take an average of 3 days to arrive in the mail, 1 day to process, and 2 days to be credited to Hector's bank account. The total collection delay is 3 + 1 + 2 = 6 days, and average daily float is 6 × $2,000 = $12,000 (i.e., on any given day the amount paid but uncollected is $12,000). Eliminating all delays would free up $12,000. By the same token, eliminating 1 day's delay frees up $2,000.

2. Cost of the (collection) float

The benefit of reducing collection delays is directly reflected in the change in average daily float. Every dollar reduction in average daily float is a dollar freed up for use in perpetuity. The change in the average daily float that any scheme to hasten collections might make is also the *most* the firm would be willing to pay for faster collections.

<u>Example: Periodic collections</u>
What is the most Priam would pay to speed up its collections by a half day? If the collections delay were reduced from 5.5 days to 5, average daily float would go from (5.5 × $10,000)/14 to (5 × $10,000)/14. i.e., from $3,928.57 to $3,571.43. So the benefit of collecting a half day faster is $357.14, and this is the most they would pay.

<u>Example: Continuous collections</u>
How much would Hector Company save if they could reduce their collection delay from 6 days to 3 days? At 3 days, average daily float is 3 × $2,000 = $6,000 and the change in average daily float is $12,000 − $6,000 = $6,000.

Lecture Tip: *The Expedited Funds Availability Act (EFAA) governs the availability of funds deposited by firms. The following rules apply as of September 1, 1990.*

Category of Funds	Availability Date
Cash or electronic payments	Day after deposit date
Government checks	Day after deposit date
Local checks	Two days after deposit
Nonlocal checks	Five days after deposit

(Source: <u>Corporate Liquidity</u>, by Kenneth L. Parkinson and Jarl G. Kallberg. Homewood, Illinois:Richard D. Irwin, Inc., 1993.)

Lecture Tip, page 582: *It may be helpful to reinforce the concept of net float through an example emphasizing the balance sheet changes resulting from an increase in collection float and a decrease in disbursement float. One could begin by having the class* *consider a firm that has credit sales of $100,000 per day. Inventory of $80,000 per day is purchased on credit. The company collects its average receivable in 30 days and takes an average of 20 days to pay its accounts payable. The balance sheet would appear as:*

Acc. Rec.	*$3,000,000*	*Acc. Pay.*	*$1,600,000*

This situation requires external funds sources (see Chapter 4) of $1,400,000. Checks, whether received or sent, will require three days for mail delivery. A negative net float of −$60,000 (−$100,000 × 3 + $80,000 × 3) exists. If the company could speed up its receivables collection by one day, only 29 days sales' would be in receivables. If the company could also delay its disbursements by one day, it would be taking 21 days to pay its payables. Net float would become a positive $120,000 (−$100,000 × 2 + $80,000 × 4). The balance sheet would initially change to:

Add. Cash	*$ 180,000*	*Acc. Pay.*	*$1,680,000*
Acc. Rec.	*$2,900,000*		

The accounts receivable debit balance is reduced by $100,000, resulting in a source of funds. Additionally, the accounts payable credit balance is increased by $80,000, resulting in an additional source of funds. The net source equals this change in float of $180,000. The additional cash can be used to reduce the external funds required ($2,900,000 − $1,680,000) to $1,220,000.

Ethics Note, page 584: *For a lengthy discussion of legal and ethical questions and issues surrounding cash management, see* Institutional Investor, *September 1985, "Cash management: Where do you draw the line", by Barbara Donnelly, pp. 69-79. The story focuses on the E.F. Hutton check kiting scandal.*

18.3 CASH COLLECTION AND CONCENTRATION

T18.3: Check Clearing Illustrated

A. Components of Collection Time

The three basic components of cash collection are:
-mail delay
-processing delay
-clearing delay

B. Cash Collection

Cash collection policies depend on the nature of the business. The firm might choose to have checks mailed to one location, numerous locations to reduce mailing time, or arrange for preauthorized payments.

C. Lockboxes

T18.4: Overview of Lockbox Processing (Fig. 18.3)

Lockboxes—special post office boxes, tended by banks on behalf of clients, to which checks are sent in an effort to reduce mail, processing, and clearing delays.

D. Cash Concentration

T18.5: Lockboxes and Concentration Banks (Fig. 18.4)

Concentration banking—sending surplus funds from remote banks to centralized banks.

Wire transfers—electronic transfer of funds - eliminates mail and check-clearing delays.

E. Accelerating Collections: An Example

18.4 MANAGING CASH DISBURSEMENTS

A. Increasing Disbursement Float

Increasing Disbursement Float-write checks on distant bank, call to verify statement, mail from remote post office.

Ethics Note: The instructor may wish to emphasize the importance of ethical behavior in the area of credit and collections. Because transactions occur so frequently and are often of such large amounts, unscrupulous financial managers tend to "cut corners" in this area more often than in some others. For example, one of the authors did some consulting work for a small firm which was routinely paid late or shorted on their billings by a large customer. The small firm suffered the costs of these actions for years because the large firm accounted for nearly three-quarters of its annual revenue and couldn't afford to lose the business. Other dubious practices include those who pay late but still take discounts, those who set invoice dates well before shipping, and those who impose large delinquency charges for late payments.

B. Controlling Disbursements

18.6: Zero-Balance Accounts (Fig. 18.5)

Zero-balance account—rather than keep cash balances in several accounts to pay checks, funds are concentrated in a central account and transferred from this account to *ZBA* accounts as checks are presented. The balance in the concentration account is typically lower than maintaining balances in several accounts.

Drafts—drafts differ from checks in that they are payable by the issuer rather than banks. Drafts are presented to the issuer by banks who act as agents. Only then do funds need to be deposited to cover them.

18.5 INVESTING IDLE CASH

A. Temporary Cash Surpluses

1. Seasonal or cyclical activities
2. Planned or possible expenditures—cash for capital expenditures, dividends, debt retirement, legal contingencies, acquisitions, etc.

B. Characteristics of Short-Term Securities

Corporate treasurers seeking to acquire liquid assets seek those with the following characteristics:

-short maturity
-low default risk
-high marketability

Lecture Tip: "Marketability" suggests that large amounts of an asset can be bought or sold quickly with little effect on the current market price. This characteristic is usually associated with financial markets which are "broad" and "deep". Broad markets are those with a large number of participants; deep markets, on the other hand, contain participants who have the ability to engage in large transactions. The market for U.S. Treasury bills epitomizes these characteristics - there are literally millions of potential buyers and sellers worldwide, and multi-million dollar transactions are common.

C. Some Different Types of Money Market Securities

> ### T18.7: Some Money Market Securities

Lecture Tip, page 594: The instructor may wish to mention that the current money market rates are presented daily in The Wall Street Journal. *Various money market instruments and their current rates can be found on the* Credit Markets *page in Section C, under the title "Money Rates." The instructor might remind the student that these rates change on a daily basis, as a function of market conditions.*

18.6 SUMMARY AND CONCLUSIONS

> ### T18.10: Solution to Problem 18.4
> ### T18.11: Solution to Problem 18.13

APPENDIX 18A—DETERMINING THE TARGET CASH BALANCE

Target cash balance—the desired cash balance as determined by the tradeoff between carrying costs and shortage costs.

Adjustment costs—costs associated with holding low levels of cash; shortage costs.

With a flexible working capital policy, the tradeoff is between the opportunity cost of cash balances and the adjustment costs of buying, selling, and managing securities.

A. The Basic Idea

> ### T18.8: Costs of Holding Cash

B. The BAT (Baumol-Allais-Tobin) Model

Define:

C = optimal cash transfer amount (amount of securities to sell)
F = the fixed cost of selling securities to replenish cash
T = the eash needed for transactions over the planning period
R = opportunity cost of cash—the interest rate on marketable securities

Assume cash is paid out at a constant rate through time.

1. *The opportunity costs*—average cash balance × interest rate = $(C/2) \times R$
2. *The trading costs*—number of transactions × cost per transfer = $(T/C) \times F$
3. *The total cost*—opportunity costs + trading costs = $(C/2) \times R + (T/C) \times F$
4. *The solution*—the minimum occurs where opportunity costs = trading costs:

$$C/2 \times R = (T/C) \times F$$

Rearranging:

$$C^2 = (2T \times F)/R$$

Solving for C:

$$C = \sqrt{(2T \times F)/R}$$

This can also be found by differentiating total cost with respect to C:

$$TC = (C/2) \times R + (T/C) \times F$$
$$\frac{\partial TC}{\partial C} = R/2 - \frac{T \times F}{C^2}$$

Setting this to zero and solving for C yields:

$$C = \sqrt{(2T \times F)/R}$$

<u>Example:</u>
    Hermes Co. has cash outflows of $500 a day, the interest rate is 10% and the cost of a transfer to cash is $25.

$$T = 365 \times \$500 = \$182,500 \quad F = \$25 \qquad R = .10$$

$$C = \sqrt{(2T \times F)/R}$$

$$= \sqrt{2 \times \$182,500 \times \$25/.10}$$

$$= \sqrt{91,250,000}$$

$$= \$9,552.49$$

C. The Miller-Orr Model: A More General Approach

The Miller-Orr model offers a general approach to handling uncertain cash flows.

T18.9: The Miller-Orr Model

1. The Basic Idea

Define:
U^* = upper limit on cash balance
L = lower limit on cash balance
C^* = target cash balance

When the cash balance, a random variable, reaches U^*, the firm transfers $U^* - C^*$ dollars from cash to securities. If the cash balance falls below L, the firm sells $C^* - L$ worth of securities to add to cash.

2. Using the Model

Need the variance of cash flow per period, σ^2, and the interest rate per period (Note: Here cash flow refers to both the amounts that go into and come out of the cash balance). The period may be anything (day, week, month) as long as these two are consistent. Given L, the target balance and upper limit are given by:

$$C^* = L + (\tfrac{3}{4} \times F \times \sigma^2/R)^{1/3} \quad \text{and} \quad U^* = 3 \times C^* - 2 \times L$$

Example:
Suppose $F = \$25$, $R = 1\%$ per month, and the variance of monthly cash flows is \$25,000,000 (i.e., a standard deviation of \$5,000 per month). Assume a minimum cash balance of \$10,000.

$$C^* = \$10,000 + (\tfrac{3}{4} \times \$25 \times \$25,000,000/.01)^{1/3}$$
$$= \$10,000 + \$3,605.62 = \$13,605.62$$

$$U^* = 3 \times \$13,605.62 - 2 \times \$10,000$$
$$= \$40,816.86 - \$20,000 = \$20,816.86$$

D. Implications of the BAT and Miller-Orr Models

From both:

-The higher the interest rate (opportunity cost), the *lower* the target balance.
-The higher the transaction cost, the higher the target balance.

From Miller-Orr:

-The greater the variability of cash flows, the higher the target balance.

E. Other Factors Influencing the Target Cash Balance

-Flexible versus restrictive short-term financing policy.
-Compensating balance requirements.
-The number and complexity of checking accounts

CHAPTER 19
CREDIT AND INVENTORY MANAGEMENT

TRANSPARENCIES

T19.1: Chapter Outline
T19.2: Credit and Inventory Management
T19.3: The Cash Flows from Granting Credit
T19.4: Length of the Credit Period
T19.5: Credit Policy Effects
T19.6: Evaluating a Proposed Credit Policy
T19.7: The Costs of Granting Credit
T19.8: The Five C's of Credit
T19.9: ABC Inventory Analysis (Fig. 19.2)
T19.10: Costs of Holding Inventory (Fig. 19.4)
T19.11: Inventory Holdings for the Eyssell Corporation (Fig. 19.5)
T19.12: Solution to Problem 19.13
T19.13: Solution to Problem 19.18
T19.14: Solution to Problem 19.22

CHAPTER ORGANIZATION

T19.1: Chapter Outline

19.1 CREDIT AND RECEIVABLES
Components of Credit Policy
The Cash Flows from Granting Credit
The Investment in Receivables

19.2 TERMS OF THE SALE
The Basic Form
The Credit Period
Cash Discounts
Credit Instruments

19.3 ANALYZING CREDIT POLICY
Credit Policy Effects
Evaluating a Proposed Credit Policy

19.4 OPTIMAL CREDIT POLICY
The Total Credit Cost Curve

19.5 CREDIT ANALYSIS
When Should Credit Be Granted?
Credit Information
Credit Evaluation and Scoring

19.6 COLLECTION POLICY
Monitoring Receivables
Collection Effort

19.7 INVENTORY MANAGEMENT
The Financial Manager and Inventory Policy
Inventory Types
Inventory Costs

19.8 INVENTORY MANAGEMENT TECHNIQUES
The ABC Approach
The Economic Order Quantity (EOQ) Model
Extensions to the EOQ Model
Managing Derived-Demand Inventories

19.9 SUMMARY AND CONCLUSIONS

APPENDIX 19A—MORE ON CREDIT POLICY ANALYSIS
Two Alternative Approaches
Discounts and Default Risk

ANNOTATED CHAPTER OUTLINE

19.1 CREDIT AND RECEIVABLES

> **T19.2: Credit and Inventory Management**

When credit is granted to other firms, it's called *trade credit*. When granted to consumers, it's called *consumer credit*.

A. Components of Credit Policy

1. *Terms of sale*—credit period, discounts and discount period, credit instrument
2. *Credit analysis*—who gets credit (and how much), and who doesn't
3. *Collection policy*—how to get borrowers to pay

B. The Cash Flows from Granting Credit

T19.3: The Cash Flows from Granting Credit

C. The Investment in Receivables

The investment in receivables depends upon the *average collection period* and the level of *average daily credit sales*.

Accounts receivable = Average daily sales × average collection period

Lecture Tip, page 612: Some students might question why the amount of investment in accounts receivable is the daily sales times ACP. They may recognize that sales contain cost plus profit, and the investment required would be the cost of the receivables, not the profit margin in the receivables account. Should this question arise, the instructor could mention that this investment analysis refers to the funds committed to this balance. If the receivables balance could be reduced by 10 days, these 10 days' receivables would be immediately freed up. Thus, the investment in receivables should be viewed in terms of the funds which are tied up for the company.

D. Organizing the Credit Function

Firms often find it cost-effective to pay others to perform one or more aspects of the credit function; by doing so, they avoid the costs of running a full-blown credit and collections department.

Captive finance companies are wholly-owned subsidiaries of large firms which perform all of the credit-granting tasks of the parents.

Lecture Tip, page 612: As noted in the text, separating the finance and non-finance lines of business by creating a captive finance subsidiary may lower the firm's overall cost of debt. Dennis E. Logue points out that this is due, in part, to the fact that "different levels of assets can support varying degrees of leverage." Put another way, this suggests that the standards an analyst would apply to the financial statements of the parent should reflect the parent's main line(s) of business, while the standards applied to the financial statements of the subsidiary should reflect the fact that it is a finance company. (See Dennis E. Logue, The Handbook of Modern Finance, second edition, Warren, Gorham, and Lamont, 1990.)

19.2 TERMS OF THE SALE

1. The credit period
2. Cash discounts and discount period
3. The credit instrument

A. The Basic Form

a/b, net *c*—e.g., 1/10, net 30
In other words, (take this discount off the invoice price)/(if you pay in this many days), (else pay the full invoice amount in this many days).

B. The Credit Period

Credit period—the length of time before the borrower is supposed to pay.

Two components: *net credit period* and *cash discount period*

1. *Invoice date*—begins the credit period, usually the shipping or billing date.

   ROG—receipt of goods
   EOM—end-of-month (The invoice date is the end of the month for all sales.)
   Seasonal dating—invoice date corresponds to "season" of goods

2. *Length of the credit period* depends upon:

   -Buyer's inventory and operating cycle
   -Perishability and collateral value
   -Consumer demand
   -Cost, profitability and standardization
   -Credit risk
   -The size of the account
   -Competition
   -Customer type

T19.4: Length of the Credit Period

C. Cash Discounts

1. *Cost of credit*—the cost of not taking discounts offered

periodic rate = (discount %)/(100 − discount %)
APR = periodic rate × 365/(net period − discount period)
EAR = $(1 + \text{periodic rate}/100)^{365/(\text{net period} - \text{discount period})} - 1$

<u>Example: Cost of Foregone Discounts</u>

On terms of 1/15, net 45 the cost of foregone discounts (assuming payment in 45 days) is:

periodic rate $= 1/(100 - 1) = 1.01\%$
APR $= 1.01\% \times 365/(45 - 15) = 1.01\% \times 12.167 = 12.29\%$
EAR $= (1 + .0101)^{12.167} - 1 = 1.130 - 1 = .130$ or 13%

2. *Trade discounts*—unlike true discounts, these are not an inducement to early payment, but are the regular terms.

3. *The cash discount and the ACP*—offering discounts generally reduces the ACP as customers pay sooner. Whether or not receivables are also reduced depends upon the effect of the discount on the amount of credit sales as well as the ACP.

Lecture Tip, page 615: The instructor may have to stress that when a company does not take advantage of discount terms such as sales terms of 2/10, net 30, the company is effectively borrowing the invoice cost for 20 days at a 2 percent cost. Some students might suspect that since the company does not have to pay its bill for 30 days, the company secures the use of the funds for 30 days. The instructor should emphasize that it is the marginal time period for funds usage, not the total time period allowed before payment, that is relevant in determining the effective annual rate. Although this is heavily emphasized under Cost of the Credit, an added classroom comment may be helpful.

D. Credit Instruments—the evidence of indebtedness

Open account—transaction evidenced by invoice and recorded on the books.
Promissory note—an IOU used when some trouble in collecting is expected.
Commercial draft—*sight draft* (due on presentation), *time draft* (due at some date), *trade acceptance* (buyer "accepts" draft, i.e., promises to pay at a later date), *banker's acceptance* (bank accepts draft, i.e., promises to pay at a later date).

International Note, page 617: Various instruments have been developed to shift the risk of nonpayment of receivables in international transactions from the seller to a financial institution. In this context, the banker's acceptance described above is actually an irrevocable letter of credit issued by a bank guaranteeing payment of the face amount. A letter of credit, in turn, is simply a promise from the buyer's bank to make payment upon receipt of the goods by the buyer. The instructor should point out that, while these guarantee arrangements add to the cost of doing business, their existence greatly facilitates international trade.

19.3 ANALYZING CREDIT POLICY

A. Credit Policy Effects

1. *Revenue effects*—price and quantity sold may be increased.

T19.5: Credit Policy Effects

---

2. *Cost effects*—the cost of running a credit scheme and collecting receivables.
3. *The cost of debt*—firm must finance receivables.
4. *The probability of nonpayment*—always get paid if you sell for cash.
5. *The cash discount*—affects payment patterns and amounts.

B. Evaluating a Proposed Credit Policy

T19.6: Evaluating a Proposed Credit Policy

<u>Define:</u>

P = price per unit
v = variable cost per unit
Q = current quantity sold per period
Q' = new quantity expected to be sold
R = periodic required return (corresponds to the ACP)

The benefit of switching is change in cash flow, i.e., (new cash flow − old cash flow):

$$(P - v) \times Q' - (P - v) \times Q = (P - v) \times (Q' - Q)$$

The periodic benefit is the gross profit × change in quantity. The PV of switching is:

$$PV = [(P - v)(Q' - Q)]/R.$$

The cost of switching is the amount uncollected for the period + the additional variable costs of production:

$$Cost = PQ + v(Q' - Q)$$

Finally, the NPV of the switch is:

$$NPV = -[PQ + v(Q' - Q)] + (P - v)(Q' - Q)/R$$

1. *A break-even application*—what change in quantity would produce a $0 NPV?

$$Q' - Q = (PQ)/[(P - v)/R - v]$$

Lecture Tip, page 618: The instructor should mention that the process for determining the NPV of a credit policy switch is no different from the process for determining the NPV of a capital asset replacement or switch. The analysis involves a comparison of the marginal costs with the marginal benefits to be realized from the switch. If a company liberalizes credit terms, the present value of the marginal profit is compared to the immediate investment in a higher receivables balance. If a company tightens credit, lower sales should be expected. The present value of the reduction in profit is compared to the cash realized from the lower amount invested in receivables.

19.4 OPTIMAL CREDIT POLICY

In principle, an optimal credit policy is one under which incremental cash flows from sales are equal to incremental costs of carrying the increase in investment in accounts receivable.

A. The Total Credit Cost Curve

T19.7: The Costs of Granting Credit

Credit policy represents the trade-off between two kinds of costs:

Carrying costs:
-the required return on receivables
-the losses from bad debts
-the costs of managing credit and collections

Opportunity costs:
-potential profit from credit sales lost

19.5 CREDIT ANALYSIS

A. When Should Credit Be Granted?

1. *A One-Time Sale*
   Let π be the percentage of *new* customers who default
   $NPV = -v + (1 - \pi)P/(1 + R)$
   The firm risks $-v$ to gain P a period later.

2. *Repeat Business*
   $NPV = -v + (1 - \pi)(P - v)/R$

Lecture Tip, page 622: The instructor might initiate this section with a discussion of the credit card offerings many banks provide for students. The instructor could mention that the default risk may be higher among college students but the marginal benefit, at 18% to 21% interest charges on unpaid balances, justifies this decision for the bank. However, the bank controls this risk with lower credit limits for riskier customer classes and providing the student with a credit card while in college allows the bank to establish student loyalty to their card.

B. Credit Information

Some typical sources of credit information are:

1. Financial statements
2. Credit reports (i.e., Dun and Bradstreet report)
3. Banks
4. The customer's payment history

C. Credit Evaluation and Scoring

T19.8: The Five C's of Credit

<u>The five Cs of credit</u>

1. Character—willingness to pay
2. Capacity—ability to pay out of cash flows
3. Capital—financial reserves
4. Collateral—pledged assets
5. Conditions—economic conditions in customer's area, line

Lecture Tip, page 625: The instructor may wish to emphasize here that credit analysis contains both quantitative and qualitative aspects. As any loan officer will tell you, using the five Cs to evaluate a potential lender reflects both types of considerations. For example, capacity and capital are measured primarily by examination of the borrower's financial statements, while character is measured by both the borrower's prior credit history, as well as by the lender's (often highly unscientific) assessment of the borrower's integrity. Complicating the decision is that the most difficult C to assess, character, is often said to be the most important determinant of repayment. After all, if a borrower is <u>unwilling</u> to repay, what difference do the other characteristics make?

Credit scoring—assigning a numerical rating to customer to indicate creditworthiness.

Ethics Note, page 625: Initially suggested for use as a credit analysis tool in the early 1940s, credit scoring models of various types have been in widespread use since the 1960s. Over the same period, however, society has displayed greater to discrimination on the basis of race, gender, national origin, etc. As such, those using credit scoring models must be extremely careful to avoid constructing models which tend to unfairly reject (even unintentionally) members of various groups. Model users who fail to pay attention to such considerations are not only acting unethically, but may find themselves subject to lawsuits and/or financial penalties.

19.6 COLLECTION POLICY

A. Monitoring Receivables

Aging schedule—a breakdown of receivables accounts by age.

<u>Example:</u>

Age of Account	Amount outstanding	% of receivables
0 - 30 days	$ 67,550	85.39%
31 - 60 days	10,480	13.25%
Over 60 days	1,075	1.36%

Lecture Tip, page 627: Wilbur Lewellen and Robert Johnson demonstrate that two of the traditional receivables monitoring tools - the number of days' sales outstanding and the aging schedule - are influenced by the pattern of sales and may be misinterpreted by managers who are unaware of this effect. Fortunately, eliminating this problem is straightforward - according to Lewellen and Johnson, one need only employ balances outstanding as a percentage of the respective original sales which generated them. Their solution is discussed in more detail in "Better Way to Monitor Accounts Receivable," Harvard Business Review, *May-June 1972, pp. 101-109.*

B. Collection Effort

<u>Usual procedures for overdue accounts</u>:

1. Send delinquency letter
2. Call customer
3. Employ collection agency
4. Sue

19.7 INVENTORY MANAGEMENT

A. The Financial Manager and Inventory Policy

B. Inventory Types

For a manufacturer, inventory is classified into one of three categories
   -*raw material, work-in-progress and finished goods.*

Things to keep in mind:

1. Classification into category is a function of the nature of the firm's business.
2. Inventory types can be different in terms of their liquidity.
3. Demand for the first two categories of inventory is demand for finished goods.

C. Inventory Costs

There are two basic types of costs associated with current assets in general and inventory in particular: *carrying costs* and *shortage costs*.

19.8 INVENTORY MANAGEMENT TECHNIQUES

A. The ABC Approach

> **T19.9:   ABC Inventory Analysis (Fig. 19.3)**

B. The Economic Order Quantity (EOQ) Model

Lecture Tip, page 631:   The EOQ model assumes the firm's inventory is sold off at a steady rate until it hits zero. Firms with seasonal demand would experience a more difficult problem determining the optimal inventory level to maintain. In Section 19.6, "Collection Policy," the text states "Firms with seasonal sales will find the percentages on the aging schedule changing during the year." The instructor might ask students to consider the impact that heavy seasonal demand would have on the EOQ model. If the heavy demand is to last for two months, the formula might be adjusted to assume annual sales based on this high level of demand. Total unit sales per year, T, in the (T/Q) component of total restocking cost would increase, suggesting a larger Q to minimize restocking costs. However, as Q increases, the (T/Q) component of restocking costs falls but the (Q/2) component of carrying costs would rise. Thus, we are finding a new optimal order quantity by trading off these two costs. The instructor could also offer the students the basic intuition that if sales increase and no additional inventory is purchased, inventory turnover would increase and the students should remember that high levels of inventory turnover imply the danger of a stock-out. As a final note, when seasonal demand is low, T would be determined based on a monthly average of low sales. It should be emphasized that the EOQ model assumes a steady rate of sales throughout the year. If sales are not constant, an adjustment may have to be applied to the formula.

> **T19.10:   Costs of Holding Inventory (Fig. 19.4)**

EOQ—the quantity which minimizes the total cost associated with inventory carrying costs and restocking costs.

Assumption: firm's inventory is *depleted* at a steady pace.

Total carrying costs
$$= \text{Average inventory} \times \text{Carrying costs per unit}$$
$$= (Q/2) \times CC$$

> ### T19.11: Inventory Holdings for the Eyssell Corporation (Fig. 19.5)

Total restocking costs
    = Fixed cost per order × Number of orders
    = F × (T/Q)

Total costs
    = Carrying costs + Restocking costs
    = (Q/2) × CC + F × (T/Q)

$$EOQ = \sqrt{\frac{2T \times F}{CC}}$$

C. Extensions to the EOQ Model

While the EOQ tells the manager the optimal amount to reorder, the manager must also consider
    1. *safety stocks*—the minimum level of inventory a firm must keep on hand.
    2. *reorder points*—to allow for delivery time.

D. Managing Derived-Demand Inventories

1. Materials Requirements Planning
2. Just-in-Time Inventory

Lecture Tip, page 631: As noted in the text, the primary advantage of a JIT system is the reduction in inventory carrying costs which, for a large manufacturing firm, can be substantial. As with every financial decision, however, there is no increase in return without a commensurate increase in risk. In this instance, the risk is that an interruption in the supply of inventory items will require the user to shut down production virtually immediately. As part of a larger program to reduce costs, General Motors adopted a variant of the Just-in-Time system, but found it necessary to temporarily halt production of some models of automobiles in early 1994 as a result of labor strikes at suppliers' plants.

19.9 SUMMARY AND CONCLUSIONS

T19.12: **Solution to Problem 19.13**
T19.13: **Solution to Problem 19.18**
T19.14: **Solution to Problem 19.22**

APPENDIX 19A—MORE ON CREDIT POLICY ANALYSIS

A. Two Alternative Approaches

1. *The One-Shot Approach*

No switch cash flow: $(P - v)Q$
Switch cash flow: invest vQ' now, receive PQ' next period
Present value of switch net cash flow: $PQ'/(1 + R) - vQ'$

NPV = Switch net benefit − No switch cash flow = $[PQ'/(1 + R) - vQ'] - (P - v)Q$
If repeated every period, the firm gets the above NPV now and in every period, giving:

$$[PQ'/(1 + R) - vQ'] - (P - v)Q + \{[PQ'/(1 + R) - vQ'] - (P - v)Q\}/R$$

This reduces to: $-[PQ + v(Q' - Q)] + (P - v)(Q' - Q)/R$.

2. *The Accounts Receivable Approach*

Periodic benefit: $(P - v) \times (Q' - Q)$
Incremental investment in receivables: $PQ + v(Q' - Q)$
Carrying cost per period: $[PQ + v(Q' - Q)] \times R$
Net benefit per period: $(P - v) \times (Q' - Q) - \{[PQ + v(Q' - Q)] \times R\}$

NPV = $((P - v) \times (Q' - Q) - \{[PQ + v(Q' - Q)] \times R\})/R$

This reduces to: $-[PQ + v(Q' - Q)] + (P - v)(Q' - Q)/R$.

Example:
Suppose we had the following for Giffie International, which is considering a change from no credit to terms of net 20.

P = \$100
v = \$75
Q = 1,000
Q' = 1,050
R = 1.5% per 20 days

Using the original method:

$$NPV = -[PQ + v(Q' - Q)] + (P - v)(Q' - Q)/R$$
$$NPV = -[\$100 \times 1,000 + \$75(1,050 - 1,000)]$$
$$+ (\$100 - \$75)(1,050 - 1,000)/.015$$
$$NPV = -\$100,000 + \$3,750 + \$1,250/.015 = -\$103,750 + \$83,333.33$$
$$= -\$20,416.67$$

Using the one-shot approach:

$$NPV = [PQ'/(1+R) - vQ'] - (P - v)Q + \{[PQ'/(1+R) - vQ'] - (P - v)Q\}/R$$
$$NPV = [(\$100 \times 1,050)/1.015 - \$75 \times 1,050] - (\$100 - \$75) \times 1,000$$
$$+ \{[(\$100 \times 1,050)/1.015 - \$75 \times 1,050] - (\$100 - \$75) \times 1,000\}/.015$$
$$NPV = [\$103,448.28 - \$78,750] - \$25,000 + \{[\$103,448.28 - \$78,750]$$
$$- \$78,750 - \$25,000\}/.015 = -301.72 - \$20,114.94$$
$$= -\$20,416.66$$

Using the accounts receivable approach:

$$NPV = ((P - v) \times (Q' - Q) - \{[PQ + v(Q' - Q)] \times R\})/R$$
$$NPV = ((\$100 - \$75) \times (1,050 - 1,000) - \{[\$100 \times 1,000 + \$75(1,050 - 1,000)]$$
$$\times .015\})/.015$$
$$= (\$1,250 - \{[\$100,000 + \$3,750] \times .015\})/.015 = (\$1,250$$
$$- \$1,556.25)/.015$$
$$= -\$20,416.66$$

To break even, Giffie needs $(PQ)/[(P - v)/R - v] = 63$ additional units.

B. Discounts and Default Risk

Define:
- π = percentage of credit sales that go uncollected
- d = percentage discount allowed for cash customers
- P' = credit price (no-discount price)
- P = cash price = $P'(1 - d)$

Assume no change in Q, then:

Net incremental cash flow = $[(1 - \pi)P' - v] \times Q - (P - v) \times Q = P'Q \times (d - \pi)$

$$NPV = -PQ + P'Q \times (d - \pi)/R$$

A break-even application: $\pi = d - R \times (1 - d)$ is the break-even default rate.

CHAPTER 20
MERGERS AND ACQUISITIONS

TRANSPARENCIES

T20.1: **Chapter Outline**
T20.2: **The Mechanics of Mergers and Acquisitions**
T20.3: **A Note on Takeovers**
T20.4: **Ten Largest Mergers, Acquisitions, and LBOs**
T20.5: **Reasons for Mergers and Acquisitions**
T20.6: **Acquisitions and EPS Growth**
T20.7: **Defensive Tactics**
T20.8: **Adoption of a Share Rights Plan (SRP) (Fig. 20.1)**
T20.9: **Evidence on Acquisitions**
T20.10: **Solution to Problem 20.2**
T20.11: **Solution to Problem 20.9**

CHAPTER ORGANIZATION

T20.1: Chapter Outline

20.1 THE LEGAL FORMS OF ACQUISITIONS
Merger or Consolidation
Acquisition of Stock
Acquisition of Assets
Acquisition Classifications
A Note on Takeovers

20.2 TAXES AND ACQUISITIONS
Determinants of Tax Status
Taxable versus Tax-Free Acquisition

20.3 ACCOUNTING FOR ACQUISITIONS
The Purchase Method
Pooling of Interests
Which is Better: Purchase or Pooling of Interests?

20.4 GAINS FROM ACQUISITIONS

Synergy
Revenue Enhancement
Cost Reductions
Tax Gains
Changing Capital Requirements
Avoiding Mistakes
A Note on Inefficient Management

20.5 SOME FINANCIAL SIDE EFFECTS OF ACQUISITIONS

EPS Growth
Diversification

20.6 THE COST OF AN ACQUISITION

Case I: Cash Acquisition
Case II: Stock Acquisition
Cash versus Common Stock

20.7 DEFENSIVE TACTICS

The Corporate Charter
Repurchase/Standstill Agreements
Exclusionary Self-Tenders
Poison Pills and Share Rights Plans
Going Private and Leveraged Buyouts
Other Devices and Jargon of Corporate Takeovers

20.8 SOME EVIDENCE ON ACQUISITIONS

20.9 SUMMARY AND CONCLUSIONS

ANNOTATED CHAPTER OUTLINE

20.1 THE LEGAL FORMS OF ACQUISITIONS

Bidder—the company making an offering to buy the stock or assets of another firm.

Target firm—the firm that is being sought.

Consideration—cash or securities offered in an acquisition or merger.

T20.2: The Mechanics of Mergers and Acquisitions

A. Merger or Consolidation

The difference between merger and consolidation is whether or not a new firm is created.

Merger—the complete absorption of one company by another (assets and liabilities). The bidder remains, the target ceases to exist.

Consolidation—a new firm is created. The joined firms cease their previous existence.

Advantages
Legally simple and relatively cheap.

Disadvantages
Must be approved by a majority vote of the shareholders of both firms, usually requiring the cooperation of both managements.

Lecture Tip, page 654: The instructor may wish to mention the recent ruling by the Delaware Chancery Court concerning the merger between Time and Warner. (Refer to lecture tips provided in IM Section 1.4.) The court ruled that the firms' directors could pursue merger talks and avoid shareholder approval, even though Time's shareholders might prefer the immediate gains offered by rival Paramount's cash bid.

B. Acquisition of Stock

Taking control by buying the voting stock of another firm with cash, securities, or both.

Tender offer—offer by one firm or individual to buy shares in another firm from any shareholder. Such deals are often contingent on the bidder obtaining a minimum percentage of the shares, otherwise no go.

Some factors involved in choosing between a tender offer and a merger:

1. No shareholder vote is required for a tender offer. Shareholders either sell or don't.
2. Tender offer bypasses the board and management of target.
3. In unfriendly combinations, a tender offer may be a way around unwilling managers.
4. In a tender offer, if the bidder ends up with less than 80% of the target's stock, it must pay taxes on any dividends paid by the target.
5. Complete absorption requires a merger. A tender offer is often the first step toward a formal merger.

Lecture Tip, page 654: The instructor may wish to add that an acquiring firm's management will typically seek prior approval from the target firm's management. If the target management refuses to grant its approval of the takeover bid, the acquiring firm may appeal directly to the target firm's shareholders. This is referred to as a hostile takeover and, should the takeover prove successful, the hostile takeover typically results in a replacement of the non-cooperating target management team. In approximately 50 percent of takeovers, a negotiated agreement between acquiring and target management had been accomplished, resulting in a friendly takeover.

C. Acquisition of Assets

In an acquisition of assets, one firm buys most or all of another's assets; liabilities aren't involved as in a merger. Transferring titles can make the process costly. Selling firm may remain in business.

D. Acquisition Classifications

1. *Horizontal acquisition*—firms in the same industry.
2. *Vertical acquisition*—firms at different steps in the production process.
3. *Conglomerate acquisition*—firms in unrelated industries.

Lecture Tip, page 655: The instructor could mention some acquisitions during the 1980s and ask the class to consider how the acquisition would be classified. The instructor might provide an example of Phillip Morris and its acquisition of Miller, General Foods, Kraft Foods, etc. Some students might argue that these product lines might relate to food retailing and the acquisitions would be horizontal acquisitions. U.S. Steel's acquisition of Marathon Oil in the early 1980s would be an example of a conglomerate acquisition. A possible example of a vertical (although it may be argued this acquisition could be considered a horizontal acquisition) would be Texaco (with excess refining capacity) and its acquisition of Getty Oil, which owned significant oil reserves.

E. A Note on Takeovers

Lecture Tip, page 656: The popularity of proxy contests as a means of gaining control has waxed and waned over the last four decades. In the 1950s, this approach was a relatively popular means of removing target firm management; those who initiated proxy contests were even referred to in the popular press as "corporate raiders"!

Tender offers came to the fore in the 1960s and 1970s. Some believe that the use of the proxy battle waned because of its relatively high cost and low probability of success. However, the ubiquity of takeover defenses and regulatory constraints has contributed to return to importance of this form of control struggle. As this note is written (March, 1993), General Electric is waging a hostile bid for control of Kemper Financial Services via proxy contest.

T20.3: A Note on Takeovers

Three means to gain control of a firm:
1. *Acquisitions*—merger or consolidation, tender offer, acquisition of assets.
2. *Proxy contests*—gaining control by electing the board of directors using proxies.
3. *Going private*—shares are all purchased by a small group of investors.
4. *Leveraged buyouts (LBOs)*—going private with borrowed money.

> ### T20.4: Ten Largest Mergers, Acquisitions, and LBOs

Lecture Tip, page 657: Just as the period of the late 1960s has been characterized as the "go-go" years of conglomeration, and the 1980s as the era of the "corporate buccaneer" and the "financially driven breakup deal", takeovers in the 1990s are characterized as "deals that basically reflect underlying strategic decisions" according to Felix Rohatyn, a general partner at Lazard, Freres & Company. Industry restructuring in response to a changing economic climate is the motive for Northrop's bid for Grumman, while the $5.5 billion merger of Columbia Healthcare Corporation and HCA-Hospital Corporation of America exemplifies the response to anticipated changes in the political climate. Bell-Atlantic's attempt to acquire Tele-Communications Inc. (later cancelled) is representative of several technology-driven combinations in the telecommunications industry.

20.2 TAXES AND ACQUISITIONS

A. Determinants of Tax Status

Tax-free—acquisition must be for a business purpose, and there must be a continuity of equity interest.
Taxable—if cash or a security other than stock is used, the acquisition is taxable.

B. Taxable versus Tax-Free Acquisition

Capital gains effect—if taxable, target's shareholders may end up paying capital gains taxes, driving up the cost of acquisition.

Write-up effect—if taxable, the target's assets may be revalued, i.e., written up, and depreciation increased. However, the Tax Reform Act of 1986 made the write up a taxable gain, making the process less attractive.

20.3 ACCOUNTING FOR ACQUISITIONS

Despite accounting differences, no cash flow effects from choice.

A. The Purchase Method

Target's assets are reported at fair market value on the bidder's books. The difference between the assets' market value and the acquisition price is *goodwill*.

<u>Example:</u>

Firm X borrows $10 million to acquire Firm Y, creating Firm XY.

Balance sheets (in millions) prior to the acquisition:

Firm X				Firm Y			
Working capital	$ 2	Equity	$20	Working capital	$ 1	Equity	$ 6
Fixed assets	18	Debt	0	Fixed assets	5	Debt	0
Total	$20	Total	$20	Total	$ 6	Total	$ 6

Firm Y's fixed assets have a fair market value of $8 million, total assets are $9 million.

Balance sheet after the acquisition:

Firm XY			
Working capital	$ 3	Equity	$20
Fixed assets	26	Debt	10
Goodwill	1		
Total	$30	Total	$30

B. Pooling of Interests

The balance sheets are added together, and the new firm is owned jointly by all the shareholders of the previously separate firms.

C. Which is Better: Purchase or Pooling of Interests?

The goodwill created by a purchase must be amortized. Similar to depreciation, it is a non-cash expense. Unlike depreciation, amortized goodwill is not tax-deductible. Thus, reported earnings (not cash flow) are lower than those under pooling. Also, the write-up of assets reduces ROA.

Lecture Tip, page 660: The American Institute of Certified Public Accountants' Accounting Principles Board (APB) Opinion 16 offers guidelines on classifying a merger as a purchase or pooling. To be treated as a pooling of interest, the merger must meet tests such as a requirement that the stockholders of the acquired firm maintain an ownership position in the combined firm and only common stock can be issued by the acquirer. The instructor is advised to refer to APB Opinion 16 for more information concerning the conditions for classifying an acquisition as a purchase or pooling.

20.4 GAINS FROM ACQUISITIONS

A. Synergy

The difference between the value of the combined firms and the sum of the values of the

T20.5:   Reasons for Mergers and Acquisitions

individual firms is the incremental net gain, $\Delta V = V_{AB} - (V_A + V_B)$.

If the value of the whole exceeds the sum of the parts, $V_{AB} > V_A + V_B$; i.e., $\Delta V > 0$ is called *synergy*.

The value of Firm B to Firm A $= V_B^* = \Delta V + V_B$. V_B^* will be greater than V_B if the acquisition produces positive incremental cash flows, ΔCF.

$\Delta CF = \Delta EBIT + \Delta Depreciation - \Delta Taxes - \Delta Capital\ requirements$

$= \Delta Revenue - \Delta Costs - \Delta Taxes - \Delta Capital\ requirements$

Lecture Tip, page 661: The instructor may wish to provide a few examples of synergies that may be realized from merger. From an operational standpoint, the merger may result in better utilization of capacity that may not be available in the short run, such as the Getty acquisition by Texaco discussed in a previous lecture tip. From a financial standpoint, the merger may provide economies of scale in flotation costs, better access to financial markets, or, should the cash flows of the two firms be less than perfectly correlated, the probability of, and costs associated with, financial distress or bankruptcy may be lowered.

B. Revenue Enhancement

1. *Marketing gains*—changes in advertising efforts, changes in the distribution network, changes in product mix.
2. *Strategic benefits (beachheads)*—acquisitions that allow a firm to enter a new industry which may become the platform for further expansion.
3. *Market power*—reduction in competition or increase in market share.

C. Cost Reductions

1. *Economies of scale*—per unit costs decline with increasing output.
2. *Economies of vertical integration*—coordinating closely related activities, technology transfers.
3. *Complementary resources (economies of scope)*—example: banks that allow insurance or stock brokerage services to be sold on premises.

D. Lower Taxes

1. *Net operating losses*—a firm with losses and not paying taxes is attractive to a firm with significant tax liabilities.
   -Carry-back and carry-forward provisions reduce incentive to merge
   -IRS may disallow or restrict use of NOL (see Lecture Tip below)

2. *Unused debt capacity*—adding debt can provide important tax savings.
3. *Surplus funds*—firms with significant free cash flow can:
 -pay dividends
 -buy back shares
 -acquire shares or assets of another firm

Lecture Tip, page 664: The IRS requires that the merger must have a justifiable business purposes for the NOL carry-over to be allowed. Additionally, if the acquisition involves cash payment to the target firm's shareholders, the acquisition is considered a taxable reorganization which results in a loss of NOLs. NOL carry-overs are allowed in tax-free reorganizations which involve an exchange of the acquiring firm's common stock for the acquired firm's common stock. Additionally, if the target firm operates as a separate subsidiary within the acquiring firm's organization, the IRS would allow the carry-over to shelter the subsidiary's future earnings but not the acquired firm's future earnings.

E. Reductions in Capital Requirements

-A firm needing capacity might acquire a firm with excess capacity rather than build new.
-Possible advantages to raising capital given economies of scale in issuing securities.
-It may reduce the investment in working capital.

F. Avoiding Mistakes

Do not ignore market values. Use as a starting point and ask, "What will change?"
Estimate only incremental cash flows. These are the basis for synergy.
Use the correct discount rate. Use the rate appropriate to the risk of the cash flows.
Be aware of transactions costs. These may be substantial, including fees to investment bankers and lawyers, and disclosure costs.

G. A Note on Inefficient Management

If management isn't doing its job, or others may simply do the job better, acquisitions are one way to replace management. Beyond the actual replacement of managers, the *threat of takeover* serves to discipline managers.

Lecture Tip, page 666: One of the fathers of modern takeover theory is Henry Manne, who published "Mergers and the Market for Corporate Control" in 1965. In this seminal work, Manne proposes the (now-commonly accepted) notion that poorly run firms are natural takeover targets because their market values will be depressed, permitting acquirers to earn large returns by running the firms successfully. This proposition has been verified empirically in dozens of academic studies over the last two decades.
*   The instructor may wish to employ Jensen's definition of the market for corporate control: "the market in which competing managerial teams compete for the right to manage corporate resources", and use statistics provided in his survey paper, as well as the follow-up by G. Jarrell, J. Brickley, and J. Netter. (See "The Market for Corporate Control: The Scientific Evidence", Journal of Financial Economics, vol. 11, April 1983, pp. 5-50, and "The Market for Corporate Control: The Evidence Since 1980", Journal of Economic Perspectives, vol. 2, Winter 1988, pp. 49-68.)*

20.5 SOME FINANCIAL SIDE EFFECTS OF ACQUISITIONS

A. EPS Growth

T20.6:   Acquisitions and EPS Growth

An acquisition may give the appearance of growth in EPS without actually changing cash flows. This happens when the bidder's stock sells for more than the target's, so that fewer shares are outstanding after the acquisition than before.

Example:

Pizza Shack wants to merge with Checkers Pizza. The merger won't create any additional value, so assuming the market isn't fooled, the new firm, Stop 'n Go Pizza, will be valued at the sum of the separate market values of the firms.

Stop 'n Go, valued at $1,875,000, is to have 125,000 shares outstanding at $15 each. 100,000 shares go to Pizza Shack stockholders and 25,000 shares go to Checkers Pizza stockholders.

Before and after merger financial positions

	Pizza Shack	Checkers Pizza	Stop 'n Go Pizza
Earnings per share	$ 1.50	$ 1.50	$1.80
Price per share	15.00	7.50	15.00
Price-earnings ratio	10	5	8.33
Number of shares	100,000	50,000	125,000
Total earnings	$ 150,000	$ 75,000	$ 225,000
Total value	$1,500,000	$ 375,000	$1,875,000

B. Diversification

A firm's attempt at diversification does not create value because stockholders could buy the stock of both firms. Firms cannot reduce their systematic risk by merging.

Lecture Tip, page 668: In earlier chapters, we pointed out that, in any publicly-held corporation, conflicts of interest will exist between the owners (stockholders) and the managers. As noted above, diversification-based mergers don't create value for shareholders; however, diversification-based mergers may reduce increase sales and reduce the total variability of firm cash flows. If managerial compensation and/or prestige is related to firm size, or if less variable cash flows reduce the likelihood of managerial replacement, then some mergers may be initiated for the wrong reasons - i.e., they will be in the interests of managers but not of stockholders.

20.6 THE COST OF AN ACQUISITION

The NPV of a merger is: $\text{NPV} = V_B^* - \text{Cost to Firm A of the acquisition,}$
where $V_B^* = \Delta V + V_B$.

Merger premium—amount paid above the stand-alone value.

Reconsider Pizza Shack's merger with Checkers Pizza. Suppose Shack acquires Checkers in a buyout. Shack has estimated the incremental value of the acquisition, ΔV, to be \$75,000. The value of Checkers to Shack is $V_C^* = \Delta V + V_C = \$75,000 + \$375,000 = \$450,000$. The Checker's stockholders are willing to sell for \$400,000. Thus the merger premium is \$25,000.

A. Case I: Cash Acquisition

Suppose Shack pays Checkers shareholders \$400,000 in cash.
$\text{NPV} = V_C^* - \text{Cost to Shack of the acquisition} = \$450,000 - \$400,000 = \$50,000$
The value of the combined firms becomes :
$V_S = V_S + (V_C^* - \text{Cost}) = \$1,500,000 + \$50,000 = \$1,550,000$
With 100,000 shares outstanding, the price per share becomes \$15.50.

B. Case II: Stock Acquisition

Suppose that instead of cash, Shack gives Checkers stockholders Shack stock at \$15 per share totaling \$400,000. Checkers shareholders end up with 26,667 (rounded) shares. The new firm will have 126,667 shares outstanding, a value of $V_S + V_C + \Delta V = \$1,950,000$, and the price per share is \$15.39.

The total consideration is 26,667 × \$15.39 = \$410,405.13. The extra \$10,405.13 comes from allowing Checkers holders proportional participation in the \$50,000 NPV.

C. Cash versus Common Stock

1. *Sharing gains.* When cash is used, the target's shareholders can't gain beyond the purchase price. Of course, they can't fall below either.
2. *Taxes.* Cash transactions are generally taxable, exchanging stock is generally tax-free.
3. *Control.* Using stock may have implications for control of the merged firm.

Lecture Tip, page 670: The instructor may add that the logic in determining the NPV of an acquisition is identical to that used in establishing the NPV of a project. However, some financial theorists argue that acquisitions reflect a "winner's curse." The argument is that the winner of an acquisition contest is that firm which (most) overestimates the true value of the target. As such, this bid is most likely to be excessive. For a more detailed discussion of the "winner's curse," see Nik Varaiya and Kenneth Ferris, "Overpaying in Corporate Takeovers: The Winner's Curse," *Financial Analysts Journal, 1987, vol. 43, no. 3. Richard Roll, in* "The Hubris Hypothesis of Corporate Takeovers" *(Journal of Business, 1986, vol. 59, no. 2 attributed the rationale for this behavior to hubris; i.e., the excessive arrogance or greed of management.*

20.7 DEFENSIVE TACTICS

T20.7: Defensive Tactics

A. The Corporate Charter

-Usually, 67% of shareholders must approve a merger. *Supermajority amendment* requires 80% or more to approve merger.
-Also, staggered terms for board members can hinder takeovers or mergers.

B. Repurchase/Standstill Agreements

Getting the bidder to agree to back off (standstill), usually by buying the bidder's stock back at a substantial premium *(targeted repurchase)*, also called *greenmail*.

Case: Ashland Oil buys off Belzbergs of Canada in a targeted repurchase. Also, established employee stock ownership plan (ESOP) with 27% of outstanding shares, and had earlier adopted a supermajority provision.

C. Exclusionary Self-Tenders

The opposite of a targeted repurchase, a tender offer for stock excluding targeted holders.

Case: Unocal made a tender offer for 29% of its shares at $26 a share *over* market price while excluding largest shareholder, Mesa Partners II (led by T. Boone Pickens).

D. Poison Pills and Share Rights Plans

T20.8: Adoption of a Share Rights Plan (SRP) (Fig. 20.1)

In a share rights plan, the firm distributes rights to purchase stock at a fixed price to existing shareholders. These can't be detached and sold or traded, can be bought back by the firm, and they can't be exercised until "triggered." Usually triggered when someone makes a tender offer.

Flip-over provision—the "poison" in the pill. Effectively, target firm's shareholders get to buy stock in the merged firm at half price.

E. Going Private and Leveraged Buyouts

Can prevent takeovers from management's point of view.

F. Other Devices and Jargon of Corporate Takeovers

1. *Golden parachutes*—compensation to top-level management in the event of a takeover.
2. *Poison puts*—forces the firm to buy stock back at a set price.
3. *Crown jewels*—a "scorched earth" strategy of threatening to sell major assets.
4. *White knights*—target of unfriendly takeover hopes to find friendly firm, white knight, to buy a large block of stock, often on favorable terms, to halt the takeover.
5. *Lockups*—option granted to friendly party (white knight) giving the right to buy stock or major assets (*crown jewels*) at a fixed price in the event of an unfriendly takeover.

Ethics Note, page 675: *In* The Law and Finance of Corporate Insider Trading: Theory and Evidence, *(Kluwer Publishing, 1993) Arshadi and Eyssell argue that an active market for corporate control will be characterized by increases in the nature and complexity of defensive tactics and by an increasing volume of pre-announcement insider trading. In the case of the former, managers facing an environment which is (from their point-of-view) increasingly hostile, will seek to defend themselves and their positions. Defensive tactics will be implemented, tested by takeover bids and in the courts, and modified.*

Trading on nonpublic information has been shown in numerous academic studies to be extremely profitable (albeit illegal); thus our earlier conclusion that financial markets are not strong-form efficient. In the case of takeover bids, insider trading is argued to be particularly endemic, because of the large potential profits involved, and because of the relatively large number of people "in on the secret". Managers, employees, investment bankers, attorneys, and financial printers have all been accused in noted takeover-related insider trading cases in the 1980s.

Anecdotal evidence of the pervasiveness of takeover-related insider trading is found in the allegations of "unusual" run-ups in the price of Grumman's stock just prior to Northrop's 1994 takeover bid. This is all the more remarkable when one considers the scope and severity of the anti-insider trading legislation enacted in the 1980s.

20.8 SOME EVIDENCE ON ACQUISITIONS

> **T20.9: Evidence on Acquisitions**

Available evidence suggests target shareholders make significant gains. The gains are larger in tender offers than in mergers. On the other hand, bidder shareholders earn comparatively little, breaking even on mergers, and making a couple of percent on tender offers.

20.9 SUMMARY AND CONCLUSIONS

> **T20.10:   Solution to Problem 20.2**
> **T20.11:   Solution to Problem 20.9**

CHAPTER 21
INTERNATIONAL CORPORATE FINANCE

TRANSPARENCIES

T21.1: Chapter Outline
T21.2: International Finance Terminology
T21.3: Global Capital Markets
T21.4: International Currency Symbols (Table 21.1)
T21.5: Exchange Rate Quotations (Table 21.2)
T21.6: Triangle Arbitrage
T21.7: Prime Rates in Selected Countries
T21.8: International Capital Budgeting: An Example
T21.9: Solution to Problem 21.3
T21.10: Solution to Problem 21.11
T21.11: Solution to Problem 21.13

CHAPTER ORGANIZATION

T21.1: Chapter Outline

21.1 TERMINOLOGY

21.2 FOREIGN EXCHANGE MARKETS AND EXCHANGE RATES
Exchange Rates
Types of Transactions

21.3 PURCHASING POWER PARITY
Absolute Purchasing Power Parity
Relative Purchasing Power Parity

21.4 INTEREST RATE PARITY, UNBIASED FORWARD RATES, AND THE INTERNATIONAL FISHER EFFECT
Covered Interest Arbitrage
Interest Rate Parity (IRP)
Forward Rates and Future Spot Rates
Putting It All Together

21.5 INTERNATIONAL CAPITAL BUDGETING
Method 1: The Home Currency Approach
Method 2: The Foreign Currency Approach
Unremitted Cash Flows

21.6 EXCHANGE RATE RISK
Short-Run Exposure
Long-Run Exposure
Translation Exposure
Managing Exchange Rate Risk

21.7 POLITICAL RISK

21.8 SUMMARY AND CONCLUSIONS

ANNOTATED CHAPTER OUTLINE

21.1 TERMINOLOGY

> **T21.2: International Finance Terminology**

American Depository Receipt (ADR)—security issued in the U.S. representing shares of a foreign stock and allowing that stock to be traded in the U.S.

Cross-rate—implicit exchange rate between two currencies quoted in a third currency (usually the U.S. dollar).

European Currency Unit (ECU)—index of 10 European currencies intended to serve as a monetary unit for the European Monetary System.

Eurobond—bonds issued in many countries but denominated in a single currency.

Eurocurrency—money deposited outside the country whose currency is involved.

Eurodollars—U.S. dollars deposited in banks outside the U.S. banking system.

Foreign bonds—bonds issued in a single country, denominated in that country's currency, but not issued by a domestic firm. Nearly half are issued in Switzerland.

Gilts—British and Irish government securities.

LIBOR (London Interbank Offer Rate)—rate most international banks charge one another for overnight Eurodollar loans.

Swaps—agreements to exchange securities, currencies, or even commodities.

> **T21.3:　Global Capital Markets**

> **Lecture Tip, page 687:** *The instructor might emphasize that Eurodollars are, as the text states, "deposits of U.S. dollars in banks located outside the United States." However, the instructor should emphasize that Eurodollars are not actual U.S. currencies deposited in a bank but are bookkeeping entries on a bank's ledger. These deposits are loaned to the Eurobank's U.S. affiliate to meet liquidity needs, or the funds might be loaned to a corporation abroad that needs the loan denominated in U.S. dollars. Money does not normally leave the country of its origination; merely the ownership is transferred to another country.*
>
> *The instructor might add that a dollar-denominated Eurobond is free of exchange rate risk for a U.S. investor, regardless of where it is issued. A foreign bond would be subject to this risk if it is not issued in the U.S. The reason is that the Eurodollar bond would pay interest in U.S. dollars, but the foreign bond would pay interest in the currency of the country in which it was issued.*

21.2 FOREIGN EXCHANGE MARKETS AND EXCHANGE RATES

Foreign exchange market—market for exchanging different country's currencies.

> **T21.4:　International Currency Symbols (Table 21.1)**

A. Exchange Rates

> **T21.5:　Exchange Rate Quotations (Table 21.2)**

In practice, almost all trading of currencies is with prices quoted in U.S. dollars.

Direct or American quote—number of U.S. dollars to buy one unit of a foreign currency. *Indirect or European exchange rate*—amount of foreign currency per U.S. dollar.

Example: Exchange Rate Quotations

The quotations in T21.5 show that it takes .8449 U.S. dollars trade for one Canadian dollar, and conversely, 1.1835 Canadian dollars trade for one U.S. dollar. That is, $100 U.S. gets you $118.35 Canadian, and $100 Canadian fetches $84.49 American.

Cross-Rates and Triangle Arbitrage Implicit in exchange rate quotations is an exchange rate between non-U.S. currencies. For there to be no arbitrage opportunities, the exchange rate between two non-U.S. currencies must equal the cross-rate. That is, (Currency 1 indirect quote)/(Currency 2 indirect quote) equals Currency 1 per unit Currency 2.

T21.6: Triangle Arbitrage

Example: Triangle Arbitrage

Suppose the indirect quote on the Japanese Yen (Currency 1) is 133.90 and the indirect quote on the South Korean Won (Currency 2) is 666.00. If the exchange rate is .1750 Yen per Won, does an arbitrage opportunity exist?

Yes. The no-arbitrage cross-rate is (133.90/666) = .20105 Yen per Won. So the Won is cheaper in Yen than in dollars. To make an arbitrage profit, first buy Yen with dollars, say ¥133900 for $1,000 U.S. Next, trade the Yen for 765,142.86 Won. Finally, trade the Won for $1,148.86 U.S. for a quick $148.86 profit.

In general:

If the exchange rate (Currency 1 per Currency 2) is less than the implied cross-rate (Currency 1 indirect quote)/(Currency 2 indirect quote), then buy Currency 1 with dollars, trade Currency 1 for Currency 2, trade Currency 2 for dollars.

If the exchange rate (Currency 1 per Currency 2) is above the implied cross-rate (Currency 1 indirect quote)/(Currency 2 indirect quote), then buy Currency 2 with dollars, trade Currency 2 for Currency 1, trade Currency 1 for dollars.

Lecture Tip, page 690: The opportunity to exploit a triangle arbitrage may appear an easy opportunity to make quick, riskless profit for the student. The instructor should mention that inequities among currency rates are slight and quickly driven to equilibrium by professional traders. For small investors, transaction costs would significantly reduce any profit realized from the triangle arbitrage.

B. Types of Transactions

Spot trade—exchange of currencies based upon current quotes (*spot exchange rate*).

Forward trade—agreement for an exchange in the future at the *forward exchange rate*. If the direct quote forward exchange rate is higher than the spot rate, the currency is selling at a *premium*; if lower, at a *discount*.

21.3 PURCHASING POWER PARITY

A. Absolute Purchasing Power Parity (PPP)

Absolute PPP states that a commodity should sell for the same real price regardless of the currency used to purchase it.

Let S_0 be the spot exchange rate (indirect quote) between a currency and the U.S. dollar at time 0. Let P_F be the foreign price of a commodity, and P_{US} be the U.S. price. Absolute PPP states:

$$P_F = S_0 \times P_{US}$$

Because of product differences, barriers to trade, tariffs, and transportation costs, absolute PPP tends to hold only for traded commodities with low transfer costs.

<u>Example: Gold</u>

Gold is a commodity that is easily traded by receipt. If gold is selling for £195 in London, and the spot rate between pounds and dollars is .5940, what price is gold likely to sell for in New York? Rearranging $P_F = S_0 \times P_{US}$ gives $P_{US} = (P_F/S_0) = $ (£195/.5940) = \$328.28.

B. Relative Purchasing Power Parity

The *change* in the exchange rate is determined by the difference in the inflation rates between two countries.

$S_0 = $ Current indirect quote spot exchange rate

$E[S_t] = $ Expected exchange rate in t periods

$h_{US} = $ Inflation rate (expected) in the U.S.

$h_F = $ Foreign country inflation rate (expected)

In general, relative PPP states the expected exchange rate t periods hence is about:

$$E[S_t] = S_0 \times [1 + (h_F - h_{US})]^t$$

<u>Currency Appreciation and Depreciation</u>—Statements such as "the dollar was stronger today" are made from the perspective of an indirect quote exchange rate. That is, a stronger dollar means more of a foreign currency is needed to buy one U.S. dollar and vice-versa for a "weaker" dollar.

Lecture Tip, page 694: When asked, "Which is better; a stronger dollar or a weaker dollar?," most students answer a stronger one. While this makes imports relatively cheaper, it makes U.S. exports relatively more expensive. In general, consumers like a stronger dollar and producers (especially exporters) a weaker one. In any event, the U.S. government has expended considerable resources in recent times to make the dollar cheaper against the yen in an effort to reduce the U.S. trade deficit with Japan.

Lecture Tip, page 695: The issue of relative PPP may be reinforced by having the students consider a product that sells in both England and the United States at identical relative prices; i.e., with a $1 to .5 pound relationship, the product would sell for $1 in the United States and .5 pounds in England. If the inflation rate is 4 percent per year in the U.S., the product would cost $1.04 in one year.

However, if, in England, inflation is expected to average 10 percent per year, the product would cost .55 pounds in one year. The student should recognize that, if they received $1.04 aftertax from an investment, they would be able to purchase the product in the United States but, if the currency rate remained at $1 to .5 pounds, they would not be able to purchase the product in England one year later since converting $1.04 to pounds would yield .52 pounds, leaving the U.S. purchaser .03 pounds short of the required price of the product in England.

Thus, to maintain parity, the dollar should rise in value (purchase more than .5 pounds in the future) to maintain relative PPP. The instructor may wish to use this simplified example to introduce the International Fisher Effect in Section 22.4.

21.4 INTEREST RATE PARITY, UNBIASED FORWARD RATES, AND THE INTERNATIONAL FISHER EFFECT

F_t = Forward exchange rate for settlement at time t

R_{US} = U.S. nominal risk-free interest rate

R_F = Foreign country nominal risk-free interest rate

A. Covered Interest Arbitrage

A covered interest arbitrage exists when an arbitrage profit can be made by converting dollars into a foreign currency, investing at that country's interest rate, taking a forward contract to convert the foreign currency back into U.S. dollars for more than could earned than by directly investing at the U.S. nominal rate. The foreign investment yields a total of $S_0 \times (1+R_F)/F_1$ per dollar. If this is greater than the U.S. yield of $(1 + R_{US})$ per dollar, an arbitrage opportunity exists.

B. Interest Rate Parity (IRP)

To prevent covered interest arbitrage, $S_0 \times (1 + R_F)/F_1 = (1 + R_{US})$ must hold. Rearranging terms gives the *interest rate parity (IRP)* condition:

$$F_1/S_0 = (1 + R_F)/(1 + R_{US}).$$

> ### T21.7: Prime Rates in Selected Countries

Useful approximations:

$$(F_1 - S_0)/S_0 = R_F - R_{US}$$

and $F_t = S_0 \times [1 + (R_F - R_{US})]^t$.

Loosely, IRP says the difference in interest rates between two countries is just offset by the change in the relative value of the currencies.

Example:
Suppose the French Franc spot rate (indirect quote) is 6.3800. If $R_F = 6\%$ and $R_{US} = 8\%$, what F_1 will prevent covered interest rate arbitrage?

$$6.3800 \times [1 + (.06 - .08)] = FF\ 6.2524$$

C. Forward Rates and Future Spot Rates

Unbiased forward rates (UFR)—states the forward rate, F_t, is equal to the *expected* future spot rate, $E[S_t]$. That is, on average, forward rates neither consistently understate nor overstate the future spot rate. That is, $F_t = E[S_t]$.

D. Putting It All Together

PPP: $E[S_1] = S_0 \times [1 + (h_F - h_{US})]$

IRP: $F_1 = S_0 \times [1 + (R_F - R_{US})]$

UFR: $F_1 = E[S_1]$

Uncovered interest parity (UIP)—combining UFR and IRP gives:

$$E[S_1] = S_0 \times [1 + (R_F - R_{US})] \text{ and } E[S_t] = S_0 \times [1 + (R_F - R_{US})]^t$$

The International Fisher Effect—combining PPP and UIP gives:

$$S_0 \times [1 + (h_F - h_{US})] = S_0 \times [1 + (R_F - R_{US})]$$

so that: $h_F - h_{US} = R_F - R_{US}$

And

$$R_{US} - h_{US} = R_F - h_F.$$

The IFE says that *real* rates must be equal across countries.

21.5 INTERNATIONAL CAPITAL BUDGETING

A. Method 1: The Home Currency Approach

This method involves converting foreign cash flows into dollars and finding the NPV.

B. Method 2: The Foreign Currency Approach

In this approach, we determine the comparable foreign discount rate, find the NPV of foreign cash flows, and convert this NPV to dollars.

T21.8: International Capital Budgeting: An Example

Example:

Pizza Shack is considering opening a store in Mexico City, Mexico. The store would cost $1.5 million, or 3,646,500,000 pesos to open. Shack hopes to operate the store for 2 years and then sell it at the end of the second year to a local franchisee. Cash flows are expected to be 250,000,000 pesos the first year, and 5 billion pesos the second year. The current spot exchange rate for Mexican pesos is 2,431.00. The U.S. risk-free rate is 7% and the Mexican risk-free rate is 10%. The required return (U.S.) is 12%.

1. The home currency approach.

Using the uncovered interest parity relation $E[S_t] = S_0 \times [1 + (R_F - R_{US})]^t$, the projected exchange rates for the store are:

$$E[S_1] = 2,431 \times [1 + (.10 - .07)]^1 = 2,503.93$$
$$E[S_2] = 2,431 \times [1 + (.10 - .07)]^2 = 2,579.05$$

Year	Cash Flow (pesos)	Expected exchange rate	Cash Flow (dollars)
0	−3,646,500,000	2,431.00	−$1,500,000
1	250,000,000	2,503.93	99,843.05
2	5,000,000,000	2,579.05	1,938,698.36

NPV = −1,500,000 + 99,843.05/1.12 + 1,938,698.36/1.12² = $134,664.04

2. The foreign currency approach.

Using the IFE, the difference in nominal rates, $R_F - R_{US}$, equals the difference in inflation rates, $h_F - h_{US}$. So a 3% inflation premium needs to be factored into the required U.S. return, giving [(1.12 × 1.03) − 1] = 15.36% considering inflation.

$$NPV_F = -3,646,500,000 + 250,000,000/1.1536 + 5,000,000,000/1.1536^2$$

$$= 327,371,337.6 \text{ pesos}$$

$$NPV_s = 327,371,337.6/2,431 = \$134,665.30$$

Note that the two approaches will produce *exactly* the same answers if the exact forms of the various parity equations are used.

C. Unremitted Cash Flows

Not all cash flows from foreign operations can be remitted to the parent.

<u>Ways foreign subsidiaries remit funds to a parent:</u>

1. Dividends
2. Management fees for central services
3. Royalties on trade names and patents

Blocked funds—funds that cannot be currently remitted.

Ethics Notes, page 702: The following case may be used as a class example to expose the class to the ethical problems involving shell corporations which attempt to conduct business on the fringe of violating international law.

In February 1989, the West German Chemical Industry Association suspended the membership of Imhausen Chemie, a major West German chemical manufacturer in response to the charge that Imhausen supplied Libya with the plant and technology to produce chemical weapons. In June 1990, the former Managing Director of Imhausen was convicted of tax evasion and violating West Germany's export control laws.

In November 1984, a shell corporation had been established in Hong Kong to conceal actual ownership of the chemical operations. In April 1987, a subsidiary of the shell corporation was established in Hamburg, West Germany for the purpose of acquiring materials from Imhausen; thus circumventing German export laws. A shipping network was established to fake end-user destinations and sell to Libya.

Reports later surfaced that Libya had constructed a chemical weapons factory. Imhausen did not deny the plant's existence but Imhausen, as well as the government of Libya, claimed that the plant was being used for the manufacture of medicinal drugs. International treaties forbade the use of chemical and biological weapons but did not restrict chemical weapons facility construction. The international community faced a further dilemma as aerial observation could not distinguish between a weapons plant and a pharmaceutical plant. Additionally, such plants could easily be switched to legitimate use in a few days.

While construction of the plant did not violate German or international law, the ease of conversion from legitimate use to weapons production raised questions regarding the technical knowledge transferred by Imhausen. The instructor could question the class as to Imhausen's responsibility in the ultimate use of the plant, despite the fact that the development of the shell corporations was a positive net present value investment.

21.6 EXCHANGE RATE RISK

Risk arising from fluctuations in exchange rates.

A. Short-Run Exposure

A great deal of international business is conducted on terms that fix costs or prices while at the same time calling for payment or receipt of funds in the future. One way to offset the risk from changing exchange rates and fixed terms is to hedge with a forward exchange agreement.

Lecture Tip, page 702: To stimulate interest in this area, the instructor might ask the students why U.S. auto producers would make a statement that the dollar was too strong and hurting their operations. One could use the example in 1985 when the dollar traded at approximately three German marks. If a U.S.-produced car costs $8,000 to produce and German competition dictated a selling price of $9,000, the U.S. auto producer would sell the car for 27,000 marks and make a profit of $1,000 (3,000 marks). This, of course, ignores excise taxes, transportation costs, etc. for simplicity.

If the dollar fell to two marks (which it soon did after the 1985 meeting of international finance ministers), the 27,000 mark selling price would generate $13,500, resulting in a profit of $5,500. The student should recognize that a weak dollar generally benefits companies that conduct operations abroad and a volatile dollar can result in a great deal of exchange rate risk. However, the instructor should also mention that a weak dollar results in higher cost products (inflation) in the United States since we now receive less foreign currency per dollar to purchase a foreign product. The foreign producer would eventually have to raise its price to compensate for the lower amount of its own currency it would receive per $1 of sales. The German producer would receive only two marks per $1 sales instead of three marks. If the product costs 2.5 marks to produce, the German producer could not sell the product at $1 in the U.S. and remain profitable.

Lecture Tip, page 702: At a jewelry store in Troy, Ohio, cultured pearls that cost $899 a few years ago now cost $3,000. The average Japanese car now costs approximately $2,000 more than its American counterpart. A local soybean farmer uses his satellite dish to keep track of commodity prices and currency rates. These are all examples of the growing importance of foreign exchange fluctuations on "average Americans". Students sometimes fail to grasp the importance and/or the relevance of distant events, particularly when they believe that they will not be personally affected by the events. Examples such as these illustrate that we are all affected by changing exchange rates, and might be used to motivate student interest. (Adapted from "Currency Waves: Global Money Trends Rattle Shop Windows in Heartland America," from The Wall Street Journal, *November 26, 1993, p. A1.)*

Lecture Tip, page 703: According to a recent Wall Street Journal *article, the earnings of H.J. Heinz Co. jumped 25% in the second quarter of 1993, but investors were cautioned about the firm's earnings weaknesses. Why? approximately 40% of the firm's earnings are attributable to overseas sales, and adverse currency fluctuations reduced dollar sales for the quarter by 7%, while reducing net earnings by 8 cents per share. The earnings increase was due to a one-time event - the sale of assets.*

B. Long-Run Exposure

Long-run changes in exchange rates can be partially offset by matching foreign assets and liabilities, and inflows and outflows.

C. Translation Exposure

U.S. based firms must translate foreign operations into dollars when calculating net income and EPS.

Problems:

1. What is the appropriate exchange rate to use for translating balance sheet accounts?

2. How should balance sheet accounting gains and losses from foreign currency translation be handled?

FASB 52 requires that assets and liabilities be translated at prevailing exchange rates. Translation gains and losses are accumulated in a special equity account and are not recognized in earnings until the underlying assets or liabilities are sold or liquidated.

D. Managing Exchange Rate Risk

For the large multinational, the net effect of fluctuating exchange rates depends on the firm's net exposure. This is probably best handled on a centralized basis to avoid duplication and conflicting actions.

21.7 POLITICAL RISK

Blocking funds and expropriation of property by foreign governments are among the routine political risks faced by multinationals. Worse, in many places acts of political terrorism are also of concern.

Blocking and expropriation can be hedged by making the operation dependent upon the parent firm, for example, for certain critical components or technical expertise.

Lecture Tip, page 705: Business Risks International has put together a list of countries in which political risk is the greatest due to governmental instability. The countries are:

1. Peru	*6. The Philippines*
2. El Salvador	*7. Sri Lanka*
3. India	*8. Northern Ireland*
4. Turkey	*9. Spain*
5. Colombia	*10. Nicaragua*

(This list appears in Understanding Business, third edition, by Nickels, McHugh, and McHugh, published by Richard D. Irwin, Inc.)

21.8 SUMMARY AND CONCLUSIONS

T21.9:   Solution to Problem 21.3
T21.10:   Solution to Problem 21.11
T21.11:   Solution to Problem 21.13

CHAPTER 22
RISK MANAGEMENT: AN INTRODUCTION TO FINANCIAL ENGINEERING

TRANSPARENCIES

T22.1: Chapter Outline
T22.2: Month-to-Month Changes in Five-Year Treasury Bond Rates (Fig. 22.4)
T22.3: Risk Profile for a Wheat Grower (Fig. 22.7)
T22.4: Risk Profile for a Wheat Buyer (Fig. 22.8)
T22.5: Payoff Profiles for a Forward Contract (Fig. 22.9)
T22.6: Sample *Wall Street Journal* Futures Price Quotations (Table 22.1)
T22.7: Illustration of an Interest Rate Swap (Fig. 22.12)
T22.8: Option Payoff Profiles (Fig. 22.14)
T22.9: Hedging with Options (Fig. 22.15)
T22.10: Solution to Problem 22.4
T22.11: Solution to Problem 22.10

CHAPTER ORGANIZATION

T22.1: Chapter Outline

22.1 HEDGING AND PRICE VOLATILITY
Price Volatility: A Historical Perspective
Interest Rate Volatility
Exchange Rate Volatility
Commodity Price Volatility
The Impact of Financial Risk: The U.S. Savings and Loan Industry

22.2 MANAGING FINANCIAL RISK
The Risk Profile
Reducing Risk Exposure
Hedging Short-Run Exposure
Cash Flow Hedging: A Cautionary Note
Hedging Long-Term Exposure

22.3 HEDGING WITH FORWARD CONTRACTS
Forward Contracts: The Basics
The Payoff Profile
Hedging with Forward Contracts

22.4 HEDGING WITH FUTURES CONTRACTS
Trading in Futures
Futures Exchanges
Hedging with Futures

22.5 HEDGING WITH SWAP CONTRACTS
Currency Swaps
Interest Rate Swaps
Commodity Swaps
The Swap Dealer
Interest Rate Swaps: An Example

22.6 HEDGING WITH OPTION CONTRACTS
Option Terminology
Options versus Forwards
Option Payoff Profiles
Option Hedging
Hedging Commodity Price Risk with Options
Hedging Exchange Rate Risk with Options
Hedging Interest Rate Risk with Options

22.7 SUMMARY AND CONCLUSIONS

ANNOTATED CHAPTER OUTLINE

22.1 HEDGING AND PRICE VOLATILITY

Hedging—reducing a firm's risk to price or rate fluctuations.

Derivative security—financial asset that has a claim to another financial asset.

A. Price Volatility: A Historical Perspective

Both security prices and rates have experienced increasing volatility over the last 30 or 40 years.

B. Interest Rate Volatility

T22.2: Month-to-Month Changes in Five-Year Treasury Bond Rates (Fig. 22.4)

The abandonment of a stable interest rate environment by the Federal Reserve in 1979 has contributed to much higher volatility in interest rates over the 1980s.

C. Exchange Rate Volatility

The breakdown of the Bretton Woods or fixed exchange rate system has caused increased volatility in international exchange rates.

D. Commodity Price Volatility

E. The Impact of Financial Risk: The U.S. Savings and Loan Industry

Lecture Tip, page 717: A discussion using the S&L industry's balance sheet structure may be appropriate to demonstrate the danger of an imbalance in the maturity structure of a financial institution's assets and liabilities.

The instructor could reference the interest-rate environment in the mid- to late-1970s, when short-term interest rates on S&L CDs (S&L liabilities) were approximately 5 percent, and long-term home mortgage rates were approximately 8 percent (the return on an S&L's assets).

The instructor could have the students consider the impact of an S&L's issuing a $100,000, 30-year mortgage in the mid-1970s. Revenue from the assets would be about $8,000 (8% × $100,000), and this would be matched against the short-term interest expense of $5,000 (5% × $100,000). This would result in a $3,000 profit in a stable interest rate environment (ignoring administrative costs and the paydown of the principal). This profit would be maintained (again, ignoring any paydown of the mortgage principal) over the 30-year period as long as the short-term CDs could be turned over at 5 percent ever period.

One could present the March-April 1980 situation in which CD rates were approximately 18 percent. The instructor might ask the students to calculate the net profit for an S&L, instructing them to remember that the mortgage rate is fixed and the CD rate is the rate at which the liabilities must be rolled over. The students should recognize that, if C.D. rates held at 18 percent for the year, revenue on the mortgage would remain at $8,000 but interest expense on the CDs which support the mortgage would be $18,000 ($100,000 × 18%), resulting in a loss of $8,000 ($8,000 − $16,000).

However, the instructor might mention, as the text states, that there was a tremendous amount of interest rate volatility following 1979. In actuality, interest rates on 90-day CDs fell to approximately 10 percent by the first week of May 1980. Additionally, 30-year Treasury yields, which are a floor yield for comparable term mortgages, were approximately 14 percent during 1980 but fell to 8 percent by 1986.

The instructor might add that many institutions have now incorporated hedging strategies to partially immunize themselves from future uncertainty.

22.2 MANAGING FINANCIAL RISK

A. The Risk Profile

A plot showing how the value of the firm is affected by changes in prices or rates.

B. Reducing Risk Exposure

Although perfect hedging may be impossible, the normal goal is to reduce financial risk to bearable levels and thereby flatten out the risk profile.

Lecture Tip, page 720:   The instructor may wish to have the students consider the concept of a reduction in risk exposure by introducing a friendly wager they could make on a baseball game—say, the Minnesota Twins versus the Oakland Athletics. The wager could be as follows: for every run the Twins win by, the student would win $10 per run (A score of Minnesota 7, Oakland 2 would result in a profit of $50), but should the Twins lose, the student would also lose $10 per run differential. The payoff could easily be plotted on a risk profile.

The instructor could then ask the students how they might reduce the risk of the bet, should they become nervous about the amount of the bet prior to the game. The instructor could add that there are many Oakland and Minnesota fans who would also like a similar wager. The students could hedge the wager by placing a similar wager on Oakland of, say, $6 per run. The combined wager could then be plotted on the risk profile, resulting in a net profit or loss of $4 per run differential, depending on the game's outcome.

The instructor could mention that if the students would have placed a $10 per run bet on Oakland to offset the $10 per run bet on Minnesota, they would have created a perfect hedge but, this perfect hedge would have resulted in zero profit.

> **T22.3:   Risk Profile for a Wheat Grower (Fig. 22.7)**
> **T22.4:   Risk Profile for a Wheat Buyer (Fig. 22.8)**

C. Hedging Short-Run Exposure

Often called *transactions exposure*—caused by the necessity of a firm entering into transactions in the near future at uncertain prices or rates.

D. Cash Flow Hedging: A Cautionary Note

Normally, hedging the risk of commodity price fluctuations or other product's price fluctuations essentially is a hedge for the firm's near-term cash flows.

E. Hedging Long-Term Exposure

Often called *economic exposure*—rooted in long-term economic fundamentals and more difficult to hedge on a permanent basis.

Lecture Tip, page 723: Metallgesellschaft AG, the 14th largest company in Germany, "stunned its shareholders last December by announcing losses of about $1 billion in its trading at the New York Mercantile Exchange and off-exchange markets in energy derivatives" according to The Wall Street Journal on March 7, 1994. Apparently, a senior executive at Metallgesellschaft AG committed the firm to deliver petroleum products "for up to 10 years into the future." He then attempted to hedge this short position using various derivative instruments. His strategy was inadequate, however, to avoid the losses due to the price drop that occurred when OPEC failed to reach an agreement in November, 1993. As a result, the firm lost approximately $1 billion and fired the executive in charge of hedging the firm's position. At the time of this writing, he has filed suit against the firm seeking $1 billion in damages for defamation and civil conspiracy.

Although it is beyond the scope of the typical undergraduate course, the use of derivative instruments by firms for hedging purposes is a rapidly growing area of interest to economists, regulators, and corporate treasurers. (The loss of $157 million in an interest rate swap arrangement in April, 1994 provides another fascinating story about the (mis)use of derivatives.)

22.3 HEDGING WITH FORWARD CONTRACTS

A. Forward Contracts: The Basics

Forward contract—contract between the *buyer*, who will take future delivery of the goods, and the *seller*, who will make future delivery, for the sale of an asset or product in the future (*the settlement date*) at a price agreed upon today (*the forward price*).

Lecture Tip, page 723: In a forward contract, both parties are legally bound to execute at the agreed to price but no money changes hands today. Suppose you want to buy the book, A Random Walk Down Wall Street for $10, but it is out of stock. The bookstore orders the book, but it will take approximately one month to be delivered. One month later, when the book arrives, the bookstore sends you a notice of the book's arrival and you go to the bookstore and buy the book for the $10 agreed-upon price. This is a forward contract. Forward contracts are common, but often are not recognized as such.

B. The Payoff Profile

T22.5: Payoff Profiles for a Forward Contract (Fig. 22.9)

A plot of gains and losses on a contract as the result of unexpected price changes.

C. Hedging with Forward Contracts

The basic concept in managing financial risk is that once we establish the firm's exposure to financial risk, we try to find a financial arrangement (such as a forward contract) with an offsetting payoff profile.

22.4 HEDGING WITH FUTURES CONTRACTS

Futures contract—identical to a forward contract except gains and losses are realized (*marked-to-market*) on a daily basis rather than only on the settlement date.

A. Trading in Futures

Typically, futures contracts are divided into two groups:
    -commodity futures contracts
    -financial futures contracts

B. Futures Exchanges

Lecture Tip, page 727: It may be beneficial to demonstrate the issue of marking-to-market and open interest with a discussion of the May corn contract presented in Table 22.1 (Transparency T22.6).

The instructor could have the students examine the May corn contract. The contract is standardized at 5,000 bushels and quoted in cents per bushel. The meaning of this contract is that a one-cent change in the contract price represents a $50 change in each outstanding contract ($.01 × 5,000 bushels)

The instructor could mention that an initial margin (cash deposit) is required by the brokerage account. Assume a $1,500 margin requirement for this transaction. The instructor could ask the class to compute a few calculations:

a)   *The settle or close on the May corn was 286 and the change was −5. What was the previous day's close?*

      Ans. *286 + 5 = 291.*

b)   *If the student <u>bought</u> one May corn contract at the previous day's settle price, what is the day's profit or loss and what is the remaining amount in the student's margin account.*

      Ans. *The corn contract would be worth $250.00 less (.05 × 5,000 bu.). Since they purchased at a higher price than the current settlement price, this amount would be deducted from their margin account and they would start the next day with $1,250.00 in their account (and hope the price on May corn increases) .*

T22.6: Sample *Wall Street Journal* Futures Price Quotations (Table 22.1)

C. Hedging with Futures

*Lecture Tip, page 729: It may be beneficial to demonstrate a futures hedge and the potential payoffs for a soybean farmer who anticipates a harvest of 100,000 bushels in September. Costs to produce the soybeans are incurred long before the harvest, but the farmer is at risk should the price for soybeans fall by harvest time. To minimize this risk, the farmer could take a **short** position in the futures contract to offset the **long** position in the soybeans she will harvest.*

Futures contract terms:

> *-Size is 5,000 bushels*
> *-September delivery at $4.50 per bushel.*

The farmer can lock-in the delivery price of soybeans at $4.50 for her harvest by selling 20 soybean futures contracts on June 1st. Note that no cash changes hands today. The 20 contracts represents delivery of 100,000 bushels (5,000 per contract × 20 contracts).

Scenario:

Date	Closing	Farmer	Net
June 1st		no money changes hands.	
June 10th	$4.60	pays $10,000	−$10,000 (100,000 × −$.10)
June 15th	$4.40	receives $20,000	+$10,000
June 30th	$4.20	receives $20,000	+$30,000
July 20th	$4.30	pays $10,000	+$20,000
August 5th	$4.40	pays $10,000	+$10,000
August 16th	$4.20	receives $20,000	+$30,000
Sept 1st	$4.20	delivers soybeans	receives $4.20 per bu + $30,000 profit on futures.

Note: *Harvest*   *Futures*   *Futures Profit*
100,000 bu. × $4.50   = 100,000 bu. × $4.20 + $30,000.

   If a bumper crop occurs and the farmer harvests 120,000 bushels, the farmer locked in the selling price of 100,000 bushels at $4.50 and would sell the remaining 20,000 bushels at $4.20 per bushel.
   However, if a poor harvest occurs and the price of soybeans is, say $4.75, the farmer might only harvest 70,000 bushels. If we can assume the original contracts were forward contracts, the farmer must buy 30,000 bushels—6 contracts—at $4.75 to make delivery. The farmer would realize a net loss of 30,000 bu. × ($4.75 − $4.50) = $7,500 on this forward arrangement. With futures, the farmer would simply offset with a long futures position. The loss would be the same.

22.5 HEDGING WITH SWAP CONTRACTS

Swap contract—an agreement by two parties to exchange or swap specified cash flows at specified intervals in the future.

A. Currency Swaps

Two firms agree to exchange a specific amount of one currency for a specific amount of another at specific dates in the future.

Lecture Tip, page 729: The following example illustrates that a currency swap is essentially a parallel loan.

Example:
    Two multinational companies with foreign projects need to obtain financing. Company A is based in England and has a U.S. project. Company B is based in the U.S. and has a British project.

1. Both firms want to avoid exchange rate fluctuations.

2. Both firms receive currency for investment at time zero and repay loan as funds are generated in the foreign project.

3. Both firms could have avoided exchange rate fluctuations if they could arrange loans in the country of the project.

        -Funds generated in England for company B (U.S.) would be in £ and repayment would be in £.

4. Both firms may have been able to borrow cheaper in their home country.

The firms arrange parallel loans *for the initial investment and use the proceeds from the project to repay the loan.*

Cash flows: Assume, fixed exchange rate = $2/£1, fixed interest rate = 10%, and a four-year loan. The matching cash flows are:

Co. A: ↓ £100,000   ↓ $20,000   ↓ $20,000   ↓ $20,000   ↓ $220,000
Co. B: ↑ $200,000   ↑ £10,000   ↑ £10,000   ↑ £10,000   ↑ £110,000

Currency swaps are similar to parallel loans and are simply a set of forward contracts.
    Firm A would take a long position and accept delivery of $200,000 for £100,000 (principal of loan). Firm A would take a series of short positions and deliver $20,000 for £10,000 (interest payments). Firm A takes a short position and delivers $200,000 for £100,000. Firm B takes the opposite side.

Result: The firms have (1) fixed the exchange rate for the entire loan period, and (2) fixed the interest rate for the entire loan period.

B. Interest Rate Swaps

C. Commodity Swaps

D. The Swap Dealer

A dealer who will take the opposite side of an agreement for a firm wishing to enter into a swap agreement.

E. Interest Rate Swaps: An Example

T22.7: Illustration of an Interest Rate Swap (Fig. 22.12)

22.6 HEDGING WITH OPTION CONTRACTS

Option contract—an agreement that gives the owner the right, but not the obligation, to buy or sell a specific asset at a specific price for a set period of time.

A. Option Terminology

Call option—a contract that gives the owner the right to buy an asset at a fixed price for a specified time.
Put option—a contract that gives the owner the right to sell an asset at a fixed price for a specified time.
Strike or exercise price—the fixed price agreed upon in the option contract.
Expiration date—the last date of the option contract.

B. Options versus Forwards

Forward contract—both parties are obligated to transact.
Option contract—contract owner has the right to transact.

C. Option Payoff Profiles

T22.8: Option Payoff Profiles (Fig. 22.14)

D. Option Hedging

Buying a put option eliminates "downside risk."

T22.9: Hedging with Options (Fig. 22.15)

E. Hedging Commodity Price Risk with Options

Futures options—a contract on an asset's current futures price.

Lecture Tip, page 736: *The instructor may wish to provide the class with an example of a farmer hedging with a futures option on wheat. A farmer, who wishes to avoid price movements against the crop (falling prices) will buy a put option on a futures contract. At a later date, if prices fall, the farmer exercises his option to enter into a futures contract. The farmer would receive a futures contract on the commodity and the cash difference between the strike price and the current commodity spot price. If the price of the commodity rises during the season, the farmer lets the option on the futures contract expire and simply sells his crop at the spot rate.*

F. Hedging Exchange Rate Risk with Options

G. Hedging Interest Rate Risk with Options

Interest rate cap—a call option on an interest rate.

Floor—a put option on an interest rate.

Collar—purchasing a cap and selling a floor.

22.7 SUMMARY AND CONCLUSIONS

T22.10: Solution to Problem 22.4
T22.11: Solution to Problem 22.10

SUPPLEMENT
OPTIONS AND CORPORATE SECURITIES

TRANSPARENCIES

TO.1: Chapter Outline
TO.2: A Sample *Wall Street Journal* Option Quotation (Table O1)
TO.3: Payoffs to a Call
TO.4: Payoffs to a Put
TO.5: Value of a Call at Expiration
TO.6: Value of a Call before Expiration
TO.7: Five Factors that Determine Option Values
TO.8: Equity as a Call Option
TO.9: Minimum Value of a Convertible Bond
TO.10: Value of a Convertible Bond
TO.11: Loan Guarantees
TO.12: Solution to Problem 9
TO.13: Solution to Problem 11
TO.14: Solution to Problem 13
TO.15: Solution to Problem 15

CHAPTER ORGANIZATION

TO.1: Chapter Outline

O.1 OPTIONS: THE BASICS
Puts and Calls
Stock Option Quotations
Option Payoffs

O.2 FUNDAMENTALS OF OPTION VALUATION
Value of a Call Option at Expiration
The Upper and Lower Bounds on a Call Option's Value
A Simple Model: Part I
Four Factors Determining Option Values

O.3 VALUING A CALL OPTION
A Simple Model: Part II
The Fifth Factor

O.4 EQUITY AS A CALL OPTION ON THE FIRM'S ASSETS
Case I: The Debt is Risk-Free
Case II: The Debt is Risky

O.5 WARRANTS
The Difference Between Warrants and Call Options
Warrants and the Value of the Firm

O.6 CONVERTIBLE BONDS
Features of a Convertible Bond
Value of a Convertible Bond

O.7 REASONS FOR ISSUING WARRANTS AND CONVERTIBLES
The Free Lunch Story
The Expensive Lunch Story
A Reconciliation

O.8 OTHER OPTIONS
The Call Provision on a Bond
Put Bonds
The Green Shoe Provision
Insurance and Loan Guarantees

O.9 SUMMARY AND CONCLUSIONS

APPENDIX A—THE BLACK-SCHOLES OPTION PRICING MODEL

ANNOTATED CHAPTER OUTLINE

O.1 OPTIONS: THE BASICS

Option: contract giving holder the right, but not the obligation, to buy (sell) an asset at a fixed price at any time on or before a given date.

Option terminology:
1. *Exercising the option*—using the option contract to buy (sell) the underlying asset.
2. *Strike or exercise price*—fixed price at which the underlying asset may be bought (sold).
3. *Expiration date*—the last day on which the option may be exercised.
4. *American option*—can be exercised at any time up to the expiration date.
5. *European option*—can only be exercised on the expiration date.

Lecture Tip, page O-2: The instructor may find it beneficial to convey the meaning of an option by having students consider a situation in which they place a down payment on a car. The instructor could ask the students what action they might take if they are interested in buying a car for an agreed-upon price of $5,000 (exercise price) from a used car dealer. However, they would like a week (option's expiration) to decide whether or not they will purchase the car.

The students should recognize that they would have to place a down payment, assumed to be $50 (option cost), with the dealer to hold the car. Over this period, the student could shop around to find a lower price (market or stock price). If they could find an identical car at a lower price, they would call the dealer and state they are not interested in purchasing the car; they would be out the $50 down payment (option cost). However, if the student, after checking around, finds that the lowest price any dealer would offer an identical car was $5,400, the value of the option to purchase at $5,000 would be $400 and they would exercise the option to purchase from the original dealer.

The instructor could introduce the time value of the option by asking the students if they would prefer the $50 down payment to hold the car for one week or four weeks. Most should recognize that they would like a longer time to check with other dealers.

The instructor could also ask the students to consider a car market in which prices are relatively flat (the price at alternative dealers is either $4,900 or $5,100) versus a market in which car prices are very uncertain (the price at alternative dealers is either $4,500 or $5,500). The students should recognize that if the price is on the high side, they would lose $100 in the flat car market but would lose $500 in the uncertain market and they should be more willing to place the down payment on the car if the market is uncertain. Thus, the option would have a higher value in an uncertain market due to the much higher variability the ending market price could attain.

A. Puts and Calls

Call option—gives holder the right, but not the obligation, to *buy* an asset at a fixed price during the option's life.

Put option—gives holder the right, but not the obligation, to *sell* an asset at a fixed price during the option's life.

The party obligated to sell (buy) the asset at the strike price is said to have *written* an option. They receive a fee at the time they write the option.

Lecture Tip, page O-2: You may wish to emphasize the symmetrical nature of options transactions by contrasting the positions of options buyers and options writers. For example, call buyers hope that the value of the underlying asset rises before their option expires. Their potential gain is unlimited, while their loss is limited to the price paid (the premium*) for the option contract.*

Call writers, on the other hand, hope the value of the underlying asset falls (or, at least, doesn't rise); their gain is limited to the premium received, while their potential (opportunity) loss is unlimited. Writers of covered *calls possess the underlying asset at the time the call is written, so the cost of delivering the underlying asset (should it become necessary) is known. Writers of* naked *calls do not own the underlying asset at the time the contract is sold. They are taking on greater risk (i.e., being forced to acquire the underlying asset at the market price) in return for the hope of greater return (receiving the option premium and never having to acquire the underlying asset).*

Lecture Tip, page O-3: *Students are invariably fascinated by the topics of* hedging *and* speculation. *The instructor may wish to take this opportunity to briefly introduce these topics via the use of options. Hedging occurs when one uses options (or some other instrument) to take a position offsetting one already held. For example, a person who owns 100 shares of General Motors stock and has watched its price rise could hedge against a temporary price decline by buying a put option contract. Should the stock price fall, she would lose on her stock position but gain on her option position. To the extent that the gains and losses offset, she has created a "perfect" hedge.*

Speculators, on the other hand, do not hold offsetting positions. Rather, they take a single position and hope that prices move in their favor. In the above example, one who owns no GM stock could speculate on its future price by buying a put option. In this case, the price decline would again result in a gain, but with no offsetting loss.

The use of options (as well as other instruments) by corporate treasurers to hedge against various occurrences has expanded dramatically in the last decade. Further discussion of some of these activities can be found in Chapter 22, "Risk Management: An Introduction to Financial Engineering".

B. Stock Option Quotations

CBOE (Chicago Board Options Exchange)—the largest organized stock options exchange. While stock options involve the shares of various companies, the firms themselves are not party to these contracts. Almost all options are "American". (The American/European appellations have no geographic meaning. Most option contracts traded throughout Europe are of the American variety.)

TO.2: A Sample *Wall Street Journal* Option Quotation (Table O1)

An option is described as " Firm / Expiration month / Strike price / Type ."

More on option contracts:

- *r* means the contract didn't trade that day; *s* indicates that no option is offered.
- Contracts are for 100 shares, so a contract costs *price × 100.*
- Options expire on the third Friday of the expiration month.
- Option prices under $3 trade in sixteenths, while those over $3 trade in eighths.

Lecture Tip, page O-3: *The instructor may wish to add that the strike prices are standardized. The various exchanges that conduct option trading offer contracts in 2 1/2 and 5 dollar intervals. The investor may trade option contracts in small-priced stocks in terms of 2 1/2 dollar intervals (Example: 10, 12 1/2, 15). Higher-priced stocks trade in 5 dollar intervals (Example: 50, 55, 60).*

C. Option Payoffs

TO.3: Payoffs to a Call
TO.4: Payoffs to a Put

For calls, when the stock price is above the exercise price at expiration, the option is *in the money*. When the stock price is below the exercise price the option is *out of the money*. (The opposite is true of puts.)

Ignoring transaction costs, since no new money is raised or invested options are a *zero-sum game*. That is, whatever one party to an options contract gains, the other party loses.

Lecture Tip, page O-4: Although the concept of a put and a call will initially seem clear to the students, students tend to have greater difficulty working with puts than calls. It may help their understanding by providing a very simplified example prior to presenting the option payoff text discussion. One could have the students consider the difference between a stock's price and the striking price (intrinsic value) for both a put and a call contract with an example showing the impact on the contracts' value given various stock price changes. The call's value equals (S − E) because the call price increases as the stock price increases relative to an agreed-upon buying price (E). The put's value equals (E − S) since the put price increases as the stock price falls relative to an agreed-upon selling price (E). Since we will let the option expire if we don't want to use it, the value of the option contract cannot be a negative number but will instead simply be zero.

Example: Consider a contract to buy or sell stock with a striking price of $30.

Strike Price(E)	Stock Price(S)	Call Value (S − E)	Put Value (E − S)
30	24	0	6
	27	0	3
	30	0	0
	33	3	0
	36	6	0

This example may help the students understand the opposite nature of puts and calls and that a call's value will fall, but a put's value will rise, as the stock price falls in value.

Lecture Tip, page O-5: The instructor may mention that Example 1 (Put Payoffs) is an example of a protective put which provides insurance should the stock price fall (answer to concept question O.1b). Such insurance could save the cost of many bottles of aspirin (or, possibly, something providing much greater pain relief!) should the stock investor experience an event such as that which occurred on Black Monday in 1987.

O.2 FUNDAMENTALS OF OPTION VALUATION

A. Value of a Call Option at Expiration

TO.5: Value of a Call Option at Expiration

Notation

S_1 = Stock price at expiration
S_0 = Stock price today
C_1 = Value of call option on the expiration date
C_0 = Price of call option today
E = Exercise price of option

If $S_1 \leq E$ then $C_1 = 0$ If $S_1 > E$ then $C_1 = S_1 - E$

B. The Upper and Lower Bounds on a Call Option's Value

TO.6 Value of a Call Option before Expiration

The Upper Bound: $C_0 \leq S_0$. A call option can never sell for more than the stock itself.

The Lower Bound: 0 or $S_0 - E$, whichever is larger. To prevent *arbitrage*, the value of a call must be greater than the stock price less the exercise price. Otherwise, buy the option, pay the exercise price, and get the stock for less than it sells for in the market.

Intrinsic value = 0 or $S_0 - E$, whichever is larger. Option value just before expiration.

C. A Simple Model: Part I

Much can be learned about influences on an option's price by examining two cases where call options and risk-free loans give the same payoffs as a straight stock investment.

Suppose a stock currently sells for $62 and its price will be either $70 or $90 in one period. Assume there is a call option on this stock with an exercise price of $65. Finally, let the one period risk-free interest rate be 10%.

1. The Basic Approach

Duplicating the payoff

1) Buy the stock. The stock will be worth either $70 or $90;
or
2) Buy the call and lend $65/(1.1) or $59.09 at 10%.

Stock value	Call value	Risk-free loan	Total payoff, call + loan
$70	$S_1 - E = \$5$	$65	$70
$90	$S_1 - E = \$25$	$65	$90

Whatever happens to the stock, the call + loan strategy has the same payoff as buying the stock. Since the stock can be purchased for $62, the current value of the call + loan must also be $62. Thus, $62 = \$59.09 + C_0 \rightarrow C_0 = \$2.91$ and $C_0 = S_0 - E/(1+R_f)$.

2. A More Complicated Case

Let the stock price be *anything* greater or equal to the exercise price in t periods. Again consider lending at the risk-free rate of 10% to receive $65 after t periods. The payoff to the call option + lending scheme is $65 + (S_1 - \$65)$, which is simply S_1. Since the stock and the (call + loan) have the same payoff, they must have the same price now. As long as the option finishes in the money its price is $C_0 = S_0 - E/(1+R_f)^t$.

D. Four Factors Determining Option Values

Since $C_0 = S_0 - E/(1+R_f)^t$:

1. *The stock price*—the higher the stock price, the greater the price of a call.
2. *The exercise price*—the higher the exercise price, the smaller the price of a call.
3. *Time to expiration*—the longer the time to expiration, the greater the price of a call.
4. *The risk-free rate*—the larger the risk-free rate, the more the call is worth.

O.3 VALUING A CALL OPTION

A. A Simple Model: Part II

When the stock price may be below the exercise price, loan the present value of the lowest stock price at the risk-free rate and buy enough calls to have the difference between the lowest and highest price.

Example:
    Suppose a stock now selling for $67 is expected to end up at $60 or $80. There is a call option with an exercise price of $70 on the stock. The risk-free rate is 9%.

Duplicating the payoff

1) Loan $55.05 at the risk-free rate. The payoff is $60 at maturity at 9%.
2) At expiration, the call will be worth either $0 ($60 stock price) or $10 ($80 stock price). If worth $10, it will take 2 calls plus the loan to make the payoff $80.

Two calls plus a risk-free loan of $55.05 have the same payoff as a share of stock, so

$$S_0 = 2 \times C_0 + \$60/(1 + .09) \Rightarrow C_0 = (\$67 - \$55.05)/2 = \$5.98$$

B. The Fifth Factor

Variance of return (σ^2)—the greater the variability in price (return), the more a call option is worth. Greater variability increases the likelihood of finishing in the money and the expected magnitude of the resulting payoff.

Example:
        Suppose the stock in the example above is expected to end up at either $55 or $85 instead of $60 or $80. What happens to the price of the call?

Duplicating the payoff

1) Loan $50.46 at the risk-free rate. The payoff is $55 at maturity at 9%.
2) At expiration the call will be worth either $0 ($55 stock price) or $15 ($85 stock price). If worth $15, it will take 2 calls plus the loan to make the payoff $85.

Two calls plus a risk-free loan of $55.05 have the same payoff as a share of stock, so

$$S_0 = 2 \times C_0 + \$55/(1 + .09) \rightarrow C_0 = (\$67 - \$50.46)/2 = \$8.27$$

Lecture Tip, page 0-13: It may be beneficial to comment on the initial example of a car down payment to offer the student additional intuition on why an option's value increases as the variance on the underlying asset increases. Students should recognize that they would be more willing to place a down payment to hold a car if they felt the possible price range could be between $4,500 and $5,500 rather than between $4,900 and $5,100 on a $5,000 asking price for a car. The potential loss of $100 (should another dealer's price actually be $5,100) should not worry them but a loss of $500 (should the other dealer's price actually be $5,500) would encourage the purchaser to desire some insurance to hold the car. If the car shopper finds another dealer actually selling the car for the lower price, the shopper simply forfeits the down payment, in which case, the value of the down payment is lost.

C. A Closer Look

Let ΔS equal the difference in the possible stock prices, and let ΔC be the difference in option values at expiration. Then the number of options needed to replicate the possible stock prices is $\Delta S/\Delta C$.

> **TO.7: Five Factors that Determine Option Values**

O.4 EQUITY AS A CALL OPTION ON THE FIRM'S ASSETS

> **TO.8: Equity as a Call Option**

The underlying asset is the value of the firm (the value of its assets). The stockholders have a call on this value with an exercise price equal to the face value of the firm's debt. If the firm's assets are worth more than the debt, the option is in the money and stockholders "exercise" by paying off the debt. If, however, the face value of the debt is greater than the value of the firm's assets, the option expires unexercised (i.e., default occurs). Thus, the bondholders can be viewed as owning the firm's assets and having written a call against them.

A. Case I: The Debt is Risk-Free

<u>The option will be in the money: Outlining the method</u>
Suppose a firm with assets currently worth $1,000 has a pure discount bond outstanding with a face value of $1,000. Assume the firm's assets will be worth $1,200 or $1,400 in one period. Finally, the risk-free rate is 11%. What is the value of the firm's equity?

<u>Duplicating the payoff</u>
Since the option is sure to finish in the money, $C_0 = S_0 - E/(1+R_f)$ can be used to value the option. The value of the equity $= C_0 = \$1,000 - \$1,000/(1.11) = \$99.10$. Thus the debt must be worth $1,000 - $99.10 = $900.90 (i.e., assets = liabilities + equity). This is confirmed by simply discounting the $1,000 debt at 11%.

B. Case II: The Debt is Risky

-Suppose all the circumstances are the same as above except the firm's assets will be worth either $900 or $1,700 in one period. How much is the debt worth? The equity?

<u>Duplicating the payoff</u>
1) The present value of a $900 payoff at 11% is $810.81.
2) At expiration the call (equity) will either be worth $0 or $700. If $700, it will take $\Delta S/\Delta C = (\$1,700 - \$900)/(\$700 - \$0) = 8/7$ calls + the risk-free loan to make the payoff $1,700.

$$S_0 = \Delta S/\Delta C \times C_0 + \$810.81 \rightarrow \$1,000 = 8/7 \times C_0 + \$810.81 \rightarrow C_0 = \$165.54$$

Since the equity is one call, it is worth $165.54. The debt must be worth at total of $1,000 - $165.54 = $834.46 (which implies a discount rate or cost of debt of 19.84%).

Lecture Tip, page O-16: The instructor might ask why a company, operating under Chapter 11 bankruptcy protection, could have a positive market equity value since the company is generally not able to pay off its creditors, should the company be liquidated. The instructor could reference the option value imbedded in the firm's assets.

One might provide a brief example:

Assets (M.V.) = $1,000	Bonds (B.V.) = $1,500
	Equity = ?

Assume the company is considering an investment in one of two projects:

1. Project A has an expected payoff of $1,000, but, because of its extremely high risk, has a NPV of only $50 .

2. Project B has an expected payoff of $400, but is considered a very secure investment, and has a NPV of $200.

Project B, with the higher NPV, would normally be preferred, but if accepted, its payoff, when combined with the current $1,000 value of assets, would fall short of the $1,500 necessary to pay off the bondholders. The only project which will possibly save the company is the lower-NPV project, Project A, with the possible high payoff at its conclusion. If project A fails, stockholders allow the bondholders to take over the firm, which would have occurred with project B anyway, whether B was successful or not.

The instructor could also use the savings and loan events of the 1980s to provide examples of risky investments undertaken due (at least in part) to their low or negative equity positions.

O.5 WARRANTS

Warrant—security issued by firms that gives the holder the right, but not the obligation, to purchase common stock directly from the company at a fixed price for a given period of time.

Sweeteners or *equity kickers*—warrants issued in combination with privately placed loans or bonds, public issues of bonds, and new stock issues.

A. The Difference between Warrants and Call Options

Although similar to call options, warrant exercise causes the firm to issue new stock in return for cash.

B. Warrants and the Value of the Firm

Suppose Ms. Burton and Mr. Peterson put up $2,000 each and buy 125 barrels of crude oil at $32 a barrel. They incorporate, issue one share each to themselves and name the firm BP Incorporated.

1. The Effect of a Call Option

Suppose Mr. Peterson immediately writes a call giving Mr. Patel the right to buy the share at $2,400 any time in the next six months.

After six months oil has gone to $40 a barrel, and the share is worth $2,500 (half of 125 barrels at $40). Mr. Patel exercises his call and pays Mr. Peterson $2,400 for the share.

The number of shares and their value is unaffected by the option transaction.

2. The Effect of a Warrant

Suppose that instead of Mr. Peterson selling a call, BP Inc. had sold a warrant to Mr. Patel. The warrant has an exercise price of $2,400.

As before, oil goes to $40 a barrel. Mr. Patel exercises his warrant, pays $2,400 to BP, and receives one share.

The firm now has oil worth $5,000 plus the $2,400 in cash from Mr. Patel. With $7,400 in assets, each of the three shares is worth $2,466.67.

Mr. Patel has gained $66.67, while Ms. Burton and Mr. Peterson now have shares worth $33.33 less than what they would have been if no warrant was issued ($2,466.67 versus $2,500). But, Burton and Peterson got the proceeds from the sale of the warrant earlier.

3. Warrant Value and Stock Value

When in the money, outstanding warrants represent claims against the value of the firm that will be reflected in the market stock price. Thus, the stock price just before and just after the exercise of warrants will be the same.

4. Earnings Dilution

Exercise of warrants increases the number of shares outstanding, and EPS decreases. Firms with significant amounts of warrants and convertibles outstanding report earnings on a *fully-diluted basis*.

0.6 CONVERTIBLE BONDS

Convertible bond—a bond that may be converted into a fixed number of shares of common stock on or before the maturity date.

A. Features of a Convertible Bond

Conversion ratio—the number of shares per $1,000 bond to be had at conversion.

Conversion price—the bond's (or preferred's) par value divided by the conversion ratio.

Conversion premium—difference between the conversion price and the current stock price divided by the current stock price.

Example:

Consider a convertible bond with a conversion price of $50 per share. The conversion ratio is 20. If the stock sells for $40 per share at issue, the conversion premium is ($50 − $40)/$40 = 25%.

B. Value of a Convertible Bond

1. *Straight bond value*—what the bond would sell for if it didn't have a conversion feature, i.e., the discounted coupons and face value at maturity.

2. *Conversion value*—what a convertible bond would be worth if converted right now.

TO.9: Minimum Value of a Convertible Bond

---

3. *Floor value for a convertible*—a convertible will not sell for less than the greater of the straight bond value or the conversion value.

TO.10: Value of a Convertible Bond

---

4. *Option value*—the convertible feature of a bond is in effect a call option on the stock. Holders in effect get a bond and a call, where the exercise price of the call is the bond. Unless the firm is forcing conversion or is in bankruptcy, the call option makes a convertible more valuable than a comparable straight bond.

O.7 REASONS FOR ISSUING WARRANTS AND CONVERTIBLES

Conventional wisdom on warrants and convertibles:

1. They make bonds "cheap"
2. They allow deferred common stock sales at relatively high prices

A. The Free Lunch Story

<u>The firm does poorly:</u>
The bonds carry a reduced rate compared to straight bonds. The warrants or convertibles are not exercised or converted. Free lunch.

<u>The firm does well:</u>
Because the conversion price is above the stock price at the time the bonds are issued, bondholders are buying the stock at "high" prices. Free lunch.

B. The Expensive Lunch Story

<u>The firm does poorly:</u>
Since the stock price falls, you can argue the firm should have sold "expensive" stock instead of bonds.

<u>The firm does well:</u>
The stock price rises and bondholders will exercise or convert at fixed prices. The firm in effect sells stock to them for less than it could get in the market.

C. A Reconciliation

The "best" course can only be seen in hindsight. If the firm does well, convertibles are better than common but worse than straight debt. On the other hand, if the firm does poorly, convertibles are better than straight debt but worse than common.

Some readers are not be completely satisfied with the hindsight argument. The key is that, in an efficient market, the choice of security is presumed to be a zero NPV proposition. That is, the potential value to the firm of issuing warrants or convertibles is reflected in bond prices. Thus, at the time of issue, unless the firm knows something the market doesn't, there is no net advantage to one or another security.

O.8 OTHER OPTIONS

A. The Call Provision on a Bond

Most corporate bonds are callable. The firm gets a call on its bonds, but since options have value, the firm pays for this feature in the form of a lower bond price, cet. par.

B. Put Bonds

A combination of a straight bond and a put option. The holder can put the bond to the issuer at a fixed price for a given period.

C. The Green Shoe Provisions

In IPOs, underwriters sometimes get the right to purchase additional shares from the issuing firm at the offer price. Since new shares are issued, this is a type of warrant.

D. Insurance and Loan Guarantees

TO.11: Loan Guarantees

Insurance and loan guarantees can be viewed as combinations of the underlying asset + a put option. If the asset declines in value, the put holder exercises by putting the asset to the put writer.

O.9 SUMMARY AND CONCLUSIONS

TO.12: Solution to Problem 9
TO.13: Solution to Problem 11
TO.14: Solution to Problem 13
TO.15: Solution to Problem 15

APPENDIX A—THE BLACK-SCHOLES OPTION PRICING MODEL

$$C_0 = S_0 \times N(d_1) - E/(1+R_f)^t \times N(d_2)$$

where

$$d_1 = [\ln(S_0/E) + (R_f + \tfrac{1}{2} \times \sigma^2) \times t]/(\sigma \times \sqrt{t})$$

$$d_2 = d_1 - \sigma \times \sqrt{t}$$

In the model, $N(d_*)$ is the probability that a standardized, normally distributed, random variable is less than or equal to d_*.

SUPPLEMENT
LEASING

TRANSPARENCIES

TL.1: Chapter Outline
TL.2: Leasing versus Buying (Fig. L1)
TL.3: Leasing and the Balance Sheet (Table L1)
TL.4: Incremental Cash Flows for Tasha Co. from Leasing instead of Buying
TL.5: Solution to Problem 7
TL.6: Solution to Problem 8

CHAPTER ORGANIZATION

TL.1: Chapter Outline

L.1 LEASES AND LEASE TYPES
Leasing versus Buying
Operating Leases
Financial Leases

L.2 ACCOUNTING AND LEASING

L.3 TAXES, THE IRS, AND LEASES

L.4 THE CASH FLOWS FROM LEASING
The Incremental Cash Flows
A Note on Taxes

L.5 LEASE OR BUY?
A Preliminary Analysis
Three Potential Pitfalls
NPV Analysis
A Misconception

L.6 A LEASING PARADOX

L.7 REASONS FOR LEASING
Good Reasons for Leasing
Bad Reasons for Leasing
Other Reasons for Leasing

L.8 SUMMARY AND CONCLUSIONS

ANNOTATED CHAPTER OUTLINE

L.1 LEASES AND LEASE TYPES

<u>Basic terminology:</u>

Lease—a contractual agreement between two parties: the lessee and the lessor.

Lessee—the party who has the right to use an asset and, in return, makes periodic payments to the asset's owner.

Lessor—the owner of the asset.

A. Leasing versus Buying

TL.2: Leasing versus Buying (Fig. L1)

The decision involves a comparison of the alternative financing methods employed to secure the use of the asset. In both cases the company ends up using the asset.

B. Operating Leases

Also called a *service lease*. Operating leases are often involved with the leasing of computers and automobiles.

-life of the lease contract is typically less than the asset's economic life; therefore, the total cost of the equipment is not recovered by the lessor over the contract's life.

-the lessor typically maintains the asset and assumes responsibility for paying taxes and insurance.

-lessee has a cancellation option prior to the contract's expiration date.

C. Financial Leases

Also called *capital leases*.

-payments are typically sufficient to cover the lessor's cost of purchasing the asset and provide the lessor a fair return (therefore, also termed a *fully amortized lease*).

-lessor is responsible for insurance, maintenance and taxes.

-generally, no cancellation clause without severe penalty.

The three financial lease types are:

1. *Tax-oriented leases*—the lessor is the owner for tax purposes.

2. *Leveraged leases*—lessor borrows a substantial portion of the purchase price on a nonrecourse basis.

3. *Sale and leaseback agreements*—lessee sells an asset to the lessor and leases it back from the lessor.

L.2 ACCOUNTING AND LEASING

TL.3: Leasing and the Balance Sheet (Table L1)

Statement of Financial Accounting Standards No. 13, "Accounting for Leases."

Financial leases—capitalized and reported on the balance sheet (a debit to the asset for the present value of the lease payments and a credit recognizing the financial obligation of the lease).

Operating leases—not disclosed on the balance sheet.

A lease is declared a capital lease if one or more of the following criteria is met:

1. Property ownership transferred to lessee by end of lease term.
2. Lessee can purchase asset below market value at lease's expiration.
3. Lease term is 75 percent of asset's economic life.
4. Present value of payments at least 90 percent of market value at inception.

Note: Often an arbitrary distinction between financial and operating leases. An advantage of operating lease classification is that balance sheet may appear stronger (such as a lower total debt to total asset ratio).

L.3 TAXES, THE IRS, AND LEASES

A valid lease from the *IRS's* perspective will meet these standards:

1. Lease term less than 80 percent of asset's economic life.

2. Contract should <u>not</u> have an option to buy at a price below fair market value when the lease contract expires.

3. Lease contract should not have a payment schedule which is initially very high and lower thereafter; it suggests that tax avoidance is the motive for the lease.

4. Lease payment plan should provide lessor a fair rate of return.

5. Renewal options must be reasonable, reflecting market value.

L.4 THE CASH FLOWS FROM LEASING

Lecture Tip, page L-8: Firms are confronted with a choice of acquiring property via a lease agreement or via a conventional loan. The analysis for the firm involves the unbundling of the lease agreement as a purchase and a finance contract. However, often firms bundle the asset as part of a lease and it is the only method available for property acquisition. The instructor may wish to mention that, as an example, large copiers and mainframe computers are often available primarily via lease agreements.

A. The Incremental Cash Flows

> **TL.4: Incremental Cash Flows for Tasha Co. from Leasing instead of Buying**

Three important cash flow differences between leasing and buying:

1. Lessee's lease payments are fully tax deductible. The aftertax lease payment is equal to the pretax payment $\times$ (1 − tax rate).

2. Lessee does not own and may not depreciate asset. Loss of depreciation tax shield occurs in the amount of Depr $\times$ tax rate.

3. Lessee does not have upfront cost of asset.

Lecture Tip, page L-8: Below is an alternative example of a lease versus buy situation:

Example:

A florist can purchase a delivery truck from her local GM dealer for $25,000. The GM dealer will also lease the van for $6,100 per year over five years. The van has an expected life of five years. If the florist wants to purchase the van she must borrow money from Boone National at a current rate of 10%. Which financing option is better?

The implied interest rate under the lease agreement is:

$$\$25{,}000 = \$6{,}100 \sum_{t=1}^{5} 1 / (1 + r)^t,$$

and solving for r yields 7%. This implies that the GM dealer is willing to loan money to the florist at 7% instead of the conventional 10% loan being offered by Boone National. Thus the decision would appear clear: lease the van.

Unfortunately, lease versus buy decisions are not this simple. The tax perspective is not straightforward; i.e., under leasing, the full lease payment is deductible for tax purposes but, under a purchase, the purchase price is only tax deductible through depreciation. The tax rules for depreciation thus impact the timing of the cash flows and therefore the evaluation of the lease versus buy decision. In addition, lease contracts are often bundled with other agreements such as maintenance, insurance, and operating expenses. Looking again at the florist's decision, the following incremental cash flows are the basis for the lease versus buy decision.

The florist has a 34% marginal tax rate and she uses the straight line depreciation method. Keeping the problem in its simplest form, the salvage value of the truck is zero at the end of the five years. To further simplify matters, the following table illustrates the incremental cash flows by subtracting the direct cash flows of the purchase option from the cash flows of the lease option.

Notes:

1. Lease Payment = $6,100 at end of each year (cash outflow).

2. Tax benefit of lease = Tax rate × Lease payment = .34 × $6,100 = $2,074 (a reduction in the cash outflow).

3. If Buy, cost of truck = $25,000 (cash outflow).

4. Lost depreciation tax shield = Depreciation × Tax rate = ($25,000/5) × .34 = $1,700. (lost benefit is a negative cash flow).

Incremental cash flows (lease − buy):

	Year 0	Year 1	Year 2	Year 3	Year 4	Year 5
Lease payment		−$6,100	−$6,100	−$6,100	−$6,100	−$6,100
Tax benefit		+$2,074	+$2,074	+$2,074	+$2,074	+$2,074
Aftertax payment		−$4,026	−$4,026	−$4,026	−$4,026	−$4,026
Cost	$25,000					
Depr. tax shield		−$1,700	−$1,700	−$1,700	−$1,700	−$1,700
Net cash flow	$25,000	−$5,726	−$5,726	−$5,726	−$5,726	−$5,726

What is the bank loan rate at which the buy option and lease option are the same?

$$\$25,000 = \$5,726 \sum_{t=1}^{5} 1 / (1 + r)^t$$

The bank would have to offer a 5% aftertax loan rate if the florist is to prefer the buy option. Note the pretax loan rate would therefore be 5% / (1 − .34) = 7.6%.

B. A Note on Taxes

Lease advantage is often a question of who can best utilize the tax shelters involved in the lease arrangement.

L.5 LEASE OR BUY?

A. A Preliminary Analysis

Leasing is advantageous if the implicit *aftertax* interest rate on the lease is less than the company's *aftertax* borrowing cost.

Lecture Tip, page L-10: *The general rule for the leasing decision is that firms should discount riskless cash flows at the aftertax rate of interest. The leasing contract is generally not subject to uncertainty. However, there is not uniform agreement as to what constitutes guaranteed cash flows since the firm must generate sufficient cash flows to make the payments and receive the tax shields. However, it is important to note, as the example in the previous lecture tip demonstrates, that the cash flows analyzed are aftertax and therefore, the "r" or hurdle rate in the solution is also the aftertax rate.*

B. Three Potential Pitfalls

Potential pitfalls using the implicit rate on the lease:

1. Cash flows are not conventional since the first cash flow is positive, so the IRR represents the rate we pay. The *lower* the IRR the better.

2. Advantage to leasing over borrowing—prefer the lower IRR. If we determine the advantage to borrowing over leasing, the cash flow signs would be reversed—prefer the higher IRR.

3. The implicit rate is based on the *net* cash flows of leasing instead of borrowing. A rate which is based only on the borrowing amount and the lease payments is not meaningful.

C. NPV Analysis

The *net advantage to leasing* can be determined by discounting the cash flows back at the lessee's aftertax borrowing rate.

L.6 A LEASING PARADOX

It is important to recognize that the cash flows to the lessee are exactly the opposite of the cash flows to the lessor. As a result, a lease arrangement is a zero-sum game. This situation presents a paradox which will be resolved in the following section:

Since, in any leasing arrangement, either one party loses and one party wins, or both parties break even, why would leasing take place?

L.7 REASONS FOR LEASING

A. Good Reasons for Leasing

1. Taxes may be reduced by leasing. A potential tax shield that cannot be used effectively by one firm can be transferred to another firm through a leasing arrangement. The firm in the higher tax bracket would want to act as the lessor and utilize the majority of the tax shields. *(The loser is the IRS)*.

2. Leasing may reduce uncertainty regarding the asset's residual value which may result in a reduction of firm value.

3. Transaction costs may be lower for leasing than buying.

4. Leasing may require few restrictive covenants than borrowing.

5. Leasing may encumber fewer assets than secured borrowing.

Lecture Tip, page L-15: *Many firms have different borrowing rates so there is potential for the lease contract to be beneficial to both the lessor and lessee. For example, if a large firm (Xerox, for example) has a very strong and stable earnings record, banks would be willing to lend at a lower rate. If the large firm desires to sell its large mainframe computer to the small company, it is in a better position to finance the loan than the small company. Thus, a lease contract is offered and the large company gets a sale. The small company gets a computer at a lower financing cost. This lease contract decision by the large firm (lessor) may also be considered a part of its credit policy in that it is designed to increase sales by offering favorable payment schedules.*

Lecture Tip, page L-15: *We tend to think of leases as involving real estate or pieces of equipment. However, there has been a virtual explosion in the number of firms who lease human assets, i.e., employees. According to The Wall Street Journal, the number of employees has grown from virtually zero in 1985 to over 1.6 million in 1994. One of the primary advantages of the arrangement is that lessees are spared the cost of providing health-care and other benefits for these people. These benefits are provided by the lessor firms; however, since they have a large number of individuals to cover, they can negotiate better prices than could the small employers who are typically the lessees.*

B. Bad Reasons for Leasing

1. By keeping leases off the books, the balance sheet and income statement may appear more favorable.

2. A firm may secure a lease arrangement when additional debt would violate a prior loan agreement.

3. Basing the lease decision on the interest rate implied by the lease payments and not on the incremental aftertax cash flows.

C. Other Reasons for Leasing

L.8 SUMMARY AND CONCLUSIONS

TL.5: Solution to Problem 7
TL.6: Solution to Problem 8

PART II

END-OF-CHAPTER

SOLUTIONS

CHAPTER 1
INTRODUCTION TO CORPORATE FINANCE

Basic

1. Capital budgeting (deciding on whether to expand a manufacturing plant), capital structure (deciding whether to issue new equity and use the proceeds to retire outstanding debt), and working capital management (modifying the firm's credit collection policy with its customers).

2. Disadvantages: unlimited liability, limited life, difficulty in transferring ownership, hard to raise capital funds. Some advantages: simpler, less regulation, the owners are also the managers, sometimes personal tax rates are better than corporate tax rates.

3. The primary disadvantage of the corporate form is the double taxation to shareholders of distributed earnings and dividends. Some advantages include: limited liability, ease of transferability, ability to raise capital, unlimited life, and so forth.

4. The treasurer's office and the controller's office are the two primary organizational groups that report directly to the chief financial officer. The controller's office handles cost and financial accounting, tax management, and management information systems, while the treasurer's office is responsibile for cash and credit management, capital budgeting, and financial planning. Therefore, the study of corporate finance is concentrated within the treasury group's functions.

5. To maximize the current market value (share price) of the equity of the firm (whether its publicly-traded or not).

6. In the corporate form of ownership, the shareholders are the owners of the firm. The shareholders elect the directors of the corporation, who in turn appoint the firm's management. This separation of ownership from control in the corporate form of organization is what causes agency problems to exist. Management may act in its own or someone else's best interests, rather than those of the shareholders. If such events occur, they may contradict the goal of maximizing the share price of the equity of the firm.

7. A primary market transaction.

8. In auction markets like the NYSE, brokers and agents meet at a physical location (the exchange) to match buyers and sellers of assets. Dealer markets like NASDAQ consist of dealers operating at dispersed locales who buy and sell assets themselves, communicating with other dealers either electronically or literally over-the-counter.

Intermediate

9. Such organizations frequently pursue social or political missions, so many different goals are conceivable. One goal that is often cited is revenue minimization; i.e., provide whatever goods and services are offered at the lowest possible cost to society. A better approach might be to observe that even a not-for-profit business has equity. Thus, one answer is that the appropriate goal is to maximize the value of the equity.

10. Presumably, the current stock value reflects the risk, timing, and magnitude of all future cash flows, both short-term *and* long-term. If this is correct, then the statement is false.

11. An argument can be made either way. At the one extreme, we could argue that in a market economy, all of these things are priced. There is thus an optimal level of, for example, ethical and/or illegal behavior, and the framework of stock valuation explicitly includes these. At the other extreme, we could argue that these are non-economic phenomena and are best handled through the political process. A classic (and highly relevant) thought question that illustrates this debate goes something like this: "A firm has estimated that the cost of improving the safety of one of its products is $30 million. However, the firm believes that improving the safety of the product will only save $20 million in product liability claims. What should the firm do?"

12. The goal will be the same, but the best course of action toward that goal may be different because of differing social, political, and economic institutions.

13. The goal of management should be to maximize the share price for the current shareholders. If management believes that it can improve the profitability of the firm so that the share price will exceed $35, then they should fight the offer from the outside company. If management believes that this bidder or other unidentified bidders will actually pay more than $35 per share to acquire the company, then they should still fight the offer. However, if the current management cannot increase the value of the firm beyond the bid price, and no other higher bids come in, then management is not acting in the interests of the shareholders by fighting the offer. Since current managers often lose their jobs when the corporation is acquired, poorly monitored managers have an incentive to fight corporate takeovers in situations such as this.

14. We would expect agency problems to be less severe in other countries, primarily due to the relatively small percentage of individual ownership. Fewer individual owners should reduce the number of diverse opinions concerning corporate goals. The high percentage of institutional ownership might lead to a higher degree of agreement between owners and managers on decisions concerning risky projects. In addition, institutions may be better able to implement effective monitoring mechanisms on managers than can individual owners, based on the institutions' deeper resources and experiences with their own management. The increase in institutional ownership of stock in the United States and the growing activism of these large shareholder groups may lead to a reduction in agency problems for U.S. corporations and a more efficient market for corporate control.

CHAPTER 2
FINANCIAL STATEMENTS, TAXES, AND CASH FLOW

Basic

1.

		Balance Sheet			
CA	$1,000	CL	$500	OE	= 5,500 – 1,700 = $3,800
NFA	4,500	LTD	1,200	NWC	= 1,000 - 500 = $500
TA	$5,500	OE	??		
		TL + OE	$5,500		

2.

Income Statement	
Sales	$300,000
Costs	175,000
EBDIT	$125,000
Depreciation	25,000
EBIT	$100,000
Interest	30,000
EBT	$70,000
Taxes	23,800
Net income	$46,200

3. Net income = divs + add. to ret. earnings; add. to ret. earnings = 46,200 – 20,000 = $26,200

4. EPS = NI / shares   = $46,200 / 30,000 = $1.54 per share
DPS = divs / shares   = $20,000 / 30,000 = $0.67 per share

5. NWC = CA – CL; CA = 500K + 500K = $1M
Book value CA   = $1M, book value NFA = $1.5M; book value assets   = 1 + 1.5 = $2.5M
Market value NFA = $2M, market value CA = $1.2M; market value assets = 2 + 1.2 = $3.2M

6. Taxes paid = 0.15($50K) + 0.25($25K) + 0.34($25K) + 0.39($140K – $100K) = $37,850

7. Average tax rate = 37,850 / 140,000 = 27.04%; marginal tax rate = 39%

8.

<u>Income Statement</u>

Sales	$5,000	OCF $= \text{EBIT} + D - T$
Costs	3,000	$= 1,550 + 450 - 455 = \$1,545$
EBDIT	$2,000	
Depreciation	450	
EBIT	$1,550	
Interest	250	
EBT	$1,300	
Taxes	455	
Net income	$845	

9.   Inc. in capital spending $= \text{NFA}_{end} - \text{NFA}_{beg} + \text{depreciation} = 3.5M - 3.4M + 400K = \$500K$

10.   Inc. in NWC $= \text{NWC}_{end} - \text{NWC}_{beg} = (\text{CA}_{end} - \text{CL}_{end}) - (\text{CA}_{beg} - \text{CL}_{beg})$
$$= (600 - 450) - (500 - 400) = 150 - 100 = \$50$$

11.   Cash flow to creditors $= \text{interest paid} - \text{net new LTD} = 575K - (\text{LTD}_{end} - \text{LTD}_{beg})$
$$= 575K - (5.9M - 5.0M) = 575K - 900K = -\$325K$$

12.   Cash flow to stockholders $= \text{dividends paid} - \text{net new equity} = 450K - [(\text{com.stk.}_{end} +$
$$\text{capital surplus}_{end}) - (\text{com.stk.}_{beg} + \text{capital surplus}_{beg})]$$
$$= 450K - [(325K + 5.975M) - (300K + 5.7M)]$$
$$= 450K - [6.3M - 6.0M] = \$150K$$

13.   Cash flow from assets $= \text{cash flow to creditors} + \text{cash flow to stockholders}$
$$= -325K + 150K = -\$175K$$
Cash flow from assets $= -\$175K = \text{OCF} - \text{inc. in NWC} - \text{inc. in cap. sp.};$
$-\$175K = \text{OCF} - (-\$75K) - (\$750K);$ $\text{OCF} = -175K + 750K - 75K = \$500K$

Intermediate

14.

<u>Income Statement</u>

Sales	$50,000	*a.* OCF $= \text{EBIT} + D - T$
Costs	30,000	$= 15,000 + 2,500 - 3,400 = \$14,100$
Gross margin	$20,000	*b.* CFB $= \text{interest} - \text{net new LTD}$
Other expenses	2,500	$= 5,000 - (-1,000) = \$6,000$
EBDIT	$17,500	*c.* CFS $= \text{dividends} - \text{net new equity}$
Depreciation	2,500	$= 3,200 - 500 = \$2,700$
EBIT	$15,000	*d.* CFA $= \text{CFB} + \text{CFS} = 6,000 + 2,700 = \$8,700$
Interest	5,000	$8,700 = \text{OCF} - \text{inc. in NWC} - \text{inc. in cap. sp.};$
EBT	$10,000	Inc. in cap. sp. $= \text{inc. in NFA} + \text{depreciation}$
Taxes	3,400	$= 2,900 + 2,500 = \$5,400$
Net income	$6,600	Inc. in NWC $= 14,100 - 5,400 - 8,700 = \$0$
Dividends	3,200	
Add. to ret. earnings	$3,400	

15. Net Income = dividends + add. to ret. earnings = $625 + 1,000 = \$1,625$
EBT = NI / (1-t) = $1,625 / 0.65 = \$2,500$
EBIT = EBT + interest = $2,500 + 500 = \$3,000$
Sales – costs = EBDIT = $10,000 – 6,000 = \$4,000$
Depreciation = EBDIT – EBIT = $4,000 – 3,000 = \$1,000$

16.

Balance Sheet

Cash	$110,000	Accounts payable	$200,000
Accounts receivable	300,000	Notes payable	300,000
Inventory	400,000	Current liabilities	$500,000
Current assets	$810,000	Long-term debt	175,000
		Total liabilities	$675,000
Tangible net fixed assets	2,000,000		
Intangible net fixed assets	750,000	Common stock	??
Total assets	$3,560,000	Accumulated ret. earnings	2,500,000
		Total liab. + owners' equity	$3,560,000

?? = $3,560,000 – 2,500,000 – 675,000 = \$385,000$

17. Owners' equity = max [(TA - TL), 0]; if TA = \$1,800, OE = \$100; if TA = \$1,500, OE = \$0

18. *a.* X: Taxes   = $0.15(\$50K) + 0.25(\$25K) + 0.34(\$5K) = \$15.45K$
      Y: Taxes   = $0.15(\$50K) + 0.25(\$25K) + 0.34(\$25K) + 0.39(\$235K) + 0.34(\$465K)$
                     = $\$272.0K$

b. Each firm has a marginal tax rate of 34% on the next \$10,000 of taxable income, despite their different average tax rates, so both firms will pay an additional \$3,400 in taxes.

19.

Income Statement

Sales	$750,000	*b.* OCF = EBIT + D – T
Costs	500,000	= $50,000 + 50,000 – 0 = \$100,000$
Gross margin	$250,000	*c.* Net income was negative because of the
Other expenses	150,000	tax deductibility of depreciation and int-
EBDIT	$100,000	erest expense. However, the actual cash
Depreciation	50,000	flow from operations was positive,
EBIT	$50,000	because depreciation is a non-cash
Interest	75,000	expense and interest is a financing, not
EBT	($25,000)	operating, expense.
Taxes	0	
a. Net income	($25,000)	

20. A firm can still pay out dividends if net income is negative; it just has to be sure there is sufficient cash flow to make the dividend payments.

Inc. in NWC = inc. in cap. sp. = net new equity = 0.

Cash flow from assets $\quad$ = OCF – inc. in NWC – inc. in cap. sp. = 100K – 0 – 0 = \$100K

Cash flow to stockholders = divs – net new equity = 25K – 0 = \$25K

Cash flow to creditors $\quad$ = cash flow from assets – cash flow to stockholders = 100K – 25K = \$75K

Cash flow to creditors $\quad$ = interest – net new LTD;

Net new LTD = interest – cash flow to creditors = 75K – 75K = \$0.

21.

Income Statement

Sales	\$4,000	*b.*	OCF = EBDIT – T = 2,000 – 238 = \$1,762
Cost of goods sold	2,000	*c.*	Inc. in NWC = $NWC_{end} - NWC_{beg}$
EBDIT	\$2,000		= $(CA_{end} - CL_{end}) - (CA_{beg} - CL_{beg})$
Depreciation	1,000		= $(2,750 - 1,250) - (2,000 - 1,000)$
EBIT	\$1,000		= 1,500 – 1,000 = \$500
Interest	300		Inc. in cap. sp. = $NFA_{end} - NFA_{beg} + D$
EBT	\$700		= 3,600 – 3,000 + 1,000 = \$1,600
Taxes	238		CFA = OCF – inc in NWC – inc in cap.sp.
a. Net income	\$462		= 1,762 – 500 – 1,600 = -\$338

The cash flow from assets can be positive or negative, since it represents whether the firm raised funds or distributed funds on a net basis. In this problem, even though net income and OCF are positive, the firm invested heavily in both fixed assets and net working capital; it had to raise a net \$338 in funds from its stockholders and creditors to make these investments.

d. Cash flow to creditors $\quad$ = interest – net new LTD = 300 – 0 = \$300

$\quad$ Cash flow to stockholders = cash flow from assets – cash flow to creditors

$\quad\quad\quad$ = -338 – 300 = -\$638 = dividends – net new equity;

Net new equity = 250 + 638 = \$888

The firm had positive earnings in an accounting sense (NI > 0) and had positive cash flow from operations. The firm invested \$500 in new net working capital and \$1,600 in new fixed assets. The firm had to raise \$338 from its stakeholders to support this new investment. It accomplished this by raising \$888 in the form of new equity. After paying out \$250 of this in the form of dividends to shareholders and \$300 in the form of interest to creditors, \$338 was left to just meet the firm's cash flow needs for investment.

22. *a.* Total assets 1993 = 354 + 1,800 = \$2,154; total liabilities 1993 = 171 + 1,150 = \$1,321

$\quad$ Owners' equity 1993 = 2,154 – 1,321 = \$833

$\quad$ Total assets 1994 = 465 + 1,995 = \$2,460; total liabilities 1994 = 205 + 1,190 = \$1,395

$\quad$ Owners' equity 1994 = 2,460 - 1,395 = \$1,065

$\quad$ *b.* NWC 1993 = CA93 – CL93 = 354 – 171 = \$183

$\quad$ NWC 1994 = CA94 – CL94 = 465 – 205 = \$260

$\quad$ Inc. in NWC 1994 = NWC94 – NWC93 = 260 – 183 = \$77

c. Inc. in cap. sp. = NFA94 – NFA93 + D94 = 1,995 – 1,800 + 540 = \$735

Inc. in cap. sp. = fixed assets bought – fixed assets sold

735 = 1,000 – fixed assets sold; fixed assets sold = 1,000 – 735 = \$265

OCF94 = EBDIT – T = 5,125 – 1,478 – (.35)(5,125 – 1,478 – 540 – 259)

$\qquad$ = 3,647 – 996.80 = \$2,650.20

Cash flow from assets = OCF – inc. in NWC – inc. in cap. sp.

$\qquad\qquad$ = 2,650.20 – 77 – 735 = \$1,838.20

d. Net new debt = LTD94 – LTD93 = 1,190 – 1,150 = \$40

Cash flow to creditors = interest – net new LTD = 259 – 40 = \$219

Net new debt = 40 = debt issued – debt retired; debt retired = 100 – 40 = \$60

Challenge

23. Liquidity measures how quickly and easily an asset can be converted to cash without significant loss in value. It's desirable for firms to have high liquidity so that they have a large factor of safety in meeting short-term creditor demands. However, since liquidity also has an opportunity cost associated with it—namely that higher returns can generally be found by investing the cash proceeds from liquidation into productive assets—low liquidity levels are also desirable to the firm. It's up to the firm's financial management staff to find a reasonable compromise between these opposing needs.

24. Inc. in cap. sp.
$$= NFA_{end} - NFA_{beg} + D$$
$$= (NFA_{end} - NFA_{beg}) + (D + AD_{beg}) - AD_{beg}$$
$$= (NFA_{end} - NFA_{beg}) + AD_{end} - AD_{beg}$$
$$= (NFA_{end} + AD_{end}) - (NFA_{beg} + AD_{beg}) = FA_{end} - FA_{beg}.$$

25. *a.* The tax bubble causes average tax rates to catch up to marginal tax rates, thus eliminating the tax advantage of low marginal rates for high income corporations.

b. Taxes paid = 0.15(\$50K) + 0.25(\$25K) + 0.34(\$25K) + 0.39(\$235K) = \$113.9K

Average tax rate = 113.9K / 335K = 34%; Marginal tax rate on next dollar of income = 34%
For corporate taxable income levels of \$335K to \$10M, average tax rates are equal to marginal tax rates.

Taxes paid = 0.34(\$10M) + 0.35(\$5M) + 0.38(\$3.333M) = \$6,416,667

Average tax rate = 6,416,667 / 18,333,333 = 35%; Marginal tax rate on next dollar of income = 35%. For corporate taxable income levels over \$18.333M, average tax rates are again equal to marginal tax rates.

c. Taxes = 0.34(\$250K) = \$85K = 0.15(\$50K) + 0.25(\$25K) + 0.34(\$25K) + X(\$150K);

X(150K) = 85K – 22.25K = 62.75K; X = 62.75K / 150K = 41.83%

26.

12/31/93 Balance Sheet			
Cash	$955	A/P	$1,050
A/R	1,444	N/P	179
Inventory	2,188	CL	$1,229
CA	$4,587	LTD	3,475
NFA	8,106	TL	$4,704
TA	$12,693		

12/31/94 Balance Sheet			
Cash	$1,190	A/P	$1,000
A/R	1,555	N/P	149
Inventory	2,275	CL	$1,149
CA	$5,020	LTD	4,300
NFA	8,315	TL	$5,449
TA	$13,335		

Owners' equity = TA − TL = 12,693 − 4,704 = $7,989

Owners' equity = 13,335 − 5,449 = $7,886

1993 Income Statement	
Sales	$1,745.00
Costs	690.00
Gross margin	$1,055.00
Other expenses	165.00
EBDIT	$890.00
Depr	184.00
EBIT	$706.00
Interest	122.00
EBT	$584.00
Taxes @ 34%	198.56
Net income	$385.44
Dividends	150.00
Add. to RE	$235.44

1994 Income Statement	
Sales	$1,900.00
Costs	770.00
Gross margin	$1,130.00
Other expenses	150.00
EBDIT	$980.00
Depr	184.00
EBIT	$796.00
Interest	148.00
EBT	$648.00
Taxes @ 34%	220.32
Net income	$427.68
Dividends	165.00
Add. to RE	$262.68

27.   1994:   OCF = EBDIT − T = 980 − 220.32 = $759.68

Inc. in NWC = $NWC_{end} - NWC_{beg}$ = $(CA - CL)_{end} - (CA - CL)_{beg}$ =
$$(5,020 - 1,149) - (4,587 - 1,229) = 3,871 - 3,358 = \$513$$

Inc. in cap. sp. = $NFA_{end} - NFA_{beg}$ + depr = 8,315 − 8,106 + 184 = $393

∴ Cash flow from assets = OCF − inc. in NWC − inc. in cap sp.
$$= 759.68 - 513 - 393 = -\$146.32$$

Cash flow to creditors = interest − net new LTD;

net new LTD   = $LTD_{end} - LTD_{beg}$.

Cash flow to creditors = 148 − (4,300 − 3,475) = −$677

Net new equity = common stock$_{end}$ − common stock$_{beg}$

Common stock + retained earnings = total owners' equity

Net new equity = $(OE - RE)_{end} - (OE - RE)_{beg}$
$$= OE_{end} - OE_{beg} + RE_{beg} - RE_{end}$$

$RE_{end} = RE_{beg}$ + add. to RE$_{94}$

$\therefore$ Net new equity $= OE_{end} - OE_{beg} + RE_{beg} - (RE_{beg} + \text{add. to } RE_{94})$

$= OE_{end} - OE_{beg} - ARE_{94}$

Net new equity $= 7{,}886 - 7{,}989 - 262.68 = -\$365.68$

Cash flow to stockholders $= \text{divs} - \text{net new equity} = 165 - (-365.68) = \$530.68$

As a check, cash flow from assets $= -\$146.32$

$= \text{cash flow from creditors} + \text{cash flow to stockholders}$

$= -\$677 + \$530.68 = -\$146.32$

CHAPTER 3
WORKING WITH FINANCIAL STATEMENTS

Basic

1. *a.* If inventory is purchased with cash, then there is no change in the current ratio. If inventory is purchased on credit, then there is a decrease in the current ratio if it was initially greater than 1.0.
    b. Reducing accounts payable with cash increases the current ratio if it was initially greater than 1.0.
    c. Reducing short-term debt with cash increases the current ratio if it was initially greater than 1.0.
    d. As long-term debt approaches maturity, the principal repayment and the remaining interest expense become current liabilities. Thus, if debt is paid off with cash, the current ratio increases if it was initially greater than 1.0.
    e. Reduction of accounts receivables and an increase in cash leaves the current ratio unchanged.
    f. Inventory sold at cost reduces inventory and raises cash, so the current ratio is unchanged.
    g. Inventory sold for a profit raises cash in excess of the inventory recorded at cost, so the current ratio increases.

2. The firm has increased inventory relative to other current assets; therefore, assuming current liability levels remain mostly unchanged, liquidity has potentially decreased.

3. A current ratio of 0.50 means that the firm has twice as much in current liabilities as it does in current assets; the firm potentially has poor liquidity. If pressed by its short-term creditors and suppliers for immediate payment, the firm might have a difficult time meeting its obligations. A current ratio of 1.50 means the firm has 50% more current assets than it does current liabilities. This probably represents an improvement in liquidity; short-term obligations can generally be met completely with a safety factor built in. A current ratio of 15.0, however, might be excessive. Any excess funds sitting in current assets generally earn little or no return. These excess funds might be put to better use by investing in productive long-term assets or distributing the funds to shareholders.

4. *a.* Quick ratio provides a measure of the short-term liquidity of the firm, after removing the effects of inventory, generally the least liquid of the firm's current assets.
    b. Cash ratio represents the ability of the firm to completely pay off its current liabilities balance if immediate payment was demanded.
    c. Interval measure gives an average estimate of how long the firm could continue operations if all its cash inflows stopped, supporting operating costs solely from existing current assets.
    d. Total asset turnover measures how much in sales are generated by each dollar of firm assets.
    e. Equity multiplier represents the leverage of an equity investor of the firm; it measures the dollars worth of firm assets each equity dollar has a claim to.
    f. Long-term debt ratio measures the percentage of total firm capitalization funded by long-term debt.

g. Times interest earned ratio provides a relative measure of how well firm operating earnings cover current interest obligations.

h. Profit margin is the accounting measure of bottom-line profit per dollar of sales.

i. Return on assets is a measure of bottom-line profit per dollar of assets.

j. Return on equity is a measure of bottom-line profit per dollar of equity.

k. Price/earnings ratio reflects how much value the market places on a dollar of accounting earnings for a firm.

5. NWC = $500 = CA – CL;   CA = $500 + $1,800 = $2,300

Current ratio = CA / CL = $2,300/$1,800 = 1.28 times

Quick ratio = (CA – inventory) / CL = ($2,300 – $600) / $1,800 = 0.94 times

6. Profit margin = net income / sales;   net income = ($5M)(0.11) = $550,000

ROA = net income / TA = $550,000 / $9M = 6.11%

ROE = net income / TE = net income / (TA – TD) = $550,000 / ($9M – $3M) = 9.17%

7. Receivables turnover = sales / receivables = $94,300 / $13,565 = 6.95 times

Days' sales in receivables = 365 days / receivables turnover = 365 / 6.95 = 52.51 days

The average collection period for an outstanding accounts receivable balance was 52.51 days.

8. Inventory turnover = COGS / inventory = $147,750 / $46,325 = 3.19 times

Days' sales in inventory = 365 days / inventory turnover = 365 / 3.19 = 114.44 days

On average, a unit of inventory sat on the shelf 114.44 days before it was sold.

9. Total debt ratio = 0.60 = TD / TA = TD / (TD + TE); 0.40(TD) = 0.60(TE)

Debt/equity ratio = TD / TE = 0.60 / 0.40 = 1.50

Equity multiplier = 1 + D/E = 2.50

10. NI = addition to retained earnings + dividends = $170K + $80K = $250K

EPS = NI / shares = $250K / 120K = $2.08 per share

DPS = dividends / shares = $80K / 120K = $0.67 per share

BVPS = TE / shares = $4M / 120K = $33.33 per share

Market-to-book ratio = share price / BVPS = $50 / $33.33 = 1.50 times

P/E ratio = share price / EPS = $50 / $2.08 = 24.0 times

11. ROE = (PM)(TAT)(EM) = (.08)(1.25)(2.0) = 20%

12. ROE = .2025 = (.09)(1.5)(EM);   EM = 1.50;   D/E = EM – 1 = 0.50

13. Decrease in inventory is a source of cash

Decrease in accounts payable is a use of cash

Decrease in notes payable is a use of cash

Increase in accounts receivable is a use of cash

Changes in cash = sources – uses = $350 – ($175 + $400 + $600) = –$825

Cash decreased by $825

14. Payables turnover = COGS / payables = $8,325 / $1,100 = 7.57 times

Days' sales in payables = 365 days / payables turnover = 365 / 7.57 = 48.23 days

The company left its bills to suppliers outstanding for 48.23 days on average. A large value for this ratio could imply that either (1) the company is having liquidity problems, making it difficult to pay off its short-term obligations, or (2) that the company has successfully negotiated lenient credit terms from its suppliers.

15. Net investment in FA = (NFA_{end} − NFA_{beg}) + depreciation = $370 + $130 = $500

The company bought $500 in new fixed assets; this is a use of cash.

16. EM = 1 + D/E = 2.10

ROE = (ROA)(EM) = .065(2.10) = 13.65%

ROE = NI / TE;   NI = (.1365)($210,000) = $28,665

17. through 19:

	1993	#17	1994	#17	#18	#19
Assets						
Current assets						
Cash	$ 9,320	(2.70%)	$ 10,050	(2.66%)	1.0783	0.985
Accounts receivable	29,720	(8.60%)	31,525	(8.35%)	1.0607	0.970
Inventory	58,500	(16.92%)	66,710	(17.66%)	1.1403	1.043
Total	$ 97,540	(28.22%)	$108,285	(28.67%)	1.1102	1.015
Fixed assets						
Net plant and equipment	248,060	(71.78%)	269,460	(71.33%)	1.0863	0.993
Total assets	$345,600	(100%)	$377,745	(100%)	1.0930	1.000
Liabilities and Owners' Equity						
Current liabilities						
Accounts payable	$ 56,250	(16.28%)	$ 51,900	(13.74%)	0.9227	0.844
Notes payable	26,200	(7.58%)	30,000	(7.94%)	1.1450	1.047
Total	$ 82,450	(23.86%)	$ 81,900	(21.68%)	0.9933	0.908
Long-term debt	50,000	(14.47%)	35,000	(9.27%)	0.7000	0.640
Owners' equity						
Common stock and paid-in surplus	$ 62,600	(18.11%)	$ 62,600	(16.57%)	1.0000	0.915
Accumulated retained earnings	150,550	(43.56%)	198,245	(52.48%)	1.3168	1.204
Total	$213,150	(61.67%)	$260,845	(69.05%)	1.2238	1.119
Total liabilities and owners' equity	$345,600	(100%)	$377,745	(100%)	1.0930	1.000

20.

	1993	Sources/Uses	1994
Assets			
Current assets			
Cash	$ 9,320	(+730) U	$ 10,050
Accounts receivable	29,720	(+1,805) U	31,525
Inventory	58,500	(+8,210) U	66,710
Total	$ 97,540	(+10,745) U	$108,285
Fixed assets			
Net plant and equipment	248,060	(+21,400) U	269,460
Total assets	$345,600	(+32,145) U	$377,745
Liabilities and Owners' Equity			
Current liabilities			
Accounts payable	$ 56,250	(- 4,350) U	$ 51,900
Notes payable	26,200	(+3,800) S	30,000
Total	$ 82,450	(- 550) U	$ 81,900
Long-term debt	50,000	(- 1,500) U	35,000
Owners' equity			
Common stock and paid-in surplus	$ 62,600	(0)	$ 62,600
Accumulated retained earnings	150,550	(+47,695) S	198,245
Total	$213,150	(+47,695) S	$260,845
Total liabilities and owners' equity	$345,600	(+32,145) S	$377,745

The firm used $32,145 in cash to acquire new assets. It raised this amount of cash by increasing liabilities and owners' equity by $32,145. In particular, the needed funds were raised entirely by internal financing (on a net basis), out of the additions to retained earnings.

21. *a.* $\quad$ CR93 = 97,540 / 82,450 = 1.183; $\qquad$ CR94 = 108,285 / 81,900 = 1.322

$\quad$ *b.* $\quad$ QR93 = (97,540 – 58,500) / 82,450 = 0.474; $\quad$ QR94 = (108,285 – 66,710) / 81,900 = 0.508

$\quad$ *c.* $\quad$ Cash ratio93 = 9,320 / 82,450 = 0.113; $\qquad$ Cash ratio94 = 10,050 / 81,900 = 0.123

$\quad$ *d.* $\quad$ NWC/TA ratio93 = (97,540 – 82,450) / 345,600 = 0.044

$\qquad$ NWC/TA ratio94 = (108,285 – 81,900) / 377,745 = 0.070

$\quad$ *e.* $\quad$ D/E93 = (82,450 + 50,000) / 213,150 = 0.621; $\quad$ D/E94 = (81,900 + 35,000) / 260,845 = 0.448

$\qquad$ EM93 = 1 + D/E93 = 1.621; $\qquad\qquad$ EM94 = 1 + D/E94 = 1.448

$\quad$ *f.* $\quad$ TDR93 = (82,450 + 50,000) / 345,600 = 0.383

$\qquad$ TDR94 = (81,900 + 35,000) / 377,745 = 0.310

$\qquad$ LTDR93 = 50,000 / (50,000 + 213,150) = 0.190

$\qquad$ LTDR94 = 35,000 / (35,000 + 260,845) = 0.118

22. Common size financial statements express all balance sheet accounts as a percentage of total assets and all income statement accounts as a percentage of total sales. Using these percentage values rather than nominal dollar values facilitates comparisons betweens firms of different size or business type. Common-base-year financial statements express each account as a ratio between their current year nominal dollar value and some reference year nominal dollar value. Using these ratios allows the total growth trend in the accounts to be measured.

23. Peer group analysis involves comparing the financial ratios and operating performance of a particular firm to a set of peer group firms in the same industry or line of business. Comparing a firm to its peers allows the financial manager to evaluate whether some aspects of the firm's operations, finance, or investment activities are out of line with the norm, and provides some guidance on appropriate actions to take to adjust these ratios if appropriate. An aspirant group would be a set of firms whose performance the company in question would like to emulate. The financial ratios of aspirant groups are often used by the financial manager as the target ratios for his or her firm; some managers' are evaluated by how well they match the performance of the identified aspirant group.

24. Return on equity is probably the most important accounting ratio that measures the bottom-line performance of the firm with respect to the equity shareholders. The Du Pont identity emphasizes the role of firm profitability, asset utilization efficiency, and financial leverage in setting the ROE figure. For example, a firm with ROE of 20% would seem to be doing well, but this figure may result from a marginally profitable firm (low profit margin) that is highly levered (high equity multiplier). If the firm's margins should erode slightly, the ROE would be heavily impacted.

25. $ROE = 0.15 = (PM)(TAT)(EM) = (PM)(S/TA)(1 + D/E)$
    $PM = [(0.15)(\$300)] / [(1 + 1)(\$500)] = .045$
    $PM = .045 = NI / S; \quad NI = .045(\$500) = \$22.50$

26. Increases in liability accounts represent a source of cash to the firm. Accounts payable are a form of short-term financing, since suppliers are providing their goods and services on credit to the firm. Thus an increase in accounts payable represents a net source of funds to the firm.

27. $CR = 1.50 = CA / CL; \quad CA = 1.50(\$500) = \$750$
    $PM = .08 = NI / sales; \quad NI = .08(\$2,500) = \$200$
    $ROE = .225 = NI / TE; \quad TE = \$200 / .225 = \$888.89$
    Long-term debt ratio $= 0.75 = LTD / (LTD + TE); \quad 1 + TE / LTD = 4/3; \quad LTD = 3(\$888.89) = \$2,666.6$
    $TD = CL + LTD = \$500 + \$2,666.67 = \$3,166.67$
    $TA = TD + TE = \$3,166.67 + \$888.89 = \$4,055.56$
    $NFA = TA - CA = \$4,055.56 - \$750 = \$3,305.56$

28. Child: profit $= \$0.75 / \$25 = 3\%;$ store: profit margin $= NI / S = \$3.375M / \$225M = 1.5\%$
    The advertisement is referring to the store's profit margin, but a more appropriate earnings measure for the firm's owners is the return on equity.
    $ROE = NI / TE = NI / (TA - TD) = \$3.375M / (\$40M - \$17M) = 14.67\%$

29. Days' sales in receivables = 16.60 days = 365 days / receivables turnover

Receivables turnover = sales / receivables; Sales = ($61,000)(365) / 16.60 = $1,341,265

PM = NI / S = $47,500 / $1,341,265 = 3.54%

TAT = S / TA = $1,341,265 / $527,000 = 2.55 times

EM = 1 + D/E = 1.85

ROE = (PM)(TAT)(EM) = (.0354)(2.55)(1.85) = 16.67%

30. Net income = (1 – t)EBT;   EBT = $4,950 / 0.66 = $7,500

EBIT = EBT + interest paid = $7,500 + $1,200 = $8,700

EBDIT = EBIT + depreciation expense = $8,700 + $1,300 = $10,000

Cash coverage ratio = EBDIT / interest = $10,000 / $1,200 = 8.33 times

31. Sales – COGS = EBDIT = $110K – $45K = $65K

EBIT = EBDIT – depreciation = $65K – $15K = $50K

DPS = dividends / shares;   dividends = $1.40(5,000) = $7K

Net income = dividends + additions to retained earnings = $7K + $12.8K = $19.8K

EBT = NI / (1 – t) = $19.8K / 0.66 = $30K

EBIT – EBT = interest paid = $50K – $30K = $20K

Times interest earned ratio = EBIT / interest = $50K / $20K = 2.50 times

32. PM = NI / S = £6,211,000 / £479,650,000 = 1.29%

As long as both net income and sales aré measured in the same currency, there is no problem; in fact, except for some market value ratios like EPS and BVPS, none of the financial ratios discussed in the text are measured in terms of currency. This is one reason why financial ratio analysis is widely used in international finance to compare the business operations of firms and/or divisions across national economic borders.

NI = .0129 ($767,440) = $9,937,000

33.   *Short-term solvency ratios:*

CR93 = ($404 + 1,115 + 2,870) / ($650 + 375 + 219) = 3.53 times

CR94 = ($247 + 1,616 + 4,225) / ($679 + 400 + 250) = 4.58 times

QR93 = ($404 + 1,115) / ($650 + 375 + 219) = 1.22 times

QR94 = ($247 + 1,616) / ($679 + 400 + 250) = 1.40 times

Cash ratio93 = $404 / ($650 + 375 + 219) = 0.325 times

Cash ratio94 = $247 / ($679 + 400 + 250) = 0.186 times

Asset management ratios:

TAT = $9,000 / $14,188 = 0.634 times

Inventory turnover = $4,500 / $4,225 = 1.07 times

Receivables turnover = $9,000 / $1,616 = 5.57 times

Long-term solvency ratios:

Debt ratio93 = ($3,400 + 650 + 375 + 219) / $12,481 = 0.372

Debt ratio94 = ($3,150 + 679 + 400 + 250) / $14,188 = 0.316

D/E93 = ($3,400 + 650 + 375 + 219) / ($500 + 1,300 + 6,397) = 0.567

D/E94 = ($3,150 + 679 + 400 + 250) / ($500 + 1,300 + 7,909) = 0.461

EM93= 1 + D/E93 = 1.567;   EM94 = 1 + D/E94 = 1.461

TIE ratio = $3,800 / $600 = 6.33 times

Cash coverage ratio = ($3,800 + 700) / $600 = 7.50 times

Profitability ratios:

PM = $2,112 / $9,000 = 23.47%

ROA = $2,112 / $14,188 = 14.89%

ROE = $2,112 / ($500 + 1,300 + 7,909) = 21.75%

34. ROE = (PM)(TAT)(EM) = (0.2347)(0.634)(1.461) = 0.2175

35. Interval measure = CA / average daily operating costs

Average daily operating costs = COGS / 365 days = $4,500 / 365 = $12.33 per day

Interval measure = ($247 + 1,616 + 4,225) / $12.33 per day = 494 days, or a little over 16 months

36.

KUIPERS ENTERPRISES

Statement of Cash Flows

For Period Ending December 31, 1994

Cash, beginning of the year	$ 404
Operating activities	
Net income	$ 2,112
Plus:	
Depreciation	$ 700
Increase in accounts payable	$ 29
Increase in other current liabilities	$ 31
Less:	
Increase in accounts receivable	$ 501
Increase in inventory	$ 1,355
Net cash from operating activities	$ 1,016
Investment activities	
Fixed asset acquisition	($ 348)
Net cash from investment activities	($ 348)

Financing activities	
Increase in notes payable	$ 25
Dividends paid	($ 600)
Decrease in long-term debt	($ 250)
Net cash from financing activities	($ 825)
Net increase in cash	($ 157)
Cash, end of year	$ 247

37. EPS = $2,112 / 400 shares = $5.28 per share
P/E ratio = $52 / $5.28 = 9.85 times
DPS = $600 / 400 shares = $1.50 per share
BVPS = ($500 + 1,300 + 7,909) / 400 shares = $24.27 per share
Market-to-book ratio = $52.00 / $24.27 = 2.14 times

CHAPTER 4
LONG-TERM FINANCIAL PLANNING AND GROWTH

Basic

1.

Pro forma income statement		Pro forma balance sheet			
Sales	$ 8,400	Assets	$ 4,200	Debt	$ 2,100
Costs	7,200			Equity	2,100
Net income	$ 1,200	Total	$ 4,200	Total	$ 4,200

Net income is $1,200, but equity only increased by $350; therefore, a dividend of $850 must have been paid. Dividends paid is the plug variable.

2.

Pro forma income statement		Pro forma balance sheet			
Sales	$ 8,400	Assets	$ 4,200	Debt	$ 1,750
Costs	7,200			Equity	2,350
Net income	$ 1,200	Total	$ 4,200	Total	$ 4,100

Dividends	$ 600	EFN = $4,200 – $4,100 = $100
Add. to RE	600	

3.

Pro forma income statement		Pro forma balance sheet			
Sales	$2,300.00	Assets	$ 5,750	Debt	$3,000.00
Costs	977.50			Equity	3,322.50
Net income	$1,322.50	Total	$ 5,750	Total	$6,322.50

EFN = $5,750 – $6,322.50 = – $572.50. No external financing is needed. There is a surplus of cash, so either debt can be retired or dividends can be paid after all.

4.

Pro forma income statement		Pro forma balance sheet			
Sales	$12,000	Assets	$48,000	Debt	$15,000
Costs	4,800			Equity	26,920
EBIT	7,200	Total	$48,000	Total	$41,920
Taxes(40%)	2,880				
Net income	$ 4,320				

Dividends	$ 2,400	Dividends = ($2,000 / $3,600)($4,320) = $2,400
Add. to RE	1,920	EFN = $48,000 – $41,920 = $6,080

5.

Pro forma income statement		_Pro forma balance sheet_			
Sales	$ 2,900	CA	$ 2,320	CL	$ 928.00
Costs	2,320	FA	4,640	LTD	1,200.00
Taxes	232			Equity	4,139.20
Net income	$ 348	Total	$ 6,960	Total	$6,267.20

Dividends $208.80   Dividends = 0.6($348) = $208.80
Add. to RE   139.20   EFN = $6,960 – $6,267.20 = $692.80

6.   ROA = NI / TA = $1,110 / $33,000 = .0336
b = 1 – 0.3 = 0.7
internal g = [0.7(.0336)] / [1 – 0.7(.0336)] = .0241 = 2.41%

7.   ROE = NI / TE = $1,110 / $13,000 = .0854
b = 1 – 0.3 = 0.7
sustainable g = [0.7 (.0854)] / [1 – 0.7(.0854)] = .0636 = 6.36%

8.   Growth may conflict with wealth maximization if negative NPV investments are undertaken merely to increase the size of the firm.

9.   ROE = NI / TE = $2,580 / $36,655 = .0704
b = 1 – 0.4 = 0.6
sustainable g = [0.6 (.0704)] / [1 – 0.6(.0704)] = .0441 = 4.41%
maximum increase in sales = $19,000(.0441) = $837.78

10.

FOLKER CORPORATION
Pro Forma Income Statement

Sales	$ 10,350
Costs	6,900
Taxable income	$ 3,450
Taxes(@34%)	1,173
Net income	$ 2,277
Dividends	$ 575
Add. to RE	1,702

11.

FOLKER CORPORATION
Balance Sheet

	($)	(%)			($)	(%)
Assets			*Liabilities and Owners' Equity*			
Current assets			Current liabilities			
Cash	$ 1,500	16.67	Accounts payable		$ 3,000	33.33
Accounts receivable	3,000	33.33	Notes payable		2,000	n/a
Inventory	3,000	33.33	Total		$ 5,000	n/a
Total	$ 7,500	83.33	Long-term debt		3,000	n/a
Fixed assets			Owners' equity			
Net plant and			Common stock and			
equipment	10,000	111.11	paid-in surplus		$ 2,500	n/a
			Retained earnings		7,000	n/a
			Total		$ 9,500	n/a
			Total liabilities and owners'			
Total assets	$17,500	194.44	equity		$17,500	n/a

12.

FOLKER CORPORATION
Pro Forma Balance Sheet

Assets		*Liabilities and Owners' Equity*	
Current assets		Current liabilities	
Cash	$ 1,725	Accounts payable	$ 3,450
Accounts receivable	3,450	Notes payable	2,000
Inventory	3,450	Total	$ 5,450
Total	$ 8,625	Long-term debt	3,000
Fixed assets		Total debt	$ 8,450
Net plant and		Owners' equity	
equipment	11,500	Common stock and	
		paid-in surplus	$ 2,500
		Retained earnings	8,702
		Total	$11,202
		Total liabilities and owners'	
Total assets	$20,125	equity	$19,652

EFN = $20,125 − $19,652 = $473

13. ROA = NI / TA = $2,277 / $20,125 = 11.31%
ROE = NI / TE = $2,277 / $11,202 = 20.33%

14. b = 1 − .6 = .4;   internal g = [.4(.12)] / [1 − .4(.12)] = 5.04%

15. b = 1 − .45 = .55;   sustainable g = [.55(.25)] / [1 − .55(.25)] = 15.94%

16. ROE = (PM)(TAT)(EM) = (.06)(1/.5)(1+.8) = 0.216
b = \$15,000 / \$20,000 = .75;   sustainable g = [.75(.216)] / [1 − .75(.216)] = 19.33%

17. ROE = (PM)(TAT)(EM) = (.04)(1.0)(2.5) = 0.10
b = 1 − .3 = .7;   sustainable g = [.7(.10)] / [1 − .7(.10)] = 7.53%

18. Full capacity sales = \$100,000 / 0.80 = \$125,000;   max sales growth = 25%

19. Fixed assets / full capacity sales = \$170,000 / \$125,000 = 1.36
Total fixed assets = 1.36(\$130,000) = \$176,800
New fixed assets = \$176,800 − \$170,000 = \$6,800

20. One plus is that it is easy to implement. A big minus is that the relationship between factors are assumed to be static, at least within each scenario. It is probably true that sales, costs, and asset needs are closely associated over the long run, but in the short run, they need not be.

21. b = 1 − .4 = .6;   sustainable g = .12 = [.6(ROE)] / [1 − .6(ROE)];   ROE = .1786
ROE = .1786 = PM(1 / 1.1)(1 + .6);   PM = (.1786)(1.1) / 1.6 = 12.28%

22. b = 1 − .3 = .7;   sustainable g = .15 = [.7(ROE)] / [1 − .7(ROE)];   ROE = .1863
ROE = .1863 = (.08)(1 / 1.5)(EM);   EM = (.1863)(1.5) / .08 = 3.494;   D/E = 2.494

23. b = 1 − .7 = .3;   internal g = .06 = [.3(ROA)] / [1 − .3(ROA)];   ROA = .1887
ROA = .1887 = (PM)(TAT);   TAT = .1887 / .10 = 1.887

24. TDR = 0.6 = TD / TA;   1 / 0.6 = TA / TD = 1 + TE / TD;   D/E = 1 / [(1 / 0.6) − 1] = 1.5
ROE = (PM)(TAT)(EM) = (.05)(1.2)(1 + 1.5) = .15;   ROA = ROE / EM = .15 / 2.5 = .06
b = 1 − .4 = .6;   sustainable g = [.6(.15)] / [1 − .6(.15)] = 9.89%

25. b = 1 − (\$400 / \$1,000) = .6;   ROE = NI / TE = \$1,000 / \$40,000 = .025
sustainable g = [.6(.025)] / [1 − .6(.025)] = 1.52%
new TA = 1.0152(\$70,000) = \$71,066;   D/E = \$30,000 / \$40,000 = .75
new TD = 3/7(TA) = 3/7(\$71,066) = \$30,457;   additional borrowing = \$30,457 − \$30,000 = \$457
ROA = NI / TA = \$1,000 / \$70,000 = .0143
internal g = [.6(.0143)] / [1 − .6(.0143)] = 0.86%

26.

HI GROW INC.

1995 Pro Forma Income Statement

Sales	$750,000
Costs	562,500
Other expenses	31,250
EBDIT	$156,250
Depreciation	25,000
EBIT	$131,250
Interest	10,000
Taxable income	$121,250
Taxes(@34%)	41,225
Net income	$ 80,025
Dividends	$ 16,840
Retained earnings	63,185

HI GROW INC.

Pro Forma Balance Sheet as of December 31, 1995

Assets		Liabilities and Owners' Equity	
Current assets		Current liabilities	
Cash	$ 12,500	Accounts payable	$ 50,000
Accounts receivable	50,000	Notes payable	10,000
Inventory	62,500	Total	$ 60,000
Total	$ 125,000	Long-term debt	75,000
Fixed assets		Total debt	$ 135,000
Net plant and		Owners' equity	
equipment	312,500	Common stock and	
		paid-in surplus	$ 25,000
		Retained earnings	263,185
		Total	$ 288,185
		Total liabilities and owners'	
Total assets	$ 437,500	equity	$ 423,185

EFN = $437,500 − $423,185 = $14,315

27. Full capacity sales = $600,000 / 0.90 = $666,667
Fixed asset utilization at full capacity = $250,000 / $666,667 = 0.375
Total fixed assets = 0.375($750,000) = $281,250
EFN = ($125,000 + $281,250) − $423,185 = − $16,935

28. D/E = $125,000 / $225,000 = 0.556;   new total debt = 0.556($288,185) = $160,103
EFN = $437,500 − ($160,103 + $288,185) = − $10,788

29.   g = 15%:   HI GROW INC.   g = 20%:   HI GROW INC.

1995 Pro Forma Income Statement		1995 Pro Forma Income Statement	
Sales	$ 690,000	Sales	$ 720,000
Costs	517,500	Costs	540,000
Other expenses	28,750	Other Expenses	30,000
EBDIT	$ 143,750	EBDIT	$ 150,000
Depreciation	25,000	Depreciation	25,000
EBIT	$ 118,750	EBIT	$ 125,000
Interest	10,000	Interest	10,000
Taxable income	$ 108,750	Taxable income	$ 115,000
Taxes(@34%)	36,975	Taxes(@34%)	39,100
Net income	$ 71,775	Net income	$ 75,900
Dividends	$ 15,104	Dividends	$ 15,972
Retained earnings	56,671	Retained earnings	59,928

HI GROW INC.
Pro Forma Balance Sheet as of December 31, 1995

Assets	g = 15%	g=20%	Liab. & OE	g = 15%	g = 20%
Current assets			Current liabilities		
Cash	$ 11,500	$ 12,000	Accounts payable	$ 46,000	$ 48,000
Accounts receivable	46,000	48,000	Notes payable	10,000	10,000
Inventory	57,500	60,000	Total	$ 56,000	$ 58,000
Total	$115,000	$120,000	Long-term debt	75,000	75,000
Fixed assets			Total debt	$ 131,000	$133,000
Net plant and			Owners' equity		
equipment	287,500	300,000	Common stock and		
			paid-in surplus	$ 25,000	$ 25,000
			Retained earnings	256,671	259,928
			Total	$ 281,671	$284,928
			Total liabilities and owners'		
Total assets	$402,500	$420,000	equity	$ 412,671	$417,928

@25%, EFN = $14,315
@20%, EFN = $420,000 – $417,928 = $2,072
@15%, EFN = $402,500 – $412,671 = – $10,171
slope of line: [$14,315 – $2,072] / [.25 – .20] = $244,860
intercept of line: $14,315 = ($244,860)(.25) + B;   B = – $46,900
equation of line: EFN = 244,860g – 46,900
EFN is zero when g is 46,900 / 244,860 = 19.15%
ROA = NI / TA = $59,400 / $350,000 = .1697;   b = $46,900 / 59,400 = .7896
internal g = [.7896(.1697)] / [1 – .7896(.1697)] = 15.47%

The two numbers are different because the equation in the book is derived from different assumptions; constant interest and depreciation expense are not factored into the book equation, nor is the spontaneously increasing accounts payable.

30.   g = 30%:

HI GROW INC.
1995 Pro Forma Income Statement

Sales	$ 780,000
Costs	585,000
Other expenses	32,500
EBDIT	$ 162,500
Depreciation	25,000
EBIT	$ 137,500
Interest	10,000
Taxable income	$ 127,500
Taxes(@34%)	43,350
Net income	$ 84,150
Dividends	$ 17,708
Retained earnings	66,442

g = 35%:

HI GROW INC.
1995 Pro Forma Income Statement

Sales	$ 810,000
Costs	607,500
Other Expenses	33,750
EBDIT	$ 168,750
Depreciation	25,000
EBIT	$ 143,750
Interest	10,000
Taxable income	$ 133,750
Taxes(@34%)	45,475
Net income	$ 88,275
Dividends	$ 18,576
Retained earnings	69,699

HI GROW INC.
Pro Forma Balance Sheet as of December 31, 1995

Assets	*g = 30%*	*g=35%*	*Liab. & OE*	*g = 30%*	*g = 35%*
Current assets			Current liabilities		
Cash	$ 13,000	$ 13,500	Accounts payable	$ 52,000	$ 54,000
Accounts receivable	52,000	54,000	Notes payable	10,000	10,000
Inventory	65,000	67,500	Total	$ 62,000	$ 64,000
Total	$130,000	$135,000	Long-term debt	99,912	99,722
Fixed assets			Total debt	$ 161,912	$163,722
Net plant and			Owners' equity		
equipment	325,000	337,500	Common stock and		
			paid-in surplus	$ 25,000	$ 25,000
			Retained earnings	266,442	269,699
			Total	$ 291,442	$294,699
			Total liabilities and owners'		
Total assets	$455,000	$472,500	equity	$ 453,354	$458,421

@30%, new total debt = 0.556($291,442) = $161,912
@35%, new total debt = 0.556($294,699) = $163,722

@25%, EFN = – $10,788
@30%, EFN = $455,000 – $453,354 = $1,646
@35%, EFN = $472,500 – $458,421 = $14,079
slope of line: [$14,079 – $1,646] / [.35 – .30] = $248,660
intercept of line: $14,079 = ($248,660)(.35) + B;   B = – $72,952
equation of line: EFN = 248,660g – 72,952
EFN is zero when g is 72,952 / 248,660 = 29.34%
ROE = NI / TE = $59,400 / $225,000 = .2640;   b = $46,900 / 59,400 = .7896
sustainable g = [.7896(.2640)] / [1 – .7896(.2640)] = 26.33%

The two numbers are different because the equation in the book is derived from different assumptions; constant interest and depreciation expense are not factored into the book equation, nor is the spontaneously increasing accounts payable.

31. ROE = (PM)(TAT)(EM) = (.05)(1 / 1.75)(1 + 0.4) = .04

sustainable g = .10 = [b(.04)] / [1 − b(.04)];   b = 2.27;   payout ratio = 1 − b = − 1.27

This is a negative dividend payout ratio of 127%, which is impossible; the growth rate is not consistent with the other constraints. The lowest possible payout rate is 0, which corresponds to b=1, or total earnings retention.

max sustainable g = .04 / (1 − .04) = 4.17%

32. The internal growth rate is greater than 15%, because at a 15% growth rate the negative EFN indicates that there is excess internal financing. If the internal growth rate is greater than 15%, then the sustainable growth rate is certainly greater than 15%, because there is additional debt financing used in that case (assuming the firm is not 100% equity-financed). As the retention ratio is increased, the firm has more internal sources of funding, so the EFN will decline. Conversely, as the retention ratio is decreased, the EFN will rise. If the firm pays out all its earnings in the form of dividends, then the firm has no internal sources of funding (ignoring the effects of accounts payable); the internal growth rate is zero in this case and the EFN will rise to the change in total assets.

33. The sustainable growth rate is greater than 20%, because at a 20% growth rate the negative EFN indicates that there is excess financing still available. If the firm is 100% equity financed, then the sustainable and internal growth rates are equal and the internal growth rate would be greater than 20%. However, when the firm has some debt, the internal growth rate is always less than the sustainable growth rate, so it is ambiguous whether the internal growth rate would be greater than or less than 20%. If the retention ratio is increased, the firm will have more internal funding sources available, and will have to take on more debt to keep the debt/equity ratio constant, so the EFN will decline. Conversely, if the retention ratio is decreased, the EFN will rise. If the retention rate is zero, both the internal and sustainable growth rates are zero, and the EFN will rise to the change in total assets.

34. EFN = increase in assets − addition to retained earnings

Increase in assets = A × g

Addition to retained earnings = (NI × b)(1 + g)

NI = PM(S)

Thus, EFN = A(g) − PM(S)b(1 + g)
     = A(g) − PM(S)b − [PM(S)b] g
     = − PM(S)b + [A − PM(S)b] g

35. Internal growth rate:

EFN	$= 0 = -\text{PM(S)}b + [\,A - \text{PM(S)}b\,]\,g$
g	$= [\,\text{PM(S)}b\,]\,/\,[\,A - \text{PM(S)}b\,]$
Since ROA	$= \text{NI}\,/\,\text{TA} = \text{PM(S)}b\,/\,A$, dividing numerator and denominator by A gives
g	$= [\,\{\,\text{PM(S)}b\,\}\,/\,A\,]\,/\,[\,\{\,A - \text{PM(S)}b\,\}\,/\,A\,]$
	$= b(\text{ROA})\,/\,[\,1 - b(\text{ROA})\,]$

Sustainable growth rate:

To maintain a constant D/E ratio with no external equity financing, EFN must equal the addition to retained earnings times the D/E ratio:

$$\text{EFN} = (\,\text{D/E}\,)[\,\text{PM(S)}b(\,1 + g\,)\,] = A(\,g\,) - \text{PM(S)}b(\,1 + g\,)$$

Solving for g and then dividing numerator and denominator by A:

g	$= \text{PM(S)}b(\,1 + \text{D/E}\,)\,/\,[\,A - \text{PM(S)}b(\,1 + \text{D/E}\,)\,]$
	$= \{\,\text{ROA}(\,1 + \text{D/E}\,)b\,\}\,/\,\{\,1 - \text{ROA}(\,1 + \text{D/E}\,)b\,\}$
	$= b(\text{ROE})\,/\,[\,1 - b(\text{ROE})\,]$

CHAPTER 5
FIRST PRINCIPLES OF VALUATION: THE TIME VALUE OF MONEY

Basic

1. $\$10,000(1.05)^{12} = \$17,958.56$; $\$7,958.56 - \$500(12) = \$1,958.56$

2. $FV = \$570(1.09)^{15}$ $= \$ \;\;\; 2,076.22$
   $FV = \$8,922(1.18)^{9}$ $= \$ \;\; 39,573.12$
   $FV = \$61,133(1.12)^{3}$ $= \$ \;\; 85,887.46$
   $FV = \$219,850(1.04)^{10}$ $= \$325,431.71$

3. $PV = \$349 / (1.06)^{5}$ $= \$ \;\;\;\; 260.79$
   $PV = \$5,227 / (1.02)^{20}$ $= \$ \;\; 3,517.62$
   $PV = \$48,950 / (1.25)^{12}$ $= \$ \;\; 3,363.82$
   $PV = \$612,511 / (1.33)^{7}$ $= \$83,205.57$

4. $FV = \$615 = \$475(1+r)^{4}$; $r = (615/475)^{1/4} - 1$ $= \;\; 6.67\%$
   $FV = \$18,350 = \$7,350(1+r)^{7}$; $r = (18,350/7,350)^{1/7} - 1$ $= 13.96\%$
   $FV = \$65,000 = \$27,175(1+r)^{11}$; $r = (65,000/27,175)^{1/11} - 1$ $= \;\; 8.25\%$
   $FV = \$200,000 = \$93,412(1+r)^{19}$; $r = (200,000/93,412)^{1/19} - 1$ $= \;\; 4.09\%$

5. $FV = \$2,550 = \$1,200(1.08)^{t}$; $t = \ln(2,550/1,200) / \ln 1.08$ $= \;\;\;\; 9.794$
   $FV = \$21,225 = \$16,310(1.12)^{t}$; $t = \ln(21,225/16,310) / \ln 1.12$ $= \;\;\;\; 2.324$
   $FV = \$175,000 = \$75,000(1.03)^{t}$; $t = \ln(175,000/75,000) / \ln 1.03$ $= \; 28.665$
   $FV = \$912,475 = \$183,650(1.29)^{t}$; $t = \ln(912,475/183,650) / \ln 1.29$ $= \;\;\;\; 6.296$

6. $FV = \$50,000 = \$5,000(1+r)^{18}$; $r = (50,000/5,000)^{1/18} - 1 = 13.65\%$

7. $FV = \$2 = \$1(1.09)^{t}$; $t = \ln 2 / \ln 1.09 = 8.043$; $t = \ln 3 / \ln 1.09 = 12.748$

8. $FV = \$10,000 = \$4,000(1+r)^{8}$; $r = (10,000/4,000)^{1/8} - 1 = 12.14\%$

9. $FV = \$20,000 = \$16,000(1.06)^{t}$; $t = \ln(20,000/16,000) / \ln 1.06 = 3.830$

10. $PV = \$225 / (1.085)^{17} = \$56.22$ million

11. $PV@10\% = \$500 / 1.1 + \$700 / 1.1^{2} + \$600 / 1.1^{3} + \$300 / 1.1^{4}$ $= \$1,688.75$
    $PV@14\% = \$500 / 1.14 + \$700 / 1.14^{2} + \$600 / 1.14^{3} + \$300 / 1.14^{4}$ $= \$1,559.83$
    $PV@20\% = \$500 / 1.2 + \$700 / 1.2^{2} + \$600 / 1.2^{3} + \$300 / 1.2^{4}$ $= \$1,394.68$

12. X@5%:   PVA = $2,000[(1 − [1/1.05]^4) / .05]   = $7,091.90

     Y@5%:   PVA = $2,500[(1 − [1/1.05]^3) / .05]   = $6,808.12; choose X

     X@20%:   PVA = $2,000[(1 − [1/1.20]^4) / .20]   = $5,177.47

     Y@20%:   PVA = $2,500[(1 − [1/1.20]^3) / .20]   = $5,266.20; choose Y

13. FV@6% = $900(1.06)^3 + $800(1.06)^2 + $700(1.06) + $600   = $3,312.79

     FV@8% = $900(1.08)^3 + $800(1.08)^2 + $700(1.08) + $600   = $3,422.86

     FV@16% = $900(1.16)^3 + $800(1.16)^2 + $700(1.16) + $600   = $3,893.29

14. PVA@12 yrs: PVA = $1,500[(1 − [1/1.12]^{12}) / .12]   = $ 9,291.56

     PVA@35 yrs: PVA = $1,500[(1 − [1/1.12]^{35}) / .12]   = $12,263.26

     PVA@60 yrs: PVA = $1,500[(1 − [1/1.12]^{60}) / .12]   = $12,486.07

     PVA@infinite yrs: PVA = $1,500 / .12   = $12,500.00

15. PVA = $55,000 = $C[(1 − [1/1.09]^7) / .09]; C = $55,000 / 5.033 = $10,927.98

16. PVA = $27,000[(1 − [1/1.07]^8) / .07] = $161,225.06; can't afford the system.

17. FVA = $600[(1.095^{10} − 1) / .095]   = $ 9,336.17

     FV@13 yrs = $9,336.17(1.095)^3 = $12,257.77

18. FVA = $17,000 = $C[(1.08^6 − 1) / .08];   C = $17,000 / 7.336 = $2,317.36

19. PVA = $7,000   = $C[(1 − [1/1.10]^6) / .10]; C = $7,000 / 4.355 = $1,607.25

20. PV = $700 / .12 = $5,833.33

21. PV = $8,500 = $700 / r ; r = $700 / $8,500 = 8.24%

22. EAR = [1+(.10/4)]^4 − 1   = 10.38%

     EAR = [1+(.16/12)]^{12} − 1   = 17.23%

     EAR = [1+(.09/365)]^{365} − 1 = 9.42%

     EAR = $e^{.21}$ − 1   = 23.37%

23. EAR = .08 = [1+(APR/2)]^2 − 1;   APR = 2[(1.08)$^{1/2}$ − 1]   = 7.85%

     EAR = .12 = [1+(APR/12)]^{12} − 1;   APR = 12[(1.12)$^{1/12}$ − 1] = 11.39%

     EAR = .17 = [1+(APR/52)]^{52} − 1;   APR = 52[(1.17)$^{1/52}$ − 1] = 15.72%

     EAR = .24 = e^{APR} − 1;   APR = ln 1.24   = 21.51%

24. Last National: EAR = [1+(.08/4)]^4 − 1 = 8.24%

     Last United: EAR = [1+(.085/2)]^2 − 1 = 8.68%

25. EAR = .09 = [1+(APR/12)]^{12} − 1; APR = 12[(1.09)$^{1/12}$ − 1] = 8.65%

     The borrower is actually paying annualized interest of 9% per year, not the 8.65% reported on the loan contract.

26. $FV = \$900[\ 1+(.11/4)\ ]^{64} = \$5,108.34$

27. FV in 3 years $= \$300[\ 1+(.04/365)\ ]^{3(365)} = \$338.25$
FV in 4 years $= \$300[\ 1+(.04/365)\ ]^{4(365)} = \$352.05$
FV in 20 years $= \$300[\ 1+(.04/365)\ ]^{20(365)} = \$667.63$

28. $PV = \$34,000\ /\ (1 + .11/365)^{365(4)} = \$21,898.69$

29. $APR = 12(25) = 300\%; \quad EAR = [1+ (.25)]^{12} - 1 = 1,355.19\%$

30. $PVA = \$26,500 = \$C[\ (1 - [\ 1\ /\ \{\ 1+(.119/12)\ \}]^{60}\ )\ /\ (.119/12)\ ]; \quad C = \$26,500\ /\ 45.06 = \$588.14$
$EAR = [1+(.119/12)]^{12} - 1 = 12.57\%$

31. $PVA = \$8,794.29 = \$263[\ (1 - [1/1.012]^{t}\ )\ /\ .012\ ]; \quad 1/1.012^{t} = 1 - [\ (\$8,794.29)(.012)\ /\ (\$263)\ ]$
$1.012^{t} = 1/(0.5987) = 1.6702; \quad t = \ln 1.6702\ /\ \ln 1.012 = 43$ months

32. $\$3(1+r) = \$4; \quad r = 4/3 - 1 = 33.33\%$ per 5 days
$APR = (365/5)33.33\% = 2,433.33\%; \quad EAR = [1+ (.3333)]^{365/5} - 1 = 131,985,968,700\%$

33. $PV = \$60,000 = \$500\ /\ r\ ; \quad r = \$500/\$60,000 = 0.83\%$ per month
Nominal return $= 12(0.83) = 10\%$ per year;   Effective return $= [1.0083]^{12} - 1 = 10.47\%$ per year

34. $FVA = \$50[\ (\ \{\ 1+(.15/12)\ \}^{240} - 1\ )\ /\ (.15/12)\ ] = \$74,861.97$

35. $EAR = [1+(.15/12)]^{12} - 1 = 16.08\%$
$FVA = \$750[\ (1.1608^{15} - 1)\ /\ .1608\ ] = \$38,986.47$

36. $PVA = \$1,000[\ (1 - [1/1.03]^{12}\ )\ /\ .03\ ] = \$9,954.00$

37. $EAR = [1+(.12/4)]^{4} - 1 = 12.55\%$
$PV = \$3,500\ /\ 1.1255 + \$4,900\ /\ 1.1255^{2} + \$5,500\ /\ 1.1255^{4} = \$10,405.23$

38. $PV = \$800\ /\ 1.098 + \$450\ /\ 1.098^{3} + \$650\ /\ 1.098^{4} = \$1,515.74$

Intermediate

39. $(.08)(10) = (1+r)^{10} - 1\ ; \quad r = 1.8^{1/10} - 1 = 6.05\%$

40. $EAR = .16 = (1+r)^{2} - 1; \quad r = (1.16)^{1/2} - 1 \quad = 7.70\%$ per 6 months
$EAR = .16 = (1+r)^{4} - 1; \quad r = (1.16)^{1/4} - 1 \quad = 3.78\%$ per quarter
$EAR = .16 = (1+r)^{12} - 1; \quad r = (1.16)^{1/12} - 1 \quad = 1.24\%$ per month

41. $EAR = [1+(.14/12)]^{12} - 1 = 14.93\%$
$PVA_1 = \$40,000[\ (1 - [1/1.1493]^{2}\ )\ /\ .1493\ ] = \$65,082.91$
$PVA_2 = \$30,000 + \$20,000[\ (1 - [1/1.1493]^{2}\ )\ /\ .1493\ ] = \$62,541.45;$ choose salary arrangement 1.

42. $\text{PVA} = \$5,000[\ (1 - [1/1.18]^8\ )\ /\ .18\ ] = \$20,387.83$

43. G: $\text{PV} = -\$25,000 + [\ \$40,000\ /\ (1+r)^6\ ] = 0;\quad (1+r)^6 = 40/25;\quad r = (1.6)^{1/6} - 1 = 8.15\%$

  H: $\text{PV} = -\$25,000 + [\ \$60,000\ /\ (1+r)^{11}\ ] = 0;\quad (1+r)^{11} = 60/25;\quad r = (2.4)^{1/11} - 1 = 8.28\%$

44. PVA falls as r increases, and PVA rises as r decreases;

  FVA rises as r increases, and FVA falls as r decreases.

  $\text{PVA@10\%} = \$400[\ (1 - [1/1.10]^8\ )\ /\ .10\ ] = \$2,133.97$

  $\text{PVA@6\%} = \$400[\ (1 - [1/1.06]^8\ )\ /\ .06\ ] = \$2,483.92$

  $\text{PVA@14\%} = \$400[\ (1 - [1/1.14]^8\ )\ /\ .14\ ] = \$1,855.55$

45. $\text{FVA} = \$10,000 = \$75.21[\ (\ \{\ 1+(.16/12)\ \}^N - 1\ )\ /\ (.16/12)\ ];$

  $1.0133^N = 1 + [\ (\$10,000)(.16/12)\ /\ 75.21\ ];\quad N = \ln 2.7728\ /\ \ln 1.0133 = 77$ payments

46. $\text{PVA} = \$12,000 = \$325[\ (1 - [1\ /\ (1+r)]^{48}\ )\ /\ r\ ];$

  solving on a financial calculator, or by trial and error, gives $r = 1.126\%$; $\text{APR} = 12(1.126) = 13.51\%$

47. $\text{PVA} = \$395[\ (1 - [\ 1\ /\ \{\ 1+(.085/12)\ \}]^{180}\ )\ /\ (.085/12)\ ] = \$40,112.13$

  balloon payment $= (\$80,000 - \$40,112.13)[1+(.085/12)]^{180} = \$142,106.65$

48. $\text{PVA} = 0.90(\$700,000) = \$5,500[\ (1 - [1\ /\ (1+r)]^{240}\ )\ /\ r\ ];$

  solving on a financial calculator, or by trial and error, gives $r = 0.7152\%$ per month

  $\text{APR} = 12(0.7152) = 8.58\%;\quad \text{EAR} = (1.007152)^{12} - 1 = 8.93\%$

49. $\text{PV} = \$50,000\ /\ 1.09^3 = \$38,609.17;$ the firm will not make a profit.

  $\$42,000 = \$50,000\ /\ (1+r)^3\ ;\quad r = (50/42)^{1/3} - 1 = 5.98\%$

50. $\text{PV@0\%} = \$2$ million; choose the 2nd payout

  $\text{PV@10\%} = \$2\ /\ 1.1^6 = \$1.129$ million; choose the 2nd payout

  $\text{PV@20\%} = \$2\ /\ 1.2^6 = \$0.670$ million; choose the 1st payout

51. $\text{PVA} = \$250,000[\ (1 - [1/1.07]^{40}\ )\ /\ .07\ ] = \$3,332,927.21$

52. $\text{PVA} = \$300[\ (1 - [1/1.12]^{22}\ )\ /\ .12\ ] = \$2,293.39$

  $\text{PV} = \$2,293.39\ /\ 1.12^3 = \$1,632.39$

53. $\text{PVA}_1 = \$1,000[\ (1 - [\ 1\ /\ \{\ 1+(.16/12)\ \}]^{48}\ )\ /\ (.16/12)\ ] = \$35,285.47$

  $\text{PVA}_2 = \$1,000[\ (1 - [\ 1\ /\ \{\ 1+(.10/12)\ \}]^{96}\ )\ /\ (.10/12)\ ] = \$65,901.49$

  $\text{PV} = \$35,285.47 + [\ \$65,901.49\ /\ (\ 1+[.16/12]\ )^{48}\ ]\ = \$70,182.10$

54. A: $\text{FVA} = \$100[\ (\ \{\ 1+(.17/12)\ \}^{84} - 1\ )\ /\ (.17/12)] = \$15,951.16$

  B: $\text{FV} = \$15,951.16 = \text{PV}e^{.12(7)};\quad \text{PV} = \$15,951.16e^{-.84} = \$6,886.28$

55. $\text{PV@t=13}:\quad \$300\ /\ .066 = \$4,545.45$

  $\text{PV@t=9}:\quad \$4,545.45\ /\ 1.066^4 = \$3,520.05$

56. PVA = $10,000 = $1,025[(1 − [1 / (1+r)]^{12}) / r];
solving on a financial calculator, or by trial and error, gives r = 3.338% per month
APR = 12(3.338) = 40.06%;   EAR = $(1.03338)^{12} − 1$ = 48.29%

57. FV@6 years = $30,000(1.08)^4 + $60,000(1.08)^3 + $75,000(1.08) = $197,397.39
FV@12 years = $197,397.39(1.08)^6 = $313,244.85

58. Monthly rate = .13/12 = .0108;   semiannual rate = $(1.0108)^6 − 1$ = 6.68%
PVA = $7,000[(1 − [1/1.0668]^{10}) / .0668] = $49,903.88
PV@t=5: $49,903.88 / 1.0668^8 = $29,751.97
PV@t=2: $49,903.88 / 1.0668^{14} = $20,186.07
PV@t=0: $49,903.88 / 1.0668^{18} = $15,586.28

59. *a.* PVA = $500[(1 − [1/1.07]^4) / .07] = $1,693.61
b. PVA = $500 + $500[(1 − [1/1.07]^3) / .07] = $1,812.16

60. PVA = $13,000 / [1+(.105/12)] = $12,887.24
PVA = $12,887.24 = $C[(1 − [1 / { 1+(.105/12) }]^{24}) / (.105/12)];   C = $597.66

Challenge

61. $17,500 = $15,750(1+r);   r = 11.11%
Because of the discount, you only get the use of $15,750, and the interest you pay on that amount is 11.11%, not 10%.

62. Net proceeds = $18,000(1 − .16) = $15,120
EAR = ($18,000/$15,120) − 1 = 19.05%

63. $500(1.12) = $500(0.98)(1+r);   r = (1.12/0.98) − 1 = 14.29%

64. EAR = (1.14/0.97) − 1 = 17.53%;   the effective rate is not affected by the loan amount, since it drop outs when solving for r (see previous problem).

65. PVA = $1,000 = ($1,331/36)[(1 − [1 / (1+r)]^{36}) / r];
solving on a financial calculator, or by trial and error, gives r = 1.635% per month
APR = 12(1.635) = 19.62%;   EAR = $(1.01635)^{12} − 1$ = 21.49%
It's called add-on interest because the interest amount of the loan is added to the principal amount of the loan before the loan payments are calculated.

66. *a.* PVA = $15,000[(1 − [1/1.09]^{12}) / .09] = $107,410.88
FVA = $107,410.88 = $C[$(1.09^{30} − 1)$ / .09];   C = $788.00
b. FV = $107,410.88 = PV(1.09)^{29} ;   PV = $8,824.29
c. FV of trust fund deposit = $10,000(1.09)^{10} = $23,673.64
FVA = $107,410.88 − $23,673.64 = $C[$(1.09^{30} − 1)$ / .09];   C = $614.33;
Worker's contribution = $614.33 − $250 = $364.33

67. $PV_1@7/1/84 = \{ \$240K[(1 - [1/1.09]^{17}) / .09] \} / 1.09^5 = \$1,332,665.80$

      $PV_2@7/1/84 = \{ \$125K[(1 - [1/1.09]^{10}) / .09] \} / 1.09^{22} = \$120,476.85$

      $PV@7/1/84 = \$875K + \$650K/1.09 + \$800K / 1.09^2 + \$1,000K / 1.09^3 + \$1,000K / 1.09^4$

                 $+ \$300K / 1.09^5 + PV_1 + PV_2$

      $PV@7/1/84 = \$3,820,262 + \$1,332,665.80 + \$120,476.85 = \$5,273,404.65$

      $EAR = .09 = (1+r)^2 - 1; \quad r = (1.09)^{1/2} - 1 = 4.40\%$ per 6 months

      $PV@1/1/84 = \$5,273,404.65 / 1.0440 = \$5,051,005.59$

      $PVA = \$5,051,005.59 = \$C[(1 - [1/1.09]^5) / .09]; \quad C = \$1,298,575.44$

68. $FVA_1 = \$1,000[(1.08^3 - 1) / .08] = \$3,246.40$

      $FV_1 = \$3,246.40(1.08)^3(1.05)^{59} = \$72,751.50$

      $FVA_2 = \$1,250[(1.08^3 - 1) / .08] = \$4,058.00$

      $FV_2 = \$4,058.00(1.05)^{59} = \$72,190.61; \quad FV = \$72,751.50 + \$72,190.61 = \$144,942.11$

The policy is not worth buying; at an 8% discount rate, it has a future value at age 65 of nearly $145K, while the policy contract will only pay off $120K.

69. $PVA = \$7,000[(1 - [1 / (1+r)]^4) / r] = FVA = \$2,000[\{ (1+r)^6 - 1 \} / r]$

      $(1+r)^{10} - 4.5(1+r)^4 + 3.5 = 0$

By trial and error, or using a root-solving calculator routine, r = 17.94%

70. $PV = \$3,000 / r = PVA = \$10,000[(1 - [1 / (1+r)]^{10}) / r]$

      $0.30(1+r)^{10} = (1+r)^{10} - 1; \quad 1/0.70 = (1+r)^{10} ; \quad r = (10/7)^{1/10} - 1 = 3.63\%$

71. $EAR = [1+(.09/365)]^{365} - 1 = 9.42\%$

      Effective 2-year rate $= 1.0942^2 - 1 = 19.72\%$

      PV@t=1 year ago: $\$5,000 / 0.1972 = \$25,356.19$

      PV today $= \$25,356.19(1.0942) = \$27,743.78$

      If first payment is 4 years from today, PV today $= \$25,356.19 / 1.1972 = \$21,179.75$

72.

$$PVA = \frac{\$C}{(1+r)} + \frac{\$C}{(1+r)^2} + \cdots + \frac{\$C}{(1+r)^N}$$

$$PVA_{due} = \$C + \frac{\$C}{(1+r)} + \cdots + \frac{\$C}{(1+r)^{N-1}}$$

$$PVA_{due} = (1+r) \cdot \left(\frac{\$C}{(1+r)} + \frac{\$C}{(1+r)^2} + \cdots + \frac{\$C}{(1+r)^N} \right)$$

$$= (1+r) \cdot PVA$$

$$FVA = \$C + \$C(1+r) + \$C(1+r)^2 + \cdots \$C(1+r)$$

$$FVA_{due} = \$C(1+r) + \$C(1+r)^2 + \cdots \$C(1+r)^N$$

$$FVA_{due} = (1+r) \cdot \left(\$C + \$C(1+r) + \cdots + \$C(1+r)^N \right)$$

$$= (1+r) \cdot FVA$$

73.   FV@t=7: $\$17,500(1.13)^7 = \$41,170.60$

      $PVA_{due} = \$41,170.60 = (1.13)\$C[(1 - [1/1.13]^6) / .13]; \quad C = \$9,114.12$

74. *a.*   APR = 52(10) = 520%;   EAR = $1.10^{52} - 1$ = 14,104.29%

     b.   \$100 = \$90(1+r);   r = 11.11% per week

         APR = 52(11.11) = 577.78%;   EAR = $1.1111^{52} - 1$ = 23,854.63%

     c.   PVA = \$53.39 = \$25[(1 − [1 / (1+r)]^4) / r];

         using trial and error or a financial calculator gives r = 30.85% per week

         APR = 52(30.85) = 1,604.43%;   EAR = $1.3085^{52} - 1$ = 118,306,303%

CHAPTER 6
VALUING STOCKS AND BONDS

Basic

1. Assuming the bond issuer wants its bonds to sell at par value when issued, the coupon rate is set equal to the required return on the bond at the time of issuance. Once set, the coupon rate is fixed throughout the life of most bonds, while the required return on any bond fluctuates over time with changes in the risk of the company, the risk of the bond, and the general level of interest rates.

2. The yield to maturity is the required rate of return on a bond expressed as a nominal annual interest rate. For noncallable bonds, the yield to maturity and required rate of return are interchangeable terms. Unlike YTM and required return, the coupon rate is not a return used as the interest rate in bond cash flow valuation, but is a fixed percentage of par over the life of the bond used to set the coupon payment amount. For the example given, the coupon rate on the bond is still 10 percent, and the YTM is 8 percent.

3. Price and yield move in opposite directions; if interest rates rise, the price of the bond will fall. This is because the fixed coupon payments determined by the fixed coupon rate are not as valuable when interest rates rise—hence, the price of the bond decreases.

4. $P = \$70(\text{PVIFA}_{8.5\%,11}) + \$1000(\text{PVIF}_{8.5\%,11}) = \$895.47$

5. $P = \$1,070 = \$105(\text{PVIFA}_{r\%,8}) + \$1000(\text{PVIF}_{r\%,8})$; $r = \text{YTM} = 9.22\%$

6. $P = \$950 = \$C(\text{PVIFA}_{7.5\%,14}) + \$1000(\text{PVIF}_{7.5\%,14})$; $C = \$69.11$; coupon rate = 6.91%

7. $P = \$43.75(\text{PVIFA}_{7.25\%/2,18}) + \$1000(\text{PVIF}_{7.25\%/2,18}) = \$1,097.91$

8. $P = \$960 = \$47.50(\text{PVIFA}_{r\%,20}) + \$1000(\text{PVIF}_{r\%,20})$; $r = 5.073\%$; YTM = 2 x 5.073 = 10.15%

9. $P = \$860 = \$C(\text{PVIFA}_{5\%,21}) + \$1000(\text{PVIF}_{5\%,21})$; $C = \$39.08$; coupon rate = 2 x 3.908 = 7.82%

10. The general method for valuing a share of stock is to find the present value of all expected future dividends. The dividend growth model presented in the text is only valid (i) if dividends are expected to occur forever, that is, the stock provides dividends in perpetuity, and (ii) if a constant growth rate of dividends occurs forever. A violation of the first assumption might be a company that is expected to cease operations and dissolve itself some finite number of years from now. The stock of such a company would be valued by the methods of this chapter by applying the general method of valuation. A violation of the second assumption might be a start-up firm that isn't currently paying any dividends, but is expected to eventually start making dividend payments some number of years from now. This stock would also be valued by the general dividend valuation method of this chapter.

11. $P_0 = D_0(1+g)/(r-g) = \$2.00(1.06)/(.13-.06) = \$30.29$

$P_3 = D_3(1+g)/(r-g) = D_0(1+g)^4/(r-g) = \$2.00(1.06)^4/(.13-.06) = \$36.07$

$P_{15} = D_{15}(1+g)/(r-g) = D_0(1+g)^{16}/(r-g) = \$2.00(1.06)^{16}/(.13-.06) = \$72.58$

12. $r = D_1/P_0 + g = \$3.00/\$70.50 + .05 = 9.26\%$

13. Dividend yield $= D_1/P_0 = 4.26\%$;   capital gains yield $= 5\%$

14. $P_0 = D_1/(r-g) = \$4.25/(.18-.09) = \$47.22$

15. $r =$ dividend yield + capital gains yield $= .055 + .05 = 10.5\%$

16. Dividend yield $= 1/2(.15) = .075 =$ capital gains yield

$D_1 = .075(\$50) = \$3.75$; $D_0(1+g) = D_1$, $D_0 = \$3.75 / (1.075) = \$3.49$

17. $P_0 = \$5.00(PVIFA_{12\%,7}) = \$22.82$

18. $r = D/P_0 = \$8.50/\$115 = 7.39\%$

Intermediate

19. *a.*   Bond price is the present value term when valuing the cash flows from a bond; YTM is the interest rate used in valuing the cash flows from a bond.

b.   If the coupon rate is higher than the required return on a bond, the bond will sell at a premium, since it provides periodic income in the form of coupon payments in excess of that required by investors on other similar bonds. If the coupon rate is lower than the required return on a bond, the bond will sell at a discount, since it provides insufficient coupon payments compared to that required by investors on other similar bonds. For premium bonds, the coupon rate exceeds the YTM; for discount bonds, the YTM exceeds the coupon rate, and for bonds selling at par, the YTM is equal to the coupon rate.

c.   Current yield is defined as the annual coupon payment divided by the current bond price. For premium bonds, the current yield exceeds the YTM, for discount bonds the current yield is less than the YTM, and for bonds selling at par value, the current yield is equal to the YTM. In all cases, the current yield plus the expected one-period capital gains yield of the bond must be equal to the required return.

20. X: $P_0 = \$90(PVIFA_{7\%,15}) + \$1000(PVIF_{7\%,15}) = \$1,182.16$

$P_1 = \$90(PVIFA_{7\%,14}) + \$1000(PVIF_{7\%,14}) = \$1,174.91$

$P_5 = \$90(PVIFA_{7\%,10}) + \$1000(PVIF_{7\%,10}) = \$1,140.47$

$P_{10} = \$90(PVIFA_{7\%,5}) + \$1000(PVIF_{7\%,5}) = \$1,082.00$

$P_{14} = \$90(PVIFA_{7\%,1}) + \$1000(PVIF_{7\%,1}) = \$1,018.69$; $P_{15} = \$1,000$

Y: $P_0 = \$60(PVIFA_{9\%,15}) + \$1000(PVIF_{9\%,15}) = \$758.18$
      $P_1 = \$60(PVIFA_{9\%,14}) + \$1000(PVIF_{9\%,14}) = \$766.42$
      $P_5 = \$60(PVIFA_{9\%,10}) + \$1000(PVIF_{9\%,10}) = \$807.47$
      $P_{10} = \$60(PVIFA_{9\%,5}) + \$1000(PVIF_{9\%,5}) = \$883.31$
      $P_{14} = \$60(PVIFA_{9\%,1}) + \$1000(PVIF_{9\%,1}) = \$972.48$; $P_{15} = \$1,000$

All else held equal, the premium over par value for a premium bond declines as maturity is approached, and the discount from par value for a discount bond declines as maturity is approached. In both cases, the largest percentage price changes occur at the shortest maturity lengths.

21. If both bonds sell at par, the initial YTM on both bonds is the coupon rate, 8 percent. If the YTM suddenly rises to 10 percent:

$P_A = \$40(PVIFA_{5\%,4}) + \$1000(PVIF_{5\%,4}) = \$964.54$
$P_B = \$40(PVIFA_{5\%,30}) + \$1000(PVIF_{5\%,30}) = \$846.28$
$\Delta P_A\% = (964.54 - 1000)/1000 = -3.55\%$
$\Delta P_B\% = (846.28 - 1000)/1000 = -15.37\%$

If the YTM suddenly falls to 6 percent:

$P_A = \$40(PVIFA_{3\%,4}) + \$1000(PVIF_{3\%,4}) = \$1,037.17$
$P_B = \$40(PVIFA_{3\%,30}) + \$1000(PVIF_{3\%,30}) = \$1,196.00$
$\Delta P_A\% = (1,037.17 - 1000)/1000 = +3.72\%$
$\Delta P_B\% = (1,196.00 - 1000)/1000 = +19.60\%$

All else the same, the longer the maturity of a bond, the greater is its price sensitivity to changes in interest rates.

22. Initially, at a YTM of 9 percent, the prices of the two bonds are:

$P_J = \$20(PVIFA_{4.5\%,20}) + \$1000(PVIF_{4.5\%,20}) = \$674.80$
$P_K = \$50(PVIFA_{4.5\%,20}) + \$1000(PVIF_{4.5\%,20}) = \$1,065.04$

If the YTM rises from 9 percent to 11 percent:

$P_J = \$20(PVIFA_{5.5\%,20}) + \$1000(PVIF_{5.5\%,20}) = \$581.74$
$P_K = \$50(PVIFA_{5.5\%,20}) + \$1000(PVIF_{5.5\%,20}) = \$940.25$
$\Delta P_J\% = (581.74 - 674.80)/674.80 = -13.79\%$
$\Delta P_K\% = (940.25 - 1,065.04)/1,065.04 = -11.72\%$

If the YTM declines from 9 percent to 7 percent:

$P_J = \$20(PVIFA_{3.5\%,20}) + \$1000(PVIF_{3.5\%,20}) = \$786.81$
$P_K = \$50(PVIFA_{3.5\%,20}) + \$1000(PVIF_{3.5\%,20}) = \$1,213.19$
$\Delta P_J\% = (786.81 - 674.80)/674.80 = +16.60\%$
$\Delta P_K\% = (1,213.19 - 1,065.04)/1,065.04 = +13.91\%$

All else the same, the lower the coupon rate on a bond, the greater is its price sensitivity to changes in interest rates.

23. $P_0 = \$1,100 = \$60(PVIFA_{r\%,18}) + \$1000(PVIF_{r\%,18})$; $r = 5.135\%$, YTM $= 2 \times 5.135 = 10.27\%$
Current yield $= \$120/\$1,100 = 10.91\%$; effective annual yield $= (1.05135)^2 - 1 = 10.53\%$

24. The company should set the coupon rate on its new bonds equal to the required return; the required return can be observed in the market by finding the YTM on outstanding bonds of the company.

$P = \$1,040 = \$40(PVIFA_{r\%,20}) + \$1000(PVIF_{r\%,20})$; $r = 3.713\%$; YTM $= 2 \times 3.713 = 7.43\%$

25. Current yield = .0901 = $100/P_0$; $P_0 = \$100/.0901 = \$1,109.88$

$P_0 = \$1,109.88 = \$100[(1 - (1/1.085)^N) / .085] + \$1,000/1.085^N$

$1,109.88(1.085)^N = 1,176.47(1.085)^N - 1,176.47 + 1,000$

$176.47 = 66.59(1.085)^N;\quad 2.6501 = 1.085^N ;\quad N = \log 2.6501 / \log 1.085 = 11.95$ years

26. Current yield = .087 = $78.75/P_0$; $P_0 = \$78.75/.087 = \$905.17 = 90.52\%$ of par $\cong$ 90 1/2

Bond closed up 1/2, so yesterday's close = 90

27. The maturity is indeterminate; a bond selling at par can have any length of maturity.

28. The value for a share of stock is determined by the marginal investor in the marketplace, who values the stock by finding the present value of all expected future dividends. An investor with a finite holding period horizon may consider the selling price into the valuation and price an N-period cash flow stream at time t=0, but since the selling price is set by the present value of all expected future dividends at the future selling date, the net result at time t=0 is simply the price of all expected future dividends forever.

29. $P_6 = D_6(1+g)/(r - g) = D_0(1+g)^7/(r - g) = \$2.50(1.065)^7/(.10 - .065) = \$111.00$

$P_3 = \$2.50(1.065)^4/(1.15) + \$2.50(1.065)^5/(1.15)^2 + \$2.50(1.065)^6/(1.15)^3 + \$111/(1.15)^3 = \$80.77$

$P_0 = \$2.50(1.065)/(1.20) + \$2.50(1.065)^2/(1.20)^2 + \$2.50(1.065)^3/(1.20)^3 + \$80.77/(1.20)^3 = \$52.68$

30. $P_5 = D_6/(r - g) = \$2.00/(.14 - .07) = \$28.57;\quad P_0 = \$28.57 / 1.14^5 = \$14.84$

31. $P_0 = \$7/(1.08) + \$8/(1.08)^2 + \$9/(1.08)^3 + \$10/(1.08)^4 = \$27.84$

32. $P_4 = D_4(1+g)/(r - g) = \$1.00(1.08)/(.16 - .08) = \$13.50$

$P_0 = \$2.25/(1.16) + \$4.00/(1.16)^2 + \$3.00/(1.16)^3 + \$14.50/(1.16)^4 = \$14.84$

33. $P_3 = D_3(1+g)/(r - g) = D_0(1+g_1)^3(1+g_2)/(r - g) = \$1.75(1.28)^3(1.05)/(.20 - .05) = \$25.69$

$P_0 = \$1.75(1.28)/(1.20) + \$1.75(1.28)^2/(1.20)^2 + \$1.75(1.28)^3/(1.20)^3 + \$25.69/(1.20)^3 = \$20.85$

34. $D_3 = D_0(1.3)^3;\quad D_4 = D_0(1.3)^3(1.2)$

$P_4 = D_4(1+g)/(r - g) = D_0(1+g_1)^3(1+g_2)(1+g_3)/(r - g) = D_0(1.3)^3(1.2)(1.06)/(.15 - .06) = 31.05D_0$

$P_0 = \$42.50 = D_0\{ (1.3/1.15) + (1.3/1.15)^2 + (1.3/1.15)^3 + [(1.3)^3(1.2) + 31.05] / 1.15^4 \}$

$D_0 = 42.50 / 23.11 = 1.84 ;\quad D_1 = 1.84(1.3) = \$2.39$

35. $P_0 = D_0(1+g)/(r - g) = \$4.00(0.94)/(.15+.06) = \$17.90$

36. $P_0 = \$92 = D_0(1+g)/(r - g)$; $D_0 = 92(.13 - .10)/(1.10) = \$2.51$

37. $P_3 = \$7.00 / .06 = \$116.67$; $P_0 = \$116.67 / 1.06^3 = \$97.96$

38. Dividend yield = .046 = $3.60 / P_0$; $P_0 = 3.60/.046 = \$78.26 \cong 78\ 1/4$

Stock closed down 3/8, so yesterday's closing price = 78 1/4 + 3/8 = 78 5/8

P/E = 16 ; EPS = $P_0 / 16 = \$4.89 = NI / shares$; NI = $4.89(1,000,000) = \$4.89M$

Challenge

39. P: $P_0 = \$95(\text{PVIFA}_{8\%,8}) + \$1000(\text{PVIF}_{8\%,8}) = \$1,086.20$

$P_1 = \$95(\text{PVIFA}_{8\%,7}) + \$1000(\text{PVIF}_{8\%,7}) = \$1,078.10$

Current yield $= 95/1,086.20 = 8.75\%$;   capital gains yield $= (1,078.10 - 1,086.20)/1,086.20$
$= -0.75\%$

D: $P_0 = \$60(\text{PVIFA}_{8\%,8}) + \$1000(\text{PVIF}_{8\%,8}) = \$885.07$

$P_1 = \$60(\text{PVIFA}_{8\%,7}) + \$1000(\text{PVIF}_{8\%,7}) = \$895.87$

Current yield $= 60/885.07 = 6.78\%$;   capital gains yield $= (895.87 - 885.07)/885.07 = +1.22\%$

All else held constant, premium bonds pay high current income while having price depreciation as maturity nears; discount bonds do not pay high current income but have price appreciation as maturity nears. For either bond, the total return is still 8%, but this return is distributed differently between current income and capital gains.

40. *a.* $P_0 = \$1,100 = \$100(\text{PVIFA}_{r\%,10}) + \$1000(\text{PVIF}_{r\%,10})$; $r = \text{YTM} = 8.48\%$

This is the rate of return you expect to earn on your investment when you purchase the bond.

b. $P_2 = \$100(\text{PVIFA}_{5.98\%,8}) + \$1000(\text{PVIF}_{5.98\%,8}) = \$1,250.01$

$P_0 = \$1,100 = \$100(\text{PVIFA}_{r\%,2}) + \$1,250.01(\text{PVIF}_{r\%,2})$; $r = \text{HPY} = 15.42\%$

The realized HPY is greater than the expected YTM when the bond was bought because interest rates have dropped by 2.5 percent; bond prices rise when yields fall.

41. $P_M = \$1,500(\text{PVIFA}_{5\%,16})(\text{PVIF}_{5\%,12}) + \$2,000(\text{PVIFA}_{5\%,12})(\text{PVIF}_{5\%,28}) + \$25,000(\text{PVIF}_{5\%,40})$
$= \$17,125.37$

$P_N = \$25,000(\text{PVIF}_{5\%,40}) = \$3,551.14$

42. *a.* $P_0 = C(1+g)/(r-g) = \$50(1.05)/(.10 - .05) = \$1,050$

b. $C_{20} = \$50$; $C_1 = \$50(1.05)^{-19} = \$19.79$

c. $P_{-20} = \$19.79/(.12 - .05) = \$282.67$;   initial proceeds from sale $= \$282.67 \times 1,000 = \$282,667$

43. W: $P_0 = D_0(1+g)/(r-g) = \$2.25(1.12)/(.18 - .12) = \$42.00$

Dividend yield $= D_1/P_0 = 2.25(1.12)/42 = 6\%$;   capital gains yield $= .18 - .06 = 12\%$

X: $P_0 = D_0(1+g)/(r-g) = \$2.25(1)/(.18 - 0) = \$12.50$

Dividend yield $= D_1/P_0 = 2.25/12.50 = 18\%$;   capital gains yield $= .18 - .18 = 0\%$

Y: $P_0 = D_0(1+g)/(r-g) = \$2.25(0.90)/(.18 + .10) = \$7.23$

Dividend yield $= D_1/P_0 = 2.25(0.90)/7.23 = 28\%$;   capital gains yield $= .18 - .28 = -10\%$

Z: $P_2 = D_2(1+g)/(r-g) = D_0(1+g_1)^2(1+g_2)/(r-g) = \$2.25(1.3)^2(1.12)/(.18 - .12) = \$70.98$

$P_0 = \$2.25(1.3)/(1.18) + \$2.25(1.3)^2/(1.18)^2 + \$70.98/(1.18)^2 = \$56.19$

Dividend yield $= D_1/P_0 = 2.25(1.3)/56.19 = 5.21\%$;   capital gains yield $= .18 - .0521 = 12.79\%$

In all cases, the required return is 18%, but this return is distributed differently between current income and capital gains. High growth stocks have an appreciable capital gains component but a relatively small current income yield; conversely, mature, negative-growth stocks provide a high current income price depreciation over time.

44. *a.* $P_0 = D_0(1+g)/(r - g) = \$3.00(1.1)/(.18 - .10) = \$41.25$

    b.   nominal $D_1 = \$3.00(1.1) = \$3.30$; $D = \$3.30/4 = \$0.825$

        $FV = \$0.825(FVIFA_{18/4\%,4}) = \$3.5295 =$ effective D_1

        nominal $D_2 = \$3.30(1.1) = \$3.63$; $D = \$3.63/4 = \$0.9075$

        $FV = \$0.9075(FVIFA_{18/4\%,4}) = \$3.8825 =$ effective D_2

        ... in general, $D_n = (1.0695)\$3.00(1.10)^n = \$3.209(1.10)^n$

        $EAR = [\ 1+(.18/4)\ ]^4 - 1 = 19.25\%$

        thus $P_0 = D_0(1+g)/(r - g) = \$3.209(1.1)/(.1925 - .10) = \$38.15$

The increased precision of accounting for the quarterly payment of dividends and quarterly compounding of these dividends, and the quarterly compounding of the required return, is often neglected in practice because the precision error involved in estimating future dividends and future expected return is much greater than the magnitudes involved in this quarterly model.

45. $P_0 = \$6.75(1.25)/(1.1375) + \$6.75(1.25)(1.2)/(1.1375)^2 + \$6.75(1.25)(1.2)(1.15)/(1.1375)^3$

    $+ \$6.75(1.25)(1.2)(1.15)(1.1)/(1.1375)^4$

    $+ \$6.75(1.25)(1.2)(1.15)(1.1)(1.05)/(.1375 - .05)(1.1375)^4 = \$122.61$

46. $P_0 = \$6.75(1.25)/(1 + r) + \$6.75(1.25)(1.2)/(1 + r)^2$

    $+ \$6.75(1.25)(1.2)(1.15)/(1 + r)^3 + \$6.75(1.25)(1.2)(1.15)(1.1)/(1 + r)^4$

    $+ \$6.75(1.25)(1.2)(1.15)(1.1)(1.05)/(r - .05)(1 + r)^4 = \$100$;

Using trial and error, or a calculator with a root solving function, gives $r = 15.66\%$

CHAPTER 7
NET PRESENT VALUE AND OTHER INVESTMENT CRITERIA

Basic

1. Payback = 2 + ($600/$900) = 2.67 years

2. Payback = 3($750) + ($250/$750) = 3.33 years
    = 6($750) + ($500/$750) = 6.67 years
    8($750) = $6,000; project never pays back if cost is $7,500

3. A: Payback = 1 + ($9K/$16K) = 1.56 years
    B: Payback = 2 + ($12K/$15K) = 2.80 years
    Using the payback criterion and a cutoff of 2.5 years, accept project A and reject project B.

4. $500/1.1 = $454.55; $600/1.1^2 = $495.87; $700/1.1^3 = $525.92; $800/1.1^4 = $546.41
    Cost = $1,000: Discounted payback = 2 + ($1,000 − $454.55 − $495.87)/$525.92 = 2.094 yrs
    Cost = $1,800: Discounted payback = 3 + ($1,800 − $454.55 − $495.87 − $525.92)/$546.41 = 3.592 yrs
    Cost = $2,500: $454.55 + $495.87 + $525.92 + $546.41 = $2,022.75; never pays back.

5. r = 0%: 4($750) = $3,000; discounted payback = regular payback = 4.00 years
    r = 5%: $750/1.05 + $750/1.05^2 + $750/1.05^3 + $750/1.05^4 = $2,659.46; $750/1.05^5 = $587.64
             discounted payback = 4 + ($3,000 − $2,659.46)/$587.64 = 4.58 years
    r = 10%: $750/1.1 + $750/1.1^2 + $750/1.1^3 + $750/1.1^4 + $750/1.1^5 = $2,843.09; never pays back.

6. Average net income = ($417,000 + $329,500 + $216,200 + $48,000) / 4 = $252,675
    Average book value = ($2M + 0) / 2 = $1M
    AAR = average net income / average book value = 25.27%

7. 0 = − $15,000 + $10,000/(1+IRR) + $10,000/(1+IRR)^3 ; IRR = 16.11% > r = 14%, so accept the project.

8. NPV = − $15,000 + $10,000/1.14 + $10,000/1.14^3 = $521.64; NPV > 0 so accept the project.
    NPV = − $15,000 + $10,000/1.18 + $10,000/1.18^3 = − $439.12; NPV < 0 so reject the project.

9. NPV = − $1,000 + $200(PVIFA$_{7\%,7}$) = $77.86 ; accept the project if r = 7%
    NPV = − $1,000 + $200(PVIFA$_{15\%,7}$) = − $167.92 ; reject the project if r = 15%
    $1,000 = $200(PVIFA$_{IRR,7}$) ; IRR = 9.20% ; indifferent about the project if r = 9.20%

10. 0 = − $600 + $200/(1+IRR) + $300/(1+IRR)^2 + $400/(1+IRR)^3 ; IRR = 20.61%

11. NPV $= -\$600 + \$200 + \$300 + \$400$ $=$ $\$300$

          $= -\$600 + \$200/1.1 + \$300/1.1^2 + \$400/1.1^3 = \$130.28$

          $= -\$600 + \$200/1.2 + \$300/1.2^2 + \$400/1.2^3 = \$6.48$

          $= -\$600 + \$200/1.3 + \$300/1.3^2 + \$400/1.3^3 = -\$86.57$

12. *a.*   L: $\$10,000 = \$200/(1+IRR) + \$500/(1+IRR)^2 + \$8,200/(1+IRR)^3 + \$4,800/(1+IRR)^4$; IRR = 10.12%

      S: $\$10,000 = \$5,000/(1+IRR) + \$6,000/(1+IRR)^2 + \$500/(1+IRR)^3 + \$500/(1+IRR)^4$; IRR = 11.46%

      $IRR_S > IRR_L$, so IRR decision rule implies accept project S. This may not be a correct decision however, because the IRR criterion has a ranking problem for mutually exclusive projects. To see if the IRR decision rule is correct or not, we need to evaluate the project NPVs.

   b.   L: NPV $= -\$10,000 + \$200/1.09 + \$500/1.09^2 + \$8,200/1.09^3 + \$4,800/1.09^4 = \$336.67$

      S: NPV $= -\$10,000 + \$5,000/1.09 + \$6,000/1.09^2 + \$500/1.09^3 + \$500/1.09^4 = \$377.54$

      $NPV_S > NPV_L$, so NPV decision rule implies accept project S.

   c.   Crossover rate: $0 = \$4,800/(1+r) + \$5,500/(1+r)^2 - \$7,700/(1+r)^3 - \$4,300/(1+r)^4$;   r = 8.73%

      At discount rates between zero and 8.73% choose project L; for discount rates greater than 8.73% choose project S; indifferent between L and S at a discount rate of 8.73%.

13. M: $\$50 = \$40/(1+IRR) + \$20/(1+IRR)^2 + \$5/(1+IRR)^3$;   IRR = 20.20%

    N: $\$50 = \$5/(1+IRR) + \$5/(1+IRR)^2 + \$65/(1+IRR)^3$;   IRR = 15.72%

Crossover rate: $0 = \$35/(1+r) + \$15/(1+r)^2 - \$60/(1+r)^3$;   r = 11.24%

r%	NPV_M	NPV_N
0	15.00	25.00
5	10.56	15.45
10	6.65	7.51
15	3.19	0.87
20	0.12	–4.75
25	–2.64	–9.52

14. *a.*   NPV $= -\$900 + \$1,200/1.1 - \$200/1.1^2 = \$25.62$;   NPV > 0 so accept the project.

   b. $\$900 = \$1,200/(1+IRR) - \$200/(1+IRR)^2 \ldots IRR^2 + (2/3)IRR - (1/9) = 0$;   IRR = 13.81% , – 80.47%

      When there are multiple IRRs, the IRR decision rule is ambiguous; in this case, if the correct IRR is 13.81%, then we would accept the project, but if the correct IRR is – 80.47%, we would reject the project.

15. PI $= [\ \$800/1.08 + \$500/1.08^2 + \$500/1.08^3\ ] / \$1,400 = 1.119$

        $= [\ \$800/1.12 + \$500/1.12^2 + \$500/1.12^3\ ] / \$1,400 = 1.049$

        $= [\ \$800/1.18 + \$500/1.18^2 + \$500/1.18^3\ ] / \$1,400 = 0.958$

16. *a.* $PI_X = \$10,000(PVIFA_{12\%,3}) / \$23,000 = 1.044$; $PI_Y = \$2,000(PVIFA_{12\%,3}) / \$4,000 = 1.201$

      The profitability index decision rule implies accept project Y, since $PI_Y > PI_X$

   b. $NPV_X = -\$23,000 + \$10,000(PVIFA_{12\%,3}) = \$1,018.31$

      $NPV_Y = -\$4,000 + \$2,000(PVIFA_{12\%,3}) = \$803.66$

      NPV decision rule implies accept X, since $NPV_X > NPV_Y$

    c.   Using the profitability index to compare mutually exclusive projects can be ambiguous when the magnitude of the cash flows for the two projects are of different scale. In this problem, project X is roughly 5 times as large as project Y and produces a larger NPV, yet the profitability index criterion implies that project Y is more acceptable.

17. *a.* $PB_A = 3 + (\$225K/\$425K) = 3.529$ years; $PB_B = \$40K/\$45K = 0.889$ years

        Payback criterion implies accept project B, because it pays back sooner than project A.

    b.   A: $\$5K/1.15 + \$15K/1.15^2 + \$15K/1.15^3 = \$25,552.72$; $\$425K/1.15^4 = \$242,995.13$

            Discounted payback $= 3 + (\$260,000 - \$25,552.72)/\$242,995.13 = 3.965$ years

        B: $\$45K/1.15 = \$39,130.43$; $\$5K/1.15^2 = \$3,780.72$

            Discounted payback $= 1 + (\$40,000 - \$39,130.43)/\$3,780.72 = 1.230$ years

        Discounted payback criterion implies accept project B, because it pays back sooner than A.

    c.   A: $NPV = -\$260K + \$5K/1.15 + \$15K/1.15^2 + \$15K/1.15^3 + \$425K/1.15^4 = \$8,547.85$

        B: $NPV = -\$40K + \$45K/1.15 + \$5K/1.15^2 + \$0.50K/1.15^3 + \$0.50K/1.15^4 = \$3,525.79$

        NPV criterion implies accept project A, because project A has a higher NPV than project A.

    d.   A: $\$260K = \$5K/(1+IRR) + \$15K/(1+IRR)^2 + \$15K/(1+IRR)^3 + \$425K/(1+IRR)^4$; IRR $= 15.9$

        B: $\$40K = \$45K/(1+IRR) + \$5K/(1+IRR)^2 + \$0.50K/(1+IRR)^3 + \$0.50K/(1+IRR)^4$; IRR $= 24$

        IRR decision rule implies accept project B, because IRR for B is greater than IRR for A.

    e.   A: $PI = [\ \$5K/1.15 + \$15K/1.15^2 + \$15K/1.15^3 + \$425K/1.15^4\ ] / \$260K = 1.033$

        B: $PI = [\ \$45K/1.15 + \$5K/1.15^2 + \$0.50K/1.15^3 + \$0.50K/1.15^4\ ] / \$40K = 1.088$

        Profitability index criterion implies accept project B, because its PI is greater than project A's.

    f.   Project A should be chosen; the NPV criterion chooses the correct project. IRR in this case gives the wrong answer because the crossover rate for the projects is 15.60% > r = 15%; PI gives the wrong answer because A is of larger scale than is B; the payback criterion give the wrong answers because B is a short-term project compared to project A.

18. NPV @ $r = 0\% = -\$176,515 + \$58,675 + \$63,116 + \$69,370 + \$72,000 = \$86,646$

    NPV @ $r = \infty = -\$176,515$

    $NPV = 0 = -\$176,515 + \$58,675/(1+IRR) + \$63,116/(1+IRR)^2 + \$69,370/(1+IRR)^3$

              $+ \$72,000/(1+IRR)^4$; IRR $= 17.41\%$

19. A payback period less than the project's life means that the NPV is positive for a zero discount rate, but nothing more definitive can be said. For discount rates greater than zero, the payback period will still be less than the project's life, but the NPV may be positive, zero, or negative, depending on whether the discount rate is less than, equal to, or greater than the IRR. The discounted payback includes the effect of the relevant discount rate. If a project's discounted payback period is less than the project's life, it must be the case that NPV is positive.

20. If a project has a positive NPV for a certain discount rate, then it will also have a positive NPV for a zero discount rate; thus the payback period must be less than the project life. Since discounted payback is calculated at the same discount rate as is NPV, if NPV is positive, the discounted payback period must be less than the project's life. If NPV is positive, then the present value of future cash inflows is greater than the initial investment cost; thus PI must be greater than 1. If NPV is positive for a certain discount rate r, then it will be zero for some larger discount rate r*; thus the IRR must be greater than the required return.

Intermediate

21. *a.* Payback period is simply the accounting break-even point of a series of cash flows. To actually compute the payback period, it is assumed that any cash flow occuring during a given period is realized continuously throughout the period, and not at a single point in time. The payback is then the point in time for the series of cash flows when the initial cash outlays are fully recovered. Given some predetermined cutoff for the payback period, the decision rule is to accept projects that payback before this cutoff, and reject projects that take longer to payback.

b. The worst problem associated with payback period is that it ignores the time value of money. In addition, the selection of a hurdle point for payback period is an arbitrary exercise that lacks any steadfast rule or method. The payback period is biased towards short-term projects; it fully ignores any cash flows that occur after the cutoff point.

c. Despite its shortcomings, payback is often used because (1) the analysis is straightforward and simple and (2) accounting numbers and estimates are readily available. Materiality considerations often warrant a payback analysis as sufficient; maintenance projects are another example where the detailed analysis of other methods is often not needed. Since payback is biased towards liquidity, it may be a useful and appropriate analysis method for short-term projects where cash management is most important.

22. *a.* The discounted payback is calculated the same as is regular payback, with the exception that each cash flow in the series is first converted to its present value. Thus discounted payback provides a measure of financial break-even because of this discounting, just as regular payback provides a measure of accounting break-even because it does not discount the cash flows. Given some predetermined cutoff for the discounted payback period, the decision rule is to accept projects that whose discounted cash flows payback before this cutoff period, and to reject all other projects.

b. The primary disadvantage to using the discounted payback method is that it ignores all cash flows that occur after the cutoff date, thus biasing this criterion towards short-term projects. As a result, the method may reject projects that in fact have positive NPVs, or it may accept projects with large future cash outlays resulting in negative NPVs. In addition, the selection of a cutoff point is again an arbitrary exercise.

c. Discounted payback is an improvement on regular payback because it takes into account the time value of money. For conventional cash flows and strictly positive discount rates, the discounted payback will always be greater than the regular payback period.

23. *a.* The average accounting return is interpreted as an average measure of the accounting performance of a project over time, computed as some average profit measure due to the project divided by some average balance sheet value for the project. This text computes AAR as average net income with respect to average (total) book value. Given some predetermined cutoff for AAR, the decision rule is to accept projects with an AAR in excess of the target measure, and reject all other projects.

b. AAR is not a measure of cash flows and market value, but a measure of financial statement accounts that often bear little semblance to the relevant value of a project. In addition, the selection of a cutoff is arbitrary, and the time value of money is ignored. For a financial manager, both the reliance on accounting numbers rather than relevant market data and the exclusion of time value of money considerations are troubling. Despite these problems, AAR continues to be used in practice because (1) the accounting information is usually available, (2) analysts often use accounting ratios to analyze firm performance, and (3) managerial compensation is often tied to the attainment of certain target accounting ratio goals.

24. *a.*   NPV is simply the present value of a project's cash flows. NPV specifically measures, after considering the time value of money, the net increase or decrease in firm wealth due to the project. The decision rule is to accept projects that have a positive NPV, and reject projects with a negative NPV.

b.   NPV is superior to the other methods of analysis presented in the text because it has no serious flaws. The method unambiguously ranks mutually exclusive projects, and can differentiate between projects of different scale and time horizon. The only drawback to NPV is that it relies on cash flow and discount rate values that are often estimates and not certain, but this is a problem shared by the other performance criteria as well. A project with NPV = $2,500 implies that the total shareholder wealth of the firm will increase by $2,500 if the project is accepted.

25. *a.*   The IRR is the discount rate that causes the NPV of a series of cash flows to be identically zero. IRR can thus be interpreted as a financial break-even rate of return; at the IRR discount rate, the net value of the project is zero. The IRR decision rule is to accept projects with IRRs greater than the discount rate, and to reject projects with IRRs less than the discount rate.

b.   IRR is the interest rate that causes NPV for a series of cash flows to be zero. NPV is preferred in all situations to IRR; IRR can lead to ambiguous results if there are non-conventional cash flows, and also ambiguously ranks some mutually exclusive projects. However, for stand-alone projects with conventional cash flows, IRR and NPV are interchangeable techniques.

c.   IRR is frequently used because it is easier for many financial managers and analysts to rate performance in relative terms, such as "12%", than in absolute terms, such as "$46,000." IRR may be a preferred method to NPV in situations where an appropriate discount rate is unknown are uncertain; in this situation, IRR would provide more information about the project than would NPV.

26. *a.*   The profitability index is the present value of cash inflows relative to the project cost. As such, it is a benefit/cost ratio, providing a measure of the relative profitability of a project. The profitability index decision rule is to accept projects with a PI greater than one, and to reject projects with a PI less than one.

b.   PI = (NPV + cost)/cost = 1 + (NPV/cost). If a firm has a basket of positive NPV projects and is subject to capital rationing, PI may provide a good ranking measure of the projects, indicating the "bang for the buck" of each particular project.

27.   PB = I / C ; $-I + C / r$ = NPV, $0 = -I + C /$ IRR so IRR = C / I; thus IRR = $1 / $ PB
For long-lived projects with relatively constant cash flows, the sooner the project pays back, the greater is the IRR.

28.   PI = (NPV + cost)/cost = 1 + (NPV/cost) ; NPV index = PI − 1

29. NPV_A @ r = 0% = $1,900 > NPV_B @ r = 0% = $1,500$

NPV_A @ r = 15% > 0 ; NPV_B @ r = 15% = 0$

For all relevant discount rates NPV_A is always greater than NPV_B; if there is a crossover rate for these two projects, it occurs when both projects have negative NPVs and thus would be rejected.

30. *a.* $I = NC$; $C = I / N$

b. $NPV = -I + C (PVIFA_{r\%,N}) > 0$; $C > I / PVIFA_{r\%,N}$

c. $PI = C (PVIFA_{r\%,N}) / I = 1.5$; $C = 1.5 I / PVIFA_{r\%,N}$

31. If the project pays back in 7 years, the accumulated total cash inflows at t = 7 must be $70,000. The worst case would be for all $70K of the inflows to occur at t = 7, and no other inflows beyond then; the best case NPV would be for an infinite cash flow to occur at $t = 7^+$.

Worst-case NPV: $NPV = -\$70,000 + \$70,000/1.16^7 = -\$45,231.93$

Best-case NPV = ∞

32. The sign of the cash flows change 4 times, so at most there can be 4 IRRs, and there are 4 in this case: 25%, 33.33%, 42.85%, and 66.67%.

$\$252 = \$1,431/(1+IRR) - \$3,035/(1+IRR)^2 + \$2,850/(1+IRR)^3 - \$1,000/(1+IRR)^4$

The project should be accepted whenever the NPV is positive;

this occurs for $r \in [.25,.3333] \cup [.4285,.6667]$.

33. *a.* $NPV = -\$400K + [\$25K(1.06)/(.12 - .06)] = \$41,667$

b. $NPV = 0 = -\$400K + [\$25K(1+g)/(.12 - g)]$; $g = 5.41\%$

CHAPTER 8
MAKING CAPITAL INVESTMENT DECISIONS

Basic

1. Management's discretion to set the firm's capital structure is applicable at the firm level. Since any one particular project could be financed entirely with equity, another project could be financed with debt, and the firm's overall capital structure remain unchanged, financing costs are not relevant in the analysis of a project's incremental cash flows according to the stand-alone principle.

2. The $5 million acquisition cost of the land six years ago is a sunk cost. The $200,000 current appraisal of the land is an opportunity cost if the land is used rather than sold off. The $7.5 million cash outlay is the initial fixed asset investment needed to get the project going. Therefore, the proper year zero cash flow to use in evaluating this project is $7.7 million.

3. Sales due solely to the new product line are 15,000($13,000) = $195 million. Increased sales of the compact car line occur because of the new product line introduction; thus 7,000($8,000) = $56 million in new sales is relevant. Erosion of luxury car sales is also due to the new mid-size cars; thus 4,000($20,000) = $80 million loss in sales is relevant. The net sales figure to use in evaluating the new line is thus $195 million + $56 million − $80 million = $171 million.

4.

Sales	$ 650,000
Variable costs	357,500
Fixed costs	125,000
Depreciation	100,000
EBT	$ 67,500
Taxes@35%	23,625
Net income	$ 43,875

5.

Sales	$ 520,500
Variable costs	281,000
Depreciation	105,800
EBT	$ 133,700
Taxes@39%	52,143
Net income	$ 81,557

$OCF = EBIT + D - T$
$$= 133,700 + 105,800 - 52,143 = \$187,357$$
Depreciation tax shield $= t_c D$
$$= .39(105,800) = \$41,262$$

6.

Sales	$ 49,350.00
Variable costs	25,000.00
Depreciation	6,175.00
EBT	$ 18,175.00
Taxes@34%	6,179.50
Net income	$ 11,995.50

a.   OCF = EBIT + D – T = 18,175 + 6,175 – 6,179.50   = \$18,170.50

b.   OCF = S – C – T = 49,350 – 25,000 – 6,179.50   = \$18,170.50

c.   OCF = (S – C)(1 – t_c) + t_cD = (49,350 – 25,000)(1 – .34) + .34(6,175) = \$18,170.50

d.   OCF = NI + D = 11,995.50 + 6,175   = \$18,170.50

7.

Year	Beg. BV	Depr.basis	MACRS%	Depr.allow.	Acc.depr.	End BV
1	\$472,000.00	\$472,000	14.29	\$ 67,448.80	\$ 67,448.80	\$404,551.20
2	404,551.20	472,000	24.49	115,592.80	183,041.60	288,958.40
3	288,958.40	472,000	17.49	82,552.80	265,594.40	206,405.60
4	206,405.60	472,000	12.49	58,952.80	324,547.20	147,452.80
5	147,452.80	472,000	8.93	42,149.60	366,696.80	105,303.20
6	105,303.20	472,000	8.93	42,149.60	408,846.40	63,153.60
7	63,153.60	472,000	8.93	42,149.60	450,996.00	21,004.00
8	21,004.00	472,000	4.45	21,004.00	472,000.00	0

8. BV_5 = \$100,000 – \$100,000($5/8$) = \$37,500

The asset is sold at a loss to book value, so the depreciation tax shield of the loss is recaptured.

Aftertax salvage value = \$20,000 + (\$37,500 – \$20,000)(0.35) = \$26,125

9. BV_4 = \$5M – \$5M(0.2000 + 0.3200 + 0.1920 + 0.1152) = \$864,000

The asset is sold at a gain to book value, so this gain is taxable.

Aftertax salvage value = \$864,000 + (\$2M – \$864,000)(1 – 0.34) = \$1,613,760

10.   A/R fell by \$5,100, and inventory increased by \$4,580, so net current assets fell by \$520

↑NWC = ↑(CA – CL) = – 520 – 1,500 = – 2,020

Net cash flow = S – C – ↑NWC = 52,775 – 39,360 – (– 2,020) = \$15,435

11.   OCF = (S – C)(1 – t_c) + t_cD = (\$1M – \$500K)(1 – 0.35) + 0.35(\$1.2M/3) = \$465,000

12.   NPV = – \$1.2M + \$465K(PVIFA$_{8\%,3}$) = – \$1,649.90

13.

Year	Cash Flow
0	– 1.2M – 100K = – 1.3M
1	465K
2	465K
3	465K + 100K + 175K(1 – 0.35) = 465K + 213.75K

NPV = – \$1.3M + \$465K(PVIFA$_{8\%,3}$) + (\$213.75K / 1.08^3) = \$68,031.74

14. D_1 = 1.2M(0.3333) = 399,960; D_2 = 1.2M(0.4444) = 533,280

D_3 = 1.2M(0.1482) = 177,840;   thus, BV_3 = 1.2M – (399,960 + 533,280 + 177,840) = 88,920

The asset is sold at a gain to book value, so this gain is taxable.

Aftertax salvage value = 88,920 + (175,000 – 88,920)(1 – 0.35) = 144,872

OCF_t = (S – C)(1 – t_c) + $t_c D_t$, so:

Year	Cash Flow
0	$-1.2M - 100K = -1.3M$
1	$(500,000)(0.65) + 0.35(399,960) = 464,986$
2	$(500,000)(0.65) + 0.35(533,280) = 511,648$
3	$(500,000)(0.65) + 0.35(177,840) = 387,244; + 100K + 144,872$

$NPV = -\$1.3M + (\$464,986/1.08) + (\$511,648/1.08^2) + (\$632,116/1.08^3) = \$70,992.35$

15. Annual depreciation charge = $\$180,000/5 = \$36,000$
Aftertax salvage value = $\$25,000(1 - 0.38) = \$15,500$
OCF = $\$65,000(1 - 0.38) + 0.38(\$36,000) = \$53,980$
$NPV = -\$180,000 - \$17,500 + \$53,980(PVIFA_{10\%,5}) + [(\$15,500+\$17,500) / 1.1^3] = \$27,617.07$

16. Annual depreciation charge = $\$950,000/5 = \$190,000$
Aftertax salvage value = $\$300,000(1 - 0.35) = \$195,000$
OCF = $\$400,000(1 - 0.35) + 0.35(\$190,000) = \$326,500$
$NPV = 0 = -\$950,000 + \$175,000 + \$326,500(PVIFA_{IRR\%,5}) + [(\$195,000-\$175,000) / (1+IRR)^3]$
$IRR = 31.70\%$

17. $300K cost savings case: OCF = $\$300,000(1 - 0.35) + 0.35(\$190,000) = \$261,500$
$NPV = -\$950,000 + \$175,000 + \$261,500(PVIFA_{18\%,5}) + [(\$195,000-\$175,000) / (1.18)^3]$
$\quad = +\$51,497.41$ (IRR = 20.87%)
$250K cost savings case: OCF = $\$250,000(1 - 0.35) + 0.35(\$190,000) = \$229,000$
$NPV = -\$950,000 + \$175,000 + \$229,000(PVIFA_{18\%,5}) + [(\$195,000-\$175,000) / (1.18)^3]$
$\quad = -\$50,135.65$ (IRR = 15.14%)
Required pretax cost-savings case:
$NPV = 0 = -\$950,000 + \$175,000 + OCF(PVIFA_{18\%,5}) + [(\$195,000-\$175,000) / (1.18)^3]$,
$\quad$ so OCF = $\$245,032.27 = (S - C)(1 - 0.35) + 0.35(\$190K);$ (S - C) = \$274,665.03

18. $NPV = -\$50,000 - \$7,500 - 10,000(PVIFA_{8\%,3}) + \$7,500/1.08^3 = -\$77,317.23$
$EAC = -\$77,317.23 / (PVIFA_{8\%,3}) = -\$30,001.68$

19. Both cases: aftertax salvage value = $\$18,000(1 - 0.35) = \$11,700$
Jazzmaster: OCF = $-\$10,000(1 - 0.35) + 0.35(\$75,000/3) = \$2,250$
$\quad NPV = -\$75,000 + \$2,250(PVIFA_{13\%,3}) + (\$11,700/1.13^3) = -\$61,578.72$
$\quad EAC = -\$61,578.72 / (PVIFA_{13\%,3}) = -\$26,079.94$
Discomaster: OCF = $-\$8,000(1 - 0.35) + 0.35(\$100,000/5) = \$1,800$
$\quad NPV = -\$100,000 + \$1,800(PVIFA_{13\%,5}) + (\$11,700/1.13^5) = -\$87,318.68$
$\quad EAC = -\$87,318.68 / (PVIFA_{13\%,3}) = -\$24,825.97$
The two sound mixers have unequal lives, so they can only be compared by expressing both over a common life, which is what the EAC method does. Thus, you prefer the Discomaster because it has the lower (less negative) annual cost.

20. Aftertax salvage value = $50,000(1 – 0.35) = $32,500

NPV = 0 = – $360,000 – $40,000 + OCF(PVIFA$_{15\%,3}$) + [($40,000+$32,500) / 1.15^3]

OCF = $352,330.07 / PVIFA$_{15\%,3}$ = $154,312.46

OCF = $154,312.46 = [(P–v)Q – FC](1 – t$_c$) + t$_c$D

154,312.46 = [(P–5.75)(70,000) – 100,000](1 – 0.35) + 0.35(360,000/3) ;   P = $9.647

Intermediate

21. Depreciation is a non-cash expense, but it is tax-deductible on the income statement. Thus depreciation causes taxes paid, an actual cash outflow, to be reduced by an amount equal to the depreciation tax shield t$_c$D. A reduction in taxes that would otherwise be paid is the same thing as a cash inflow, so the effects of the depreciation tax shield must be added in to get the total incremental aftertax cash flows.

22. All else the same, firm Y will always have the higher NPV estimate, because with accelerated depreciation methods, a larger percentage of the total allowable depreciation is taken up-front compared to straight-line methods; thus the present value of the depreciation tax shield is higher in the case of accelerated methods, leading to higher NPV estimates.

23. The EAC approach is appropriate when comparing mutually exclusive projects with different lives that will be replaced when they wear out. This type of analysis is necessary so that the project's have a common-life span over which they can be compared; in effect, each project is assumed to exist over an infinite horizon of N-year repeating projects. Assuming that this type of analysis is valid implies that the project cash flows remain the same forever, thus ignoring the possible effects of, among other things: (1) inflation, (2) changing economic conditions, (3) the increasing unreliability of cash flow estimates that occur far into the future, and (4) the possible effects of future technology improvement that could alter the project cash flows.

24. D$_1$ = $200,000(0.20) = $40,000   D$_2$ = $200,000(0.32) = $64,000

D$_3$ = $200,000(0.192) = $38,400   D$_4$ = $200,000(0.1152) = $23,040

BV$_4$ = $200,000 – ($40,000 + $64,000 + $38,400 + $23,040) = $34,560

The asset is sold at a gain to book value, so this gain is taxable.

Aftertax salvage value = $34,560 + ($50,000 – $34,560)(1 – 0.34) = $44,750.40

OCF$_1$ = $85,000(1 – 0.34) + 0.34($40,000) = $69,700

OCF$_2$ = $85,000(1 – 0.34) + 0.34($64,000) = $77,860

OCF$_3$ = $85,000(1 – 0.34) + 0.34($38,400) = $69,156

OCF$_4$ = $85,000(1 – 0.34) + 0.34($23,040) = $63,933.60

NPV = – $200,000 – $15,000 + ($69,700 – $5,000)/1.13 + ($77,860 – $5,000)/1.13^2

+ ($69,156 – $5,000)/1.13^3 + ($63,933.60 + $30,000 + $44,750.40)/1.13^4 = $28,837.53

25. OCF$_A$ = – $100,000(1 – 0.34) + 0.34($300,000/3) = – $32,000

NPV$_A$ = – $300,000 – $32,000(PVIFA$_{10\%,3}$) = – $379,579.26

OCF$_B$ = – $85,000(1 – 0.34) + 0.34($400,000/4) = – $22,100

NPV$_B$ = – $400,000 – $22,100(PVIFA$_{10\%,4}$) = – $470,054.03

If the system will not be replaced when it wears out, then system A should be chosen, because it has the more positive NPV.

26. $EAC_A = -\$379,579.26 / (PVIFA_{10\%,3}) = -\$152,634.44$

$EAC_B = -\$470,054.03 / (PVIFA_{10\%,4}) = -\$148,288.32$

27. Aftertax salvage value = $\$200,000(1 - 0.34) = \$132,000$

$NPV = 0 = -\$100,000 - \$1,800,000 - \$200,000 + OCF(PVIFA_{14\%,4}) - \$50,000(PVIFA_{14\%,4})$
$\qquad + [(\$132,000+\$400,000) / 1.14^4]$

$OCF = \$1,930,698.91 / PVIFA_{14\%,4} = \$662,625.10$

$OCF = \$662,625.10 = [(P-v)Q - FC](1 - t_c) + t_cD$

$662,625.10 = [(P-0.20)(10,000,000) - 300,000](1 - 0.34) + 0.34(1,800,000/4) ; \quad P = \$0.3072$

28. At a given price, taking accelerated depreciation compared to straight-line depreciation causes the NPV to be higher; similarly, at a given price, lower net working capital investment requirements will cause the NPV to be higher. Thus NPV would be zero at a lower price in this situation. In the case of a bid price, you could submit a lower price and still break-even, or submit the higher price and make a profit.

Challenge

29. $D_1 = \$9.75M(0.1429) = \$1,393,275$ $\qquad D_2 = \$9.75M(0.2449) = \$2,387,775$

$D_3 = \$9.75M(0.1749) = \$1,705,275$ $\qquad D_4 = \$9.75M(0.1249) = \$1,217,775$

$D_5 = \$9.75M(0.0893) = \$870,675$ $\qquad$ total depreciation D_1-$D_5 = \$7,574,775$

$BV_5 = \$9,750,000 - \$7,574,775 = \$2,175,225$

Market value of asset in year 5 = $0.28(\$9.75M) = \$2,730,000$

The asset is sold at a gain to book value, so this gain is taxable.

Aftertax salvage value = $\$2,175,225 + (\$2,730,000 - \$2,175,225)(1 - 0.38) = \$2,519,185.50$

Year 0 cash flow = $-\$9,750,000 - \$875,000 = -\$10,625,000$

$\uparrow NWC_t = 0.35(S_{t+1} - S_t)$ if $S_{t+1} > S_t$; $\uparrow NWC_t = 0$ otherwise

$OCF_t = NI_t + D_t$

Year:	1	2	3	4	5
Sales	$8,400,000.00	$9,450,000.00	$9,975,000.00	$10,395,000.00	$7,875,000.00
VC	6,000,000.00	6,750,000.00	7,125,000.00	7,425,000.00	5,625,000.00
FC	200,000.00	200,000.00	200,000.00	200,000.00	200,000.00
Depr	1,393,275.00	2,387,775.00	1,705,275.00	1,217,775.00	870,675.00
EBIT	$ 806,725.00	$ 112,225.00	$ 944,725.00	$ 1,552,225.00	$1,179,325.00
Taxes	306,555.50	42,645.50	358,995.50	589,845.50	448,143.50
NI	$ 500,169.50	$ 69,579.50	$ 585,729.50	$ 962,379.50	$ 731,181.50
OCF	$1,893,444.50	$2,457,354.50	$2,291,004.50	$2,180,154.50	$1,601,856.50
NWC	367,500.00	183,750.00	147,000.00		(1,573,250.00)
Cap.Sp.					(2,519,185.50)
CFA	$1,525,944.50	$2,273,604.50	$2,144,004.50	$2,180,154.50	$5,694,292.00

$$NPV = -\$10,625,000 + CFA_1/1.1 + CFA_2/1.1^2 + CFA_3/1.1^3 + CFA_4/1.1^4 + CFA_5/1.1^5$$
$$= -\$723,161.25 \text{ @ } 10\% \; ; \;\; IRR = 7.75\%$$

30. $D_1 = \$330,000(0.3333) = \$110,000$ $D_2 = \$330,000(0.4444) = \$146,641$

$D_3 = \$330,000(0.1482) = \$48,906$ $D_4 = \$330,000(0.0741) = \$24,453$

Aftertax salvage value = $\$45,000(1 - 0.35) = \$29,250$

$OCF_1 = (S - C)(1 - 0.35) + 0.35(\$110,000)$

$OCF_2 = (S - C)(1 - 0.35) + 0.35(\$146,641)$

$OCF_3 = (S - C)(1 - 0.35) + 0.35(\$\ 48,906)$

$OCF_4 = (S - C)(1 - 0.35) + 0.35(\$\ 24,453)$

$OCF_5 = (S - C)(1 - 0.35)$

$NPV = 0 = -\$330,000 - \$20,000 + (S - C)(0.65)(PVIFA_{12\%,5}) + 0.35\{\ \$110,000/1.12$
$+ \$146,641/1.12^2 + \$48,906/1.12^3 + \$24,453/1.12^4\} + (\$29,250 + \$20,000)/1.12^5$

$(S - C)(0.65)(PVIFA_{12\%,5}) = \$234,580.16 \; ; \;\; (S - C) = \$100,115.11$

31. *a.* $OCF_t = (S - C)(1 - t_c) + t_c D_t = (\$80M - \$40M)(1 - 0.38) + 0.38(\$90M/4) = \$33.35M$

$NPV = -\$90M - \$8M + \$33.35M(PVIFA_{16\%,4}) + \$8M/1.16^4 = -\$262,347$

b.   OCF is the same in all cases; only aftertax salvage value of the asset is changing.

Abandon after 3 years: $BV_3 = \$90M - \$90M(^3/_4) = \$22.5M$

Asset is sold at a gain to book value, so this gain is taxable.

Aftertax salvage value = $\$22.5M + (\$35M - \$22.5M)(1 - 0.38) = \$30.25M$

$NPV = -\$90M - \$8M + \$33.35M(PVIFA_{16\%,3}) + \$38.25M/1.16^3 = \$1,405,572$

Abandon after 2 years: $BV_2 = \$90M - \$90M(^1/_2) = \$45M$

Asset is sold at a gain to book value, so this gain is taxable.

Aftertax salvage value = $\$45M + (\$60M - \$45M)(1 - 0.38) = \$54.30M$

$NPV = -\$90M - \$8M + \$33.35M(PVIFA_{16\%,2}) + \$62.30M/1.16^2 = \$1,833,532$

Abandon after 1 year: $BV_1 = \$90M - \$90M(^1/_4) = \$67.5M$

Asset is sold at a gain to book value, so this gain is taxable.

Aftertax salvage value = $\$67.5M + (\$75M - \$67.5M)(1 - 0.38) = \$72.15M$

$NPV = -\$90M - \$8M + \$33.35M/1.16 + \$80.15M/1.16 = -\$155,172.41$

The NPV for the project is actually maximized if it is abandoned after 2 years of operation. This problem shows that the economic life and physical life of a project are not always the same. For project assets that keep their value in their marketplace, short-term projects with abandonment will often be more profitable than long-term projects.

32. New computer: initial cost = $\$400,000$

$OCF = \$70,000(1 - 0.35) + 0.35(\$400,000/5) = \$73,500$

aftertax salvage value = $\$50,000(1 - 0.35) = \$32,500$

$NPV = -\$400,000 + \$73,500(PVIFA_{9\%,5}) + \$32,500/1.09^5 = -\$92,987.86$

$EAC = -\$92,987.86 / PVIFA_{9\%,5} = -\$23,906.48$

Old computer: current depreciation = $60,000 per year

written off in 3 years implies current book value = $180,000

current market value = $100,000 implies:

current cost = $100,000 + 0.35($180,000 − $100,000) = $128,000

in two years, book value is $60,000 implies asset is sold at a loss:

aftertax salvage value = $50,000 + 0.35($60,000 − $50,000) = $53,500

$OCF = t_c D = 0.35(\$60,000) = \$21,000$

$NPV = -\$128,000 + \$21,000(PVIFA_{9\%,2}) + \$53,500/1.09^2 = -\$46,028.79$

$EAC = -\$46,028.79 / PVIFA_{9\%,2} = -\$26,165.93$

Incremental cash flows:

Year	$CF_{new} - CF_{old}$	
0	− $272,000	
1	52,500	NPV = − $46,959.08 (just the difference in NPVs)
2	− 1,000	
3	73,500	
4	73,500	
5	106,000	

a.   If we just look at replacing the computer without worrying about what will happen in two years, the NPV is − $46,959 and we should not replace the old system.

b.   If the computer systems will always be replaced at the end of their lives, we should buy the new system because it has the lower EAC.

33. a. $OCF = [\ (10-5.75)(70,000) - 100,000\ ](1 - 0.35) + 0.35(360,000/3) = \$170,375$

$NPV = -\$400,000 + \$170,375(PVIFA_{15\%,3}) + [(\$40,000+\$32,500) / 1.15^3] = \$36,674.41$

If the project has a positive NPV at a price of $10, then the bid price must be something lower than $10; similarly, if price remains at $10, then the break-even level of quantity must be something lower than 70,000 units, and the break-even level of fixed costs must be something greater than $100,000.

b. $NPV = 0 = -\$360,000 - \$40,000 + OCF(PVIFA_{15\%,3}) + [(\$40,000+\$32,500) / 1.15^3]$

$OCF = \$352,330.07 / PVIFA_{15\%,3} = \$154,312.46$

$OCF = \$154,312.46 = [\ (P-v)Q - FC\ ](1 - t_c) + t_c D$

$154,312.46 = [\ (10-5.75)(Q) - 100,000\ ](1 - 0.35) + 0.35(360,000/3);\ \ Q = 64,186$

c. $NPV = 0 = -\$360,000 - \$40,000 + OCF(PVIFA_{15\%,3}) + [(\$40,000+\$32,500) / 1.15^3]$

$OCF = \$352,330.07 / PVIFA_{15\%,3} = \$154,312.46$

$OCF = \$154,312.46 = [\ (P-v)Q - FC\ ](1 - t_c) + t_c D$

$154,312.46 = [\ (10-5.75)(70,000) - FC\ ](1 - 0.35) + 0.35(360,000/3);\ \ FC = \$124,711.60$

CHAPTER 9
PROJECT ANALYSIS AND EVALUATION

Basic

1.   *a.*   Total variable costs = $0.72 + $1.90 = $2.62

    b.   Total costs = variable costs + fixed costs = $2.62(350,000) + $510,000 = $1,427,000

    c. $Q = (FC+OCF)/(P - v)$

         Q_{cf} = $510,000/($4.25 - $2.62) = 312,883

         Q_{acc} = ($510,000 + $160,000)/($4.25 - $2.62) = 411,043

2.   Total costs = ($8.90 + $29)(90,000) + $700,000 = $4,111,000

     Marginal cost = cost of producing one more unit = $37.90

     Average cost = total cost/total quantity = $4,111,000/90,000 = $45.68

     Minimum acceptable total revenue = 4,000($37.90) = $151,600. Additional units should be produced only if the cost of producing those units can be recovered.

3.   For the base-case scenario, the nominal estimates for the variables should be used. For the worst-case scenario, the variables should be adjusted to their worst-possible values as far as NPV is concerned. In the case of price and quantity therefore, these values should be adjusted downward; for costs, the values should be adjusted upwards.

     P = 250(0.85) = $212.50;   Q = 100,000(0.85) = 85,000;

     v = 135(1.15) = $155.25;   FC= 8,000,000(1.15) = $9,200,000

4.   An estimate for the impact of changes in price on the profitability of the project can be found from the sensitivity of NPV with respect to price; $\Delta NPV/\Delta P$. This measure can be calculated by finding the NPV at any two different price levels and forming the ratio of the changes in these parameters. Whenever a sensitivity analysis is performed, all other variables are held constant at their base-case values.

5.   *a.*   D = $960,000/6 = $160,000 per year. Q_{acc} = ($750,000 + $160,000)/($19.95 - $12) = 114,465

         DOL = 1 + FC/OCF = 1 + FC/D = 1 + [$750,000/$160,000] = 5.688

    b. OCF_{base} = [(P - v)Q - FC](1 - t) + tD = [(19.95 - 12)(150K) - 750K](0.65) + 0.35(160K) = $343,625

         NPV_{base} = -$960,000 + $343,625($PVIFA_{12\%,6}$) = $452,782.34

         Say Q = 160,000: OCF_{new} = [(19.95 - 12)(160K) - 750K](0.65) + 0.35(160K) = $395,300

         NPV_{base} = -$960,000 + $395,300($PVIFA_{12\%,6}$) = $665,239.32

         $\Delta NPV/\Delta S$ = ($665,239.32 - $452,782.34)/(160,000 - 150,000) = +$21.246

         If sales were to drop by 500 units then, NPV would drop by 21.246(500) = $10,622.85

    c.   Say v = $13: OCF_{new} = [(19.95 - 13)(150K) - 750K](0.65) + 0.35(160K) = $246,125

         $\Delta OCF/\Delta v$ = ($246,125 - $343,625)/($13 - $12) = - 97,500

         If variable costs fell by $1 then, NPV would rise by $97,500

6. $OCF_{best} = \{[(19.95)(1.1) - (12)(0.9)](150K)(1.1) - 750K(0.9)\}(0.65) + 0.35(160K) = \$812,551.25$
$NPV_{best} = -\$960,000 + \$812,551.25(PVIFA_{12\%,6}) = \$2,380,729.16$
$OCF_{worst} = \{[(19.95)(0.9) - (12)(1.1)](150K)(0.9) - 750K(1.1)\}(0.65) + 0.35(160K) = -\$62,998.75$
$NPV_{worst} = -\$960,000 - \$62,998.75(PVIFA_{12\%,6}) = -\$1,219,013.52$

7. (1): $Q_{cf} = \$18M/(\$8K - \$6.5K) = 12,000$; $Q_{acc} = (\$18M + \$12M)/(\$8K - \$6.5K) = 20,000$
   (2): $Q_{cf} = \$40K/(\$60 - \$35) = 1,600$; $Q_{acc} = (\$40K + \$180K)/(\$60 - \$35) = 8,800$
   (3): $Q_{cf} = \$250/(\$5 - \$3) = 125$; $Q_{acc} = (\$250 + \$400)/(\$5 - \$3) = 325$

8. (1): $Q_{acc} = 45,000 = (\$275K + D)/(\$40 - \$25)$; $D = \$400,000$
   (2): $Q_{acc} = 150,000 = (\$3M + \$1.5M)/(P - \$60)$; $P = \$90$
   (3): $Q_{acc} = 7,500 = (\$175K + \$125K)/(\$90 - v)$; $v = \$50$

9. $Q_{acc} = [\$2,500 + (\$4,500/3)]/(\$50 - \$25) = 160$; $Q_{cf} = \$2,500/(\$50 - \$25) = 100$
   $NPV = 0$ implies $\$4,500 = OCF(PVIFA_{15\%,3})$; $OCF = \$1,970.90$.
   $Q_{finc} = (\$2,500 + \$1,970.90)/(\$50 - \$25) = 179$; $DOL = 1 + (\$2,500/\$1,970.90) = 2.268$

10. $Q_{cf} = FC/(P-v)$; $10,000 = \$100,000/(P-\$10)$; $P = \$20$
   $Q_{acc} = (FC+D)/(P-v)$; $14,500 = (\$100,000 + D)/(\$20 - \$10)$; $D = \$45,000$
   $D = I / N$; $I = 5(\$45,000) = \$225,000$
   $OCF_{finc} = I/(PVIFA_{10\%,5}) = \$225,000/3.7908 = \$59,354.43$
   $Q_{finc} = (\$100,000 + \$59,354.43)/(\$20 - \$10) = 15,935$

11. $DOL = \%\Delta OCF/\%\Delta Q$; $\%\Delta OCF = 3[(30K-25K)/25K] = 60\%$
   The new level of operating leverage is lower since FC/OCF is smaller.

12. $DOL = 3 = 1 + \$100,000/OCF$; $OCF = \$50,000$.   New $OCF = \$50,000(1.6) = \$80,000$
   New $DOL = 1 + (\$100,000/\$80,000) = 2.25$

13. $DOL = 1 + (\$75,000/\$200,000) = 1.375$ $\%\Delta Q = (5,600 - 5,000)/5,000 = 12\%$
   $\%\Delta OCF = DOL(\%\Delta Q) = 1.375(12) = 16.5\%$ New $OCF = \$200,000(1.165) = \$233,000$
   DOL at 5,600 units $= 1 + (\$75,000/\$233,000) = 1.322$

14. Forecasting risk is the risk that a poor decision is made because of errors in projected cash flows. The danger is greatest with a new product because the cash flows are probably harder to predict.

15. The option to abandon reflects our ability to reallocate assets if we find our initial estimates were too optimistic. The option to expand reflects our ability to increase cash flows from a project if we find our initial estimates were too pessimistic. Since the option to expand can increase cash flows and the option to abandon can reduce losses, failing to consider these two options will generally lead to an underestimate of a project's NPV.

16. $DOL = 1.5 = 1 + FC/OCF$; $FC = (1.5 - 1)\$6,000 = \$3,000$
   $\%\Delta Q = (9,000 - 8,000)/8,000$ or $(7,000 - 8,000)/8,000 = \pm12.5\%$; $\%\Delta OCF = 1.5(\pm12.5) = 18.75\%$
   OCF at 9,000 units $= \$6,000(1.1875) = \$7,125$; OCF at 7,000 units $= \$6,000(0.8125) = \$4,875$

17. DOL at 9,000 units = 1 + \$3,000/\$7,125 = 1.421;   DOL at 7,000 units = 1 + \$3,000/\$4,875 = 1.615

Intermediate

18. It is true that if average revenue is less than average cost, the firm is losing money. This much of the statement is therefore correct. At the margin, however, accepting a project with a marginal revenue in excess of its marginal cost clearly acts to increase operating cash flow.

19. *a.*   IRR = 0%;   payback = N years; $NPV = I \{(1/N)(\text{PVIFA}_{r\%,N}) - 1\}$

   b.   IRR = –100%;   payback = ∞; $NPV = -I$

   c.   IRR = r %;   payback < N years; $NPV = 0$

20. Accounting break-even is unaffected (taxes are zero at that point).

Cash break-even is lower (assuming a tax credit).

Financial break-even will be higher (because of taxes paid).

21. OCF @ 100K units = [(\$17 – \$12)(100K) – \$250K](0.66) + 0.34(\$450K/3) = \$216,000

OCF @ 101K units = [(\$17 – \$12)(101K) – \$250K](0.66) + 0.34(\$450K/3) = \$219,300

Sensitivity = $\Delta OCF/\Delta Q$ = (\$219,300 – \$216,000)/(101,000 – 100,000) = +\$3.30

OCF will increase by \$3.30 for every additional unit sold.

22. DOL @ 100,000 units = 1 + (\$250,000/\$216,000) = 2.157

Q_{acc} = [\$250,000 + (\$450,000/3)]/(\$17 – \$12) = 80,000

DOL @ 80,000 units = 1 + (\$250,000/\$150,000) = 2.667

23. *a.*   Sales = 75(1±0.12) = 84, 66;   variable costs = \$14,000(1±0.12) = \$15,680, \$12,320

   Fixed costs = \$175,000(1±0.12) = \$196,000, \$154,000

   OCF_{base} = [(\$20K – \$14K)(75) – \$175K](0.65) + 0.35(\$720K/4) = \$241,750

   NPV_{base} = –\$720,000 + \$241,750($\text{PVIFA}_{8\%,4}$) = \$80,706.66

   OCF_{worst} = [(\$20K – \$15.68K)(66) – \$196K](0.65) + 0.35(\$720K/4) = \$120,928

   NPV_{worst} = –\$720,000 + \$120,928($\text{PVIFA}_{8\%,4}$) = –\$319,471.13

   OCF_{best} = [(\$20K – \$12.32K)(84) – \$154K](0.65) + 0.35(\$720K/4) = \$382,228

   NPV_{best} = –\$720,000 + \$382,228($\text{PVIFA}_{8\%,4}$) = \$545,987.62

   b.   Say FC are \$176K: OCF = [(\$20K – \$14K)(75) – \$176K](0.65) + 0.35(\$720K/4) = \$241,100

   NPV = –\$720,000 + \$241,100($\text{PVIFA}_{8\%,4}$) = \$78,553.78

   $\Delta NPV/\Delta FC$ = (\$78,553.78 – \$80,706.66)/(\$176,000 – \$175,000) = –2.153

   For every dollar FC increase, NPV falls by \$2.15.

   c. Q_{cf} = \$175,000/(\$20K – \$14K) = 29.17

   d. Q_{acc} = [\$175,000 + (\$720,000/4)]/(\$20K – \$14K) = 59.17

   At this level of output, DOL = 1 + (\$175,000/\$180,000) = 1.972

   For each 1% increase in unit sales, OCF will increase by 1.972%.

24. *a.* $NPV_{base} = -\$345,000 + \$70,000(PVIFA_{17\%,10}) = -\$18,897.75$

   b. $\$300,000 = (\$35)Q(PVIFA_{17\%,9})$; $Q = 300,000/[35(4.4506)] = 1,925.92$

   Abandon the project if $Q < 1,926$ units, because NPV(abandonment) > NPV (project CF's)

   c.   The $300,000 is the market value of the project. If you continue with the project in one year, you forego the $300,000 that could have been used for something else.

25. *a.*   Success: PV future CF's $= \$35(2,800)(PVIFA_{17\%,9}) = \$436,155.49$

   Failure: from #24, $Q = 1,200 < 1,926$ so you will abandon the project; PV = $300,000

   Expected value of project at year $1 = [(\$436,155.49+\$300,000)/2] + \$70,000 = \$438,077.75$

   $NPV = -\$345,000 + (\$438,077.75)/1.17 = \$29,425.42$

   b.   If we couldn't abandon the project, PV future CF's $= \$35(1,200)(PVIFA_{17\%,9}) = \$186,923.78$

   Gain from option to abandon = $300,000 - $186,923.78 = $113,076.22

   Option is 50% likely to occur: value $= \frac{1}{2}(\$113,076.22)/1.17 = \$48,310.17$

26.   Success: PV future CF's $= \$35(5,600)(PVIFA_{17\%,9}) = \$872,310.98$

   Failure: from #24, $Q = 1,200 < 1,926$ so you will abandon the project; PV = $300,000

   Expected value of project at year $1 = [(\$872,310.98+\$300,000)/2] + \$70,000 = \$656,155.49$

   $NPV = -\$345,000 + (\$656,115.49)/1.17 = \$215,816.66$

   If no expansion allowed, PV future CF's $= \$35(2,800)(PVIFA_{17\%,9}) = \$436,155.49$

   Gain from option to expand = $872,310.98 - $436,155.49 = $436,155.49

   Option is 50% likely to occur: value $= \frac{1}{2}(\$436,155.49)/1.17 = \$186,391.24$

27. *a.*   From the tax-shield definition of OCF (Chapter 8):

   $OCF = [(P-v)Q - FC](1-t) + tD$; $(OCF-tD)/(1-t) = (P-v)Q - FC$

   $\{FC + [(OCF-tD)/(1-t)] \}/(P-v) = Q$

   b. $Q_{cf} = \{\$500,000+[-0.38(\$700,000)/0.62]\}/(\$40,000-\$20,000) = 3.548 = 4$

   $Q_{acc} = \{\$500,000+[\$700,000-(\$700,000(0.38)/0.62)]/(\$40,000-\$20,000) = 60$

   $OCF_{finc} = \$3,500,000/PVIFA_{20\%,5} = \$1,170,328.96$; thus $Q_{finc} = 97.93 = 98$

   c.   At the accounting break-even point, net income = 0, so $OCF = NI+D = D$

   $Q_{acc} = \{FC+[(D-tD)/(1-t)]\}/(P-v) = \{FC+[D(1-t)]\}/(P-v) = (FC+D)/(P-v) = (FC+OCF)/(P-v)$

   The tax rate has cancelled out in this case.

28. $DOL = \%\Delta OCF/\%\Delta Q = [\{(OCF_1-OCF_0)/OCF_0\} / \{(Q_1-Q_0)/Q_0\}]$

   $OCF_1 = [(P-v)Q_1 - FC](1-t) + tD$; $OCF_0 = [(P-v)Q_1 - FC](1-t) + tD$;

   $OCF_1-OCF_0 = (P-v)(1-t)(Q_1-Q_0)$; $(OCF_1-OCF_0)/OCF_0 = (P-v)(1-t)(Q1-Q0) / OCF_0$;

   $\{(OCF1-OCF0)/OCF0\}[(Q_1-Q_0)/Q_0] = [(P-v)(1-t)Q_0]/OCF_0 =$

   $[OCF_0-tD+FC(1-t)]/OCF_0$;

   $DOL = 1 + [FC(1-t)-tD]/OCF_0$

29. *a.*   OCF = [($120 – $90)(25K) – $200K](0.62) + 0.38($1.25M/3) = $436,000

            NPV = –$1.25M – $90K + $436K(PVIFA$_{17\%,9}$) + [$90K+$100K(1–.38)]/1.14^5 = $235,767.34

     b.   OCF$_{worst}$ = {[(120)(0.9) – (90)(1.15)](25K) – 200K(1.15)}(0.62) + 0.38(250K) = $22,150

            NPV$_{worst}$ = –$1.25M – $90K(1.05) + $22,150(PVIFA$_{17\%,9}$) +

                       [$90K(1.05)+$100K(0.85)(1–.38)]/1.14^5 = –$1,192,006.19

            OCF$_{best}$ = {[(120)(1.1) – (90)(0.85)](25K) – 200K(0.85)}(0.62) + 0.38(250K) = $849,850

            NPV$_{best}$ = –$1.25M – $90K(0.95) + $849,850(PVIFA$_{17\%,9}$) +

                       [$90K(0.95)+$100K(1.15)(1–.38)]/1.14^5 = $1,663,540.87

30. Try Q = 26,000: OCF = [($120 – $90)(26K) – $200K](0.62) + 0.38($1.25M/5) = $454,600

      ΔOCF/ΔQ = ($454,600–$436,000)/(26,000–25,000) = +$18.60

      NPV = –$1.25M – $90K + $454.6K(PVIFA$_{17\%,9}$) + [$90K+$100K(1–.38)]/1.14^5 = $299,622.65

      ΔNPV/ΔQ = ($299,622.45–$235,767.34)/(26,000–25,000) = +$63.86

      You wouldn't want Q to fall below the point where NPV = 0:

      $235,767.34 = $63.86($\Delta$Q) ; ΔQ = 3,692.21 ; Q$_{min}$ = 25,000 – 3,692.21 = 21,308

31. At Q$_{cf}$, OCF=0: 0 = [($120 – $90)Q$_{cf}$ – $200K](0.62) + 0.38($1.25M/5) ; Q$_{cf}$ = 1,559

      Q$_{acc}$ = [$200,000+{$1,250,000/5}]/($120–$90); Q$_{acc}$ = 15,000

      From #30, Q$_{finc}$ = 21,308

32. DOL = 1 + {$200,000(1–0.38) – 0.38($1,250,000/5)}/ $436,000 = 1.0665

      Thus a 1% rise leads to a 1.0665% rise in OCF. If Q rises to 26,000, then ΔQ = 4%,

      so %ΔOCF = 4(1.0665) = 4.2661%

      From #30, ΔOCF/OCF = {$454,600–$436,000}/$436,000 = 0.042661

CHAPTER 10
SOME LESSONS FROM CAPITAL MARKET HISTORY

Basic

1. R = [$1.75 + ($46 – $54)] / $54 = – 11.57%

2. Dividend yield = $1.75 / $54 = 3.24% ; Capital gains yield = ($46 – $54) / $54 = – 14.81%

3. R = [$1.75 + ($65 – $54)] / $54 = 23.61%
   Dividend yield = $1.75 / $54 = 3.24% ; Capital gains yield = ($65 – $54) / $54 = 20.37%

4. $r \approx .08 – .06 = 2\%$; $r = [1.08 / 1.06] – 1 = 1.89\%$

5. R = (1.025)(1.07) – 1 = 9.68%

6. h = [1.18 / 1.14] – 1 = 3.51%

7. r = [1.14 / 1.05] – 1 = 8.57%

8. r = [1.14 / 1.16] – 1 = – 1.72%. A negative real rate of return implies that the inflation rate exceeds the nominal rate, which could occur if either inflation was much higher than expected after the fact, or if the nominal return on investment was much lower than expected after the fact.

9. *a.* Dollar return = $110 + ($925 – $965) = $70
   b. R = $70 / $965 = 7.25%
   c. r = [1.0725 / 1.04] – 1 = 3.13%

10. *a.* From Figure 10.10, R = 12.1%
    b. From Figure 10.10, h = 3.2%. Thus r = [1.121 / 1.032] – 1 = 8.62%

11. Long-term government bonds: r = [1.049 / 1.032] – 1 = 1.65%
    Long-term corporate bonds: r = [1.055 / 1.032] – 1 = 2.23%

12. $\overline{X} = \left[\sum_{i=1}^{N} x_i \right] \Big/ N = \dfrac{[.14 + .03 – .06 + .11 + .09]}{5} = 6.20\%$; $\overline{Y} = \left[\sum_{i=1}^{N} y_i \right] \Big/ N = \dfrac{[.22 – .05 – .15 + .28 + .17]}{5} = 9.40\%$

$$s_X^2 = \left[\sum_{i=1}^{N}(x_i - \bar{x})^2\right]\Big/(N-1)$$

$$= \frac{1}{5-1}\left\{(.14-.026)^2 +(.03-.026)^2 +(-.06-.026)^2 +(.11-.026)^2 +(.09-.026)^2\right\} = .00789$$

$$s_Y^2 = \frac{1}{5-1}\left\{(.22-.094)^2 +(-.05-.094)^2 +(-.15-.094)^2 +(.28-.094)^2 +(.17-.094)^2\right\} = .03413$$

$$s_X = \sqrt{.00789} = 0.0888 = 8.88\% \quad ; \quad s_Y = \sqrt{.03413} = 0.1847 = 18.47\%$$

13.

Year	Small stock return	T-bill return	Risk premium
1980	39.88%	11.24%	28.64%
1981	13.88	14.71	–0.83
1982	28.01	10.54	17.47
1983	39.67	8.80	30.87
1984	–6.67	9.85	–16.52
1985	24.66	7.72	16.94
1986	6.85	6.16	0.69
	146.28	69.02	77.26

a. Small stocks: average return = 146.28 / 7 = 20.90% ; T-bills: average return = 69.02 / 7 = 9.86%

b. Small stocks: variance = 1/6{ $(.3988-.2090)^2$ + $(.1388-.2090)^2$ + $(.2801-.2090)^2$ + $(.3967-.2090)^2$
$\qquad$ + $(-.0667-.2090)^2$ + $(.2466-.2090)^2$ + $(.0685-.2090)^2$ } = 0.0297
$\qquad$ standard deviation = $(0.0297)^{1/2}$ = 0.1724 = 17.24%

$\quad$ T-bills: variance = 1/6{ $(.1124-.0986)^2$ + $(.1471-.0986)^2$ + $(.1054-.0986)^2$ + $(.0880-.0986)^2$
$\qquad$ + $(.0985-.0986)^2$ + $(.0772-.0986)^2$ + $(.0616-.0986)^2$ } = 0.0007547
$\qquad$ standard deviation = $(0.0007547)^{1/2}$ = 0.0275 = 2.75%

c. Average observed risk premium = 77.26 / 7 = 11.04%
$\qquad$ variance = 1/6{ $(.2864-.1104)^2$ + $(-.0083-.1104)^2$ + $(.1747-.1104)^2$ + $(.3087-.1104)^2$
$\qquad$ + $(-.1652-.1104)^2$ + $(.1694-.1104)^2$ + $(.0069-.1104)^2$ } = 0.0298
$\qquad$ standard deviation = $(0.0298)^{1/2}$ = 0.1726 = 17.26%

d. Before the fact, for most assets the risk premium will be positive; investors demand compensation over and above the risk-free return to invest their money in the risky asset. After the fact, the observed risk premium can be negative if the asset's nominal return is unexpectedly low, the risk-free return is unexpectedly high, or any combination of these two events.

14. a. Average return = (1/5){.05–.11+.02+.27+.07 }/5 = .06 = 6%

$\quad$ b. Variance = 1/4{ $(.05-.06)^2$ + $(-.11-.06)^2$ + $(.02-.06)^2$ + $(.27-.06)^2$ + $(.07-.06)^2$ } = 0.0187
$\qquad$ Standard deviation = $(0.0187)^{1/2}$ = 0.1367 = 13.67%

15. a. $\bar{r}$ = (1.06/1.045) – 1 = 1.44%

$\quad$ b. $\overline{RP} = \bar{R} - \bar{R}_f = .06-.048 = 1.20\%$

16. $\bar{r}_f = (1.048 / 1.045) - 1 = 0.29\%$; $\overline{rp} = \bar{r} - \bar{r}_f = 1.44 - 0.29 = 1.15\%$

17. T-bill rates were highest in the early eighties. This was during a period of high inflation and is consistent with the Fisher effect.

18. On average, the only return that is earned is the required return—investors buy assets with returns in excess of the required return (positive NPV), bidding up the price and thus causing the return to fall to the required return (zero NPV); investors sell assets with returns less than the required return (negative NPV), driving the price lower and thus the causing the return to rise to the required return (zero NPV).

19. The market is not weak form efficient.

20. Yes, historical information is also public information; weak form efficiency is a subset of semistrong form efficiency.

Intermediate

21. A negative real rate implies that the inflation rate exceeds the nominal rate. Certainly this has happened in the past, but it is unlikely that securities would be priced before the fact with a negative real rate. A negative inflation rate implies that the real rate exceeds the nominal rate. This is unlikely to occur, but it is not impossible. However, in all cases the nominal rate itself cannot be less than zero, since an investor can always hold cash.

22. $P_1 = \$80(PVIFA_{10\%,6}) + \$1,000(PVIF_{10\%,6}) = \$912.89$
    $R = [\ \$80 + (\$912.89 - \$1,078.50)\ ]/\$1,078.50 = -.0794$
    $r = [\ (1 - .0794)/1.038\ ] - 1 = -11.31\%$

23. $Pr(\ R<-3.3\ or\ R>14.1\ ) \approx \frac{1}{3}$, but we are only interested in one tail here; $Pr(\ R<-3) \approx \frac{1}{6}$
    95% level: $R \in\ \mu \pm 2\sigma = 5.4 \pm 2(8.7) = -12.0\%$ to 22.8%
    99% level: $R \in\ \mu \pm 3\sigma = 5.4 \pm 3(8.7) = -20.7\%$ to 31.5%

24. $\mu = 17.1\%$; $\sigma = 35.4\%$. Doubling your money is a 100% return, so if the return distribution is normal, $z = (100-17.1)/35.4 = 2.34$ standard deviations above the mean; this corresponds to a probability of $\approx 1\%$, or once every 100 years. Tripling your money would be $z = (200-17.1)/35.4 = 5.17$ standard deviations above the mean; this corresponds to a probability of (much) less than 0.5%, or once every 200 years. (The actual answer is $\approx.0001\%$, or about once every 1 million years).

25. It is impossible to lose more than –100 percent of your investment. Therefore, return distributions are truncated on the lower tail at –100 percent.

26. Ignoring trading costs, on average, such investors merely earn what the market offers; the trades all have zero NPV. If trading costs exist, then these investors lose by the amount of the costs.

27. Unlike gambling, the stock market is a positive sum game; everybody can win. Also, speculators provide liquidity to markets and thus help to promote efficiency.

Challenge

28. $z = (0 - 12.3)/20.5 = -0.6000$; $\Pr(R \leq 0) = 27.43\%$

29. *a.* $z_1 = (10 - 5.9)/8.4 = 0.4881$; $\Pr(R \geq 10\%) = 1 - \Pr(R \leq 10\%) = 1 - .6873 = 31.27\%$
    $z_2 = (0 - 5.9)/8.4 = -0.7024$; $\Pr(R \leq 0) \approx 24.12\%$

  b. $z_3 = (10 - 3.7)/3.3 = 1.9091$; $\Pr(R \geq 10\%) = 1 - \Pr(R \leq 10\%) = 1 - .9719 = 2.81\%$
    $z_4 = (0 - 3.7)/3.3 = -1.1212$; $\Pr(R \leq 0) \approx 13.11\%$

  c. $z_5 = (-4.18 - 5.9)/8.4 = -1.2000$; $\Pr(R \leq -4.18\%) \approx 11.51\%$
    $z_6 = (10.38 - 3.7)/3.3 = 2.0242$; $\Pr(R \geq 10.38\%) = 1 - \Pr(R \leq 10.38\%) = 1 - .9785 = 2.15\%$

30. The EMH only says, within the bounds of increasingly strong assumptions about the information processing of investors, that assets are fairly priced. An implication of this is that, on average, the typical market participant cannot earn excessive profits from a particular trading strategy. However, that does not mean that a few particular investors cannot outperform the market over a particular investment horizon. Certain investors who do well for a period of time get a lot of attention from the financial press, but the scores of investors who do not do well over the same period of time generally get considerably less attention from the financial press.

31. *a.*   If the market is not weak form efficient, then this information could be acted on and a profit earned from following the price trend. Under *ii, iii,* and *iv,* this information is fully impounded in the current price and no abnormal profit opportunity exists.

  b.   Under *ii,* if the market is not semistrong form efficient, then this information could be used to buy the stock "cheap" before the rest of the market disovers the financial statement anomaly. Since *ii* is stronger than *i,* both imply that a profit opportunity exists; under *iii* and *iv,* this information is fully impounded in the current price and no profit opportunity exists.

  c.   Under *iii,* if the market is not strong form efficient, then this information could be used as a profitable trading strategy, by noting the buying activity of the insiders as a signal that the stock is underpriced or that good news is imminent. Since *i* and *ii* are weaker than *iii,* all three imply that a profit opportunity exists. Under *iv,* this information does not signal any profit opportunity for traders; any pertinent information the manager-insiders may have is fully reflected in the current share price.

CHAPTER 11
RETURN, RISK, AND THE
SECURITY MARKET LINE

Basic

1. total value = 50($30) + 20($45) = $2,400
   $weight_1 = 50(\$30)/\$2,400 = .625$; $weight_2 = 20(\$45)/\$2,400 = .375$

2. $E[r_p] = (\$500/\$1,500)(0.20) + (\$1,000/\$1,500)(0.14) = .16$

3. $E[r_p] = .40(.08) + .35(.15) + .25(.25) = .147$

4. $E[r_p] = .18 = .22x_H + .12(1 - x_H)$; $x_H = 0.6$
   investment in H = 0.6($100,000) = $60,000 ;   investment in L = (1 − 0.6)($100,000) = $40,000

5. $E[r] = .25(.05) + .75(.25) = .20$

6. $E[r] = .10(-.05) + .70(.12) + .20(.30) = .139$

7. $E[r_A] = .15(.02) + .60(.09) + .25(.18)\quad = .1020$
   $E[r_B] = .15(-.15) + .60(.18) + .25(.50)\quad = .2105$
   $\sigma^2_A = .15(.02 - .102)^2 + .60(.09 - .102)^2 + .25(.18 - .102)^2 = .002616$; $\sigma_A = [.002616]^{1/2} = .0511$
   $\sigma^2_B = .15(-.15 - .2105)^2 + .60(.18 - .2105)^2 + .25(.50 - .2105)^2 = .0410$; $\sigma_B = [.0410]^{1/2} = .2025$

8. $E[r_p] = .30(.10) + .50(.20) + .20(.30) = .190.$

9. *a.*   boom: $E[r_p] = (.12 + .16 + .25)/3 = .1767$;   bust: $E[r_p] = (.10 + .04 + 0)/3 = .0467$
   $E[r_p] = .65(.1767) + .35(.0467) = .1312$
   b.   boom: $E[r_p] = .25(.12) + .25(.16) + .50(.25) = .195$; bust: $E[r_p] = .25(.10) + .25(.04) + .50(0) = .03\text{\textit{5}}$
   $E[r_p] = .65(.195) + .35(.035) = .139$
   $\sigma^2_p = .65(.195 - .139)^2 + .35(.035 - .139)^2 = .005824$; $\sigma_p = [.005824]^{1/2} = .0763$

10. *a.*   boom: $E[r_p] = .30(.10) + .40(.35) + .30(.20)\quad = .230$
    good: $E[r_p] = .30(.07) + .40(.15) + .30(.10)\quad = .111$
    poor: $E[r_p] = .30(.04) + .40(-.05) + .30(0)\quad = -.008$
    bust: $E[r_p] = .30(0) + .40(-.40) + .30(-.08)\quad = -.184$
    $E[r_p] = .20(.230) + .50(.111) + .25(-.008) + .05(-.184) = .0903$
    b. $\sigma^2_p = .20(.230 \pm .0903)^2 + .50(.111 - .0903)^2 + .25(-.008 - .0903)^2 + .05(-.184 - .0903)^2$
    $\sigma^2_p = .01030$; $\sigma_p = [.01030]^{1/2} = .1015$

11. Some of the risk in holding any asset is unique to the asset in question. By investing in a variety of assets, this unique portion of the total risk can be eliminated at little cost. On the other hand, there are some risks that affect all investments. This portion of the total risk of an asset cannot be costlessly eliminated. In other words, systematic risk can be controlled, but only by a costly reduction in expected returns.

12. If the market expected the growth rate in the coming year to be 2 percent, then there would be no change in security prices if this expectation had been fully anticipated and priced. However, if the market had been expecting a growth rate different than 2 percent and the expectation was incorporated into security prices, then the government's announcement would most likely cause security prices in general to change; prices would drop if the anticipated growth rate had been more than 2 percent, and prices would rise if the anticipated growth rate had been less than 2 percent.

13. *a.* systematic
    b. unsystematic
    c. both; probably mostly systematic
    d. unsystematic
    e. unsystematic
    f. systematic

14. *a.* a change in systematic risk has occurred; market prices in general will most likely decline.
    b. no change in unsystematic risk; company price will most likely stay constant.
    c. no change in systematic risk; market prices in general will most likely stay constant.
    d. a change in unsystematic risk has occurred; company price will most likely decline.
    e. no change in systematic risk; market prices in general will most likely stay constant.

15. $\beta_p = .20(1.10) + .40(.95) + .25(1.40) + .15(.70) = 1.055$

16. $\beta_p = 1.0 = \frac{1}{3}(0) + \frac{1}{3}(1.20) + \frac{1}{3}(\beta_X)$; $\beta_X = 1.80$

17. $E[r_i] = .07 + (.15 - .07)(0.9) = .142$

18. $E[r_i] = .12 = .06 + .05\beta_i$; $\beta_i = 1.20$

19. $E[r_i] = .15 = .05 + (E[r_{mkt}] - .05)(1.25)$; $E[r_{mkt}] = .13$

20. $E[r_i] = .10 = r_f + (.16 - r_f)(0.5)$; $r_f = .04$

21. *a.* $E[r_p] = (.11 + .08)/2 = .095$
    b. $\beta_p = 0.45 = x_S(0.80) + (1 - x_S)(0)$; $x_S = 0.45/0.80 = .5625$; $x_{rf} = 1 - .5625 = .4375$
    c. $E[r_p] = .10 = .11x_S + .08(1 - x_S)$; $x_S = \frac{2}{3}$; $\beta_p = \frac{2}{3}(0.80) + \frac{1}{3}(0) = 0.533$
    d. $\beta_p = 1.75 = x_S(0.80) + (1 - x_S)(0)$; $x_S = 1.75/0.80 = 2.1875$; $x_{rf} = 1 - 2.1875 = -1.1875$
        The portfolio is invested 218.75% in the stock and −118.75% in the risk-free asset. This represents borrowing at the risk-free rate to buy more of the stock.

22. $\beta_p = x_W(1.25) + (1 - x_W)(0) = 1.25x_W$

$E[r_W] = .20 = .06 + MRP(1.25)$; $MRP = .14/1.25 = .112$

$E[r_p] = .06 + .112\beta_p$; slope of line = MRP = .112 ; $E[r_p] = .06 + .112\beta_p = .06 + .14x_W$

x_W	$E[r_p]$	β_p	x_W	$E[r_p]$	β_p
0%	.060	0	100%	.200	1.2500
25	.095	0.3125	125	.235	1.5625
50	.130	0.6250	150	.270	1.8750
75	.165	0.9375			

23. $E[r_i] = .05 + .123\beta_i$

$.20 > E[r_M] = .05 + .123(1.2) = .1976$;   M plots above the SML and is undervalued.

$E[r_N] = .05 + .123(0.9) = .1607 > .16$;   N plots below the SML and is overvalued.

24. $[.20 - r_f]/1.2 = [.16 - r_f]/0.9$; $r_f = .04$

Intermediate

25. No to both questions. The portfolio expected return is a weighted average of the asset returns, so it must be less than the largest asset return and greater than the smallest asset return.

26. False. The variance of the individual assets is a measure of the total risk. The variance on a well-diversified portfolio is a function of systematic risk only.

27. Yes, the standard deviation can be less than that of every asset in the portfolio. However, β cannot be less than the smallest beta because β_p is a weighted average of the individual asset betas.

28. $E[r_{p1}] = (.123 + .054)/2 = 8.85\%$

$E[r_{p2}] = (.176 + .037)/2 = 10.65\%$

29. $(E[r_A] - r_f)/\beta_A = (E[r_B] - r_f)/\beta_B$

$RP_A/\beta_A = RP_B/\beta_B$; $\beta_B/\beta_A = RP_B/RP_A$

30.   *a.*   boom: $E[r_p] = .30(.20) + .30(.30) + .40(1.00) = .550$

         normal: $E[r_p] = .30(.10) + .30(.05) + .40(.30) = .165$

         bust: $E[r_p] = .30(0) + .30(-.20) + .40(-.80) = -.380$

         $E[r_p] = .20(.550) + .70(.165) + .10(-.380) = .1875$

         $\sigma^2_p = .20(.55 - .1875)^2 + .70(.165 - .1875)^2 + .10(-.380 - .1875)^2 = .05884$

         $\sigma_p = [.05884]^{1/2} = .2426$

   b. $RP_i = E[r_i] - r_f = .1875 - .0525 = .135$

   c. $(1 + E[r_i]) = (1 + h)(1 + e[r_i])$; $e[r_i] = [1.1875/1.05] - 1 = .1310$

         real risk-free rate = $[1.0525/1.05] - 1 = .0024$

         $rp_i = e[r_i] - $ real $r_f = .1310 - .0024 = .1286$

31. $x_A = x_B = \$60,000/\$200,000 = .30$; $x_C + x_{rf} = 1 - x_A - x_B = .40$

$\beta_p = 1.0 = x_A(1.20) + x_B(0.85) + x_C(1.40) + x_{rf}(0)$; $x_C = .275$, invest $.275(\$200,000) = \$55,000$ in C.

$x_{rf} = .40 - .275 = .125$;   invest $.125(\$200,000) = \$25,000$ in the risk-free asset.

32. $E[r_p] = .10 = x_D(.20) + x_F(.15) + (1 - x_D - x_F)(.05)$

$\beta_p = .60 = x_D(1.5) + x_F(1.15) + (1 - x_D - x_F)(0)$

solving these two equations in two unknowns gives $x_D = -\frac{1}{9}$, $x_F = \frac{2}{3}$; so $x_{rf} = \frac{4}{9}$

investment in F $= \frac{2}{3}(\$100,000) = \$66,667$

33. $E[r_A] = .15(.14) + .60(.24) + .25(.28) = .235$; $.235 = .06 + .08\beta_A$, $\beta_A = 2.1875$

$\sigma^2_A = .15(.14 - .235)^2 + .60(.24 - .235)^2 + .25(.28 - .235)^2 = .001875$; $\sigma_A = [.001875]^{1/2} = .04330$

$E[r_B] = .15(-.18) + .60(.10) + .25(.40) = .133$; $.133 = .06 + .08\beta_B$, $\beta_B = 0.9125$

$\sigma^2_B = .15(-.18 - .133)^2 + .60(.10 - .133)^2 + .25(.40 - .133)^2 = .033171$; $\sigma_B = [.033171]^{1/2} = .18213$

Although stock B has more total risk than A, it has much less systematic risk, since its beta is much smaller than A's. Thus A has more systematic risk, and B has more unsystematic and more total risk. Since unsystematic risk can be diversified away, A is actually the "riskier" stock despite the lack of volatility in its returns. Stock A will have a higher risk premium and a greater expected return.

Challenge

34. Yes. It is possible, in theory, to construct a zero beta portfolio of risky assets whose return would be equal to the risk-free rate. It is also possible to have a negative beta; the return would be less than the risk-free rate. A negative beta asset would carry a negative risk premium because of its value as a diversification instrument.

35. want $\beta_{mkt} = 1.0 = \beta_p = x_A(1.15) + (1 - x_A)(0.80)$; $x_A = .5714$

$E[r_{mkt}] = E[r_p] = .5714(.18) + (1 - .5714)(.15) = .1671$

$E[r_A] = .18 = r_f + (.1671 - r_f)(1.15)$; $r_f = .0814$

CHAPTER 12
LONG-TERM FINANCING:
AN INTRODUCTION

Basic

1. Common stock account = 6,000($1) = $6,000
    Total = $6,000 + $125,000 + $300,000 = $431,000

2. | | |
    |---|---|
    | Common stock (8,000 shares outstanding, $1 par value) | $ 8,000 |
    | Capital surplus ($125,000 + 2,000×$39) | 203,000 |
    | Retained earnings | 300,000 |
    | Total | $511,000 |

    Market/book ratio = $40/($511,000/8,000) = 0.626

3. The stock is called treasury stock.

Common stock (6,000 shares outstanding, $1 par value	$ 6,000
1,000 shares are treasury stock)	
Capital surplus	125,000
Retained earnings	300,000
Less: Treasury stock (1,000×$40)	40,000
Total	$391,000

4. a. 750,000[1/(5+1)] + 1 = 125,001
    b. $\frac{1}{2}$(750,000) + 1 = 375,001

5. Corporate bond yields are generally higher. Corporations that hold the preferred stock of other corporations get a partial tax exclusion on the dividends they receive, so they are willing to pay more for this tax advantaged cash flow and hence accept a lower pretax yield. Corporations are the biggest investors in outstanding preferred stock primarily because of this tax feature on received dividends.

6. P = $6.00/.08 = $75.00

7. The main differences are that debt has no ownership claim on the firm, the interest paid on debt is a tax deductible expense while dividends paid on common stock are not, and unpaid debt is a liability of the firm. Firms may be motivated to disguise equity issues as debt to gain the tax benefits of debt while realizing the bankruptcy benefits of equity. Some of the characteristics of preferred stock that make it similar to debt include:

1.   Preferred stockholders receive a stated dividend.

2.   In case of liquidation, preferred stockholders get a stated amount.

3.   Preferred stock usually carries credit ratings.

4.   Preferred stock is sometimes convertible into common stock.

5.   Preferred stock is sometimes callable.

6.   Preferred stock often has a sinking fund provision.

7.   Preferred stock may have an adjustable dividend.

8.   A good guess would be:

0.80($10M) = $8M in internal funding,

0.20($10M) = $2M in external funding, more likely debt than equity.

Historically, U.S. firms have looked to internal funding sources first, then external debt, and finally equity as a last resort.

9.   Dual classes of stock refers to separation of the common stock owners of the firm into two distinct groups, based on some characteristic usually including differential voting rights and different shares in distributed earnings. Firms may authorize more than one class of stock in order to protect the entrenched management, often the firm's founders, while still having ready access to the equity capital markets. Multiple classes of stock are controversial in the United States because of the historical tradition of one share, one vote.

10. The two most basic options are liquidation or reorganization, though creative alternatives like negotiated postponements may exist.

11. PV = $24M/.12 = $200M; this firm is worth more dead ($250M) than alive and should be liquidated.

12. *g, f, d, b, c, a, e.*

13. *a.*   Probably lowers the coupon, but it depends on what the floating rate is tied to.

b.   Raises the coupon; investors require a higher return as compensation for the risk that their bonds will be called away from them in the event of falling interest rates.

c.   Lowers the coupon; investors will accept a lower return for the opportunity to put back the bond to the issuer in the event of rising interest rates.

d.   Lowers the coupon; investors will accept a lower return for the opportunity to convert into shares.

e.   Lowers the coupon; investors will accept a lower return because the risk of a loss is reduced by the pledge of hard assets as secured collateral.

f.   Lowers the coupon; investors will accept a lower return because the risk of insufficient cash flow to meet interest obligations is reduced.

14. *a.* $P_0 = \$1{,}000/1.09^{10} = \$422.41$

   b. $P_1 = \$1{,}000/1.09^9 = \$460.43$;   year 1 interest deduction = $\$460.43 - \$422.41 = \$38.02$

   $P_9 = \$1{,}000/1.09 = \$917.43$;   year 10 interest deduction = $\$1{,}000 - \$917.43 = \$82.57$

   c.   Total interest = $\$1{,}000 - \$422.41 = \$577.59$

   Annual interest deduction = $\$577.59/10 = \$57.76$

   d.   The company will prefer straight-line methods when allowed because the valuable interest deductions occur earlier in the life of the bond.

Challenge

15. *a.*   The coupon bonds have a 10% coupon which matches the 10% required return, so they will sell at par; # of bonds = $\$10M/\$1{,}000 = 10{,}000$.

   For the zeroes, $P_0 = \$1{,}000/1.1^{20} = \$148.64$; $\$10M/\$148.64 = 67{,}275$ bonds will be issued.

   b.   Coupon bonds: repayment = $10{,}000(\$1{,}000) = \$10M$

   Zeroes: repayment = $67{,}275(\$1{,}000) = \$67.275M$

   c.   Coupon bonds: $(10{,}000)(\$100)(1-.35) = \$650{,}000$ cash outflow

   Zeroes: $P_1 = \$1{,}000/1.1^{19} = \$163.51$;   year 1 interest deduction = $\$163.51 - \$148.64 = \$14.86$

   $(67{,}275)(\$14.86)(1-.35) = \$350{,}000$ cash inflow

   During the life of the bond, the zero generates cash inflows to the firm in the form of the interest tax shield of debt.

   d.   Coupon bonds: NPV = $+\$10M - \$650K(\text{PVIFA}_{10\%,20}) - \$10M(\text{PVIF}_{10\%,20}) = -\$2.98M$

   Zeroes: NPV = $+\$10M + \$350K(\text{PVIFA}_{10\%,20}) - \$67.275M(\text{PVIF}_{10\%,20}) = -\$2.98M$

APPENDIX 12A

1.   NPV = $[\$1{,}000(.18-.15)/.15] - \$180 = \$200 - \$180 = \$20$

2.   NPV = $0 = [\$1{,}000(.18-r)/r] - \$180$; $r = .18/1.18 = 15.25\%$

3.   P = $\$1{,}000 = [\$C + \{^1\!/_2(\$C/.10) + {}^1\!/_2(\$1{,}080)\}]/1.08$;   C = \$90, or 9%

4.   P = $\$1{,}000 = [\$80 + \{^1\!/_2(\$80/.10) + {}^1\!/_2(\$1{,}000 + x\,)\}]/1.08$; $x = \$200$

5.   P = $[\$80 + \{^1\!/_2(\$80/.10) + {}^1\!/_2(\$1{,}125)\}]/1.08 = \$965.28$

6.   P = $[\$80 + \{^1\!/_2(\$80/.10) + {}^1\!/_2(\$80/.06)\}]/1.08 = \$1{,}061.73$ if no call provision present.

   Cost of the call provision = $\$1{,}061.73 - \$965.28 = \$96.45$

7.   # bonds outstanding = $\$50M/\$1{,}000 = 50{,}000$

   NPV = $0 = [\$50M(.12-r)/r] - \$9M - 50{,}000(\$150)$; $r = 9.02\%$

8.   NPV = $[\$50M(.12-.09)](\text{PVIFA}_{9\%,10}) - \$9M - 50{,}000(\$150) = -\$6{,}873{,}513$

Challenge

9.   NPV = $0 = [\$50M(.12-r)](PVIFA_{r\%,10}) - \$9M - 50,000(\$150)$

$0 = -\$16.5M + \$6M(PVIFA_{r\%,10}) - (\$50M)r[\{1-(1/[1+r])^N\}/r]$

$0 = -\$16.5M + \$6M(PVIFA_{r\%,10}) - \$50M + \$50M(1/[1+r])^N$

$0 = -\$66.5M + \$6M(PVIFA_{r\%,10}) + \$50M(PVIF_{r\%,10})$; $r = 7.248\%$

10.   NPV = $\{\$1,000(.18-.15)(1-.35)\}/\{.15(1-.35)\} - \$180(1-.35) = \$200 - \$117 = \$83$

The net effect of the taxes is to make refunding more attractive because of the tax deductibility of the call premium, which is a cost. The difference between the NPV here and in Problem 1 is simply the $63 tax savings from deducting the call premium.

11.   *a.* $P = \$1,175 = \$100(PVIFA_{YTM\%,10}) + \$1,000(PVIF_{YTM\%,10})$;   YTM = 7.46%

     b. $P_0 = \$1,175 = \$100(PVIFA_{YTC\%,3}) + \$1,000(PVIFA_{YTC\%,3})$;   YTC = 1.10%

The yield on the investment has fallen because you're not getting as many coupon payments as you were planning on and the principal is being returned to you sooner than expected.

     c. $\$1,175 = \$100(PVIFA_{7.46\%,2}) + (\$1,000 + x)(PVIFA_{7.46\%,2})$; $x = \$149.28$

CHAPTER 13
ISSUING SECURITIES TO THE PUBLIC

Basic

1. *a.* new market value = 20,000($45) + 5,000($35) = $1,075,000
    b. number of rights needed = 20,000 old shares/5,000 new shares = 4 rights per new share
    c. P_X = $1,075,000/25,000 shares = $43
    d. value of a right = $45 − $43 = $2
    e. A rights offering usually costs less, it protects the proportionate interests of existing share-holders, and protects against underpricing.

2. *a.* maximum subscription price = current share price = $30; minimum is anything > $0
    b. number of new shares = $30 million/$20 = 1.5 million shares
        number of rights needed = 7,125,000 old shares/1,500,000 new shares = 4.75
    c. P_X = [4.75($30) + $20]/5.75 = $28.26;   value of a right = $30 − $28.26 = $1.74
    d. before offer: portfolio = (1,000 shares)($30) = $30,000
        after offer: portfolio = (1,000 shares)($28.26) + (1,000 rights)($1.74) = $30,000

3. P_X = $67.50 = [N($75) + $50]/(N + 1);   N = 2.333
    number of new shares = $15M/$50 = 300,000;   number of old shares = 2.333(300,000) = 700,000

4. The evidence suggests that the costs associated with non-underwritten rights offerings are substantially less than those of cash offers.

5. He could have done worse since his access to the oversubscribed and, presumably, underpriced issues was restricted while the bulk of his funds were allocated to stocks from the undersubscribed and, quite possibly, overpriced issues.

6. IPOs are not always underpriced. Your ability to make money is directly related to your ability to purchase only the IPOs that are underpriced.

7. If you receive 1,000 shares of each, the profit is 1,000($4) − 1,000($2) = $2,000.
    Expected profit = 500($4) − 1,000($2) = $0. This is an example of the winner's curse.

8. X(1 − .06) = $25M;   X = $26,595,744.68 required total proceeds from sale.
    number of shares offered = $26,595,744.68/$40 = 664,894

9. X(1 − .06) = $25.350M;   X = $26,968,085.11 required total proceeds from sale.
    number of shares offered = $26,968,085.11/$40 = 674,202

10. net amount raised = (2M shares)($9) – $150,000 = $17.85M

total direct costs = $150,000 + ($10 – $9)(2M shares) = $2.15M

total indirect costs = $70,000 + ($12 – $10)(2M shares) = $4.07M

total costs = $2.15M + $4.07M = $6.22M

flotation cost percentage = $6.22M/$17.85M = 34.85%

11. number of rights needed = 25,000 old shares/10,000 new shares = 2.5 rights per new share.

a. P_X = [2.5($30) + $30]/3.5 = $30.00; no change.

b. P_X = [2.5($30) + $20]/3.5 = $27.14; price drops by $2.86 per share.

c. P_X = [2.5($30) + $10]/3.5 = $24.29; price drops by $5.71 per share.

12. *a.* number of shares after offering = 5M + $40M/$50 = 5.8M

new book value per share = [5M($75) + 800K($50)]/5.8M = $71.55

$EPS_0 = NI_0/shares_0$ = $15M/5M shares = $3 per share; $(P/E)_0$ = $50/$3 = 16.67

$EPS_1 = NI_1/shares_1$ = $16.5M/5.8M shares = $2.84 per share;

$P_1 = (P/E)_0(EPS_1)$ = 16.67($2.84) = $47.41

old market-to-book = $50/$75 = 0.667; new market-to-book = $47.41/$71.55 = 0.663

Accounting dilution has occurred because new shares were issued when the market-to-book ratio was less than one; market value dilution has occurred because the firm financed a negative NPV project: NPV = –$40M + [5.8M($47.41) – 5M($50)] = –$15M

b. For the price to remain unchanged when the P/E ratio is constant, EPS must remain constant. NI_1 = (5.8M shares)($3 per share) = $17.4M

13. $ROE_0 = NI_0/TE_0$ = $15,000/$200,000 = .075

$NI_1 = (ROE_0)(TE_1)$ = .075($200,000 + $75,000) = $20,625

EPS_0 = $15,000/3,000 shares = $5; number of new shares = $75,000/$60 = 1,250

EPS_1 = $20,625/4,250 shares = $4.85; $(P/E)_0$ = $60/$5 = 12; P_1 = 12($4.85) = $58.24

$BVPS_0 = TE_0/shares_0$ = $200,000/3,000 shares = $66.67 per share;

$BVPS_1 = TE_1/shares_1$ = ($200,000 + $75,000)/4,250 shares = $64.71 per share

market-to-book$_0$ = $60/$66.67 = 0.9; market-to-book$_1$ = $58.24/$64.71 = 0.9

NPV = –$75,000 + [$58.24(4,250) – $60(3,000)] = –$7,500

Dilution takes place here because the market-to-book ratio is less than one and the firm is investing in a negative NPV project.

14. P_1 = $60 = 12(EPS$_1$); EPS$_1$ = $5.00. NI_1 = EPS$_1$(4,250 shares) = $21,250

ROE_1 = $21,250/$275,000 = .0773

If the share price after the offering is $60, then the project NPV is:

NPV = –$75,000 + [$60(4,250) – $60(3,000)] = $0

Accounting dilution still takes place, as BVPS still falls from $66.67 to $64.71, but no market dilution takes place because the firm is investing in a zero NPV project.

Intermediate

15. number of new shares = $\$80M/\$P_S$; N = # old shares/#new shares = $8M/(\$80M/\$P_S) = .10P_S$

$P_X = \$35 = [N(\$50) + \$P_S]/(N + 1) = [50(.1P_S) + P_S]/(.1P_S + 1) = 6P_S/(1+.1P_S)$; $P_S = \$14.00$

16. $P_X = [NP_{RO} + P_S]/(N+1)$

value of a right $= P_{RO} - P_X = P_{RO} - \{ [NP_{RO} + P_S]/(N+1) \}$

$= [(N+1)P_{RO} - NP_{RO} - P_S]/(N+1) = [P_{RO} - P_S]/(N+1)$

17. net proceeds to company = $\$12(1 - .075) = \$11.10$ per share

new shares offered = $\$1.11M/\$11.10 = 100,000$

number of rights needed = 250,000 old shares/100,000 new shares = 2.5 rights per new share

$P_X = [2.5(\$30) + \$12]/3.5 = \$24.86$

value of a right = $\$30 - \$24.86 = \$5.14$;   proceeds from selling rights = $5,000(\$5.14) = \$25,714$

18. $P_X = [4(\$40) + \$20]/5 = \$36$; the stock is correctly priced.

value of a right = $\$40 - \$36 = \$4$; the rights are underpriced.

You can create an immediate profit on the ex rights day if the stock is selling for $36 and the rights are selling for $3 by executing the following transactions:

Buy 4 rights in the market for 4($3) = $12. Use these rights to purchase a new share at the subscription price of $20. Immediately sell this share in the market for $36, creating an instant $4 profit.

19. *a.*   The price will probably go up because IPOs are generally underpriced. This is especially true for smaller issues such as this one.

   b.   It is probably safe to assume that they are having trouble moving the issue, and it is likely that the issue is not substantially underpriced.

CHAPTER 14
COST OF CAPITAL

Basic

1. $r_E = [\$2.50(1.06)/\$50] + .06 = 11.30\%$

2. $r_E = .04 + 1.25(.12 - .04) = 14.00\%$

3. $r_{E1} = .05 + .90(.095) = .1355;$ $r_{E2} = [\$3.75(1.03)/\$32.50] + .03 = .1488$
    $r_E = (.1355 + .1488)/2 = 14.22\%$

4. $g_1 = (.58 - .45)/.45 = .2889;$ $g_2 = (.69 - .58)/.58 = .1897$
    $g_3 = (.80 - .69)/.69 = .1594;$ $g_3 = (.90 - .80)/.80 = .1250$
    $g = (.2889 + .1897 + .1594 + .1250)/4 = .1907$
    $r_E = [\$0.90(1.1907)/\$17.50] + .1907 = 25.20\%$

5. $r_P = \$5/\$80 = 6.25\%$

6. $P_0 = \$930 = \$30(PVIFA_{r\%,24}) + \$1,000(PVIF_{r\%,24});$ $r = 3.433\%$
    pretax cost of debt = YTM = 2 x 3.433 = 6.87%
    $r_D = .0687(1 - .35) = 4.46\%$

7. *a.* $P_0 = \$1,080 = \$45(PVIFA_{r\%,26}) + \$1,000(PVIF_{r\%,26});$ $r = 4.00\%$
        pretax cost of debt = YTM = 2 x 4.00 = 8.00%
    b. $r_D = .0800(1 - .38) = 4.96\%$
    c.   The aftertax rate is more relevant because that is the actual cost to the company.

8. $BV_D = \$50M + \$30M = \$80M$
    $MV_D = 1.08(\$50M) + 0.48(\$30M) = \$68.4M$
    $P_Z = \$480 = \$1,000(PVIF_{r\%,9});$ $r = 8.50\%;$ $r_Z = .0850(1 - .38) = 5.27\%$
    $r_D = (.0496 + .0527)/2 = 5.11\%$

9. *a.*   WACC = .35(.18) + .10(.08) + .55(.10)(1 − .35) = 10.68%
    b.   Since interest is tax deductible and dividends are not, we look at the aftertax cost of debt, which
        is .10(1 − .35) = 6.5%. Hence, on an aftertax basis, debt is cheaper than the preferred stock.

10. WACC = .20(5/8) + .12(3/8)(1 − .34) = 15.47%

11. WACC = .0975 = .16(E/V) + .1025(D/V)(1 − .39)
    .0975(V/E) = .16 + .1025(.61)(D/E)
    .0975(D/E + 1) = .16 + .0625(D/E);   .0350(D/E) = .0625;   D/E = 1.787

12. *a.* $BV_E = 12.8M(\$18) = \$230.4M$; $\quad BV_D = \$100M + \$75M = \$175M$

$V = 230.4 + 175 = \$405.4M$: $\quad E/V = 230.4/405.4 = 0.568$; $\quad D/V = 1 - E/V = 0.432$

b. $MV_E = 12.8M(\$29) = \$371.2M$; $\quad BV_D = 0.94(\$100M) + 0.87(\$75M) = \$159.25M$

$V = 371.2 + 159.25 = \$530.45M$: $\quad E/V = 371.2/530.45 = 0.700$; $\quad D/V = 1 - E/V = 0.300$

c. The market value weights are more relevant.

13. $r_E = [\$2.00(1.08)/\$29] + .08 = .1545$

$P_1 = \$940 = \$35(PVIFA_{r\%,26}) + \$1,000(PVIF_{r\%,26})$; $\quad r = 3.87\%$, $YTM = 7.74\%$

$P_2 = \$870 = \$27.5(PVIFA_{r\%,16}) + \$1,000(PVIF_{r\%,16})$; $\quad r = 3.85\%$, $YTM = 7.71\%$

$r_D = (1 - .35)(.0774 + .0771)/2 = .0502$

$WACC = .70(.1545) + .30(.0502) = 12.32\%$

14. *a.* $WACC = .10 = (1/3)(.19) + (2/3)(1 - .35)r_D$; $\quad r_D = 8.46\%$

b. $WACC = .10 = (1/3)r_E + (2/3)(.07)$; $\quad r_E = 16.00\%$

15. $MV_D = 2,500(\$1,000)(1.03) = \$2.575M$; $\quad MV_E = 75,000(\$50) = \$3.75M$

$MV_P = 10,000(\$80) = \$0.800M$; $\quad V = 2.575 + 3.750 + 0.800 = \$7.125M$

$r_E = .06 + .85(.05) = 10.25\%$

$P_0 = \$1,030 = \$38.75(PVIFA_{r\%,16}) + \$1,000(PVIF_{r\%,16})$; $\quad r = 3.62\%$, $YTM = 7.243\%$

$r_D = (1 - .34)(.07243) = 4.78\%$

$r_P = \$5/\$80 = 6.25\%$

$WACC = .0478(2.575/7.125) + .1025(3.75/7.125) + .0625(0.8/7.125) = 7.82\%$

16. *a.* $MV_D = 250,000(\$1,000)(0.935) = \$233.75M$; $\quad MV_E = 5M(\$40) = \$200M$

$MV_P = 750,000(\$75) = \$56.25M$; $\quad V = 233.75 + 200 + 56.25 = \$490M$

$E/V = 200/490 = .4082$; $\quad D/V = 233.75/490 = .4770$; $\quad P/V = 56.25/490 = .1148$

b. For projects equally as risky as the firm itself, the WACC should be used as the discount rate.

$r_E = .04 + 1.2(.06) = 11.20\%$

$P_0 = \$935 = \$55(PVIFA_{r\%,30}) + \$1,000(PVIF_{r\%,30})$; $\quad r = 5.971\%$, $YTM = 11.94\%$

$r_D = (1 - .34)(.1194) = 7.88\%$

$r_P = \$7/\$75 = 9.33\%$

$WACC = .1120(.4082) + .0933(.1148) + .0788(.4770) = 9.40\%$

17. *a.* Projects Y and Z.

b. Using the firm's overall cost of capital as a hurdle rate, projects Y and Z. However, after considering risk via the SML:

$E[W] = .06 + .60(.16 - .06) = .12 < .13$, so accept W.

$E[X] = .06 + .85(.16 - .06) = .145 > .14$, so reject X.

$E[Y] = .06 + 1.15(.16 - .06) = .175 < .18$, so accept Y.

$E[Z] = .06 + 1.50(.16 - .06) = .21 > .20$, so reject Z.

c. Project W would be incorrectly rejected; project Z would be incorrectly accepted.

18. *a.* He should look at the weighted average flotation cost, not just the debt cost.

b. $f_T = .04(1/3) + .14(2/3) = .1067$

c. $X(1 - .1067) = \$2.4M$; $\quad X = \text{cost} = 2.4/(1 - .1067) = \$2.687M$

Even if the specific funds are actually being raised completely from debt, the flotation costs and hence true investment cost should be valued as if the firm's target capital structure is used.

19. $f_T = .50(.13) + .10(.06) + .40(.03) = .083$
$X(1 - .083) = \$5M; \quad X = \text{cost} = 5/(1 - .083) = \$5.453M$

Intermediate

20. The primary advantage of the DCF model is its simplicity. The method is disadvantaged in that (1) the model is applicable only to firms that actually pay dividends; many do not; (2) even if a firm does pay dividends, the DCF model requires a constant dividend growth rate forever; (3) the estimated cost of equity from this method is very sensitive to changes in g, which is a very uncertain parameter; and (4) the model does not explicitly consider risk, although risk is implicitly considered to the extent that the market has impounded the relevant risk of the stock into its market price. While the share price and most recent dividend can be observed in the market, the dividend growth rate must be estimated. Two common methods of estimating g are to use analysts' earnings and payout forecasts, or determine some appropriate average historical g from the firm's available data.

21. Two primary advantages of the SML approach are that the model explicitly incorporates the relevant risk of the stock, and the method is more widely applicable than is the DCF model, since the SML doesn't make any assumptions about the firm's dividends. The primary disadvantages of the SML method are (1) three parameters, the risk-free rate, the expected return on the market, and beta must be estimated, and (2) the method essentially uses historical information to estimate these parameters. The risk-free rate is usually estimated to be the yield on very short maturity T-bills and is hence observable; the market risk premium is usually estimated from historical risk premiums and hence is not observable. The stock beta, which is unobservable, is usually estimated either by determining some average historical beta from the firm and the market's return data, or using beta estimates provided by analysts and investment firms.

22. The appropriate aftertax cost of debt to the company is the interest rate it would have to pay if it were to issue new debt today. Hence, if the YTM on outstanding bonds of the company is observed, the company has an accurate estimate of its cost of debt. If the debt is privately-placed, the firm could still estimate its cost of debt by (1) looking at the cost of debt for similar firms in similar risk classes, (2) looking at the average debt cost for firms with the same credit rating (assuming the firm's private debt is rated), or (3) consulting analysts and investment bankers. Even if the debt is publicly traded, an additional complication is when the firm has more than one issue outstanding; these issues rarely have the same yield because no two issues are ever completely homogeneous.

23. *a.* This only considers the dividend yield component of the required return on equity.

b. This is the current yield only, not the promised yield to maturity. In addition, it is based on the book value of the liability, and it ignores taxes.

c. Equity is inherently more risky than debt (except, perhaps, in the unusual case where a firm's assets have a negative beta). For this reason, the cost of equity exceeds the cost of debt. If taxes are considered in this case, it can be seen that at reasonable tax rates, the cost of equity does exceed the cost of debt.

24. $R_{sup} = .12 + .75(.08) = 18\%$

Both should proceed. The appropriate discount rate does not depend on which company is investing; it depends on the risk of the project. Since Superior is in the business, it is closer to a pure play. Therefore, its cost of capital should be used. With an 18% cost of capital, the project has an NPV of $1 million regardless of who takes it.

25. If the different operating divisions were in much different risk classes, then separate cost of capital figures should be used for the different divisions; the use of a single, overall cost of capital would be inappropriate. If the single hurdle rate were used, riskier divisions would tend to horde the investment projects, since their return would exceed the hurdle rate despite the fact that they may actually plot below the SML and hence be unprofitable projects on a risk-adjusted basis. The typical problem encountered in estimating the cost of capital for a division is that it rarely has its own securities traded on the market, so it is difficult to observe the market's valuation of the risk of the division. Two typical ways around this are to use a pure play proxy for the division, or to use subjective adjustments of the overall firm hurdle rate based on the perceived risk of the division.

26. WACC $= (3/4)(.10) + (1/4)(.22) = 13\%$;   project discount rate $= 13\% + 3\% = 16\%$

NPV $= -$ cost $+$ PV cash flows;   PV $= [\$9M(1.05)/(.16 - .05)] = \$85.909M$

The project should only be undertaken if its cost is less than $85.909M.

27. total costs $= \$2M + \$150,000 = \$2.15M$; $\$2.15M(1 - f_T) = \$2M$; $f_T = .0698$

$f_T = .0698 = .12(E/V) + .05(D/V)$; $.0698(D/E + 1) = .12 + .05(D/E)$;   D/E $= 2.54$

Challenge

28. $f_T = (4/7)(.15) + (3/7)[(1/5)(0) + (4/5)(.035)] = .0977$

$X(1 - .0977) = \$12M$;   X $=$ cost $= 12/(1 - .0977) = \$13.300M$

WACC $= (4/7)(.19) + (3/7)[(1/5)(WACC) + (4/5)(.11)(1 - .35)]$;   WACC $= .1456$

NPV $= -\$13.300M + [\$2M/.1456] = \$440,246$

29. The $5 million cost of the land 6 years ago is a sunk cost and irrelevant; the $200,000 appraised value of the land is an opportunity cost and is relevant. The relevant market value capitalization weights are:

$MV_D = 10,000(\$1,000)(0.88) = \$8.8M$; $MV_E = 400,000(\$30) = \$12M$

$MV_P = 20,000(\$90) = \$1.8M$;   V $= 8.8 + 12 + 1.8 = \$22.6M$

$r_E = .04 + 1.2(.06) = 11.20\%$

$P_0 = \$880 = \$45(PVIFA_{r\%,20}) + \$1,000(PVIF_{r\%,20})$;   r $= 5.50\%$, YTM $= 11.01\%$

$r_D = (1 - .34)(.1101) = 7.27\%$

$r_P = \$6/\$90 = 6.67\%$

a. $f_T = (12/22.6)(.12) + (1.8/22.6)(.07) + (8.8/22.6)(.04) = .0849$

$X(1 - .0849) = \$8M;\quad X = cost = 8/(1 - .0849) = \$8,741,901$

$CF_0 = -\$200,000 - \$8,741,901 = -\$8,941,901$

b. $WACC = .02 + \{(12/22.6)(.112) + (1.8/22.6)(.0667) + (8.8/22.6)(.0727)\} = .1131$

c. $BV_5 = \$3M;\quad$ aftertax salvage value $= \$1M + .34(\$3M - \$1M) = \$1.68M$

d. $OCF = [(P-v)Q - FC](1 - t) + tD$

$\quad\quad = [(250-150)(40,000) - 1,000,000](1 - .34) + .34(\$8M/8) = \$2,320,000$

e. $Q = (FC + D)/(P - v) = (\$1M + \$1M)/(\$250 - \$150) = 20,000$

f.

Year	Cash Flow
0	–$9,541,901
1	$2,320,000
2	$2,320,000
3	$2,320,000
4	$2,320,000
5	$4,600,000

IRR = 12.44%

NPV = $301,254

discount rate = WACC = 11.31%

CHAPTER 15
FINANCIAL LEVERAGE AND CAPITAL STRUCTURE POLICY

Basic

1. *a.*

EBIT:	$2,500	$5,000	$7,000
Interest:	0	0	0
NI:	$2,500	$5,000	$7,000
EPS:	$ 2.50	$ 5.00	$ 7.00
ΔEPS%:	−50	—	+40

b. MV $60,000/1,000 shares = $60 per share; $24,000/$60 = 400 shares bought back

EBIT:	$2,500	$5,000	$7,000
Interest:	2,400	2,400	2,400
NI:	$ 100	$2,600	$4,600
EPS:	$ 0.17	$ 4.33	$ 7.67
ΔEPS%:	−96.15	—	+76.92

2. *a.*

EBIT:	$2,500	$5,000	$7,000
Interest:	0	0	0
Taxes:	875	1,750	2,450
NI:	$1,625	$3,250	$4,550
EPS:	$ 1.63	$ 3.25	$ 4.55
ΔEPS%:	−50	—	+40

b. MV $60,000/1,000 shares = $60 per share; $24,000/$60 = 400 shares bought back

EBIT:	$2,500	$5,000	$7,000
Interest:	2,400	2,400	2,400
Taxes:	35	910	1,610
NI:	$ 65	$1,690	$2,990
EPS:	$ 0.11	$ 2.82	$ 4.98
ΔEPS%:	−96.15	—	+76.92

3. *a.* market-to-book ratio = 1.0, so TE = MV = $60,000; ROE = NI/$60,000

ROE:	.0417	.0833	.1167
ΔROE%:	−50	—	+40

b. now, TE = $60,000 − $24,000 = $36,000; ROE = NI/$36,000

ROE:	.0028	.0722	.1278
ΔROE%:	−96.15	—	+76.92

c.

no debt, ROE:	.0271	.0542	.0758
ΔROE%:	−50	—	+40
with debt, ROE:	.0018	.0469	.0831
ΔROE%:	−96.15	—	+76.92

4.   *a.*   Plan I: NI = $900K ;   EPS = $900K/300K shares = $3.00

          Plan II: NI = $900K − .09($6M) = $360K ;   EPS = $360K/200K shares = $1.80

          Plan I has the higher EPS when EBIT is $900,000.

   b.   Plan I: NI = $2.1M ;   EPS = $2.1M/300K shares = $7.00

          Plan II: NI = $2.1M − .09($6M) = $1.56M ;   EPS = $1.56M/200K shares = $7.80

          Plan II has the higher EPS when EBIT is $2,100,000.

   c.   EBIT/300K = [EBIT − .09($6M)]/200K ;   EBIT = $1.62M;   EPS = $1.62M/300K = $5.40

5.   P = $6M/100K shares bought with debt = $60 per share

     V_1 = $60(300K shares) = $18M; V_2 = $60(200K shares) + $6M debt = $18M

6.   *a.*

	I	*II*	*all-equity*
EBIT:	$2,500	$2,500	$2,500
Interest:	700	280	0
NI:	$1,800	$2,220	$2,500
EPS:	$ 2.40	$ 2.47	$ 2.50

         The all-equity plan has the highest EPS; Plan I has the lowest EPS.

   b.   Plan I vs. all-equity: EBIT/1,000 = [EBIT − .08($8,750)]/750;   EBIT = $2,800

         Plan II vs. all-equity: EBIT/1,000 = [EBIT − .08($3,500)]/900;   EBIT = $2,800

         The break-even levels of EBIT are the same because of M&M Proposition I.

   c.   [EBIT − .08($8,750)]/750 = [EBIT − .08($3,500)]/900 ;   EBIT = $2,800

         This break-even level of EBIT is the same as in part (b) again because of M&M Proposition I.

   d.

	I	*II*	*all-equity*
EBIT:	$2,500	$2,500	$2,500
Interest:	700	280	0
Taxes:	684	844	950
NI:	$1,116	$1,376	$1,550
EPS:	$ 1.49	$ 1.53	$ 1.55

         The all-equity plan still has the highest EPS; Plan I still has the lowest EPS.

         Plan I vs. all-equity: EBIT(.62)/1,000 = [EBIT − .08($8,750)](.62)/750;   EBIT = $2,800

         Plan II vs. all-equity: EBIT(.62)/1,000 = [EBIT − .08($3,500)](.62)/900;   EBIT = $2,800

         [EBIT − .08($8,750)](.62)/750 = [EBIT − .08($3,500)](.62)/900 ;   EBIT = $2,800

         The break-even levels of EBIT do not change because the addition of taxes reduces the income of all three plans by the same percentage; therefore, they do not change relative to one another.

7.   I: P = $8,750/250 shares bought with debt = $35 per share;   II: P = $3,500/100 shares = $35

     This shows that when there are no corporate taxes, the stockholder does not care about the capital structure decision of the firm. This is M&M Proposition I without taxes.

8.   *a.*   EPS = $1,000/400 shares = $2.50; Smith's cash flow = $2.50(80 shares) = $200

   b.   V = $75(400) = $30,000;   D = 0.30($30,000) = $9,000

         $9,000/$75 = 120 shares are bought;   NI = $1,000 − .11($9,000) = $10

         EPS = $10/280 shares = $.036;   Smith's cash flow = $.036(80 shares) = $2.86

   c.   Sell 24 shares of stock and lend the proceeds at 11%: interest cash flow = 24($75)(.11) = $198

         cash flow from shares held = $.036(56 shares) = $2.00;   total cash flow = $200.

d. The capital structure is irrelevant because shareholders can create their own leverage or unlever the stock to create the payoff they desire, regardless of the capital structure the firm actually chooses.

9. *a.* EBIT = \$37,500 − .10(\$125K) = \$25K;   Jones' cash flow = \$25K(\$25K/\$125K) = \$5K
   R = \$5,000/\$25,000 = 20%

   b. Sell all XYZ shares: nets \$25,000. Borrow \$25,000 at 10%: interest cash flow = −\$2,500
   Use the proceeds from selling shares and the borrowed funds to buy ABC shares:
   Jones' cash flow from ABC = \$37,500(\$50K/\$250K) = \$7,500. Jones' total cash flow = \$5,000
   R = \$5,000/\$25,000 net investment = 20%

   c. $R_E = R_U + (R_U - R_D)(D/E)(1 - t)$
   ABC: R_E = .15;   XYZ: R_E = .15 + (.15 − .10)(1)(1) = .20

   d. WACC = $(E/V)R_E + (D/V)R_D(1 - t)$
   ABC: WACC = (1)(.15) + (0)(.10) = .15;   XYZ: WACC = (1/2)(.20) + (1/2)(.10) = .15
   When there are no corporate taxes, the cost of capital for the firm is unaffected by the capital structure; this is M&M Proposition I without taxes.

10. V = EBIT/WACC;   EBIT = .12(\$30M) = \$3.6M

11. V = V_U + T_CD;   V = \$30M = EBIT(.66)/.12 + 0 ;   EBIT = \$5.455M, WACC = 12%
    Because of taxes, EBIT for an all-equity firm would have to be higher for the firm to still be worth \$30M.

12. *a.* WACC = .115 = $(1/2.5)R_E$ + (1.5/2.5)(.08)(.65); R_E = .2095
    b. .2095 = R_U + (R_U − .08)(1.5)(.65) ; R_U = .1456
    c. .115 = $(1/2)R_E$ + (1/2)(.08)(.65); R_E = .1780
    .115 = $(2/3)R_E$ + (1/3)(.08)(.65); R_E = .1465
    .115 = $(1)R_E$ + (0)(.08)(.65); R_E = R_U = WACC = .115

13. *a* all-equity financed: WACC = R_U = R_E = .14
    b. $R_E = R_U + (R_U - R_D)(D/E)(1 - t)$ = .14 + (.14 − .10)(.40/.60)(.61) = .1563
    c. $R_E = R_U + (R_U - R_D)(D/E)(1 - t)$ = .14 + (.14 − .10)(.70/.30)(.61) = .1969
    d. $WACC_A = (E/V)R_E + (D/V)R_D(1 - t)$ = .60(.1563) + .40(.10)(.61) = .1182
    $WACC_B = (E/V)R_E + (D/V)R_D(1 - t)$ = .30(.1969) + .70(.10)(.61) = .1018

14. *a.* V = V_U = \$25,000(.65)/.15 = \$108,333.33
    b. V = V_U + T_CD = \$108,333.33 + .35(\$50,000) = \$125,833.33

15. $R_E = R_U + (R_U - R_D)(D/E)(1 - t)$ = .15 + (.15 − .09)(\$50,000/\$75,833.33)(.65) = .1757
    WACC = .1757(\$75,833.33/\$125,833.33) + .09(.65)(\$50,000/\$125,833.33) = .1291
    When there are corporate taxes, the overall cost of capital for the firm declines the more highly leveraged is the firm's capital structure. This is M&M Proposition I with taxes.

Intermediate

16. Business risk is the equity risk arising from the nature of the firm's operating activity, and is directly related to the systematic risk of the firm's assets. Financial risk is the equity risk that is due entirely to the firm's chosen capital structure. As financial leverage, or the use of debt financing, increases, so does financial risk and hence the overall risk of the equity.

17. No, it doesn't follow. While it is true that the equity and debt costs are rising, the key thing to remember is that the cost of debt is still less than the cost of equity. Since we are using more and more debt, the WACC does not necessarily rise.

18. Because many relevant factors such as bankruptcy costs, tax asymmetries, and agency costs cannot easily be identified or quantified, it's practically impossible to determine the precise debt/equity ratio that maximizes the value of the firm. However, if the firm's cost of new debt suddenly becomes much more expensive, it's probably true that the firm is too highly leveraged.

19. The more capital-intensive industries such as steel and mining tend to have higher debt/equity ratios. In addition, industries with more seasonal variation in earnings and sales, such as confectionary products and appliances, tend to have lower debt/equity ratios than industries with more predictable earnings streams, as do industries with a high concentration of growth and startup firms such as pharmaceuticals and communication equipment. These observed variations across industries are consistent with the notion that firms with higher EBIT volatility issue less debt, and the notion that firms with low tax rates or alternative tax shelters may not fully take advantage of the interest tax shield due to debt.

20. $\text{WACC} = .078 = (2/3)R_E + (1/3)(.07)(.65)$; $R_E = .0943$
    $R_E = .0943 = R_U + (R_U - .07)(1/2)(.65)$; $R_U = .0883$
    $V_L = V_U + T_C D = \text{EBIT}(1 - t)/R_U + T_C D = \$2,880(.65)/.0883 + .35(\$8,000)$
    $\quad = \$21,200 + \$2,800 = \$24,000$
    Applying M&M Proposition I with taxes, the firm has increased its value by \$2,800 by issuing debt. As long as M&M Proposition I holds, that is, there are no bankruptcy costs and so forth, then Clines should continue to increase its debt/equity ratio to maximize the value of the firm.

21. no debt: $V = V_U = \$12,000(.62)/.22 = \$33,818.18$
    50% debt: $V = \$33,818.18 + .38(V/2)$; $V = \$41,750.84$
    100% debt: $V = \$33,818.18 + .38V$; $V = \$54,545.45$

Challenge

22. $R_E = R_U + (R_U - R_D)(D/E)(1 - t)$
    $\text{WACC} = (E/V)R_E + (D/V)R_D(1 - t) = (E/V)[R_U + (R_U - R_D)(D/E)(1 - t)] + (D/V)R_D(1 - t)$
    $\quad = R_U[(E/V) + (E/V)(D/E)(1 - t)] + R_D(1 - t)[(D/V) - (E/V)(D/V)]$
    $\quad = R_U[(E/V) + (D/V)(1 - t)] = R_U\{[(E+D)/V\} - t(D/V)] = R_U[1 - t(D/V)]$

23. $R_E = (\text{EBIT} - R_D D)(1 - t)/E = \{\text{EBIT}(1 - t)/E\} - \{R_D(D/E)(1 - t)\}$

$= R_U V_U/E - \{R_D(D/E)(1 - t)\} = R_U(V_L - tD)/E - \{R_D(D/E)(1 - t)\}$

$= R_U(E + D - tD)/E - \{R_D(D/E)(1 - t)\} = R_U + (R_U - R_D)(D/E)(1 - t)$

24. M&M Proposition II, with $R_D = R_f$:

$R_E = R_A + (R_A - R_f)(D/E)$

CAPM: $R_E = \beta_E(R_M - R_f) + R_f$; $R_A = \beta_A(R_M - R_f) + R_f$:

$R_E = \beta_E(R_M - R_f) + R_f = \{1 + (D/E)\}[\beta_A(R_M - R_f) + R_f] - R_f(D/E)$

$\beta_E = \beta_A[1 + D/E]$

25. $\beta_E = \beta_A[1 + D/E]$; $\beta_E = 1.0, 2.0, 6.0, 21.0$

The equity risk to the shareholder is composed of both business and financial risk. Even if the assets of the firm are not very risky, the risk to the shareholder can still be large if the financial leverage is high. These higher levels of risk will be reflected in the shareholder's required rate of return R_E, which will increase with higher debt/equity ratios.

CHAPTER 16
DIVIDENDS AND DIVIDEND POLICY

Basic

1. It would not be irrational to find low-dividend, high-growth stocks. The university should be indifferent between receiving dividends or capital gains since it does not pay taxes on either one (ignoring possible restrictions on invasion of principal, etc.). It would be irrational, however, to hold municipal bonds. Since the university does not pay taxes on the interest income it receives, it does not need the tax break associated with the municipal bonds. Therefore, it should prefer to hold higher yielding, taxable bonds.

2. aftertax dividend = $1.50(1 – .28) = $1.08; ex-dividend price = $30 – $1.08 = $28.92

3. *a.* new shares outstanding = 3,000(1.15) = 3,450; new shares issued = 450
   capital surplus on new shares = 450($19) = $8,550

Common stock ($1 par value)	$ 3,450
Capital surplus	68,550
Retained earnings	231,000
	$303,000

   b. new shares outstanding = 3,000(1.50) = 4,500; new shares issued = 1,500

Common stock ($1 par value)	$ 4,500
Capital surplus	60,000
Retained earnings	238,500
	$303,000

4. *a.* new shares outstanding = 3,000(10) = 30,000. The equity accounts are unchanged except the par value of the stock is now $0.10 per share.

   b. new shares outstanding = 3,000(1/3) = 1,000. The equity accounts are unchanged except the par value of the stock is now $3.00 per share.

5. *a.* $50(4/7) = $28.57
   b. $50(1/1.10) = $45.45
   c. $50(1/1.375) = $36.36
   d. $50(5/3) = $83.33
   e. *a:* 250,000(7/4) = 437,500;   *b:* 250,000(1.1) = 275,000;
       c: 250,000(1.375) = 343,750;   *d:* 250,000(3/5) = 150,000.

6. Wednesday, December 27 is the ex-dividend day. Remember not to count January 1 because it is a holiday, and the exchanges are closed. Anyone who buys the stock before December 27 is entitled to the dividend, assuming they do not sell it again before December 27.

7. P_0 = $100,000 equity/4,000 shares = $25. P_X = $25 – $1.25 = $23.75.
   $1.25(4,000 shares) = $5,000; the equity and cash accounts will both decline by $5,000.

8. Repurchasing the shares will reduce shareholders' equity by $5,000.
shares bought = $5,000/$25 = 200; new shares outstanding = 3,800.
After repurchase, share price = $95,000 equity/3,800 shares = $25. The repurchase is effectively the same as the cash dividend because you either hold a share worth $25, or a share worth $23.75 and $1.25 in cash. If you participate in the repurchase according to the dividend payout percentage, you are unaffected.

9. P_0 = $200,000 equity/5,000 shares = $40.   new shares outstanding = 5,000(1.10) = 5,500
P_X = $200,000/5,500 shares = $36.36

10. new shares outstanding = 375,000(1.06) = 397,500
capital surplus for new shares = 22,500($7) = $157,500

Common stock ($1 par value)	$ 397,500
Capital surplus	2,607,500
Retained earnings	5,045,000
	$8,050,000

11. The equity accounts are unchanged except the new par value of the stock is $0.20 per share.
Dividends this year = $0.40(375,000 shares)(5/1 split) = $750,000
Last year's dividends = $750,000/1.125 = $666,666.67
Dividends per share last year = $666,666.67/375,000 shares = $1.78

12. equity portion of capital outlays = $250 – $180 = $70;   D/E = 1/2 implies capital structure is 2/3 equity and 1/3 debt. Therefore, new borrowings = $35; total capital outlays = $105.

13. *a.*   payout ratio = DPS/EPS = $1/$3 = 1/3
b.   equity portion of capital outlays = 8M shares ($3 – $1) = $16M
D/E ratio = $10M/$16M = 0.625

14. *a.*   maximum capital outlays with no equity financing = $125,000 + 2($125,000) = $375,000.
b.   If planned capital spending is $500,000>$375,000, then no dividend will be paid and new equity will be issued.
c.   No, they do not maintain a constant dividend payout because, with the strict residual policy, the dividend will depend on the investment opportunities and earnings. As these two things vary, the dividend payout will also vary.

15. *a.*   maximum investment with no equity financing = $24M + .75($24M) = $42M; debt = $18M
b.   D/E = .75 implies capital structure is 3/7 debt and 4/7 equity.
equity portion of investment funds = 4/7($28M) = $16M. Residual = $24M – $16M = $8M
dividend per share = $8M/5M shares = $1.60
c.   borrowing = $28M – $16M = $12M;   addition to retained earnings = $16M
d.   dividend per share = $24M/5M shares = $4.80;   no new borrowing will take place

Intermediate

16. $P_0 = \$0.65/1.16 + \$25/1.16^2 = \$19.14$
$\$19.14 = D/1.16 + D/1.16^2 ;$ $D = \$11.92$
$P_1 = \$25/1.16 = \$21.55$
You want $1,625(\$11.92) = \$19,375$ in one year, but you'll only get $1,625(\$0.65) = \$1,056.25$.
Thus sell $(\$19,375 - \$1,056.25)/\$21.55 = 850$ shares at time 1.
time 2 cash flow $= \$25(1,625 - 850) = \$19,375$

17. you only want \$50 in year 1, so buy $(\$1,056.25 - \$50)/\$21.55 = 46.69$ shares at time 1.
year 2: $(1,625 + 46.69)(\$25) = \$41,792.25$
$PV = \$50/1.16 + (\$41,792.25)/1.16^2 = \$31,101.55$
$PV = 1,625(\$0.65)/1.16 + 1,625(\$25)/1.16^2 = \$31,101.55$

18. *a.*   cash dividend: DPS $= \$3,000/250$ shares $= \$12$; $P_X = \$40 - \$12 = \$28$ per share.
wealth of a shareholder = a share worth \$28 plus \$12 cash = \$40.
repurchase: $\$3,000/\$40 = 75$ shares will be repurchased. If you choose to let your shares be repurchased, you have \$40 in cash; if you keep your shares, they're still worth \$40.

b.   dividends: EPS $= \$4$;   P/E $= \$28/\$4 = 7$
repurchase: EPS $= \$4(250)/175 = \$5.71$;   P/E $= \$40/\$5.71 = 7$

c.   A share repurchase would seem to be the preferred course of action. Only those shareholders who wish to sell will do so, giving the shareholder a tax timing option that he or she doesn't get with a dividend payment.

19. No, because the money could be better invested in stocks that pay dividends in cash that will benefit the fundholders directly.

20. The change in price is due to the change in dividends, not to the change in dividend *policy*. Dividend policy can still be irrelevant without a contradiction.

21. The stock price dropped because of an expected drop in future dividends. Since the stock price is the present value of all future dividend payments, if the expected future dividend payments decrease, then the stock price will decline.

22. The plan will probably have little effect on shareholder wealth. The shareholders can reinvest on their own, and the shareholders must pay the taxes on the dividends either way. However, the shareholders who take the option may benefit at the expense of the ones who don't (because of the discount). Also as a result of the plan, the firm will be able to raise equity by paying a 10% flotation cost (the discount), which may be a smaller discount than the market flotation costs of a new issue for some companies.

23. If these firms just went public, they probably did so because they were growing and needed the additional capital. Growth firms typically pay very small cash dividends, if they pay a dividend at all. This is because they have numerous projects, and they therefore reinvest the earnings in the firm instead of paying cash dividends.

24. *a.* First, it probably is not a good time to raise dividends if earnings are not good, and it is not certain that the higher dividend can be maintained. It would be worse to raise the dividend and then to later cut it back again. Second, if the firm can invest the money profitably, then it should do so. That is the basis for positive net present value projects.

    b. On theoretical grounds, there is nothing inherently wrong with "borrowing to pay dividends," but most practitioners would probably feel that this is not the soundest financial policy. For example, it may have adverse capital structure consequences, or may limit the firm's accessibility to the capital markets if it has to borrow again in the near future for real investment needs. In any case, if the firm needs the money to fund profitable investments, it should probably not raise the dividend.

    c. Neither one, really. Its dividend policy should probably be based on its long-range capital needs.

    d. The company should not be too worried about the little old lady in Iowa. If she wants higher dividends, she can sell her stock in Clark and buy stock in a company that pays a higher dividend, or she can sell off portions of Clark stock as needed to achieve the cash flow she desires.

25. The chief drawback to a strict dividend policy is the variability in dividend payments. This is a problem because investors tend to want a somewhat predictable cash flow. Also, if there is information content to dividend announcements, then the firm may be inadvertently telling the market that it is expecting a downturn in earnings prospects when it cuts a dividend, when in reality its prospects are very good. In a compromise policy, the firm maintains a relatively constant dividend. It increases dividends only when it expects earnings to remain at a sufficiently high level to pay the larger dividends, and it lowers the dividend only if it absolutely has to.

Challenge

26. If both firms have the same aftertax return of 18%, than D must have a higher pretax return to compensate for the taxation of dividends. Of the 18% gain, D pays 5.5% in dividends, of which only $5.5(.65) = 3.575\%$ is kept aftertax. Together with D's capital gain of $18 - 5.5 = 12.5\%$, the price for D is $1.16075/1.18 = .9837$ of U; thus the pretax required return is $(1.18 - .9837)/.9837 = 19.96\%$.

27. *a.* $P_0 - P_X = D$

    b. $P_0 - P_X = .72D$

    c. $P_0 - P_X = .8472D$

    d. $P_0 - P_X = D[1 - (.34)(.30)]/.66 = 1.361D$

    e. Since different investors have widely varying tax rates on ordinary income and capital gains, then dividend payments have different aftertax implications for different investors. This differential taxation among investors is one aspect of what we have called the clientele effect.

CHAPTER 17
SHORT-TERM FINANCE
AND PLANNING

Basic

1. *a.* Use: The cash balance declined by $200 to pay the dividend.
   b. Source: The cash balance increased by $500 assuming the goods bought on payables credit were sold for cash.
   c. Use: The cash balance declined by $900 to pay for the fixed assets.
   d. Use: The cash balance declined by $625 to pay for the higher level of inventory.
   e. Use: The cash balance declined by $1,200 to pay for the redemption of debt.

2. *a.* N   *b.* N   *c.* N
   d. I   *e.* D   *f.* I
   g. N   *h.* D   *i.* I
   j. D   *k.* D   *l.* N
   m. I   *n.* D   *o.* D

3. Cash = $3,500 + $900 − $2,000 + $975 − $2,375 = $1,000
   Current assets = $1,400 + $975 + 1,000 = $3,375

4. Carrying costs will decrease because they are not holding goods in inventory. Shortage costs will probably increase depending on how close the suppliers are and how well they can estimate need. The operating cycle will decrease because the inventory period is decreased.

5. *a.* I   *b.* I   *c.* D
   d. N   *e.* D   *f.* N

6. Since the cash cycle equals the operating cycle minus the accounts payable period, it is not possible for the cash cycle to be longer than the operating cycle if the accounts payable period is positive. Moreover, it's unlikely that the accounts payable period would ever be negative, since that implies that the firm pays its bills before they are incurred.

7. first letter is cash cycle,   *a.* D; D   *b.* D; N   *c.* I; I
   second is operating cycle.   *d.* D; D   *e.* I; N   *f.* I; I

8. *a.* 72-day collection period implies all receivables outstanding from previous quarter are collected in the current quarter, and (90-72)/90 = ⅕ of current sales are collected.

	Q1	Q2	Q3	Q4
Beginning receivables	$300	$460	$500	$560
Sales	575	625	700	600
Cash collections	415	585	640	680
Ending receivables	$460	$500	$560	$480

b. 54-day collection period implies all receivables outstanding from previous quarter are collected in the current quarter, and $(90-54)/90 = 2/5$ of current sales are collected.

	Q1	Q2	Q3	Q4
Beginning receivables	$300	$345	$375	$420
Sales	575	625	700	600
Cash collections	530	595	655	660
Ending receivables	$345	$375	$420	$360

c. 36-day collection period implies all receivables outstanding from previous quarter are collected in the current quarter, and $(90-36)/90 = 3/5$ of current sales are collected.

	Q1	Q2	Q3	Q4
Beginning receivables	$300	$230	$250	$280
Sales	575	625	700	600
Cash collections	645	605	670	640
Ending receivables	$230	$250	$280	$240

9. Inventory turnover $= \$22,893/\{\frac{1}{2}[\$4,925+\$5,150]\} = 4.545$ times
    Inventory period $= 365$ days$/4.545 = 80.32$ days
    Receivables turnover $= \$47,115/\{\frac{1}{2}[\$3,019+\$3,380]\} = 14.726$ times
    Receivables period $= 365$ days$/14.726 = 24.79$ days
    Operating cycle $= 80.32 + 24.79 = 105.10$ days
    Payables turnover $= \$22,893/\{\frac{1}{2}[\$7,516+\$7,952]\} = 2.960$ times
    Payables period $= 365$ days$/2.960 = 123.31$ days
    Cash cycle $= 105.10 - 123.31 = -18.21$ days
    The firm is receiving cash on average 18.21 days before it pays its bills.

10. number of periods $= 365/48 = 7.604$;   EAR $= (1 + 03/97)^{7.604} - 1 = 26.06\%$

11. a. The payables period is zero since Van Meter pays immediately.
         Payment in each period $= 0.45$ times next period sales.

	Q1	Q2	Q3	Q4
Payment of accounts	$247.50	$202.50	$270.00	$348.75

b. Since the payables period is 90 days, payment in each period = 0.45 times current period sales.

	Q1	*Q2*	*Q3*	*Q4*
Payment of accounts	$279.00	$247.50	$202.50	$270.00

c. Since the payables period is 60 days, payment in each period = 2/3 of last quarter's orders, and 1/3 of this quarter's orders, or 2/3(.45) times current sales + 1/3(.45) next period sales.

	Q1	*Q2*	*Q3*	*Q4*
Payment of accounts	$268.50	$232.50	$225.00	$296.25

12. Since the payables period is 60 days, payables in each period = 2/3 of last quarter's orders, and 1/3 of this quarter's orders, or 2/3(.6) times current sales + 1/3(.6) next period sales.

	Q1	*Q2*	*Q3*	*Q4*
Payment of accounts	$140.00	$156.00	$102.00	$116.00
Wages, taxes, other expenses	30.00	45.00	27.00	22.50
Long-term financing expenses (interest and expenses)	30.00	30.00	30.00	30.00
Total	$200.00	$231.00	$159.00	$168.50

13. *a.* November sales = ($50,000 – $38,000)/0.20 = $60,000
b. December sales = $38,000/0.75 = $50,666.67
c. January collections = .20($60,000) + .55($50,666.67) + .25($80,000) = $59,866.67
February collections = .20($50,666.67) + .55($80,000) .25($105,000) = $80,383.33
March collections = .20($80,000) + .55($105,000) + .25($130,000) = $106,250.00

14. Sales collections = .40 times current month sales + .50 times previous month sales.

	April	*May*	*June*
Beginning cash balances	$300,000	$316,000	$406,500
Cash receipts			
Cash collections from credit sales	221,000	210,000	222,900
Total cash available	$521,000	$526,000	$629,400
Cash disbursements			
Purchases	95,000	100,000	94,000
Wages, taxes, and expenses	15,000	14,500	17,200
Interest	5,000	5,000	5,000
Equipment purchases	90,000	0	10,000
Total cash disbursements	$205,000	$119,500	$126,200
Ending cash balance	$316,000	$406,500	$503,200

15. *a.*   Valley Piping finances its current assets with a combination of short-term and long-term borrowing, whereas Mountain Valve finances its current assets with short-term borrowing only (very little cash).

  b.   Valley Piping has a higher investment on an absolute basis, and Mountain Valve has a higher investment on a relative basis. The relative basis is more important for determining working capital policy because the absolute basis does not consider the size of the firm and how that should affect policy.

  c.   Mountain Valve is more likely to incur carrying costs because it has a lower inventory turnover. For the same reason, Valley Piping is more likely to incur shortage costs, but since its inventory turnover is 1.22, its chances of being short may not be that great either.

Intermediate

16. *a.*   Borrow $10M for one month, pay $75,000 in interest, but you only get the use of $9.2M.
  $$EAR = (1 + \$75,000/\$9.2M)^{12} - 1 = 10.23\%$$

  b.   to end up with $3M, must borrow $3/.92 = \$3,260,869.57$
  total interest paid = $\$3,260,869.57(1.0075)^4 - \$3,260,869.57 = \$98,932.15$

17. *a.* $EAR = 1.0125^4 - 1 = 5.09\%$

  b.   opportunity cost = $.15(\$25M)(1.0125)^4 - .15(\$25M) = \$191,045.01$
  interest cost = $\$50M(1.025)^4 - \$50M = \$5,190,644.55$
  $EAR = \$5,381,689.56/\$50M = 10.76\%$

  c. $EAR = 1.025^4 - 1 = 10.38\%$

18. *a.*   36-day collection period means sales collections = $3/5$ current sales + $2/5$ old sales
  30-day payables period means payables = $2/3$ current orders + $1/3$ old orders
  Q1: cash inflow = $\$65 + 3/5(\$160) - 1/3(.55)(\$160) - 2/3(.55)(\$227) - .24(\$160) - \$15 = -\$4.97$
  Q2: cash inflow = $2/5(\$160) + 3/5(\$227) - 1/3(.55)(\$227) - 2/3(.55)(\$269) - .24(\$227) - \$15 = -\$9.53$
  Q3: cash inflow = $2/5(\$227) + 3/5(\$269) - 1/3(.55)(\$269) - 2/3(.55)(\$241) - .24(\$269)$
  $\qquad\qquad - \$15 - \$150 = -\$115.04$
  Q4: cash inflow = $2/5(\$269) + 3/5(\$241) - 1/3(.55)(\$241) - 2/3(.55)(\$205) - .24(\$241) - \$15 = \$60.01$

STREAMLINE, INC.
Cash Balance (in millions)

	Q1	Q2	Q3	Q4
Beginning cash balance	$25.00	$20.03	$ 10.50	-$104.54
Net cash inflow	-4.97	-9.53	-115.04	60.01
Ending cash balance	20.03	10.50	-104.54	-44.53
Minimum cash balance	15.00	15.00	15.00	15.00
Cumulative surplus (deficit)	$ 5.03	($4.50)	($119.54)	($59.53)

b.   Q1: excess funds at start of quarter of $10 deposited for 1 quarter earns $0.30 in income
Q2: excess funds of $5.33 invested for 1 quarter earns .03($5.33) = $0.16 in income
Q3: shortfall of $4.04 borrowed for 1 quarter requires .04($4.04) = $0.16 in interest expense
Q4: shortfall of $115.20 and old $4.04 requires .04($115.20 + $4.04) = $4.77 in interest expense

STREAMLINE, INC.
Short-Term Financial Plan
(in millions)

	Q1	Q2	Q3	Q4
Beginning cash balance	$15.00	$15.00	$ 15.00	$15.00
Net cash inflow	–4.97	–9.53	–115.04	60.01
New short-term investments	0	0	0	0
Income on short-term investments	0.30	0.16	0	0
Short-term investments sold	4.67	5.33	0	0
New short-term borrowing	0	4.04	115.20	0
Interest on short-term borrowing	0	0	–0.16	–4.77
Short-term borrowing repaid	0	0	0	–55.24
Ending cash balance	$15.00	$15.00	$ 15.00	$15.00
Minimum cash balance	15.00	15.00	15.00	15.00
Cumulative surplus (deficit)	$ 0	$ 0	$ 0	$ 0
Beginning short-term investments	$10.00	$ 5.33	$ 0	$ 0
Ending short-term investments	5.33	0	0	0
Beginning short-term debt	0	0	4.04	119.24
Ending short-term debt	0	4.04	119.24	64.00

19.   *a.*

STREAMLINE, INC.
Short-Term Financial Plan
(in millions)

	Q1	Q2	Q3	Q4
Beginning cash balance	$25.00	$25.00	$ 25.00	$25.00
Net cash inflow	–4.97	–9.53	–115.04	60.01
New short-term investments	0	0	0	0
Income on short-term investments	0	0	0	0
Short-term investments sold	0	0	0	0
New short-term borrowing	4.97	9.73	115.63	0
Interest on short-term borrowing	0	–0.20	–0.59	–5.21
Short-term borrowing repaid	0	0	0	–54.80
Ending cash balance	$25.00	$25.00	$ 25.00	$25.00
Minimum cash balance	25.00	25.00	25.00	25.00
Cumulative surplus (deficit)	$ 0	$ 0	$ 0	$ 0

	Q1	Q2	Q3	Q4
Beginning short-term investments	$ 0	$ 0	$ 0	$ 0
Ending short-term investments	0	0	0	0
Beginning short-term debt	0	4.97	14.70	130.33
Ending short-term debt	4.97	14.70	130.33	75.53

b.

STREAMLINE, INC.
Short-Term Financial Plan
(in millions)

	Q1	Q2	Q3	Q4
Beginning cash balance	$ 5.00	$ 5.00	$ 5.00	$ 5.00
Net cash inflow	−4.97	−9.53	−115.04	60.01
New short-term investments	0	0	0	0
Income on short-term investments	0.60	0.47	0.20	0
Short-term investments sold	4.37	9.06	6.57	0
New short-term borrowing	0	0	108.27	0
Interest on short-term borrowing	0	0	0	−4.33
Short-term borrowing repaid	0	0	0	−55.68
Ending cash balance	$ 5.00	$ 5.00	$ 5.00	$ 5.00
Minimum cash balance	5.00	5.00	5.00	5.00
Cumulative surplus (deficit)	$ 0	$ 0	$ 0	$ 0
Beginning short-term investments	$20.00	$15.63	$ 6.57	$ 0
Ending short-term investments	15.63	6.57	0	0
Beginning short-term debt	0	0	0	108.27
Ending short-term debt	0	0	108.27	52.59

Since cash has an opportunity cost, the firm can boost its profit if it keeps its minimum cash balance low and invests the cash instead. However, the tradeoff is that in the event of unforeseen circumstances, the firm may not be able to meet its short-run obligations if not enough cash is available.

Challenge

20. *a.* For every $1 borrowed, you pay $0.03 in interest and get to use $0.96.

EAR $= (1 + .03/.96)^4 - 1 = 13.10\%$

   b. Now for every $1 borrowed, you only get the use of $0.9575

EAR $= (1 + .03/.9575)^4 - 1 = 13.13\%$

21. You're paying $100,000 in interest, but you only get the use of $740,000, the combination of the discount loan ($100,000) and the compensating balance ($160,000).

EAR $= \$100,000/\$740,000 = 13.51\%$

With the commitment fee, the usable funds are now only $738,000.

EAR $= \$100,000/\$738,000 = 13.55\%$

CHAPTER 18
CASH AND LIQUIDITY MANAGEMENT

Basic

1. Net disbursement float is more desirable because the bank thinks the firm has more money than it actually does, and the firm is therefore receiving interest on funds it has already spent.

2. The firm has a net disbursement float of $500,000. If this is an ongoing situation, the firm may be tempted to write checks for more than it actually has in its account.

3. Average daily float = 5($84,000)/30 = $14,000 (assuming a 30-day month)

4. *a.* Disbursement float = 6($35,000) = $210,000
   Collection float = 4($45,000) = $180,000
   Net float = $210,000 – $180,000 = $ 30,000
   b. Collection float = 5($45,000) = $225,000
   Net float = $210,000 – $225,000 = –$ 15,000

5. *a.* Collection float = 3($4,000) = $12,000
   b. The firm should pay no more than $12,000 to eliminate the float.
   c. Maximum daily charge = $12,000(.00025) = $3.00

6. *a.* Total float = 3($8,000) + 7($5,000) = $59,000
   b. Average daily float = $59,000/30 = $1,966.67 (assuming a 30-day month).
   c. Average daily receipts = ($8,000 + $5,000)/30 = $433.33
   Weighted average delay = 3($8,000/$13,000) + 7($5,000/$13,000) = 4.54 days

7. Average daily collections = $25(15,000) = $375,000
   PV = (2 day reduction)($375,000) = $750,000
   Cost = $100/.00015 = $666,667 ; the firm should take the lockbox service; NPV = $83,333.
   Annual savings = $750,000(1.00015)^{365} – $750,000 = $42,204.13
   Annual cost = $100(FVIFA$_{365,.015\%}$) = $37,514.78
   Annual net savings = $42,204.13 – $37,514.78 = $83,333[(1.00015)^{365} – 1] = $4,689.35

8. *a.* Average daily float = [.3(8,000)($50)(2) + .7(8,000)($75)(3)]/30 = $50,000.
   On average, there is $50,000 that is uncollected and not available to the firm.
   b. Total collections = .3(8,000)($50) + .7(8,000)($75) = $120K + $420K = $540K
   Weighted average delay = 2(120K/540K) + 3(420K/540K) = 2.78 days
   Average daily float = 2.78[$540K/30 days] = $50,000
   c. The most the firm should pay is the total amount of the average float, or $50,000.
   d. 1.1 = (1+r)^{365}; r = .02612% per day
   Daily cost of the float = $50,000(.0002612) = $13.06
   e. 1.5[$540K/30] = $27,000

393

9. *a.*   PV = 2(500)($1,600) = $1.6M

    b.   NPV = $1.6M – [$0.50(500)/.0002] = $350,000

    c.   Net cash flow = $1.6M(.0002) – $0.50(500) = $70 per day

    Net cash flow = 2($1,600)(.0002) – $0.50 = $0.14 per check

10. *a.*   2($90,000) = $180,000

    b.   Average daily rate = $1.11^{1/365} - 1 = .0286\%$ per day

    $180,000(.000286) = $51.47

    c.   Monthly rate = $1.11^{1/12} - 1 = .8735\%$ per month

    NPV = 0 = $180,000 – X/.008735 ;   X = $1,572.23

11. $300,000(4)(52/2)(.0003) = $9,360

12. NPV = $2M – ($500K – $400K) = $1.9M; proceed with the new system.

    Net savings = $1.9M(.08) = $152,000

Intermediate

13. PV = 3(450)($2,000) = $2.7M

    Daily interest rate = $1.06^{1/365} = .01597\%$ per day

    NPV = $2.7M – [$0.40(450)/.0001597] = $1,572,562; the lockbox system should be accepted.

    With the fee, NPV = $1,572,562 – [$100,000/.06] = $94,104.75; the lockbox system should still be accepted.

14. Daily interest rate = $1.05^{1/365} = .01337\%$ per day

    NPV = 0 = ($3,000)(2)N – [$0.30(N)/.0001337] – [$20,000/.0001337]

    N = 106.50 ≈ 107 customers per day

15. *a.*   About the only disadvantage to holding T-bills are the generally lower yields compared to alternative money market investments.

    b.   Some ordinary preferred stock issues pose both credit and price risks that are not consistent with most short-term cash management plans.

    c.   The primary disadvantage of NCDs is the normally large transactions sizes, which may not be feasible for the short-term investment plans of many smaller to medium-sized corporations.

    d.   The primary disadvantages of the commercial paper market are the higher default risk characteristics of the security, and the lack of an active secondary market which may excessively restrict the flexibility of corporations to meet their liquidity adjustment needs.

    e.   The primary disadvantages of RANs is that some possess non-trivial levels of default risk, and also corporations are somewhat restricted in the type and amount of these tax-exempts they can hold in their portfolios.

    f.   The primary disadvantage of the repo market is the generally very short maturities available.

Challenge

16. *a.*   FVA = .9985(4)($400,000)(FVIFA$_{14,.02\%}$) = $22,395,500.28

   b.   FVA = {4($400,000 − $1,000)(FVIFA$_{14,.02\%}$)}/1.0002 = $22,368,597.42
   Laurel should not go ahead with the plan.

   c.   {4($400,000 − $X)(FVIFA$_{14,.02\%}$)}/1.0002 = $22,395,500.28 ;   X = $520.12

APPENDIX 18A

1. *a.*   D: this will lower the trading costs which will cause a decrease in the target cash balance.

   b.   D: this will increase the holding cost which will cause a decrease in the target cash balance.

   c.   I: this will increase the amount of cash that the firm has to hold in non-interest bearing accounts, so they will have to raise the target cash balance to meet this requirement.

   d.   D: if the credit rating improves, then the firm can borrow easier, allowing it to lower the target cash balance and borrow if a cash shortfall occurs.

   e.   I: if the cost of borrowing increases, the firm will need to hold more cash to protect against cash shortfalls as its borrowing costs become more prohibitive.

   f.   D: this depends somewhat on what the fees apply to, but if direct fees are established, then the compensating balance may be lowered, thus lowering the target cash balance. If, on the other hand, fees are charged on the number of transactions, then the firm may wish to hold a higher cash balance so they are not transferring money into the account as often.

2. $C^* = [2(\$2,800)(\$6)/.08]^{1/2}$ = $648.07
   The initial balance should be $648.07, and whenever the balance drops to $0, another $648.07 should be transferred in.

3.   holding cost = ($250)(.09) = $22.50
   trading cost = [($40,000)($5)]/[($250)(2)] = $400
   total cost = $22.50 + $400 = $422.50
   $C^* = [2(\$40,000)(\$5)/.09]^{1/2}$ = $2,108.19
   They should increase their average daily cash balance to $2,108.19/2 = $1,054.09, which would minimize the costs. New total cost = ($1,054.09)(.09) + [($40,000)($5)]/[2($1,054.09)] = $189.74

4. *a.*   opportunity cost = ($750)(.14)/2 = $52.50
   trading cost = ($3,000)($80)/$750 = $320
   The firm keeps too little in cash because the trading costs are much higher than the opportunity costs.

   b. $C^* = [2(\$3,000)(\$80)/.14]^{1/2}$ = $1,851.64

5.   Total cash = 12($250,000) = $3M
   $C^* = [2(\$3M)(\$400)/.06]^{1/2}$ = $200,000

The company should invest $600,000 - $200,000 = $400,000 of its current cash holdings in marketable securities, to bring the cash balance down to the optimal cash level.

Over the rest of the year, sell securities $3M/$200,000 = 15 times.

6. The lower limit is the minimum balance allowed in the account, and the upper limit is the maximum balance allowed in the account. When the account balance drops to the lower limit, $45,000 - $25,000 = $20,000 in marketable securities will be sold, and the proceeds deposited in the account. This moves the account balance back to the target cash level. When the account balance rises to the upper limit, then $125,000 - $45,000 = $80,000 of marketable securities will be purchased. This expenditure brings the cash level back down to the target balance of $45,000.

7. $C^* = \$1,250 + [\frac{3}{4}(\$100)(\$70)^2/.00025]^{1/3} = \$2,387.03$
   $U^* = 3(\$2,387.03) - 2(\$1,250) = \$4,661.09$
   When the balance in the cash account drops to $1,250, the firm sells $2,387.03 - $1,250 = $1,137.03 of marketable securities. The proceeds from the sale are used to replenish the account back to the optimal target level of C^*. Conversely, when the upper limit is reached, the firm buys $4,661.09 - $2,387.03 = $2,274.06 of marketable securities. This expenditure lowers the cash level back down to the optimal level of $2,387.03.

8. As variance increases, the upper limit and the spread will increase, while the lower limit remains unchanged. The lower limit does not change because it is an exogeneous variable set by management. As the variance increases, however, the amount of uncertainty increases. When this happens, the target cash balance and therefore the upper limit and the spread will need to be higher. If the variance drops to zero, then the lower limit, the target balance, and the upper limit will all be the same.

9. Daily rate $= 1.1^{1/365} - 1 = .02612\%$ per day
   $C^* = \$30,000 + [\frac{3}{4}(\$1.15M)(\$500)/.0002612]^{1/3} = \$41,819.76$
   $U^* = 3(\$41,819.76) - 2(\$30,000) = \$65,459.27$

10. $\$1,500 = [2(\$25,000)(\$3)/r]^{1/2}$; $r = 6.67\%$

CHAPTER 19
CREDIT AND INVENTORY MANAGEMENT

Basic

1. Terms of sale, credit analysis, and collection policy.

2. The credit period, the type of credit instrument, the cash discount, and the discount period.

3. *a.* 90 days until account overdue; remittance: 400($60) = $24,000
    b. 3% discount; 30 day discount period; remittance: .97($24,000) = $23,280
    c. implicit interest: $24,000 − $23,280 = $720; 90 − 30 = 60 days credit

4. *1.* Perishability and collateral value
    2. Consumer demand
    3. Cost, profitability, and standardization
    4. Credit risk
    5. The size of the account
    6. Competition
    7. Customer type

    If the credit period exceeds a customer's operating cycle, then the firm is financing the receivables and other aspects of the customer's business that go beyond the purchase of the selling firm's merchandise.

5. *a.* B: A is likely to sell for cash only, unless the product really works. If it does, then they might grant longer credit periods to entice buyers.
    b. A: Landlords have significantly greater collateral, and that collateral is not mobile.
    c. A: Since A's customers turn over inventory less frequently, they have a longer inventory period and thus will most likely have a longer credit period as well.
    d. B: Since A's merchandise is perishable and B's is not, B will probably have a longer credit period.
    e. A: Rugs are fairly standardized and they are transportable, while carpets are custom fit and are not particularly transportable.

6. *a.* A sight draft is a commercial draft that is payable immediately.
    b. A time draft is a commercial draft that does not require immediate payment.
    c. A bankers acceptance is when a bank guarantees the future payment of a commercial draft.
    d. A promissory note is an IOU that the customer signs.
    e. A trade acceptance is when the buyer accepts the commercial draft and promises to pay it in the future.

7. Trade credit is usually granted on open account. The invoice is the credit instrument.

8. Credit costs: cost of debt, probability of default, and the cash discount

No-credit costs: lost sales

The sum of these are the carrying costs.

9. *1.* Character: determines if a customer is willing to pay his or her debts.

2. Capacity: determines if a customer is able to pay debts out of operating cash flow.

3. Capital: determines the customer's financial reserves in case problems occur with operating cash flow.

4. Collateral: assets that can be liquidated to pay off the loan in case of default.

5. Conditions: customer's ability to weather an economic downturn and whether such a downturn is likely.

10. Receivables turnover = 365/45 = 8.111 times

Average receivables = $85 million/8.111 = $10,479,452

11. *a.* ACP = .4(15 days) + .6(60 days) = 42 days

b. Average balance = 500($1,200) = 600,000

12. Average accounts receivable = 10 weeks sales = 10($90,000) = $900,000

13. nominal interest rate = .03/.97 = .0309 for 60 − 15 = 45 days

EAR = $(1.0309)^{365/45} - 1 = 28.03\%$

a. .02/.98 = .0204;   EAR = $(1.0204)^{365/45} - 1 = 17.81\%$

b. EAR = $(1.0309)^{365/15} - 1 = 109.84\%$

c. EAR = $(1.0309)^{365/50} - 1 = 24.90\%$

14. Receivables turnover = 365/57 = 6.404 times

Annual credit sales = 6.404($250,000) = $1.601M

15. Total credit sales = 6,500($500) = $3.25M

ACP = .35(10) + .65(45) = 32.75 days

Receivables turnover = 365/32.75 = 11.145 times

Average receivables = $3.25M/11.145 = $291,609.59

If the firm increases the cash discount, then more people will pay sooner, thus lowering the average collection period. If the ACP declines, receivables turnover increases, which will lead to a decrease in average receivables.

16. ACP = 30 + 15 = 45 days

Receivables turnover = 365/45 = 8.111 times

Receivables = $4M/8.111 = $493,150.68

17. *a.* NPV = –$32 + (1 – .125)($40)/1.03 = $1.98 per unit; fill the order.

b. NPV = 0 = –$32 + (1 – π)($40)/1.03 ; π = .1760 = 17.60%

c. NPV = –$32 + (1 – .125)($40 – $32)/.03 = $201.33 per unit; fill the order.

NPV = 0 = –$32 + (1 – π)($40 – $32)/.03 ; π = .8800 = 88.00%

d. It is assumed that if a person has paid his or her bills in the past, then they will pay their bills in the future. This implies that if someone doesn't default when credit is first granted, then they will be a good customer far into the future, and the possible gains from the future business outweigh the possible losses from granting credit the first time.

18. Cost of switching = $520(600) + $280(650 – 600) = $326K

Perpetual benefit of switching = ($520 – $280)(650 – 600) = $12,000

NPV = –$326K –$326K/1.015 + $12,000/(1.015)(.015) = $140,995

The firm will have to bear the cost of sales for two months before they receive any revenue from credit sales, which is why the initial cost is for two months. Receivables will grow over the two month credit period, and then will remain about stable with payments and new sales offsetting one another.

19. The three main categories of inventory are: raw material (initial inputs to the firm's production process), work-in-progress (partially completed products), and finished goods (products ready for sale). From the firm's perspective, the demand for finished goods is independent from the demand for the other types of inventory. The demand for raw material and work-in-progress is derived from, or dependent on, the firm's needs for these inventory types in order to achieve the desired levels of finished goods.

20. JIT systems reduce inventory amounts. Assuming no adverse effects on sales, inventory turnover will increase. Since assets will decrease, total asset turnover will also increase. Recalling the Du Pont equation, an increase in total asset turnover, all else being equal, has a positive effect on ROE.

21. Carrying costs should be equal to order costs. Since the carrying costs are low relative to the order costs, the firm should increase the inventory level.

22. Carrying costs = (8,000/2)($25) = $100,000

Order costs = (52)($1,500) = $78,000

EOQ = [2(52)(8,000)($1,500)/$25]$^{1/2}$ = 7,065

The firm's policy is not optimal, since the costs are not equal. Brooks should decrease the order size and increase the number of orders.

23. Carrying costs = (250/2)($12) = $1,500

Restocking costs = 52($900) = $46,800

EOQ = [2(52)(250)($900)/$12]$^{1/2}$ = 1,396.42

Number of orders per year = 52(250)/1,396.42 = 9.31 times

The firm's policy is not optimal, since the costs are not equal. Brooks should increase the order size and decrease the number of orders.

Intermediate

24. Carrying costs = $(Q/2) \times CC$;   restocking costs = $F \times (T/Q)$

$CC \times (Q/2) = F \times (T/Q)$

$Q^2 = 2 \times F \times T / CC$

$Q = [2F \times T / CC]^{1/2} = \text{EOQ}$

25. Cash flow approach:

Cash flow from old policy = ($30 – $18)(5,000) = $60,000

Cash flow from new policy = ($34 – $18)(5,400) = $86,400

Incremental cash flow = $86,400 – $60,000 = $26,400

NPV = –($30)(5,000) – ($18)(5,400 – 5,000) + $26,400/.02 = $1.163M

Accounts receivable approach:

Carrying cost = [$30(5,000) + $18(5,400 – 5,000)](.02) = $3,144

NPV = ($26,400 – $3,144)/(.02) = $1.163M

One-shot approach:

Present value of new sales next month = $34(5,400)/1.02 = $180,000

Net benefit = $180,000 – $18(5,400) = $82,800

NPV for one month = $82,800 – $60,000 = $22,800

NPV = $22,800 + $22,800/(.02) = $1.163M

26. Cash flow from old policy = ($30 – $20)(15,000) = $150,000

Cash flow from new policy = ($33 – $21)(15,000) = $180,000

Incremental cash flow = $180,000 – $150,000 = $30,000

NPV = –($30)(15,000) – ($21 – $20)(15,000) + ($30,000)/.015 = $1.535M; make the switch.

Challenge

27. Incremental cash flow = ($30 – $18)Q – ($30 – $18)(5,000) = 12Q – 60,000

NPV = 0 = –($30)(5,000) – ($18)(Q – 5,000) + (12Q – 60,000)/.02

150,000 = –18Q + 90,000 + 600Q – 3,000,000

582Q = 3,060,000 ;   Q* = 5,257.73

28. Incremental cash flow = (P – $18)(5,100) – ($30 – $18)(5,000) = 5,100P – 151,800

NPV = 0 = –($30)(5,000) – ($18)(5,100 – 5,000) + (5,100P – 151,800)/.02

150,000 + 1,800 = 255,000P – 7,590,000

255,000P = 7,741,800 ;   P = $30.36

29. Incremental cash flow = (P – $21)(15,000) – ($30 – $20)(15,000) = 15,000P – 465,000

NPV = 0 = –($30)(15,000) – ($21 – $20)(15,000) + (15,000P – 465,000)/.015

150,000 + 15,000 = 1,000,000P – 31,000,000

31,165,000 = 1,000,000P ;   P = $31.16

30. The company places an order every six days. Number of orders per year = 365/6 = 60.83 times.

The next order should be placed after the close of business Thursday.

APPENDIX 19A

1. Cash flow from old policy = 50,000($700) = $35M
   Cash flow from new policy = 50,000($790)(1 – .10) = $35.55M
   Incremental cash flow = $35.55M – $35M = $550,000
   NPV = –$35M + $550,000/.01 = –$7.25M

2. *a.* 67.90/70 = .97; credit terms: 3/10, net 30
   b. 8,000($67.90) = $543,200 (at a maximum)
   c. Since the quantity sold does not change, variable cost is the same under either plan.
   d. No, because $d - \pi = 3 - 5 = -2\%$, the NPV will be negative; NPV = –8,000($67.90) + (8,000)($70)(.03 – .05)/(.01) = –$1.663M.
   The breakeven credit price is $P(1+r)/(1-\pi) = \$67.90(1.01)/(.95) = \$72.19$, which implies that the breakeven discount is $1 - (67.90/72.19) = 5.94\%$.
   NPV = –8,000($67.90) + (8,000)($72.19)(.0594 – .05)/(.01) = 0

3. *a.* NPV = $-7(\$400) + (1 - .15)(7)(\$950)/1.0125^2 = \$2,713.79$; the order should be taken.
   b. NPV = $0 = -7(\$400) + (1 - \pi)(7)(\$950)/1.0125^2$; $\pi = .5684 = 56.84\%$
   c. Effectively the cash discount is $100/$950 = 10.53%. Since the discount rate is less than the default rate, credit should not be granted. The firm would be better off taking the $850 up-front than taking an 85% chance of making $950.

4. *a.* Cash discount = 1 – ($20/$22) = .0909 = 9.09%
   Default probability = 1 – .90 = .10
   Since the default probability is greater than the cash discount, credit should not be granted; the NPV of doing so is negative.
   b. Due to the increase in both quantity sold and credit price when credit is granted, an additional incremental cost is entailed of (6,500)($13 – $12) + (6,800 – 6,500)($13) = $10,400.
   NPV = $0 = -\$10,400 -(6,500)(\$20) + \{ 6,800[(1 - .1)P - \$13] - 6,500(\$20 - \$12) \}/ \{1.008^3 - 1\}$;
   140,400 = (6,120P/.0242) – 5,803,449 ;   P = $23.50
   c. NPV = $0 = -\$10,400 - (6,500)(\$20) - (6,800)(\$0.50) + \{ 0.9(6,800)(\$22 - \$13) \}/ \{1.008^3 - 1\}$
       = $2.133M ; credit should be extended.

5.

Old Cashflow	$= (P - v)Q$
New Cashflow	$= (P - v)(1 - \alpha)Q' + \alpha Q'\left[(1 - \pi)P' - v\right]$

Incremental Cashflow $= -(P - v)Q + (P - v)(1 - \alpha)Q' + \alpha Q'\left[(1 - \pi)P' - v\right]$

$$= (P - v)(Q' - Q) + \alpha Q'\left[(1 - \pi)P' - P\right]$$

Thus, NPV $= (P - v)(Q' - Q) - \alpha P Q' + \dfrac{\left[(P - v)(Q' - Q) + \alpha Q'\{(1 - \pi)P' - P\}\right]}{R}$

CHAPTER 20
MERGERS AND ACQUISITIONS

Basic

1. $25M – $22M = $3M

2. In the purchase method, assets must be recorded at market value and goodwill is created to account for the excess of the purchase price over this recorded value. In the pooling of interests method, the balance sheets of the two firms are simply combined; no goodwill is created.

    There is no direct impact of the choice of accounting method on the cash flows of the firms.

    EPS will probably be lower under the purchase method because reported income is usually lower due to the required amortization of the goodwill created in the purchase.

3. *a.* Greenmail refers to the practice of paying unwanted suitors who hold an equity stake in the firm a premium for their shares over the market value, to eliminate the potential takeover threat.
    b. A white knight refers to an outside bidder that a target firm brings in to acquire it, rescuing the firm from a takeover by some other unwanted hostile bidder.
    c. A golden parachute refers to lucrative compensation and termination packages granted to management in the event the firm is acquired.
    d. The crown jewels usually refer to the most valuable or prestigious assets of the firm, which in the event of a hostile takeover attempt the target sometimes threatens to sell.
    e. Shark repellant generally refers to any defensive tactic employed by the firm to resist hostile takeover attempts.
    f. A corporate raider usually refers to a person or firm that specializes in the hostile takeover of other firms.
    g. A poison pill is an amendment to the corporate charter granting the shareholders the right to purchase shares at little or no cost in the event of a hostile takeover, thus making the acquisition prohibitively expensive for the hostile bidder.
    h. A tender offer is the legal mechanism required by the SEC when a bidding firm goes directly to the shareholders of the target firm in an effort to purchase their shares.
    i. A leveraged buyout refers to the purchase of the shares of a publicly-held company and its subsequent conversion into a privately-held company, financed primarily with debt.

4. *i)* Pooling of interests: assets = equity = 20,000($25) + 20,000($12) = $740,000
    ii) Purchase method: assets from X = 20,000($25) = $500,000 (book value)
                                   assets from Y = 20,000($18) = $360,000 (market value)
    Purchase price of Y = 20,000($18 + $5) = $460,000, so goodwill = $100,000.
    Total assets XY = total equity XY = $500K + $360K + $100K = $960,000

5.

Nelson Manufacturing, post-merger

Current assets	$ 2,000	Current liabilities	$ 1,150
Fixed assets	9,000	Long-term debt	2,050
		Equity	7,800
Total	$11,000		$11,000

6. goodwill created = $6,000 – ($4,000 market value FA) – ($1,000 market value CA) = $1,000

Nelson Manufacturing, post-merger

Current assets	$ 2,000	Current liabilities	$ 400
Fixed assets	10,000	Long-term debt	7,600
Goodwill	1,000	Equity	5,000
Total	$13,000		$13,000

7.

The Runny Cheese Company, post-merger

Current assets	$2,200	Current liabilities	$ 625
Other assets	550	Long-term debt	1,000
Net fixed assets	$3,750	Equity	4,875
Total	$6,500		$6,500

8. goodwill created = $1,300 – ($900 mkt value FA) – ($250 mkt value CA and other assets) = $150

The Runny Cheese Company, post-merger

Current assets	$2,200	Current liabilities	$ 500
Other assets	550	Long-term debt	2,300
Net fixed assets	3,900	Equity	4,000
Goodwill	150		
Total	$6,800		$6,800

9. *a.* V^*_{BBC} = $30M + ($2.4M/.08) = $60M

Cash cost = $40M ;   equity cost = .40($45M + $60M) = $42M

b. NPV cash = $60M – $40M = $20M

NPV stock = $60M – $42M = $18M

c. Acquire BBC for $40M cash.

10. *a.* EPS = ($132,000 + $375,000)/[150,000 + $\frac{1}{3}$(60,000)] = $2.98

The market price of International Rail will remain unchanged if it is a zero NPV acquisition.

P = 26.4($375,000)/150,000 = $66 ;   therefore, new P/E = $66/$2.98 = 22.13

b. NPV = 0 = V^* + ΔV – cost = $132,000(10) + ΔV – ($\frac{1}{3}$)(60,000) ; ΔV = 0.

Although there is no value to the synergy, it is possible that International Rail is motivated to purchase Wilton Trucking for other than financial reasons.

11. *a.* NPV = 250($15) + $1,000 – 250($18) = $250

b. [1,000($25) + $250]/1,000 = $25.25

c. merger premium = 250($18 – $15) = $750

d. 250($\frac{3}{5}$) = 150 new shares of B

V_{BT} = 1,000($25) + 250($15) + $1,000 = $29,750

P = $29,750/1,150 = $25.87

e. NPV = 250($15) + $1,000 – 150($25.87) = $869.57

Intermediate

12. The cash offer is better for T's shareholders, because they get $18 a share instead of $^3/_5(\$25.87) = \$15.52$ per share.
$250X[\$29,750/(1,000 + 250X)] = 250(\$18)$; $29,750X = 18,000 + 4,500X$; $X = .7129$
Equivalently, from part (*b*), $X = \$18/\$25.25 = .7129$

13. One of the primary advantages of a taxable merger is the write-up in the basis of the target firm's assets, while one of the primary disadvantages of the capital gains tax that is payable. The situation is the reverse for a tax-free merger.
The basic determinant of tax status is whether or not the old stockholders will continue to participate in the new company, which is usually determined by whether they get any shares in the bidding firm. An LBO is usually taxable because the acquiring group pays off the current stockholders in full, usually in cash.

14. Economies of scale occur when average cost declines as output levels increase. A merger in this particular case might make sense because Eastern and Western may need less total capital investment to handle the peak power needs, thereby reducing average generation costs.

15. Among the defensive tactics often employed by management are seeking white knights, threatening to sell the crown jewels, appealing to regulatory agencies and the courts (if possible), and targeted share repurchases. Frequently antitakeover charter amendments are available as well, such as poison pills, poison puts, golden parachutes, lockup agreements, and supermajority amendments, but these require shareholder approval so they can't be immediately used if time is short. While target firm shareholders may benefit from management actively fighting acquisition bids, in that it encourages higher bidding and may solicit bids from other parties as well, there is also the danger that such defensive tactics will discourage potential bidders from seeking the firm in the first place, which harms the shareholders.

16. cost = 300($35) = $10,500 ;   A gives up $10,500/$100 = 105 shares
    a.   EPS = ($1,200 + $500)/1,105 = $1.54
    b.   old P/E = $100/$1.20 = 80 times;   new P = $1.54(80) = $128.21
    c.   new P/E = $100/$1.54 = 65 times
    d.   P = [(1,000)($100) + 300($25)]/1,105 = $97.29
          P/E = $97.29/$1.54 = 63.2 times
          At a bid price of $35 per share, this is a negative NPV acquisition for A. They should revise their bid downward until the NPV = 0.

17. NPV $= V^*_B - \text{cost}$
         $= \Delta V + V_B - \text{cost}$
         $= \Delta V - (\text{cost} - V_B)$
         $= \Delta V - \text{merger premium}$

Challenge

18. *a.* $EPS_W = \$525K/150K$ shares $= \$3.50$ per share ; $P_W = 14(\$3.50) = \$49$
$R_E = [\$2.25(1.05)/\$49] + .05 = .0982$
$P_W = \$2.25(1.07)/(.0982 - .07) = \$85.33$
$V_W{}^* = 150,000(\$85.33) = \$12,799,367$

b. Gain $= \$12,799,367 - 150,000(\$49) = \$5,449,367$

c. NPV $= \$12,799,367 - 150,000(\$53) = \$4,849,367$

d. $X = \$12,799,367/150,000 = \$85.33$

e. $P_G = [\$40M + \$12,799,367]/1,775,625 = \$29.74$
NPV $= \$12,799,367 - 275,625(\$29.74) = \$4,603,478$

f. Yes, the acquisition should go forward and Galesburg should make the $53 per share cash offer.

g. $P_W = \$2.25(1.06)/(.0982 - .06) = \$62.41$; $V_W{}^* = 150,000(\$62.41) = \$9,361,682$
Gain $= \$9,361,682 - 150,000(\$49) = \$2,011,682$
NPV cash $= \$9,361,682 - 150,000(\$53) = \$1,411,682$
$P_G = [\$40M + \$9,361,682]/1,775,625 = \$27.80$
NPV stock $= \$9,361,682 - 275,625(\$27.80) = \$1,699,415$

In this situation, with the lower projected growth rate, the acquisition should still go forward but the offer should be made as an exchange of stock in this case rather than a cash bid.

WOW!

CHAPTER 21
INTERNATIONAL CORPORATE FINANCE

Basic

1.   *a.* $100(Lit 1,681.60/$1) = Lit 168,160

      b.   .05947¢

      c.   Lit 3M($.0005947/Lit 1) = $1,784.10

      d.   Singapore dollar

      e.   Mexican peso

      f.   (SFr 1.4330/$1)($0.2827/BF 1) = SFr .0405/BF 1 ;   this is a cross rate.

      g.   Most valuable: Kuwaiti dinar = $3.3784

         Least valuable: Polish zloty = $0.00004549

2.   *a.*   £100, since (£100)($1.4853/£1) = $148.53

      b.   FF 100, since (£100)($1.4853/£1)(FF 5.8403/$1) = FF 867.46

      c.   (FF 5.8403/$1)($1.4853/£1) = FF 8.6746/£1 ;   1/8.6746 = £0.1153/FF 1

3.   *a.* F_{180} = ¥104.24 (per $). The yen is selling at a premium because it is more expensive in the forward market than in the spot market ($0.009593 versus $0.009510).

      b. F_{90} = DM 1.7289 = $0.5784/DM 1. The dollar is selling at a premium because it is more expensive in the forward market than in the spot market (DM 1.7351 versus DM 1.7188).

      c.   The value of the dollar will fall relative to the yen, since it takes more dollars to buy one yen in the future than it does today. Conversely, the value of the dollar will rise relative to the deutsche mark, because it will take less dollars to buy one deutsche mark in the future than it does today.

4.   *a.*   The U.S. dollar, since (Can$1)/(Can$1.30/$1) = $0.7692

      b.   (Can$1.95)/(Can$1.30/$1) = $1.50. Among the reasons that absolute PPP doesn't hold are tariffs and other barriers to trade, transactions costs, taxes, and differential tastes.

      c.   The U.S. dollar is selling at a discount, because it is less expensive in the forward market than in the spot market (Can$1.25 versus Can$1.30).

      d.   The Canadian dollar is expected to appreciate in value relative to the dollar, because it takes less Canadian dollars to buy one U.S. dollar in the future than it does today.

      e.   Interest rates in the United States are probably higher than they are in Canada.

5.   *a.*   The dollar is selling at a premium, because it is more expensive in the forward market than in the spot market (SFr 1.53 versus SFr 1.50).

      b.   The franc is expected to depreciate relative to the dollar, because it will take more francs to buy one dollar in the future than it does today.

      c.   Inflation in Switzerland is higher than in the United States, as are interest rates.

6.   *a.*   (¥120/$1)($1.50/£1) = ¥180/£1

     b.   The yen is quoted too low relative to the pound. Take out a loan for $1 and buy ¥120. Use the ¥120 to purchase pounds at the cross-rate—120/175 = £0.6857. Use the pounds to buy back dollars and repay the loan—£0.6857(1.50) = $1.0286; arbitrage profit is 2.86¢ per dollar used.

7.   The exchange rate will increase, as it will take progressively more deutsche marks to purchase a dollar. This is the relative PPP relationship.

8.   *a.*   The Australian dollar is expected to weaken relative to the dollar, because it will take more A$ in the future to buy one dollar than it does today.

     b.   The inflation rate in Australia is higher.

     c.   Nominal interest rates in Australia are higher; relative real rates in the two countries are the same.

9.   A Yankee bond is most accurately described by d.

10.   France: R_{FC} = (FF 5.9033 – FF 5.8403)/FF 5.8403 + .04 = 5.08%

       Japan: R_{FC} = (¥104.25 – ¥105.15)/¥105.15 + .04 = 3.14%

       Switzerland: R_{FC} = (SFr 1.4334 – SFr 1.4330)/SFr 1.4330 + .04 = 4.03%

11.   US: $12M(1.0075)^4$ = $12,364,070

       Great Britain: ($12M)(£0.60/$1)(1.01)^4/(£0.62/$1) = $12,084,434; invest in U.S.

12.   Relative PPP: FF 4 = (FF 5)(1 + {$h_{FC} - h_{US}$})^4 ; $(4/5)^{1/4} - 1$ = – .0543

       Inflation in the U.S. is expected to exceed that in France by 5.43% over this period.

13.   No change in exchange rate: profit = 60,000[$170 – {(W 121,245)/(W 808.28/$1)}]   = $1,200,000

       If exchange rate rises: profit = 60,000[$170 – {(W 121,245)/1.1(W 808.28/$1)}]   = $2,018,182

       If exchange rate falls: profit = 60,000[$170 – {(W 121,245)/0.9(W 808.28/$1)}]   = $ 200,000

       Breakeven: $170 = 121,245/$S_T$; S_T = W 713.21/$1 = – 11.76% decline

14.   *a.* $R_{US} \approx 1.07^{1/2} - 1$ = 3.44% ; $R_G \approx 1.09^{1/2} - 1$ = 4.40%

         If IRP holds, then F_{180} = (DM 1.70)(1 + {.0440 – .0344}) = DM 1.7164

         Since given F_{180} = DM 1.75, an arbitrage exists; the forward premium is too high.

         Borrow DM 1 today at 4.40% interest. Agree to a 180-day forward contract at DM 1.75. Convert the loan proceeds into DM 1/DM 1.70 = $0.5882 today. Invest these dollars at 3.44%, ending up with $0.6085. Convert the dollars back into deutsche marks as $0.6085(DM 1.75/$1) = DM 1.0648. Repay the DM 1 loan, ending with a profit of 1.0648 – 1.0440 = DM 0.0208.

     b. F_{180} = (DM 1.70)(1 + {.0440 – .0344}) = DM 1.7164

15.   *a.* $h_{NETH} \approx$ .07 + .04 – .05 = 6%

     b. h_{CAN} = .09 + .04 – .05 = 8%

     c. h_{FRA} = .12 + .04 – .05 = 11%

16. *a.*   The yen is expected to get stronger, since it will take less yen to buy one dollar in the future than it does today.

    b. $h_{US} - h_{JAP} \approx$ (¥109 − ¥110)/¥110 = − .0091; $1.0091^4 - 1 = .0369$

        The approximate inflation differential between the U.S. and Japan is 3.69% annually.

17.   Relative PPP: $E[S_1] = 100\{1 + (.20 - .05)\}^1 =$ HUF 115.00

                                   $E[S_2] = 100\{1 + (.20 - .05)\}^2 =$ HUF 132.25

                                   $E[S_5] = 100\{1 + (.20 - .05)\}^5 =$ HUF 201.14

Intermediate

18. *a.*   False. If prices are rising faster in Great Britain, it will take more pounds to buy the same amount of goods that one dollar can buy; the pound will depreciate relative to the dollar.

    b.   False. The forward market would already reflect the projected deterioration of the deutsche mark relative to the dollar. Only if you feel that there might be additional, unanticipated weakening of the deutsche mark that isn't reflected in forward rates today will the forward hedge protect you against additional declines.

    c.   True. The market would only be correct on average, while you would be correct all the time.

19. *a.*   American exporters: their situation in general improves because a sale of the exported goods for a fixed number of DMs will be worth more dollars.

        American importers: their situation in general worsens because the purchase of the imported goods for a fixed number of DMs will cost more in dollars.

    b.   American exporters: they would generally be better off if the British government's intentions result in a strengthened pound.

        American importers: they would generally be worse off if the pound strengthens.

    c.   American exporters: would generally be worse off because their goods would become more expensive in Ireland, reducing sales. If the sale price were kept at a fixed number of punts, Irish sales would be worth less dollars.

        American importers: would generally be better off, since Irish goods would cost less in dollars to pay for.

    d.   American exporters: would generally be much worse off, because an extreme case of fiscal expansion like this one will make American goods prohibitively expensive to buy, or else Brazilian sales if fixed in cruzeiros would become worth an unacceptably low number of dollars.

        American importers: would generally be much better off, because Brazilian goods will become much cheaper to purchase in dollars.

20.   IRP is the most likely to hold because it presents the easiest and least costly means to exploit any arbitrage opportunities. Relative PPP is least likely to hold since it depends on the absence of market imperfections and frictions in order to hold strictly.

21. *a.*   Implicitly, it is assumed that interest rates won't change over the life of the project, but the exchange rate is projected to decline because the Euroswiss rate is lower than the Eurodollar rate.

b. $E[S_t] = (SFr\ 2.25)\{1 + (.05 - .08)\}^t = 2.25(.97)^t$

t	SFr	$E[S_t]$	US$
0	−15.75M	2.2500	−$7M
1	+5M	2.1825	$2,290,950.75
2	+5M	2.1170	$2,361,804.89
3	+5M	2.0535	$2,434,850.40
4	+5M	1.9919	$2,510,155.05

NPV @ 11% = $414,671.93

c. $R_{SFr} = 1.11(.97) - 1 = 7.67\%$

NPV $= -15.75M + 5M\{ 1/1.0767 + 1/1.0767^2 + 1/1.0767^3 + 1/1.0767^4\} = $ SFr 933,011.86

$= 933,011.86/2.25 = \$414,671.94$

Challenge

22. *a.* $1 + r_{US} = (1 + R_{US})/(1 + h_{US}) = (1 + R_{FC})/(1 + h_{FC}) = 1 + r_{FC}$

b. $E[S_T] = F_T = S_0 \times [(1 + R_{FC})/(1 + R_{US})]^T$

c. $E[S_T] = S_0 \times [(1 + h_{FC})/(1 + h_{US})]^T$

d.   *Home currency approach:*

$E[S_T] = (FF\ 5)[1.07/1.05]^T = (FF\ 5)(1.019)^T$

NPV $= - [FF\ 20M/(FF\ 5)] + \{FF\ 9M/[1.019(FF\ 5)]\}/1.1 + \{FF\ 9M/[1.019^2(FF\ 5)]\}/1.1^2 +$
$\{FF\ 9M/[1.019^3(FF\ 5/\$1)]\}/1.1^3 = \$316,230.72$

Foreign currency approach:

$R_{FC} = 1.10(1.07/1.05) - 1 = 0.121$

NPV $= -\ FF\ 20M + (FF\ 9M)/1.121 + (FF\ 9M)/1.121^2 + (FF\ 9M)/1.121^3 = FF\ 1.5812M$

NPV ($) $= FF\ 1.5812M/(FF\ 5/\$1) = \$316,230.72$

CHAPTER 22
RISK MANAGEMENT: AN INTRODUCTION TO FINANCIAL ENGINEERING

Basic

1. Since the firm is selling futures, it wants to be able to deliver the lumber; therefore it is a supplier. Since a decline in lumber prices would reduce the income of a lumber supplier, it has hedged its price risk by selling lumber futures. Losses in the spot market due to a fall in lumber prices are offset by gains on the short position in lumber futures.

2. Buying call options gives the firm the right to purchase pork bellies; therefore it must be a consumer of pork bellies. While a rise in pork belly prices is bad for the consumer, this risk is offset by the gain on the call options; if pork belly prices actually decline, the consumer enjoys lower costs while the call option expires worthless.

3. Forward contracts are usually designed by the parties involved for their specific needs and are rarely sold in the secondary market; forwards are somewhat customized financial contracts. All gains and losses on the forward position are settled at the maturity date. Futures contracts are standardized to facilitate their liquidity and allow them to be effectively traded on organized futures exchanges. Gains and losses on futures are marked-to-market daily. The default risk is greatly reduced with futures, since the exchange acts as an intermediary between the two parties, guaranteeing performance; default risk is also reduced because the daily settlement procedure keeps large loss positions from accumulating. You might prefer to use forwards instead of futures if your hedging needs were different from the standard contract size and maturity dates offered by the futures contract.

4. Initial contract value = ($1,187 per ton)(10 tons per contract) = $11,870
   Final contract value = ($1,300 per ton)(10 tons per contract) = $13,000
   Gain on futures contract = $13,000 − $11,870 = $1,130

5. Initial contract value = ($0.8745 per lb.)(25,000 lbs. per contract) = $21,862.50
   $F_T = \$1.00$: Final contract value = ($1.00 per lb.)(25,000 lbs. per contract) = $25,000
   since this is a short position, there is a net loss of $25,000 − $21,862.50 = $3,137.50
   $F_T = \$0.70$: Final contract value = ($0.70 per lb.)(25,000 lbs. per contract) = $17,500
   since this is a short position, there is a net gain of $21,862.50 − $17,500 = $4,362.50

6. Cost = $0.72 per barrel = ($0.72 per barrel)(1,000 barrels per contract) = $720 per contract
   $F_T = \$14$: the option finishes out of the money; loss = $720
   $F_T = \$17$: the option finishes in the money; gain = ($17 − $15)(1,000) − $720 = $1,280

7. The firm is hurt by declining oil prices, so it should sell oil futures contracts. The firm may not be able to create a perfect hedge because the quantity of oil it needs to hedge doesn't match the standard contract size on crude oil futures, or perhaps the exact settlement date the company requires isn't available on these futures (exposing the firm to basis risk), or maybe the firm produces a different grade of crude oil than that specified for delivery in the futures contract.

8. The firm is directly exposed to fluctuations in the price of natural gas, since it is a natural gas user. In addition, the firm is indirectly exposed to fluctuations in the price of oil. If oil becomes less expensive relative to natural gas, its competitors will enjoy a cost advantage relative to the firm.

9. Buying the call options is a form of insurance policy for the firm. If cotton prices rise, the firm is protected by the call, while if prices actually decline, they can just allow the call to expire worthless. However, options hedges are costly because of the initial premium that must be paid. The futures contract can be entered into at no initial cost, with the disadvantage that the firm is locking in one price for cotton; it can't profit from cotton price declines.

10. The call options give the manager the right to purchase oil futures contracts at a futures price of $18 per barrel. The manager will exercise the option if the price rises above $18. Selling put options obligates the manager to buy oil futures contracts at a futures price of $18 per barrel. The put holder will exercise the option if the price falls below $18. The payoffs are:

Oil futures price:	$10	$15	$18	$21	$26
Value of call option position:	0	0	0	3	8
Value of put option position:	– 8	– 3	0	0	0
Total value:	– $8	– $3	$0	$3	$8

The payoff profile is identical to that of a forward contract with a $18 strike price.

11. The put option on the bond gives the owner the right to sell the bond at the option's strike price. If bond prices decline, the owner of the put option profits. However, since bond prices and interest rates move in opposite directions, if the put owner profits from a decline in bond prices, he would also profit from a rise in interest rates. Hence a call option on interest rates is conceptually the same thing as a put option on bond prices.

12. The company would like to lock in the current low rates, or at least be protected from a rise in rates, allowing for the possibility of benefit if rates actually fall. The former hedge could be implemented by selling bond futures; the latter could be implemented by buying put options on bond prices or buying call options on interest rates.

13. A swap contract is an agreement between parties to exchange assets over several time intervals in the future. The swap contract is usually an exchange of cash flows, but not necessarily so. Since a forward contract is also an agreement between parties to exchange assets in the future, but at a single point in time, a swap can be viewed as a series of forward contracts with different settlement dates. The firm participating in the swap agreement is exposed to the default risk of the dealer, in that the dealer may not make the cash flow payments called for in the contract. The dealer faces the same

risk from the contracting party, but can more easily hedge its default risk by entering into an offsetting swap agreement with another party.

14. The firm will borrow at a fixed rate of interest, receive fixed rate payments from the dealer as part of the swap agreement, and make floating rate payments back to the dealer; the net position of the firm is that it has effectively borrowed at floating rates.

Intermediate

15. Transactions exposure is the short-term exposure due to uncertain prices in the future. Economic exposure is the long-term exposure due to changes in overall economic conditions. There are a variety of instruments available to hedge transaction exposure, but very few long-term hedging instruments exist. It is much more difficult to hedge against economic exposure, since fundamental changes in the business generally must be made to offset long-run changes in the economic environment.

16. *a.* You're concerned about a rise in copper prices, so you would buy 100,000/25,000 = 4 September copper futures contracts. By doing so, you're effectively locking in the settle price on March 3, 1994 of $0.8755 per pound of copper, or $87,550.

b. final contract value = ($1.20 per lb.)(25,000 lbs. per contract)(4 contracts) = $120,000
gain = $120,000 − $87,550 = $32,450. While the price of the copper your firm needs has become $32,450 more expensive since March, your profit from the futures position has netted out this higher cost.

17. The risk is that the dollar will strengthen relative to the yen, since the fixed yen payments in the future will be worth less dollars. Since this implies a decline in the $/¥ exchange rate, the firm should sell yen futures.

18. *a.* Buy oil and natural gas futures contracts, since these are probably your primary resource costs. If it is a coal-fired plant, a cross-hedge might be implemented by selling natural gas futures, since coal and natural gas prices are somewhat negatively related in the market; coal and natural gas are somewhat substitutable.

b. Buy sugar and cocoa futures, since these are probably your primary commodity inputs.

c. Sell corn futures, since a record harvest implies low corn prices.

d. Buy silver and platinum futures, since these are primary commodity inputs required in the manufacture of photographic equipment.

e. Sell natural gas futures, since excess supply in the market implies low prices.

f. Assuming the bank doesn't resell its mortgage portfolio in the secondary market, buy bond futures.

g. Sell stock index futures, using an index most closely associated with the stocks in your fund; such as the S&P 100 or the Major Market Index for large blue-chip stocks.

h. Buy Swiss franc futures, since the risk is that the dollar will weaken relative to the franc over the next six month, which implies a rise in the $/SFr exchange rate.

i. Sell deutsche mark futures, since the risk is that the dollar will strengthen relative to the DM over the next three months, which implies a decline in the $/DM exchange rate.

Challenge

19. The financial engineer can replicate the payoffs of owning a put option by selling a forward contract and buying a call. For example, suppose the forward contract has a settle price of $60 and the exercise price of the call is also $60. The payoffs below show that the position is the same as owning a put with an exercise price of $60:

Price of coal:	$50	$55	$60	$65	$70
Value of call option position:	0	0	0	5	10
Value of forward position:	10	5	0	–5	–10
Total value:	$10	$5	$0	$0	$0
Value of put position:	$10	$5	$0	$0	$0

The payoffs for the combined position are exactly the same as those of owning a put. This means that, in general, the relationship between puts, calls, and forwards must be such that the cost of the two strategies will be the same, or an arbitrage opportunity exists. In general, given any two of the instruments, the third can be synthesized.

20. *a.* ABC has a comparative advantage relative to XYZ in borrowing at fixed interest rates, while XYZ has a comparative advantage relative to ABC in borrowing at floating interest rates. Since the spread between ABC and XYZ's fixed rate costs is 2% while their differential is only 1% in floating rate markets, there is an opportunity for a 1% total gain by entering into a fixed for floating rate swap agreement.

   b. If the swap dealer must capture ¼% of the available gain, there is ¾% left for ABC and XYZ. Any division of that gain is feasible; in an actual swap deal, the divisions would probably be negotiated by the dealer. One possible combination is ¼% for ABC and ½% for XYZ:

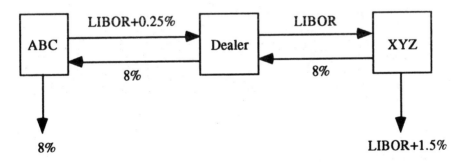

SUPPLEMENT
OPTIONS AND CORPORATE SECURITIES

Basic

1. A call option confers the right, without the obligation, to buy an asset at a given price on or before a given date. A put option confers the right, without the obligation, to sell an asset at a given price on or before a given date. You would buy a call option if you expect the price of the asset to increase. You would buy a put option if you expect the price of the asset to decrease. A call option has unlimited potential profit, while a put option has limited potential profit; the underlying asset's price cannot be less than zero.

2.   *a.*   The buyer of a call option pays money for the right to buy....
      b.   The buyer of a put option pays money for the right to sell....
      c.   The seller of a call option receives money for the obligation to sell....
      d.   The seller of a put option receives money for the obligation to buy....

3. The intrinsic value of a call option is $\max\{S - E, 0\}$. It is the value of the option at expiration.

4. The value of a put option at expiration is $\max\{E - S, 0\}$. By definition, the intrinsic value of an option is its value at expiration, so $\max\{E - S, 0\}$ is the intrinsic value of a put option.

5. The call is selling for less than its intrinsic value; an arbitrage opportunity exists. Buy the call for $10, exercise the call by paying $35 in return for a share of stock, and sell the stock for $50. You've made a riskless $5 profit.

6. The prices of both the call and the put option should increase. The higher level of downside risk still results in an option price of zero, but the upside potential is greater since there is a higher probability that the asset will finish in the money.

7. False. The value of a call option depends on the total variance of the underlying asset, not just the systematic variance.

8.   *a.* $C_0 = \$42 - [\$40/1.06] = \$4.26.$ Intrinsic value = $2
      b. $C_0 = \$42 - [\$20/1.06] = \$23.13.$ Intrinsic value = $22
      c. $P_0 = \$0$; there is no possibility that the put will finish in the money. Intrinsic value = $0.

9.   *a.*   The calls are in the money. The intrinsic value of the calls is $4.
      b.   The puts are out of the money. The intrinsic value of the puts is $0.
      c.   The Mar call and the Oct put are mispriced. The call is mispriced because it is selling for less than its intrinsic value. If the option expired today, the arbitrage would be to buy the call for $3.50, exercise it and pay $55 for a share of stock, and sell the stock for $59. Riskless profit of $0.50. The October put is mispriced because it sells for less than the July put. To take advantage of this, sell the July put for $3.63 and buy the October put for $3.25, for a cash inflow of

$0.38. The exposure of the short position is completely covered by the long position in the October put, with a positive cash inflow today.

10. a. 60(100 shares/contract)($7) = $42,000
     b. S_T = $95: value = 60(100)($95 – $80) = $90,000
         S_T = $86: value = 60(100)($86 – $80) = $36,000
     c. initial cost = 25(100)$4.25 = $10,625 ;   maximum gain = 25(100)($80) – $10,625 = $189,375
         terminal value = 25(100)($80 – $55) = $62,500 ;   net gain = $62,500 – $10,625 = $51,875
     d. S_T = $55: net loss = $10,625 – $62,500 = – $51,875
         S_T = $100: net gain = $10,625
         breakeven S_T: $10,625 = 25(100)($80 – S_T) ; S_T = $75.75. For terminal stock prices above $75.75, the writer of the put option makes a net profit (ignoring the effects of the time value of money).

11. a. C_0 = $90 – [$75/1.05] = $18.57
     b. $90 = 2$C_0$ + [$80/1.05] ; C_0 = $6.90

12. a. C_0 = $25 – [$10/1.06] = $15.57
     b. $25 = 4$C_0$ + [$20/1.06] ; C_0 = $1.53

13. $1,800/(100 shares per contract) = $18 = C_0
     S_0 = ($20/$15)($18) + [$30/1.08] = $51.78

14. a. E_0 = $750 – [$400/1.09] = $383.03
     b. D_0 = $750 – $383.03 = $366.97 ;   interest rate = [$400/$366.97] – 1 = 9%
     c. The value of the equity will increase. The debt requires a higher return, therefore the present value of the debt is less while the value of the firm does not change.

15. a. $1,100 = 1.5$E_0$ + [$700/1.07] ; E_0 = $297.20 ; D_0 = $1,100 – $297.20 = $802.80
     b. $1,100 = (13/9)$E_0$ + [$600/1.07] ; E_0 = $373.33. The stockholders will prefer the new asset structure because their potential gain increases while their potential loss remains unchanged.

16. Conversion ratio = $1,000/$150 = 6.67
     Conversion value = 6.67($50) = $333.33

17. a. straight-bond value = $40(PVIFA$_{5\%,24}$) + $1,000/1.05^{24} = $862.01
         conversion ratio = $1,000/$60 = 16.67 ;   conversion value = 16.67($65) = $1,083.33
         The minimum value for this bond is the convertible floor value of $1,083.33
     b. The option embedded in the bond adds the extra value.

18. a. straight bond value = $50(PVIFA$_{8\%,30}$) + $1,000/1.08^{30} = $662.27
         conversion ratio = $1,000/$80 = 12.5 ;   conversion value = 12.5($35) = $437.50
         The minimum value for this bond is the straight bond floor value of $662.27
     b. conversion premium = ($80 – $35)/$35 = 129%

19. bond value component: $\$70(\text{PVIFA}_{12\%,15}) + \$1,000/1.12^{15} = \$659.46$
warrant component = $\$1,000 - \$659.46 = \$340.54$;   price of one warrant = $\$340.54/25 = \$13.62$

20. $\$13.62/2 = \$6.81 = S_{min}$; the warrants can't sell for more than the stock.
conversion price = $\$1,000/(25)(2) = \$20 = S_{max}$; the conversion value of the bond can't be > $\$1,000$.

21. *a.* $P_0 = [(\$700,000 - \$200,000) + 80(10)(100)]/\{5,000 + 10(100)\} = \$96.67$
     $W_0 = 10(\$96.67) - 10(\$80) = \$166.67$

   b.   Before warrant expiration:

Assets		Liabilities and Equity	
Assets	$700,000	Debt	$200,000
		Equity	483,333
		Warrants	16,667
	$700,000		$700,000

   After warrant expiration:

Assets		Liabilities and Equity	
Assets	$780,000	Debt	$200,000
		Equity	580,000
	$780,000		$780,000

   c. The effective exercise price is $66.67

Intermediate

22. The call option will sell for more since it provides an unlimited profit opportunity, while the potential profit from the put is limited (the stock price cannot fall below zero).

23. The value of a call option will increase, and the value of a put option will decrease.

24. *a.* $C_0 = \max\{\$60 - [\$75/1.08],0\} = \$0$. The option isn't worth anything.
   b.   The stock price is too low for the option to finish in the money. The minimum return on the stock required to get the option in the money is $(75 - 60)/60 = 25\%$, which is much higher than the risk-free rate of interest.

25. B is the more typical case; A presents an arbitrage opportunity. Buy the bond for $900 and immediately convert it into stock that can be sold for $1,000. A riskless $100 profit results.

26. *a.*   conversion ratio = 40 (given) ;   conversion price = $\$1,000/40 = \$25$
      conversion premium = $(\$25 - \$19)/\$19 = 31.6\%$
   b.   straight bond value = $\$30(\text{PVIFA}_{5\%,20}) + \$1,000/1.05^{20} = \$750.76$
      conversion value = $40(\$19) = \$760.00$
   c. $\$750.76 = 40S$; $S = \$18.77$

    d.   There are actually two option values to consider with a convertible bond. The conversion option value, defined as the market value less the floor value, and the speculative option value, defined as the floor value less the straight bond value. When the conversion value is less than the straight-bond value, the speculative option is worth zero.

        conversion option value = \$780 – \$760 = \$20

        speculative option value = \$760 – 750.76 = \$9.24

        total option value = \$20 + \$9.24 = \$29.24

Challenge

27. straight bond value = $\$50(\text{PVIFA}_{8\%,30}) + \$1{,}000/1.08^{30} = \$662.27$

conversion value = $\$38.50(\$1{,}000/\$120) = \$320.83$

$\$320.83(1.12)^n = \$1{,}250$; $n = 12$ years. The bond will be called in 12 year, forcing conversion.

bond value = $\$50(\text{PVIFA}_{8\%,12}) + \$1{,}250/1.08^{12} = \$773.92$

APPENDIX 23A

A1. *a.* $d_1 = -2.3441$; $d_2 = -2.5209$; $N(d_1) = .0095$; $N(d_2) = .0059$

        $C = \$25(.0095) - [\$40/1.08^{1/2}](.0059) = \$0.01$

   b. $d_1 = 1.4101$; $d_2 = 1.1070$; $N(d_1) = .9207$; $N(d_2) = .8658$

        $C = \$35(.9207) - [\$25/1.06^{3/4}](.8658) = \$11.51$

   c. $d_1 = .2239$; $d_2 = .0118$; $N(d_1) = .5886$; $N(d_2) = .5047$

        $C = \$70(.5886) - [\$70/1.05^{1/2}](.5047) = \$6.72$

   d. $d_1 = -.0720$; $d_2 = -.3548$; $N(d_1) = .4713$; $N(d_2) = .3614$

        $C = \$45(.4713) - [\$50/1.09^{1/2}](.3614) = \$3.91$

   e. $S = 0$, so $C = 0$

   f. $T = \infty$, so $C = S = \$90$

   g. $E = 0$, so $C = S = \$50$

   h. $\sigma = 0$, so d_1 and d_2 go to $+\infty$, so $N(d_1)$ and $N(d_2)$ go to 1. This is the no risk call option formula given in the text. $C = S - E/(1+r)^t$; $C = \$70 - [\$65/1.07^{.75}] = \$8.22$

   i.   for $\sigma = \infty$, d_1 goes to $+\infty$ so $N(d_1)$ goes to 1, and d_2 goes to $-\infty$ so $N(d_2)$ goes to 0; $C = S = \$30$

A2. using $S = \$1{,}300$, $E = \$1{,}000$, $T = 1$, $r = .08$, $\sigma = .10^{1/2} = .3162$:

$d_1 = 1.2408$; $d_2 = .9245$; $N(d_1) = .8927$; $N(d_2) = .8224$

$E = \$1{,}300(.8927) - [\$1{,}000/1.08](.8224) = \$398.97$; $D = \$1{,}300 - \$398.97 = \$901.03$

Intermediate

A3. *a.*   project A: using $S = \$1,380$, $E = \$1,000$, $T = 1$, $r = .08$, $\sigma = .20^{1\!/2} = .4472$:

$d_1 = 1.1227$; $d_2 = .6755$; $N(d_1) = .8692$; $N(d_2) = .7503$

$E_A = \$1,380(.8692) - [\$1,000/1.08](.7503) = \$504.78$

$D_A = \$1,380 - \$504.78 = \$875.22$

project B: using $S = \$1,410$, $E = \$1,000$, $T = 1$, $r = .08$, $\sigma = .08^{1\!/2} = .2828$:

$d_1 = 1.6390$; $d_2 = 1.3562$; $N(d_1) = .9494$; $N(d_2) = .9125$

$E_B = \$1,410(.9494) - [\$1,000/1.08](.9125) = \$493.76$

$D_B = \$1,410 - \$493.76 = \$916.24$

b.   Stockholders prefer project A. The value of the option to default is worth more than the additional $30 in NPV.

c.   Yes. If the same group of investors have equal stakes in the firm as bondholders and stockholders, then total firm value matters and project B should be chosen, since it increases the value of the firm to $1,410 instead of $1,380.

d.   Stockholders may have an incentive to take on more risky, less profitable projects if the firm is leveraged; the higher the firm's debt load, all else the same, the greater is this incentive.

SUPPLEMENT
LEASING

Basic

1. *a.* Leasing is a form of secured borrowing. It reduces a firm's cost of capital only if it is cheaper than other forms of secured borrowing. The reduction of uncertainty is not particularly relevant; what matters is the NAL.

b. The statement is not always true. For example, a lease often requires an advance lease payment or security deposit and may be implicitly secured by other assets of the firm.

c. Leasing would probably not disappear, since it does reduce the uncertainty about salvage value and the transactions costs of transferring ownership. However, the use of leasing would be greatly reduced.

2. A lease must be disclosed on the balance sheet if one of the following criteria is met:

1. The lease transfers ownership of the asset by the end of the lease. In this case, the firm essentially owns the asset and will have access to its residual value.

2. The lessee can purchase the asset at a price below its fair market value (bargain purchase option) when the lease ends. The firm essentially owns the asset, and will have access to most of its residual value.

3. The lease term is for 75% or more of the estimated economic life of the asset. The firm basically has access to the majority of the benefits of the asset, without any responsibility for the consequences of its disposal.

4. The present value of the lease payments is 90% or more of the fair market value of the asset at the start of the lease. The firm is essentially purchasing the asset on an installment basis.

3. The lease must meet the following IRS standards for the lease payments to be tax deductible:

1. The lease term must be less than 80% of the economic life of the asset. If the term is longer, the lease is considered to be a conditional sale.

2. The lease should not contain a bargain purchase option, which the IRS interprets as an equity interest in the asset.

3. The lease payment schedule should not provide for very high payments early and very low payments late in the life of the lease. This would indicate that the lease is being used simply to avoid taxes.

4. Renewal options should be reasonable and based on the fair market value of the asset at renewal time. This indicates that the lease is for legitimate business purposes, not tax avoidance.

4. As the term implies, off-balance sheet financing involves financing arrangements that are not required to be reported on the firm's balance sheet. Such activities, if reported at all, appear only in the footnotes to the statements. Operating leases (those that do not meet the criteria in problem 2) provide off-balance sheet financing. For accounting purposes, total assets will be lower and some financial ratios may be artificially high. Financial analysts are generally not fooled by such practices. There are no economic consequences, since the cashflows of the firm are not affected by how the lease is treated for accounting purposes.

5. The lessee may not be able to take advantage of the depreciation tax shield and may not be able to obtain favorable lease arrangements for "passing on" the tax shield benefits. The lessee might also need the cash flow from the sale to meet immediate needs, but will be able to meet the lease obligation cash flows in the future.

6. Since the relevant cash flows are all aftertax, the aftertax discount rate is appropriate.

7. depreciation tax shield = ($900,000/4)(.35) = $ 78,750 ; aftertax debt cost = .09(1 − .35) = .0585
aftertax lease payment = ($275,00)(1 − .35) = $178,750
                                                                    $257,500
NAL = $900,000 − $257,500(PVIFA$_{5.85\%,4}$) = $4,662.02 ; NAL is positive so you should buy.

8. NAL = − $4,662.02

9. NAL = 0 = $900,000 − X(PVIFA$_{5.85\%,4}$) ; X = $258,840.80
aftertax lease payment = $258,840.80 − $78,750 = $180,090.80
breakeven lease payment = $180,090.80/(1 − .35) = $277,062.77

10. If the tax rate is zero, there is no depreciation tax shield foregone, the aftertax lease payment is the same as the pretax payment, and the aftertax cost of debt is the same as the pretax cost.
cost of debt = .09, annual cost of leasing = leasing payment = $275,000
NAL = $900,000 − $275,000(PVIFA$_{9\%,4}$) = $9,077.03

11. The lessor breaks even with a payment of $277,062.77 (from problem 9).
Lessee: breakeven payment— NAL = 0 = $900,000 − PMT(PVIFA$_{9\%,4}$) ; PMT = $277,801.80
Total payment range = $277,801.80 − $277,062.77 = $739.03

12. the appropriate depreciation percentages for a 3-year ACRS class asset are (.3333, .4444, .1482, .0741) leasing cost cashflows are:

year 1: ($900,000)(.3333)(.35) + $178,750 = $283,739.50
year 2: ($900,000)(.4444)(.35) + $178,750 = $318,736.00
year 3: ($900,000)(.1482)(.35) + $178,750 = $225,433.00
year 4: ($900,000)(.0741)(.35) + $178,750 = $202,091.50

NAL = $900,000 − $283,739.50/1.0585 − $318,736/1.0585^2 + $225,433/1.0585^3 + $202,091.50/1.0585
NAL = $3,604.97
The machine should still be leased, but it is less advantageous to do so than it was previously. This is because of the accelerated tax benefits due to depreciation, which represents a cost in the decision to lease compared to an advantage of the decision to purchase.

Intermediate

13. The pretax cost savings are not relevant to the lease versus buy decision, since the firm will definitely use the equipment and realize the savings regardless of the financing choice made.

depreciation tax shield lost = ($3M/5)(.34) = $204,000 ;   aftertax debt cost = .10(1 − .34) = .066
aftertax lease payment = $710,000(1 − .34) = $468,600
                                                $672,600

NAL = $3M − $672,600(1.066)(PVIFA$_{6.6\%,5}$) = $28,436.98 ; the equipment should be leased.

maximum payment: NAL = 0 = $3M − X(1.066)(PVIFA$_{6.6\%,5}$) ; X = $679,036.58
aftertax lease payment   = $679,036.58 − $204,0000 = $475,036.58
breakeven payment   = $475,036.58/(1 − .34) = $719,752.40

14. The aftertax residual value of the asset is a cost to the leasing decision, occurring at the end of the project life (year 5). Also, the residual value is not really a debt-like cash flow, since there is uncertainty associated with it at year 0. Nevertheless, although a higher discount rate may be appropriate, we'll use the aftertax cost of debt to discount the residual value as is common in practice.

NAL = 0 = $3M − X(1.066)(PVIFA$_{6.6\%,5}$) − $250,000/1.066^5; X = $637,928.62
aftertax lease payment   = $637,928.62 − $204,0000 = $433,928.62
breakeven payment   = $433,928.62/(1 − .34) = $657,467.61

15. NAL = $2.89M − $672,600(1.066)(PVIFA$_{6.6\%,5}$) + $110,000/1.066^5 = −$1,652.01.
With the security deposit, the firm should now buy the equipment rather than lease it, because the NAL is less than zero.

Challenge

16. loan payment: $900,000 = PMT(PVIFA$_{9\%,4}$) ; PMT = $277,801.80
aftertax payment = payment − interest tax shield: total cash flow

year 1: $277,801.80 − ($900,000)(.09)(.35)   = $249,451.80   −$ 8,048.20
year 2: $277,801.80 − ($703,198.20)(.09)(.35) = $255,651.06   −$ 1,848.94
year 3: $277,801.80 − ($488,684.24)(.09)(.35) = $262,408.25 $ 4,908.25
year 4: $277,801.80 − ($254,864.02)(.09)(.35) = $269,773.58 $12,273.58

NAL = 0 − $8,048.40/1.0585 − $1,848.94/1.0585^2 + $4,908.25/1.0585^3 + $12,273.58/1.0585^4
NAL = $4,662.02
The NAL is the same because the present value of the aftertax loan payments, discounted at the aftertax cost of capital (which is the aftertax cost of debt) equals $900,000.

PART III

SELECTED

TRANSPARENCY

MASTERS

Balance Sheet

	Beg	End		Beg	End
Cash	$100	$150	A/P	$100	$150
A/R	200	250	N/P	200	200
Inv	300	300	C/L	300	350
C/A	$600	$700	LTD	$400	$420
NFA	400	500	C/S	50	60
			R/E	250	370
				$300	$430
Total	$1000	$1200	Total	$1000	$1200

Income Statement

Sales	$2000
Costs	1400
Depreciation	100
EBIT	500
Interest	100
Taxes	200
Net income	$200
Addition to R/E	$120
Dividends	80

A. Cash flow from assets

1. Operating cash flow

$= \text{EBIT} + \underline{\quad Dep. \quad} - \text{Taxes}$

$= \$500 + 100 - 200$

$= \$\underline{400}$

2. Addition to NWC (NWC spending)

$= \underset{End}{\underline{NWC}} - \underset{Beg.}{\underline{NWC}}$

$= \$350 - \$\underline{300}$

$= \$\underline{50}$

3. Capital spending

$= \underset{End}{\underline{NFA}} + \text{Dep} - \underset{Beg.}{\underline{NFA}}$

$= \$500 + 100 - 400$

$= \$\underline{200}$

4. Cash flow from assets

$= \text{OCF} - \text{NWC sp.} - \text{Cap. sp.}$

$= \$400 - 50 - 200 = \$150$

B. Cash flow to B/H and S/H

1. Cash flow to B/H

$= \text{Int. paid} - \underline{NET\ NEW\ DEBT}$

$= \$100 - \$20$

$= \$80$

2. Cash flow to S/H

$= \text{Div. paid} - \underline{NET\ NEW\ EQUITY}$

$= \$80 - \$10$

$= \$70$

Check: $150 from assets = $80 to B/H + $70 to S/H ✓

---

1. Return on equity (ROE) can be decomposed as follows:

ROE   = Net income/Total equity
           = Net income/Total equity × Total assets/Total assets
           = Net income/Total assets × Total assets/Total equity

           = ___ROA___ × *Equity multiplier*

Check: 6.86% × 1.56 = 10.7% ✓

2.   Return on assets (ROA) can be decomposed as follows:

ROA   = Net income/Total assets × Sales/Sales
           = Net income/Sales × Sales/Total assets

           = _Prof. Mar._ × _Tot. Asset T/O_

Check: 17.8% × .385 = 6.86% ✓

3.   Putting it all together gives the Du Pont identity:

ROE   = ROA × Equity multiplier

           = *Profit margin* × *Total asset turnover* × *Equity mult.*

Check: 17.8% × .385 × 1.56 = 10.7% ✓

4.   Profitability (or the lack thereof!) thus has three parts:

- Operating efficiency
- _Asset use_ efficiency
- Financial leverage

Recent Financial Statments

Income statement			Balance sheet		
Sales	$100	Assets	$50	Debt	$20
Costs	90			Equity	30
Net	$ 10	Total	$50	Total	$50

Assume that:

1. sales are projected to rise by 25%
2. the debt/equity ratio stays at 2/3
3. costs and assets grow at the same rate as sales

Pro Forma Financial Statements

Income statement			Balance sheet		
Sales	$125	Assets	$62.5	Debt	25
Costs	112.5			Equity	37.5
Net	$ 12.5	Total	$62.5	Total	$ 62.5

What's the plug? (the dividend)

Suppose that:

1. half of net income is paid out in dividends
2. new equity sales are not feasible.

Something will have to give; these assumptions are not consistent. In fact, given these assumptions, the maximum possible growth rate is 20 %. Why? Stay tuned.

Income Statement
(projected growth = 30%)

	Original	Pro forma
Sales	$2000	$2600 (+30%)
Costs	1700	2210 (= 85% of sales)
Taxable	300	390
Taxes (34%)	102	132.6
Net income	198	257.4
Dividends	66	85.8 (= 1/3 of net)
Retained	132	171.6 (= 2/3 of net)

Preliminary Balance Sheet

	Orig.	% of sales		Orig.	% of sales
Cash	$100	5%	A/P	$ 60	3%
A/R	120	6%	N/P	140	7%
Inv	140	7%	Total	200	10
Total	$360	18 %	LTD	$200	n/a
NFA	640	32%	C/S	10	n/a
			R/E	590	n/a
				$600	n/a
Total	$1000	50%	Total	$1000	n/a

Note that the ratio of total assets to sales is $1000/$2000 = 0.50. This ratio is the _cap. intensity_ *ratio*. It is the reciprocal of tot. asset t/o   .

The Percentage of Sales Approach, Continued

	Proj.	(+/-)		Proj.	(+/-)
Cash	$130	$30	A/P	$78	$ 18
A/R	156	36	N/P	140	–
Inv	182	42	Total	$218	$ 18
Total	$468	$108	LTD	200	-
NFA	832	192	C/S	10	-
			R/E	761.6	171.6
				$771.6	$171.6
Total	$1300	$300	Total	$1189.6	$171.6

Financing needs are $300, but internally generated sources are only $189.60. The difference is *external financing needed*:

$$EFN = \$300 - 189.60 = \$110.40$$

One possible financing strategy:

1. Borrow short-term first
2. If needed, borrow long-term next
3. Sell equity as a last resort

Constraints:

1. Current ratio must not fall below 2.0.
2. Total debt ratio must not rise above 0.40.

The Percentage of Sales Approach: A Financing Plan

Determine maximum borrowings:

1. • $468/CL = 2.0 implies maximum CL = $234
   • Maximum short-term borrowing = $234 - $218 = $ 16

2. • .40 × $1300 = $520 = maximum debt
   • $520 - 234 = $286 = maximum long-term debt
   • Maximum long-term borrowing = $286 - 200 = $ 86

3. • Total new borrowings = $16 + 86 = $ 102
   • Shortage = $ 110.4 - 102 = $ 8.4

A possible plan:

New short-term debt = $ 8.0
New long-term debt   =   43.0
New equity   =   59.4
                       $110.4

Completed *Pro Forma* Balance Sheet

	Proj.	(+/-)		Proj.	(+/-)
Cash	$130	$ 30	A/P	$ 78	$ 18
A/R	156	36	N/P	148	8
Inv	182	42	Total	$226	$ 26
Total	$468	$108	LTD	243	43
NFA	832	192	C/S	69.4	59.4
			R/E	761.6	171.6
				$831	$231
Total	$1300	$300	Total	$1300	$300

So far, 100% capacity has been assumed. Suppose that, instead, current capacity use is 80%.

1. **At 80% capacity:**

    - $2000 = .80 × full capacity sales
    - $2000/.80 = $<u>2500</u> = full capacity sales

2. **At full capacity, fixed assets to sales will be:**

    - $640/$<u>2500</u> = 25.60%

3. **So, NFA will need to be just:**

    - 25.60% × $2600 = $<u>665.6</u>, not $832
    - $832 - $665.60 = $<u>166.4</u> *less* than originally projected

4. **In this case, original EFN is substantially overstated:**

    - New EFN = $110.40 - $166.40 = -$<u>56</u>, a <u>*surplus*</u>

Moral of the story: *Assumptions matter. Don't blindly apply approach.*

Key issue:

- What is the relationship between sales growth and financing needs?

Recent Financial Statements

Income statement		Balance sheet			
Sales	$100	Assets	$50	Debt	$20
Costs	90			Equity	30
Net	$ 10	Total	$50	Total	$50

Assume that:

1. costs and assets grow at the same rate as sales
2. 60% of net income is paid out in dividends
3. no external financing is available (debt or equity)

Q. What is the *maximum* growth rate achievable?

A. The maximum growth rate is given by

$$\text{Internal growth rate (IGR)} = \frac{ROA \times b}{1 - ROA \times b}$$

- ROA = $10/50 = 20\%$
- b = $1 - .60 = .40$

- IGR = $(20\% \times .40)/[1 - (20\% \times .40)]$
       = $.08/.92 = 8.7\%$ (= 8.695656 ... %)

Assume sales do grow at 8.7 percent:

Pro Forma Financial Statements

Income statement		Balance sheet			
Sales	$108.70	Assets	$54.35	Debt	$20.00
Costs	97.83			Equity	34.35
Net	$ 10.87	Total	$54.35	Total	$54.35

Dividends	$6.52
Add to R/E	4.35

Now assume:

1. no external *equity* financing is available
2. the current debt/equity ratio is optimal

Q. What is the *maximum* growth rate achievable now?

A. The maximum growth rate is given by

$$\text{Sustainable growth rate (SGR)} = \frac{ROE \times b}{1 - ROE \times b}$$

- ROE $= \$10/30 = 1/3 \ (= 33.333 \ldots \%)$
- b $= \$1 - .60 = .40$

- SGR $= (1/3 \times .40)/[1 - (1/3 \times .40)]$
  $= 15.385\% \ (= 15.38462 \ldots \%)$

Assume sales do grow at 15.385 percent:

Pro Forma Financial Statements

Income statement		Balance sheet			
Sales	$115.38	Assets	$57.69	Debt	$ 20
Costs	103.85			Equity	34.61
Net	$ 11.53	Total	$57.69	Total	$54.61
Dividends	$6.92			EFN	$ 3.08
Add to R/E	4.61				

If we borrow the $3.08, the debt/equity ratio will be:

$$\$23.08 \,/\, 34.61 = 2/3$$

So, everything checks out.

Thus, sustainable growth depends on four factors:

1. *profitability* (operating efficiency)
2. *asset management efficiency* (capital intensity)
3. *financial policy* (capital structure)
4. dividend policy

Key result: Given fixed values for these 4 variables, the SGR is the only g.

Notice that

1. $110 $= \$100 \times (1 + .10)$
2. $121 $= \$110 \times (1 + .10) = \$100 \times 1.1 \times 1.1 = \$100 \times 1.1^2$
3. $133.10 $= \$121 \times (1 + .10) = \$100 \times 1.1 \times 1.1 \times 1.1$
              $= \$100 \times \underline{1.1^3}$

In general, the future value, FV_t, of $1 invested today at r% for t periods is

$$FV_t = \$1 \times (1 + r)^t$$

The expression $(1 + r)^t$ is called the *future value factor*.

Q.   Deposit $5000 today in an account paying 12%. How much will you have in 6 years? How much is simple interest? How much is compound interest?

A.   Multiply the $5000 by the future value factor:

$5000 \times (1 + r)^t$ $= \$5000 \times \underline{1.12^6}$
                         $= \$5000 \times 1.9738227$
                         $= \$9869.1135$

At 12%, the simple interest is .12 × $5000 = $ <u>600</u> per year. After 6 years, this is 6 × $600 = $ <u>3600</u> ; the compound interest is thus $ <u>4869.11</u> - $3600 = $ <u>1269.11</u>

Q. Suppose you need $20,000 in three years to pay tuition at MU. If you can earn 8% on your money, how much do you need today?

A. Here we know the future value is $20,000, the rate (8%), and the number of periods (3). What is the unknown present amount (called the *present value*)? From before:

$$FV_t = (1 + r)^t$$
$$\$20,000 = PV \times \underline{1.08^3}$$

Rearranging:

$$PV = \$20,000/(1.08)^3$$
$$= \$\underline{15,876.65}$$

In general, the present value, PV, of a $1 to be received in t periods when the rate is r is

$$PV = \frac{\$1}{(1 + r)^t}$$

Basic Vocabulary:

1. The expression $1/(1 + r)^t$ is called the *present value factor* or, more often, <u>discount factor</u>

2. The r is usually called the <u>discount factor</u>

3. The approach is often called <u>DCF valuation</u>

Notice that $FV_t = PV \times \underline{(1 + r)^t}$

Rearranging, we get that, in general, the relationship between present value, PV, future value, FV_t, the discount rate, r, and the length of time t is:

$$PV = \frac{FV_t}{(1 + r)^t}$$

This is the *basic present value equation.*   It has four components, and, given any three, we can solve for the fourth.

Q.   Deposit $5000 today in an account paying r. If we will get $10,000 in 10 years, what *rate of return* are we being offered?

A.   The PV is $5000. The FV is $10,000. The time, t, is 10 years. From the basic PV equation:

PV $= FV_t/(1 + r)^t$
$5000 $= \$10,000/(1 + r)^{10}$

Three ways to find r:

   1.   Hit relevant buttons on financial calculator.
   2.   Solve equation for r:

$(1 + r)^{10} = 2$
$(1 + r) = \underline{2^{1/10}} = 1.0717735$
    $r \approx 7.2\%.$

   3.   Know the rule of 72.

Benjamin Franklin died on April 17, 1790. In his will, he gave 1,000 pounds sterling to Massachusetts and the city of Boston. He gave a like amount to Pennsylvania and the city of Philadelphia. The money was paid to Franklin when he held political office, but he believed that politicians should not be paid for their service (!).

Franklin originally specified that the money should be paid out 100 years after his death and used to train young people. Later, however, after some legal wrangling, it was agreed that the money would be paid out 200 years after Franklin's death in 1990. By that time, the Pennsylvania bequest had grown to about $2 million; the Massachusetts bequest had grown to $4.5 million. The money was used to fund the Franklin Institutes in Boston and Philadelphia.

Q. Assuming that 1,000 pounds sterling was equivalent to 1,000 dollars, what rate did the two states earn (the dollar didn't become the official U.S. currency until 1792)?

A. For Pennsylvania, the future value is $ __2M__ and the present value is $ _1000_ . There are 200 years involved, so we need to solve for r in the following:

$$\underline{\$1000} = \underline{\$2M} /(1 + r)^{200}$$

$$(1 + r)^{200} = \underline{2000}$$

Solving for r, the Pennsylvania money grew at about 3.87% per year. The Massachusetts money did better; check that the rate of return in this case was 4.3%. Small differences can add up!

Q.   Deposit $5000 today in an account paying 10%. If we will need $10,000, how long will we have to wait.?

A.   The PV is $<u>5000</u>. The FV is $<u>10,000</u>. The rate is 10%. From the basic PV equation:

PV $= FV_t / ((1 + r)^t$

$5000 $= \$10,000/(1.10)^t$

Three ways to find t:

1.   Hit relevant buttons on financial calculator.

2.   Solve equation for t:

$(1.10)^t = 2$

$\log(1.10)^t = \log(2)$

t $= \log(2)/\log(1.10) \approx .693/.0953$

               $= 7.27$ years

3.   Know the rule of 72.

Present value for annuities--a short cut

Q. Suppose you need $20,000 each year for the next three years to pay tuition. Important: you need the first $20,000 in exactly one year. If you can earn 8% on your money, how much do you need today?

A. Here we know the periodic cash flows are $20,000 each. Using the most basic approach:

$$PV = \$20,000/1.08 + \$20,000/\underline{1.08}^2 + \$20,000/1.08^3$$
$$= \$18,518.52 + \$\underline{17,146.78} + \$15,876.65$$
$$= \$51,541.94$$

Using the shortcut:

$$PV = \$20,000 \times \{ 1 - \frac{1}{1.08^3} \}/.08$$
$$= \$20,000 \times 2.577097$$
$$= \$\underline{51,541.94}$$

In the previous example, we had $1000 per year for 5 years at 6% per year.

$$PV = \$1000 \times \{ 1 - \frac{1}{1.06^5} \}/.06$$
$$= \$1000 \times \{1 - .74726\}/.06$$
$$= \$1000 \times 4.212362$$
$$= \$4212.364$$

Suppose the cash flow was $1000 per year *forever*. This is called a *perpetuity* (or *consol*). In this case, the PV is easy to calculate:

$$PV = C/r = \$1000/\underline{.06} = \$16.666.66 \ldots$$

More on annuities

Notice that, as with the basic PV equation, there are only four pieces here, PV, C, r, and t. Given any three, we can find the fourth.

Finding C:

Q. You want to buy a Mazda Miata to go cruising. It costs $17,000. With a 10% down payment, the bank will loan you the rest at 12% per year (1% per month) for 60 months. What will your payment be?

A. You will borrow __.90__ × $17,000 = $ __15,300__ . This is the amount today, so it's the __PV__ . The rate is __1%__ , and there are __60__ periods:

$$\$ \underline{15,300} = C \times \{\ \underline{1 - \frac{1}{1.01^{60}}}\ \}/.01$$
$$= C \times \{1 - .55045\}/.01$$
$$= C \times 44.955$$

$$C = \$15,300/44.955$$
$$C = \$\underline{340.34}$$

Q. Suppose you owe $2000 on a VISA card, and the interest rate is 2% per month. If you make the minimum monthly payments of $50, how long will it take you to pay it off?

A. A *long* time:

$$\$2000 = \$50 \times \{\ \underline{1 - \frac{1}{1.02^{t}}}\ )\}/.02$$
$$.80 = 1 - 1/1.02^{t}$$
$$1.02^{t} = 5.0$$
$$t = \underline{81.27} \text{ months, or about } \underline{6.8} \text{ years}$$

Finding the discount rate

Q. Suppose you are offered an investment that will pay you $8000 per year for the next 12 years for $50,000. Is this a good deal?

A. Depends on the return:

$\underline{\$ 50,000} = \$\underline{\ 8,000} \times \{1 - 1/(1 + r)^{12}\}/r$

Good news: can't be solved algebraically
Bad news: solve it with trial and error (or get a financial calculator)

Try r = 10%:

PV = $8000 \times \{1 - 1/(1.10)^{12}\}/.10 = \$\underline{54,510}$ (nice guess)

Is 10% too high or too low?

Try r = 12%:

PV = $8000 \times \{1 - 1/(1.12)^{12}\}/.12 = \$\underline{49,555}$ (a little high)

From here it's "plug and chug," check that $\underline{11.8\%}$ is close.

Q. Suppose you deposit $2,000 each year for the next three years into an account that pays 8%. How much will you have in three years? Important: you make the first deposit in exactly one year.

A. Here we know the periodic cash flows are $2,000 each. Using the most basic approach:

$$FV = \$2,000 \times 1.08^{\underline{2}} + \$2,000 \times 1.08^{\underline{1}} + \$2,000$$
$$= \$2332.80 \qquad + \ \$2,160 \qquad + \$2,000$$
$$= \$6,492.80$$

Using the shortcut:

$$FV = \$2,000 \times (\underline{\ 1.08^{3} - 1\ })/.08$$
$$= \$2,000 \times 3.2464$$
$$= \$6,492.80$$

In a previous example, we had $2,000 per year for 5 years at 10% per year.

$$FV = \$2000 \times (\underline{\ 1.10^{5} - 1\ })/.10$$
$$= \$1000 \times (1.61051 - 1)/.10$$
$$= \$1000 \times 6.1051$$
$$= \$12,210.20$$

With annuity future values there are still only four pieces, FV, r, t, and C. Given any three of these you can find the fourth. The procedures are the same as those for annuity PV's.

What about perpetuity future values?

EARs and APRs

Q. If a rate is quoted at 16%, compounded semiannually, then the actual rate is 8% per six months. Is 8% per six months the same as 16% per year?

A. <u>No</u>. If you invest $1000 for one year at 16%, then you'll have $1160 at the end of the year. If you invest at 8% per period for two periods, you'll have

$$FV = \$1000 \times (1.08)^2$$
$$= \$1000 \times 1.1664$$
$$= \$1166.40,$$

or $6.40 more. Why? What rate per year is the same as 8% per six months?

The *Effective Annual Rate (EAR)* is <u>16.64</u> %. The "16% compounded semiannually" is the quoted or stated rate, not the effective rate.

By law, in consumer lending, the rate that must be quoted on a loan agreement is equal to the rate per period multiplied by the number of periods. This rate is called the <u>ANNUAL PERC. RATE</u> *(APR)*.

Q. A bank charges 1% per month on car loans. What is the APR? What is the EAR?

A. The APR is <u>1%</u> × <u>12</u> = <u>12</u> %. The EAR is:

$$EAR = \underline{\quad 1.01^{12} \quad} - 1 = 1.126825 - 1 = 12.6825\%$$

The APR is thus a quoted rate, not an effective rate!

In general, if we let q be the quoted rate and m be the number of periods, then the general relationship between the quoted rate and the effective rate is:

$$1 + EAR = \left(1 + \frac{q}{m} \right)^m$$

Q. If a VISA card quotes a rate of 18% APR, what is the EAR?

A. Assuming that the billing period is monthly (which it usually is), then the APR is the quoted rate, and the number of periods is 12. The EAR is thus

$$1 + EAR = \left(1 + \frac{.18}{12} \right)^{12}$$
$$= 1.015^{12}$$
$$= 1.1956$$
$$EAR = \underline{19.56} \%$$

Q. Suppose a bank wants to offer a savings account that has quarterly compounding and an EAR of 7%. What rate must it quote?

A. Here we have to find the unknown quoted rate:

$$\underline{\qquad} = (1 + q/\underline{4})^4$$
$$1.07 \underline{\qquad} = 1 + q/4$$
$$1.018245 = 1 + q/4$$
$$q = 6.8234\%$$

How to lie, cheat, and steal with interest rates

> **RIPOV RETAILING**
> Going out (for) business sale!
>
> *note sleazy ad!*
>
> **$1000 instant credit!**
> **12% simple interest!**
> **Three years to pay!**
> **Low, low monthly payments!**

Your payment is calculated as:

1. Borrow $1000 today at 12% per year for three years, you will owe $1000 \times 1.12^3 = \$1404.93$.

2. To make it easy on you, make 36 low, low payments of $1404.93/36 = \$39.03$.

3. Is this a 12% loan? __HAH!__

$$\$\,1{,}000 = \$\,39.03 \times (1 - 1/(1 + r)^{36})/r$$

$$r = 1.96\% \text{ per month}$$

$$\text{APR} = 12 \times 1.96\% = 23.52\%$$
$$\text{EAR} = 1.0196^{12} - 1 = 26.23\% \ (!)$$

You want to buy a house for $140,000. The bank will loan you 80% of the purchase price. The mortgage terms are "30 years, monthly payments, 9% APR, 2 points, 10 year balloon."

Q.   What will your payments be?   What will the balloon payment be? What is the EAR on the mortgage?

A.   You will borrow .80 × $140,000 = $112,000. The interest rate is 9%/12 = .75% per month. There are 360 payments, so your payment is

$$\$\underline{112,000} = C \times (1 - 1/1.0075^{360})/.0075$$
$$= C \times 124.2819$$
$$C = \$\underline{901.15} \text{ per month}$$

If you pay two "points," you will actually only get $.\underline{98} \times$ $112,000 = $\underline{109,760}$. The monthly interest rate is thus

$$\$\underline{109,760} = \$\underline{901.18} \times (1 - 1/(1 + r)^{360})/r$$

$$r = .\underline{769}\% \text{ per } \underline{month}$$

$$\text{APR} = \underline{9.227}$$
$$\text{EAR} = \underline{9.628}$$

After 10 years, you owe $\underline{240}$ payments of $901.18 each. The balloon payment is the $\underline{PV}$ of these payments:

$$\text{Balloon} = \$901.18 \times (1 - 1/1.0075^{\underline{240}})/.0075$$
$$= \$\underline{100,161.31}$$

When a corporation (or government) wants to borrow money, it often sells a *bond*. An investor gives the corporation some money for the bond. The corporation promises to give the investor:

1. Regular *coupon* payments every period until the bond matures.

2. The *face value* of the bond when it matures.

If a bond has five years to maturity, an $80 annual coupon, and a $1000 face value, its cash flows would look like this:

Time	0	1	2	3	4	5
Coupons		$80	$80	$80	$80	$80
Face value						$1000
						$1080

How much is the bond worth? It depends on current interest rates. If the going rate on bonds like this one is 10%, then this bond is worth $924.18. Why? Stay tuned.

Suppose a bond currently sells for $932.90. It pays an annual coupon of $70, and it matures in 10 years. It has a face value of $1000. What are its coupon rate, current yield, and yield to maturity (YTM)?

1. The *coupon rate* (or just "coupon") is the annual dollar coupon expressed as a percentage of the face value:

    Coupon rate = $70/$ 1000 = 7%

2. The *current yield* is the annual coupon divided by the price:

    Current yield = $ 70 / 932.90 = 7.5%

3. The *yield to maturity* (or just "yield") is the rate that makes the price of the bond just equal to the present value of its future cash flows. It is the unknown r in:

    $$ \$ 932.90 = \$ 70 \times (1 - 1/(1 + r)^{10})/r + \$ 1000 /(1 + r)^{10} $$

    The only way to find the yield is trial and error:

    a. Try 10%: $70 \times (1 - 1/(1.10)^{10})/.10 + \$1000/(1.10)^{10} = \$816$

    b. Try 9%: $70 \times (1 - 1/(1.09)^{10})/.09 + \$1000/(1.09)^{10} = \$872$

    c. Try 8%: $70 \times (1 - 1/(1.08)^{10})/.08 + \$1000/(1.08)^{10} = \$933$

    ($\therefore$) The yield to maturity is 8%

1. Constant growth example:

Suppose a stock has just paid a $5 per share dividend. The dividend is projected to grow at 5% per year indefinitely. If the required return is 9%, then the price today is

P_0 = $D_1/(r - g)$
= $5 × ($\underline{1.05}$)/($.09$ - $\underline{.05}$)
= $5.25/.04
= $131.25 per share

What will the price be in a year? It will rise by 5%:

P_t = $D_{t+1}/(r - g)$
P_1 = $D_{\underline{2}}/(r - g)$ = ($\underline{5.25}$ × 1.05)/(.09 - .05) = $137.8125

2. The required return:

Suppose a stock has just paid a $5 per share dividend. The dividend is projected to grow at 5% per year indefinitely. If the stock sells today for $65 5/8, what is the required return?

P_0 = $D_1/(r - g)$
$(r - g)$ = D_1/P_0
r   = $D_1/P_0 + g$
             = $5.25/$65.625 + .05
             = dividend yield ($\underline{8\%}$) + capital gain yield ($\underline{5\%}$)
             = 13%

Nonconstant Growth

Suppose a stock has just paid a $5 per share dividend. The dividend is projected to grow at 10% for the next two years, the 8% for one year, and then 6% indefinitely. The required return is 12%. What is the stock value?

Time	Dividend	
0	$5.00	
1	$ 5.5	(10% growth)
2	$6.05	(10% growth)
3	$6.534	(8% growth)
4	$6.926	(6% growth)

At time 3, the value of the stock will be:

$$P_3 = D_4/(r - g) = \$6.926/(.12 - .06) = \$115.434.$$

The value today of the stock is thus:

$$P_0 = D_1/(1 + r) + D_2/(1 + r)^2 + D_3/(1 + r)^3 + P_3/(1 + r)^3$$

$$= \$5.5/1.12 + \$6.05/1.12^2 + \$6.534/1.12^3 + \$115.434/1.12^3$$

$$= \$96.55$$

The cash flows are

Year	Cash flow
0	-$ 252
1	1431
2	-3035
3	2850
4	-1000

What's the IRR?

at 25.00%:   NPV = _$ 0_

at 33.33%:   NPV = _$ 0_

at 42.86%:   NPV = _$ 0_

at 66.67%:   NPV = _$ 0_

Two questions:

1. What's going on here?

2. How many IRRs can there be?

Background info:

1. Sales of 10,000 units/year @$5/unit. Life of 3 years.
2. Variable cost/unit is $3. Fixed costs are $5000/year.
3. Fixed assets are $21,000. Depreciation is $7000/year. No salvage value.
4. Net working capital is $10,000. Req. return is 20%.

Pro Forma Financial Statements

Projected Income Statements

Sales	$50,000
Var. costs	30,000
	$20,000
Fixed costs	5,000
Depreciation	7,000
"EBIT"	$ 8,000
Taxes (34%)	2,720
Net income	$ 5280

Projected Balance Sheets

	0	1	2	3
NWC	$ 10,000	$10,000	$10,000	$10,000
NFA	21,000	14,000	7,000	0
Total	$31,000	$24,000	$17,000	$10,000

A. Project operating cash flows:

EBIT	$8,000
Depreciation	+7,000
Taxes	-2,720
OCF	$12,280

B. Project total cash flows:

	0	1	2	3
OCF		$12,280	$12,280	$12,280
NWC Sp.	-10,000			+10,000
Cap. Sp.	-21,000			
Total	-31,000	$12,280	$12,280	$22,280

C. Valuation:

NPV= -$31,000 + $12,280/1.20^1 + $12,280/1.20^2 + $22,280/1.20^3
    = $655

IRR = 21%

PBP= 2.3 years

AAR= $5280/{(31,000 + 24,000 + 17,000 + 10,000)/4} = 25.76%

1. Fixed asset spending is zero.
2. Net working capital spending is $200:

	0	1	Change	S/U
A/R	$100	$200	+100	U
INV	100	150	+50	U
-A/P	100	50	-50	U
NWC	$100	$300		

(∴) NWC Spending = $ _200_

3. Operating cash flow is $100:

Sales	$300
Costs	200
Depreciation	0
EBIT	$100
Tax	0
Net	$100

(∴) OCF = $100

(∴) Cash flow   = OCF - NWC spending - FA spending
                     = -$ _100_

What really happened?

Cash sales   = $300 - _100_   = $200 (collections)
Cash costs   = $200 + _50_ + _50_ = $300 (disbursements

Cash flow   = $200 - 300   = -$100 (cash in – cash out

A.   The deductions on a $30,000, 5-year property:

Year	(%)	($)
1	20%	$6,000
2	32%	9,600
3	19.20%	5,760
4	11.52%	3,456
5	11.52%	3,456
6	5.76%	1,728
	100%	$30,000

B.   Salvage values, book values, and taxes

Year	Book	Salvage	Tax	
0	$30,000			
1	24,000			
2	14,400	20,000	1904	(= 5600 × .34)
3	8,640			
4	5,184	2,000	−1083	(= −3184 × .34)
5	1,728			
6	0			

C.   Land and real estate

D.   Recapture versus capital gains

Background:

1. NWC investment = $40; cost = $60; 3 year life
2. Sales = $100; costs = 50; straight line depreciation to $0
3. Salvage = $10; tax rate = 34%; Payback = ?

- The aftertax salvage is $10 - ($10 - 0) $\times$ .34 = $6.6
- OCF = (100 - 50 - 20) + 20 - (100 - 50 - 20) $\times$ .34 = $39.8

The cash flows are thus:

	0	1	2	3
OCF		$39.8	$39.8	$39.8
Add. NWC	-40			40
Cap. Sp.	-60			6.6
	-100	$39.8	$39.8	$86.4

NPV = $28.76 (@12%)

PBP = 2.24 years

Background:

1. No NWC; cost = $200,000; 3 year MACRS
2. Cost saving = $70,000/year; 4 year life; salvage is $50,000
3. Tax rate = 39%; r = 10%; find NPV

Depreciation:

Year	(%)	($)
1	33.33%	$66,660
2	44.44%	88,880
3	14.82%	29,640
4	7.41%	14,820
	100%	$200,000

The aftertax salvage is $50,000 - ($50,000 - 0) × .39 = $30,500

The cash flows are thus:

	0	1	2	3	4
AT saving		$42,700.0	$42,700.0	$42,700.0	$42,700.0
Tax shield		25,997.4	34,663.2	11,559.6	5,779.8
"OCF"		$68,697.4	$77,363.2	$54,259.6	$48,479.8
Cap. Sp.	-200,000				30,500
	-200,000	$68,697.4	$77,363.2	$54,259.6	$78,979.8

NPV = $21,099.02 (IRR = 14.77%)

Evaluating Cost Cutting Proposals

In thousands of dollars:

Cost   = $900
Depreciation = $180
Life   = 5 years
Salvage   = $330
Savings   = $500/year, pretax
Add. to NWC   = –$220 (note the minus sign)

1. *Aftertax* cost saving: $500 × (*1 – .34*) = $ _*330*_ /year.

2. Depreciation *tax shield*: $180 × _*.34*_ = $ _*61.2*_ /year.

3. *Aftertax* salvage value: $330 – ($330 – 0) × .34 = $ _*217.8*_

4. The cash flows are thus:

	0	1	2	3	4	5
AT saving		$330.0	$330.0	$330.0	$330.0	$330.0
Tax shield		61.2	61.2	61.2	61.2	61.2
"OCF"		*391.2*	*391.2*	$391.2	$391.2	$391.2
NWC Sp.	*220*					*–220*
Cap. Sp.	-900					217.8
	–680	$391.2	$391.2	$391.2	$391.2	*389*

The IRR is about 50%, so it looks good!

Background (in $000):

1. Bid calls for 20 units/year; 3 years
2. Costs are $25/unit hardware; $10 unit other; $35 total
3. Cap. spending of $250; depreciation = $250/5 = $50/year
4. Salvage in 3 years is half of cost, $125.
5. NWC investment of $60,000
6. r = 16%; tax rate = 39%

The aftertax salvage is $125 - ($_125_ - _100_) × .39 = $115.25

The cash flows are:

	0	1	2	3
OCF		$OCF	$OCF	$OCF
Add. to NWC	-$60			60
Cap. Sp.	-250			$115.25
	-$310	$OCF	$OCF	$OCF + 175.25

Find OCF such that NPV is zero at 16%:

$+\$310,000 - 175,250/1.16^3 = OCF \times (1 - 1/1.16^3)/.16$

$\$197,724.74 = OCF \times 2.2459$

$OCF = \$\ \underline{88,038.5}\ /year$

If OCF is to be $88,038.50/year, what price do we have to bid?

OCF	= Net income + depreciation
$88,038.50	= Net income + $ *50,000*
Net income	= *38,038.50*

Sales	?
Costs	700,000.00
Depreciation	50,000.00
EBIT	$ *62,338*
Tax	24,319.70
Net income	$38,038.50

Sales = $62,358.20 + 50,000 + 700,000 = $812,358.20/year

The bid price should be $812,358.20/ *20* = *$40,618* /unit

The Unequal Lives Problem

This problem comes up when we have *both* of the following:

1. Mutually exclusive investments
2. The investment will be *repeated*--it's not a "one-shot" deal

	Jazz	Disco
Cost	= $45	= $65
Life	= 3 yrs.	= 5 years
Op. Cost	= $5/yr.	= $4/yr.
r	= 12%	

PV(costs) for Jazz: $\$45 + \$5 \times (1 - 1/1.12^3)/.12 = \$\underline{57.01}$

PV(costs) for Disco: $\$65 + \$4 \times (1 - 1/1.12^5)/.12 = \$\underline{79.42}$

For each investment, find the *equivalent annual cost (EAC)*; i.e., the cash amount paid every year that has the same PV.

EAC for Jazz: $\$\underline{57.01} = EAC \times (1 - 1/1.12^3)/.12$

EAC $= \$\underline{23.74}$

EAC for Disco: $\$79.42 = EAC \times (1 - 1/1.12^5)/.12$

EAC $= \$\underline{22.03}$ ✓

Background:
1. Price = $ 5/unit; variable costs = $3/unit.
2. Fixed costs are $10,000/year
3. Initial cost is $20,000; life is 5 years; .depreciation is $4,000/year, no salvage.
4. Ignore taxes; r = 20%

In general, if taxes are ignored:

> **Q = (Fixed costs + OCF) / (Price - variable cost)**

A. Accounting break-even

= (Fixed costs + depreciation)/(Price - variable cost)
= ($10,000 + $ _4,000_)/($5 - $3) = 7000 units

IRR = _0_ ; NPV _<0_ (= -$ _8,038_)

B. Cash break-even

Q = (Fixed costs + _$0_)/(Price - variable cost)
= $10,000/($5 - $3) = _5,000_ units

IRR = _-100%_ ; NPV = _-20,000_

B. Financial break-even

Q = (Fixed costs + $6,688)/(Price - variable cost)
= $16,688/($5 - $3) = 8,344 units

IRR = _20%_ ; NPV = _$0_

Key issues:

- What is the difference between a real and a nominal return?
- How can we convert from one to the other?

Background:

We have $1000, and Diet Coke costs $2.00/six pack. We can buy 500 six packs. Suppose the rate of inflation is 5%, so that the price rises to $2.10 in one year. We invest the $1000, and it grows to $1100 in one year. What's our return in dollars? In six packs?

A. *Dollars.* Our return is

($1100 - $1000)/$1000 = $100/$1000 = _10%_ .

(∴) The percentage increase in the amount of green stuff is 10%; our return is 10%.

B. *Six packs.* We can buy $1100/$2.10 = _523.81_ six packs, so our return is

(523.81 - 500)/500 = 23.81/500 = 4.76%

(∴) The percentage increase in the amount of brown stuff is 4.76%; our return is 4.76%.

Key issues:

- How are average returns measured?
- How is volatility measured?

Average returns:

Your portfolio has had returns of 10%, –7%, 28%, and -11% over the last four years.

Your *average annual return* is simply:

[.10 + (-.07) + .28 + (-.11)]/4 = ___5___ % per year

Return volatility:

The usual measure of volatility is the *standard deviation,* which is the square root of the _variance_ :

Year	Actual return	Average return	Return deviation	Squared deviation
1	.10	.05	.05	.0025
2	-.07	.05	-.12	.0144
3	.28	.05	.23	.0529
4	-.11	.05	-.16	.0256
Total	.20		.00	.0954

The variance, σ^2 or Var(R) = .0954/(___3___) = .0318

The standard deviation, σ or SD(R) = $\sqrt{.0318}$ = .1783 or 17.83%

Key issues:

What is a risk premium?
What is the reward for bearing risk?

Risk premiums:

The risk premium is the difference between a risky investment's return and a riskless return:

Investment	Average return	Standard deviation	Risk premium
Common stocks	12.1%	20.9%	_8.4_ %
Small stocks	17.8%	35.6%	14.2%
Long-term T-bonds	4.7%	8.5%	1.1%
Short-term T-bills	3.6%	3.3%	0.0%

Using market history:

• Suppose the current T-bill rate is 5%. An investment has "average" risk relative to a typical share of stock. It offers a 10% return. Is this a good investment?

Suppose an investment is similar to buying small company equities. If the T-bill rate is 5%, what return would you demand?

Key issues:

* What is the relationship between risk and return?
* What does security market equilibrium look like?

The fundamental conclusion is that the ratio of risk premium to beta is the same for every asset. In other words, the reward-to-risk ratio is *constant* and equal to

$$Reward/risk\ ratio = \frac{E(R_i) - R_f}{\beta_i}$$

Example:

Asset A has an expected return of 12% and a beta of 1.40. Asset B has an expected return of 8% and a beta of 0.80. Are these assets valued correctly relative to each other if the risk-free rate is 5%?

a. For A, $(.12 - .05)/1.40 =$ ___.05___

b. For B, $(.08 - .05)/0.80 =$ __.0375__

What would the risk-free rate have to be for these assets to be correctly valued?

$$(.12 - R_f)/1.40 = (.08 - R_f)/0.80$$

$R_f =$ ___$2\frac{2}{3}$ %___

Key issues:

- **What is the CAPM?**
- **What are the components of an expected return?**

The market as a whole has a beta of 1. It plots on the SML, so:

$$E(R_M) - R_f = \frac{E(R_i) - R_f}{\beta_i}$$

Rearranging, the Capital Asset Pricing Model is

$$E(R_i) = R_f + [E(R_M) - R_f] \times \beta_i$$

The expected return on a risky asset thus depends on:

1. *Pure time value of money.*

2. *Reward for bearing systematic risk*

3. *Amount of systematic risk*

Example: The historic risk premium has been about 8.5%. The risk-free rate is currently about 5%. GTE has a beta of about .85. What return should you expect from GTE?

$$E(R_{GTE}) = 5\% + \underline{\quad 8.5 \quad} \times .85$$
$$= 12.225\%$$

Common stock and other shareholders' equity	
Common stock, $1 par value, authorized 100,000,000 shares in 1990; issued 54,234,665	$54,235
Capital in excess of par value	88,554
Retained earnings	973,493
	$1,116,282
Less 2,559,333 shares of treasury stock	31,224
	$1,085,058

- **Par vs. nonpar**

- **Authorized vs. issued**

- **Capital surplus**

- **Retained earnings**

Shareholder Rights

- Corporate democracy: cumulative vs. straight voting

  Example: There are a total of 1000 shares, and 3 directors are up. How many shares do you need to win a seat with straight voting? Cumulative voting?

- Proxy voting and proxy fights

- Dividends

- Classes of stock

Effects of a Stock Sale

Before:

Common stock and other shareholders' equity	
Common stock, $1 par value	$10,000
Capital surplus	90,000
Retained earnings	800,000
Total	$900,000

After: sell 100 share at $40 per share:

Common stock and other shareholders' equity	
Common stock, $1 par value	$ 10,100
Capital surplus	93,900
Retained earnings	800,000
Total	$ 904,000

Key issues:

- How does a rights offering work?
- What is the value of a right?

Mechanics of a rights offering:

1. Early steps same as cash offer (SEC approval, etc.)
2. You are notified that you can buy 1 new share at a special "subscription" price for every N that you currently own (or: you have 1 right for every share you own, and it takes N rights to buy 1 new share--same thing).
3. You can (1) buy the stock, (2) sell your rights, or (3) do nothing.

Subscription price and the number of rights:

Suppose a firm with 200,000 shares out wants to raise $1 million. Current price is $40 per share. The subscription price, the number of new shares that have to be sold and the number of rights needed to buy 1 share are related like this:

Subscription price	Number of new shares	Number of rights to buy 1 share
$25	40,000	5
$20	50,000	4
$10	100,000	2
$5	200,000	1

Effect on share price (subscription price = $20):

1. Firm sets "holder of record" day. Beginning 4 days before, the stock sells "ex rights." Before that it sells "rights-on, cum rights, or with rights" at $40.

2. After rights offering, _250 K_ shares are out. Total value is old $8 million plus new $1 million = $_9_ million.

3. New ex rights stock price is $9 million/250,000 =$_36_

Value of a right:

The stock sells for $40 "rights-on," vs. $36 "ex rights," so the value of right is $4. Consider acquiring 5 shares:

1. Buy 4 shares "with rights" at $40. Exercise your rights and buy new share at $20. Total for 5 shares is $_180_ or $_36_ /share.

2. Buy 4 × 5 = 20 rights for $_80_ and buy 5 shares @$20. Total cost of 5 shares is $180 or $36/share.

3. Buy 5 @ $36, total cost is $180.

Dividend Growth Approach

Implementing the approach

1. Need the current price and annual dividend from financial press (Ch. 6). Suppose these are $50 and $5 respectively.

2. Need an estimate of the *future* growth rate in dividends:

   a. Analyst forecasts
   b. Historical
   c. Other

3. Suppose g is estimated at 9%, then, using the approach,

$$R_E = D_1 / P_0 + g$$

$$= \$5 \times (\underline{\quad 1.09 \quad})/\$50 + .09$$

$$= \underline{\quad 19.90 \quad} \%$$

Advantages of the approach

1. Easy to do/widely recognized

Disadvantages

1. Only strictly applicable to steady dividend payers.

2. Sensitive to *g* estimates

3. No direct adjustment for risk

Implementing the approach

1. Need the risk-free rate from financial press--usually the Treasury bill rate, say 6%.

2. Need *estimates* of market risk premium and security beta.

    a. Risk premium historical--___8.5___% (Ch. 10)
    b. Beta--historical
        (1) Investment services
        (2) Estimate from historical data

3. Suppose the beta is 1.40, then, using the approach:

    $$R_E = R_f + \beta_E \times (R_M - R_f)$$

    $$= 0.06 + 1.40 \times \underline{\ \ .085\ \ }$$

    $$= 17.9\%$$

Advantages of the approach

1. Widely applicable

2. Explicit risk adjustment

Disadvantages

1. Need estimates of β_E and market risk premium.

Cost of debt

1.   Cost of debt, R_D, is the interest rate on new borrowing.

2.   Cost of debt is *observable*:

     a. Yield on currently outstanding debt.
     b. Yields on newly-issued similarly-rated bonds.

3.   Historic debt cost is irrelevant.

     Example: We sold a 20-year, 12% bond 10 years ago at par. It is currently priced at 86. What is our cost of debt?

     The *yield to maturity* (Ch. 6) is ___14.8___%, so this is what we use as the cost of debt, not 12%.

Cost of preferred

1.   Preferred stock is a perpetuity, so the cost is

     $R_P = D/P_0$

2.   Notice that cost is simply the dividend yield.

     Example: We sold an $8 preferred issue 10 years ago. It sells for $120/share today.

     The dividend yield *today* is $___8___/$___120___ = 6.67%, so this what we use as the cost of preferred.

Capital structure weights

1. Let: E = the *market* value of the equity.
                 D = the *market* value of the debt.

   Then: $V = E + D$
                  $1 = E/V + D/V = 100\%$

2. Thus, the firm's capital structure weights are E/V and D/V.

3. The *unadjusted weighted average cost of capital* is then

   WACC (unadjusted) $= (E/V) \times R_E + (D/V) \times R_D$,

   a simple weighted average of the equity and debt costs.

The weighted average cost of capital (adjusted)

1. Interest payments on debt are tax-deductible, so the *aftertax* cost of debt is the pretax cost multiplied by (1 - corporate tax rate).

   Aftertax cost of debt $= R_D \times (\underline{\hspace{1cm} 1 - T_c \hspace{1cm}})$

2. The weighted average cost of capital that we actually use is thus

   WACC $= (E/V) \times R_E + (D/V) \times R_D \times (1 - T_c)$

Ignoring taxes:

A.   **With no debt:**

$$EPS = EBIT/500,000$$

B.   **With $2,500,000 in debt at 10%:**

$$EPS = (EBIT - \$\underline{250,000})/250,000$$

C.   **These are equal when:**

$$EPS_{BE} = EBIT_{BE}/\underline{500,000} = (EBIT_{BE} - \$250,000)/250,000$$

D.   **With a little algebra:**

$$EBIT_{BE} = \$500,000$$

So $EPS_{BE} = \$\underline{1}$/share

The interest tax shield and firm value

For simplicity: (1) perpetual cash flows
                   (2) no depreciation
                   (3) no fixed asset or NWC spending

A firm is consider going from zero debt to $400 at 10%:

	Firm U (unleveraged)	Firm L (leveraged)
EBIT	$200	$200
Interest	0	$40
Tax (40%)	$80	$64
Net income	$120	$96
Cash flow from assets	$120	$ _136_

- Tax saving = $16 = __.40__ × $40 = $T_c \times R_D \times D$

MM Proposition I (with taxes)

- PV(tax saving)   = $16/__.10__ = $ __160__
                      = $(T_c \times R_D \times D)/R_D = T_c \times D$

$$V_L = V_U + T_c \times D$$

Taxes and firm value: an example

- EBIT   = $100
- T_c = 30%
- R_U = 12.5%

Q.   Suppose debt goes from $0 to $100 at 10%, what happens to equity value, E?

V_U = $100 × (__1 − .30__)/.125 = $560

V_L = $560 + .30 × $__100__ = $590, so E = $__490__.

WACC and the cost of equity (MM Proposition II with taxes)

With taxes:

$$R_E = R_U + (R_U - R_D) \times (D/E) \times (1 - T_c)$$

R_E = __.125__ + (__.125__ - .10) × (__100 / 490__) × (1 - .30)

     = 12.86%

WACC = (__490 / 590__) × .1286 + (100/590) × .10 × (1 - .30)

     = 11.86%

(∴) The WACC decreases as more debt financing is used. Optimal capital structure is all debt!

Accounting treatment of splits and stock dividends

A. Before:

Common ($1 par; 1 million shares)	$1M
Add. paid in capital	9M
Retained earnings	100M
Total equity	$110M
Market price per share	$50

B. "Small" stock dividend (10%)

- 100,000 new shares at $50 each = $5M, so

Common ($1 par; 1.1 million shares)	$1.1M
Add. paid in capital	*13.9* M
Retained earnings	*95* M
Total equity	$110M
Market price per share	$50

C. A 4-for-1 stock split

D. A "large" stock dividend (300%)

Dividend policy versus cash dividends

An illustration of dividend irrelevance

- **Original dividends**

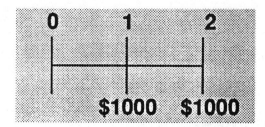

if $R_E = 20\%$: P_0 (total) $= \$1000/1.2 + \$1000/1.2^2 = \$\underline{1527.78}$

- **New dividend plan**

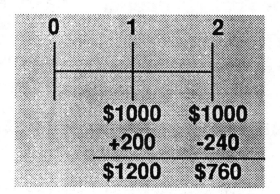

P_0 (total) $= \$1200/1.2 + \$760/1.2^2 = \$\underline{1527.78}$

An illustration of "homemade" dividends

- **Original dividends if you own 10% of the stock**

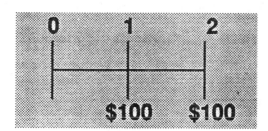

- **Dividends under new plan**

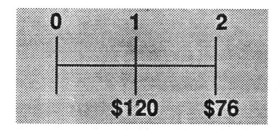

- **Undo the new plan**

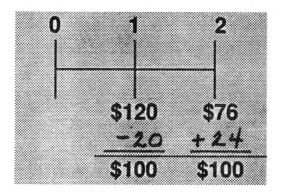

- **ADRs (DRIPs)**

A residual policy

- Net income (projected) = $200M

- D/E (target) = 2/3 (E/V = __60__%; D/V = __40__%)

- Capital budget (planned) = $260

- Maximum capital spending with no outside equity:

$$.60 \times X = \$200M \Rightarrow X = \$\underline{\;333\;^1/_3\;}\;M$$

- (∴) A dividend will be paid

- New equity needed   = .60 × $260 = $ _156 M_
New debt needed   = .40 × $260 = $ _104 M_

- Dividend = $ _200 M_ - $156 = $ __44__ M

Dividend stability

- Constant payout

- Constant dividend